Politics and Ethnicity

Perspectives on Comparative Politics

Published by Palgrave Macmillan

The Struggle against Corruption: A Comparative Study
  Edited by Roberta Ann Johnson
Women, Democracy, and Globalization in North America: A Comparative Study
  By Jane Bayes, Patricia Begne, Laura Gonzalez, Lois Harder, Mary
  Hawkesworth, and Laura Macdonald
Politics and Ethnicity: A Comparative Study
  By Joseph Rudolph
Immigration Policy and the Politics of Immigration: A Comparative Study
  By Martin Schain
Politics, Policy, and Health Care: A Comparative Study
  By Paul Godt
Social Movements in Politics, Second Edition
  By Cyrus Ernesto Zirakzadeh

Politics and Ethnicity

A Comparative Study

Joseph Rudolph

POLITICS AND ETHNICITY

First published in 2006 by
PALGRAVE MACMILLAN™
175 Fifth Avenue, New York, N.Y. 10010 and
Houndmills, Basingstoke, Hampshire, England RG21 6XS
Companies and representatives throughout the world.

PALGRAVE MACMILLAN is the global academic imprint of the Palgrave Macmillan division of St. Martin's Press, LLC and of Palgrave Macmillan Ltd. Macmillan® is a registered trademark in the United States, United Kingdom and other countries. Palgrave is a registered trademark in the European Union and other countries.

ISBN-13: 978–1–4039–6233–1 (hardback)
ISBN-10: 1–4039–6233–2 (hardback)
ISBN-13: 978–1–4039–6234–8 (paperback)
ISBN-10: 1–4039–6234–0 (paperback)

Library of Congress Cataloging-in-Publication Data

Rudolph, Joseph R. (Joseph Russell), 1942–
    Politics and ethnicity: a comparative study / by Joseph Rudolph.
        p. cm.—(Perspectives on comparative politics)
    Includes index.
    ISBN 1–4039–6233–2 (alk. paper)
    1. Ethnicity—Political aspects. 2. Ethnic relations—Political aspects. 3. Politics and culture. 4. Political anthropology. I. Title. II. Series.

GN495.6.R83 2006
305.8—dc22   2005058654

A catalogue record for this book is available from the British Library.

Design by Newgen Imaging Systems (P) Ltd., Chennai, India.

First edition: August 2006

10 9 8 7 6 5 4 3 2 1

Printed in the United States of America.

To those mentors who shaped my life,
and to my family, friends,
and those four-legged companions
who so enriched it.

A Snake, having made his hole close to the porch of a cottage, inflicted a mortal bite on the Cottager's infant son. Grieving over his loss, the Father resolved to kill the Snake. The next day, when it came out of its hole for food, he took up his axe, but by swinging too hastily, missed its head and cut off only the end of its tail. After some time, the Cottager, afraid that the Snake would bite him also, endeavored to make peace, and placed some bread and salt in the hole. The Snake, slightly hissing, said "There can henceforth be no peace between us; for whenever I see you I shall remember the loss of my tail, and whenever you see me you will be thinking of the death of your son."

No one truly forgets injuries in the presence of him who caused the injury.

Aesop, ca. 600 B.C.
(Translated by George Fyler Townsend)

CONTENTS

Part 3 Nigeria: Ethnopolitics in the Multinational Third World

Conclusion

LIST OF TABLES

All books in this series, Perspectives in Comparative Politics, are designed to be scholarly, topic-oriented studies of a particular problem, accessible to upper-division students as well as to graduate students and professors. They begin with an introductory chapter, covering the relevant literature and laying out the problem, and end with a concluding chapter, summarizing what has been learned about the problems in the three or more nations covered, and elucidating the important comparative lessons learned. *Politics and Ethnicity: A Comparative Study*, by Joseph Rudolph, follows that format. It offers parallel consideration of its topic in France, the Czech Republic, and Nigeria, preceded by a chapter on "Ethnicity and Politics in the Contemporary World," and followed by "Concluding Reflections on Managing Ethnopolitical Conflict in the Contemporary World."

Despite adherence to the overall design, however, every book in the series has its own very special character. The topics, the countries chosen as case studies, and, above all, the author ensure this rich variety. Professors adopting different books in the series for classroom use will always find the comforting familiarity of the expected design, but also the surprise and delight of engaging new ideas presented by authors working from long experience, deep understanding, and passion. The authors in this series care deeply about their topics, and it shows. They maintain impeccable loyalty to the norms of objective scholarship, and at the same time demonstrate how well such scholarship can serve argument for change. Students learn about the topic and the cases, but they also learn, by the example set, important lessons about the comparative method and the norms of scholarship.

The present book illustrates these features remarkably well. Joseph Rudolph takes on one of the most difficult and vexing problems of international politics today: the prevalence of ethnic conflict. He points out how this problem has been widely studied, from three major theoretical approaches, yet very seldom *comparatively*. Writing with exceptional clarity and persuasiveness, he sets out to rectify that omission.

One of the everlasting arguments in comparative studies is whether to compare the similar or the different. Some feel more comfortable comparing different kinds of apples; others find it more enlightening to assemble different kinds of fruit; still others contrast fruit with other food groups, and some wonder about the relative value of food, shelter, and love. The level of abstraction matters, but there is no single answer to the argument. It all depends. Rudolph easily persuades us, in his preface and throughout the book. Ethnic conflict takes so many forms and creates such horrific problems not only for those caught up in the specific battles but also for all of us caught up—sometimes quite desperately ourselves—in the quest for international peace and development, that we must perforce seek the insights of broader comparison. This book promises those insights, and it delivers.

I am very pleased indeed to have this book join the series Perspectives in Comparative Politics.

—Kay Lawson

AUTHOR'S FOREWORD

When this book was conceived more than a decade ago, there was still a Soviet Union. There was still a Czechoslovakia. The turmoil in Yugoslavia had yet to turn violent. The bloody war in Rwanda in which Hutus and Tutsis would kill one another in the tens of thousands in days was still years away. London was still adamant in rejecting the demands of the Scots and Welsh for their own regional assemblies. No avowedly anti-immigrant party had ever been included within the cabinet of a modern democratic state, much less had their leader been placed on the ballot in a run-off election for the presidency of one of the leading states in the Western world.

"Ethnic cleansing" was yet to become a part of the vocabulary of politics in today's world, and peacekeeping implied largely an existing peace in areas where the protagonists had tired of the fighting. "Peacekeeping" did not involve trying to stop an ongoing civil war, let alone entail enforcing an uneasy peace or building postconflict institutions designed to bring self-government to ethnic communities who only a short while before were trying to kill one another. And the United States had yet to enunciate the doctrine of preemptive action in the aftermath of the terrorist attacks on New York and Washington on September 11, 2001, or attempt to implement that doctrine only to find itself deeply involved in the unfamiliar ground of trying to fashion democratic governments for the quarreling members of multinational societies previously controlled effectively, if then, by ruthless authoritarian regimes.

These developments have prolonged the completion of this book, but more importantly they have regularly testified to the continuing importance of ethnic and national identity, the persistence of ethnic conflict, and the still prevalent need to find means of managing it in our time. Class, contrary to the theories of Marx more than a century ago, has not fully replaced ethnicity in the politics of even highly industrial states; nor have postindustrial, quality of life concerns in the late industrial and postindustrial states of the advanced democratic world, contrary to the forecasts of postindustrial theorists half a century ago. Rather, the desire for autonomy and national self-determination and the freedom to pursue one's "cultural traditions" have often been recast as quality of life issues in today's world.

To be sure, the headline grabbing accounts of ethnic conflict, intolerance, and bloodletting present a distorted view of ethnic conflict in not just the developed world, but in much of the developing world as well. Most ethnic conflict, and indeed ethnonational conflict, does not end in political violence. It does, however, pose a challenge to policy makers in a world where migrations are again gathering momentum and the ethnically homogeneous state has—excluding a few small island states—become essentially extinct. Moreover, as new states emerge and as older states restructure their regimes and seek to find democratic means of controlling the multiethnic and usually multinational communities confronting them, prior models of ethnic balancing and proportionality in distributing power at the center, federal autonomy for territorialized minorities, and guaranteed minority rights have found frequent replication, most recently in the state-building processes unfolding in both the postcommunist and developing worlds.

In order to canvass these developments while simultaneously focusing in detail on the problems of responding to ethnic and national demands in the policy processes of states in the developed democratic, democratizing postcommunist, and developing worlds, this book adopts a combination of case studies and comparative frameworks, with case studies exploring the principal forms of ethnic conflict in each of these arenas, followed in each section by a chapter placing the case study in a comparative context, and a concluding chapter focusing on the contemporary trends involving the management of ethnic conflict in the contemporary world.

The Case Studies

Choosing the case study from the multiethnic and often multinational states of the advanced democratic world was particularly difficult given the differing ways in which the principal forms of ethnic conflict are now unfolding in the policy processes of Western democracies; that is, the foreign worker–immigrant issue and demands by territorialized ethnic minorities for autonomy. To be sure, the latter is absent in the United States unless the issue is stretched to include the periodic statehood movements in Puerto Rico and Native American reservation politics, which provide interesting but scarcely representative examples of the many faces of ethnic conflict in developed systems. Further, although interesting, the U.S. approach to dealing with intermingled ethnic and racial minorities is largely unique to the United States as an immigrant society.

The United Kingdom was much more tempting as a case study, offering as it does not only examples of the peaceful accommodation of ethnoterritorial demands (the assemblies for Wales and Scotland, the diplomatic efforts to resolve the continuing Irish question), but an assortment of immigration/race issues lacing its public policy deliberations. France, however, has *the* antiforeigner movement in the West spearheaded by its National Front party and it faces the ultimate policy dilemma of democratic governments trying to cope with anti-immigrant sentiment because so many of those viewed as "foreigners" by the indigenous French population are, by virtue of their birth in France, now French citizens. Meanwhile, and cementing the choice of France for the case study of ethnopolitics in the developed democratic world, ethnoregional politics in France have been far more typical of the nature and treatment of ethnoterritorial demands in the developed world than the challenges London faces in Northern Ireland.

For the section devoted to ethnopolitics in the democratizing postcommunist world, two broad considerations affected the choice of the former country of Czechoslovakia as the case study. First, its peaceful partition in 1993 provides a clear illustration of the fact that ethnonational demands, even when involving separatism, have not resulted throughout postcommunist Europe in the dreadful ethnic warfare the world witnessed when Yugoslavia violently broke apart. Second, both states born of the former Czechoslovakia have subsequently become epicenters for the overt discrimination found throughout Central Europe against the Romany: a large, despised, and almost uniquely powerless minority lacking even an outsider, home state to protect their interests.

Finally, for the highly diverse, democratic, and nondemocratic developing world, the selection is Nigeria, Africa's most populous state and, were it not for Nigeria's internal problems, Africa's natural leader. More importantly, Nigeria's problems with accommodating territorial minorities have been and remain similar to those faced by postcolonial governments elsewhere. Finally, the conflict-management devices that a succession of Nigerian governments have employed to deal with ethnic unrest are not only the same instruments that other multiethnic states in the developing world have repeatedly utilized in order to control ethnic conflict within their own borders but find echoes in those formulas that the United States and other international actors have recently employed in their efforts to erect pluralistic governing institutions in postwar Afghanistan, Iraq, Bosnia, and Kosovo.

ACKNOWLEDGMENTS

No one truly writes a book by themself; certainly not an academic work and much less one that has been as long in progress as this one. Given the length of debts to be acknowledged, it is best to be general. In that vein, sincere appreciation is expressed to those in the broader academic community and my classrooms alike, off of whom I have bounced ideas and from whom I have learned much. In a like manner, I am also indebted to my University, the Fulbright program, the United States State Department, and the Organization for Security and Cooperation in Europe for their research support and the other means they provided, which enabled me to do large parts of the field work on which portions of this book are based. More particularly, anyone who works or otherwise plows this particular field of study owes an enormous debt to Walker Connor for his pioneering work in it, as well as to such earlier scholars of nationalism as Rupert Emerson and Anthony Smith, and those before and after who have expanded our knowledge of the broad, interdisciplinary arena that tries to house the politics of ethnicity and nationalism. Beyond the general, however, there are two to whom I owe special thanks for enabling this book to migrate from conceptualization to publication.

First, this book would almost certainly not have been undertaken without the participation of my friend and long-term collaborator Robert Thompson. Bob was to be the coauthor, but shortly after the first contract was signed, he went over to the dark side to be a full-time administrator, leaving the project entirely to me (thanks a lot, Bob). Still, his influence on the completed work goes far beyond the specific credit given to him in the notes buried throughout the text, and I remain grateful for all that I learned from Bob in our years of working together.

Second, special thanks is owed to our Series Editor Kay Lawson for staying with me and the project for so long. Had I been informed sometime along the way that dealing with me had driven her into self-imposed exile in France, perhaps toiling with an easier species, such as two or three hundred French cats, I would feel a pang of guilt, but not surprise. Certainly without her mix of good-humored prodding and encouragement, the book would probably have lost its other would-be coauthor long ago. *Merci, mille fois*, Kay.

CHAPTER ONE

Ethnicity and Politics in the Contemporary World

Public policy conflicts arising from the contemporary and past interactions of ethnic groups and involving some aspect of ethnicity or ethnic identification are common, frequently volatile issues on the agendas of virtually every political system. The examples are obvious. They include such conflicts or issues as the war between the Bosnians and Serbs in the former Yugoslavia, the problems between Jews and Palestinians on the West Bank and Gaza, the legality of race-based college scholarships and congressional districts in the United States, the rights of illegal immigrants and guest workers, the future of Northern Ireland.

Given the prevalence of ethnic conflict in contemporary domestic and international affairs, it is essential for students of comparative politics to understand the significance and dynamics of the relationships between ethnicity and politics, and to appreciate the varieties of ethnopolitics, the factors affecting the intensity of ethnic conflict, and the success of policy makers in managing it. Obtaining such an analytical handle on this broad, diverse, and challenging political arena requires a careful mix of both comparative and case study methodology.

Ethnopolitical Conflict: Approaching the Field

Ethnicity, Nationalism, and Ethnopolitics

Insofar as much of the more publicized conflicts in the contemporary world revolve around the fusing of ethnic identity and national identity, let us begin with the basics: working definitions of these pivotal terms.

Ethnicity and Ethnic Groups

Traditionally, ethnicity was largely defined in terms of shared genetic, racial, and sometimes linguistic traits, usually visibly apparent and hence detectable by outsiders. Moreover, these definitions of ethnic communities were not limited to those of geneticists and linguists. Statesmen too got in the act, most famously at Versailles after World War I, when the joining of the northern Slavic lands and the southern lands formerly ruled by the Austrian-Hungarian empire into, respectively, Czechoslovakia and Yugoslavia were celebrated as triumphs of the principle of national self-determination for Slavs. Ethnicity, however, is self- as well as other-defined, and the Czechs and the Slovaks in the north, and the principal groups in the south (the Serbs and Croats) saw themselves as separate ethnic entities possessing distinct histories, linguistic nuances, and religions, and in the world of ethnic politics what matters is how a group sees itself, not how others define it. Consequently, unless otherwise noted, and recognizing that a broad and inclusive definition of ethnicity does raise issues pertaining to analytical precision, we will be defining an ethnic group broadly—as opposed to narrowly in terms of biological similarities—as a people "who identify themselves or are identified by others in cultural terms, such as language, religion, tribe, nationality, and possibly race."[1]

So viewed, ethnicity has long been a basis of political as well as social association, defying both the predictions of the Marxists who a century and a half ago foresaw social class replacing such primordial bases of political association as ethnicity and language, and the postindustrial theorists of the mid-twentieth century, who saw such concerns being eclipsed by quality of life issues.

The Nation, Nationalism, and Ethnonationalism

Even where ethnicity functions in the context of a multiethnic society with an overarching sense of patriotism, as in the United States, self-conscious ethnic identity can exert a powerful impact on a political process. In the twentieth century, however, the most significant political expressions of ethnicity have occurred where it has become the building block of nations seeking either self-determination or to preserve their ethnic purity. Unfortunately, the term "nation" has acquired wide usage in the popular vocabulary of politics without retaining the precision of meaning necessitated by the term's importance. Accordingly, although a broad definition of ethnicity is required to appreciate its role in contemporary politics, we prefer to return to basics and define the "nation" more narrowly, lest it lose all meaning in a world in which journalists speak of the territorial entities that are countries, the governments that are states, and people that are their populations interchangeably as "nations," and in which "nation-building" has become a common but misleading term almost daily employed to characterize postconflict international activity in such ethically and nationally diverse areas as Bosnia, Afghanistan, and Iraq.

As Walker Connor has observed, whereas the ethnic group *can* be "other-defined," nations are necessarily self-defining. To use Rupert Emerson's still imminently serviceable definition, a nation is "the largest community which, when the chips are down, effectively commands men's loyalty, overriding the claims both of the lesser communities within it and those which cut across it or potentially enfold it within a still greater society."[2] The concept of nation-building—that is, of instilling through the art of politics this paramount sense of national identity in a political community lacking it—acquired its initial currency in the mid-twentieth century, when the process of decolonization rapidly bestowed statehood on an increasing number of multinational countries. Half a century later, their efforts at nation-building have been largely abandoned precisely because people usually develop this paramount level of identification with those with whom they already have much in common. Thus, the developing world remains overwhelmingly multinational and the ethnic group remains, as it was in the case of the Slovaks, Serbs, Croats, and Czechs, the primary building block of nations, and the basis of the latter's argument for political self-determination, normally referred to as nationalism or—more precisely—as what Walker Connor labels "ethnonationalism."[3] Among the states in today's world, however, the ideal outcome of national self-determination, the nation-state in which the people identify with one another as members of a single nation and with the government as *their* government, remains very much the minority case.

Ethnic Identity, Ethnic Movements, and Ethnopolitics

Beyond the meanings assigned to these critical concepts, the still growing literature on ethnic politics and conflict has elsewhere mirrored the increasing importance of the ethnic factor in the political processes of developed and developing, democratic and nondemocratic political processes during the last third of the twentieth century. Unfortunately, in too many instances this literature has developed in an alternately ambiguous or compartmentalized manner, failing on the one hand to distinguish clearly between those factors explaining the persistence of the ethnic factor in modern politics versus those affecting its influence in the modern world, while on the other hand providing neither broad, cross-country studies of ethnic conflict nor comparative explorations of the various types of ethnic conflict to be found in the contemporary world.

There have been notable exceptions to these generalizations, especially the latter, such as Joseph Rothschild's *Ethnopolitics: A Conceptual Framework;*[4] however, they have been too few. Thus, although an extensive number of excellent case studies of different ethnic conflicts are available, comparisons have often been hindered by the authors' almost implicit assumption of uniqueness underlying each of these individual studies. Where comparative studies exist, they have generally suffered from one or both of two defects. Even comparative studies such as Saul Newman's work on ethnonational parties and politics in the developed world have usually focused only on one source of ethnic conflict—most notably ethnoterritorial conflict—and here the tendency has been to separate the study of conflict in the multinational politics of the developing world from its examination in the states of North America and Western Europe.[5] Other manifestations of this segregated approach in the study of ethnic politics are not hard to find, especially in the literature studying ethnoterritorial politics in *domestic* relations apart from the study of its impact on the international system; for example, Daniel Patrick Moynihan's *Pandaemonium: Ethnicity in International Politics.*[6] The tools for managing ethnic conflict in the international system do differ from those where such conflicts occur entirely inside a polity; however, the absence of virtually any effort to explore the linkages between the actors involved in, and the prospects for managing in-system versus international manifestations of nationalism is nonetheless regrettable.

The profuse amount of work on foreign workers, immigrants, and—especially in the United States—nonspatial ethnic minorities has tended to flow in similar, compartmentalized channels. Studies tend to focus primarily on politics in the developed Western world, and are normally compartmentalized both conceptually (from the study of other forms of ethnic conflict) and spatially (from the study of the politics involving foreign workers, for example, in other parts of the world).[7] Where commentators do survey various forms of conflict in this context, they usually link ethnic conflict to the study of other forms of cleavage in the same political process, not to similar forms of ethnic conflict in other systems.[8]

This compartmentalized approach to the study of ethnic conflict has, to be sure, had its advantages. Scholars have been able to generate a large number of solid analyses covering a broad range of ethnic conflicts. Yet there is also something less than satisfying about the approach. Understanding what ethnicity is, and tracing it into the political process requires also understanding what it is not, where its boundaries fall, and how its political impact differs, not only in terms of where it manifests itself but in terms of how and in what form it emerges in a political process. Conceptualization and case studies require the development of a broader framework for analysis, lest they lead to a process of conceptual reification or studies resting on the somewhat unsatisfying, unproven assumption of the comparability or noncomparability of different types of ethnic conflict, policy demands, and governmental responses, or generalizations of an untested or nontestable nature.

Primordial, Constructionist, and Structuralist Theory: Competing Explanations of Ethnopolitics?

In one important manner, however, the study of ethnic and national identity, ethnic mobilization and nationalism, and the interaction of these forces with political processes has perhaps not been sufficiently segmented. Allowing for overlap, the three theoretical models that have undergirded the study of ethnopolitics during the last 40 years focus on three separate but not always clearly differentiated subjects. *Primordial theory*, which views ethnicity as a natural trait rooted in the individual's birth into an ancestral gene pool or shared cultural network, centers on the *origin and durability* of ethnic identify.[9] As such, it is akin to but not entirely dependent on the narrow, biological definition of ethnicity. *Constructionist theory* is more about the *adaptability* of ethnic identity as a means of explaining its durability. Related to the broad definition of ethnicity we are employing here, constructionism treats ethnicity as an evolving concept in which, "over time and space, economic, political and religious structures emerge with specific configurations that may be labeled ethnic."[10]

In contrast to both primordial and constructionist theory, *instrumentalist* theory focuses on the *utility* of ethnic identity as a tool of politics, used in a similar fashion by both individuals and groups in order to achieve their personal agendas. Here, the emphasis is on political leaders—political entrepreneurs and demagogues who mobilize communities around perhaps latent or forgotten ethnic identities and grievances—not the groups themselves, and the area of concern is the political process, not the historical origin of the group or the changing environment in which it exists or defines itself.[11]

The failure to differentiate among the central concerns of these explanations of ethnicity and ethnopolitics has occasionally led to their use on an "either-or" basis. A more fruitful approach would be to view them in a "where," "when," and "how" manner. In many tracts of the developing world, the primordial approach remains an immensely useful starting point for understanding the manner in which individuals see themselves in life. On the other hand, as Martin Heisler and others have noted, in the advanced developed world, where individuals are a part of a pluralistic as well as highly differentiated social and political universe, "neither individual identity nor the structure of the collectivity is likely to be based in its essence on ethnicity."[12] Here, the constructionist approach to ethnicity provides a better point of departure. As for the structuralist approach, it can explain ethnic mobilization and conflict at some point in time in any area of the contemporary multiethnic world, though the opportunities to manipulate the ethnic factor have perhaps been most prevalent in the Third World, where first decolonization and then subsequent regime failures have presented local demagogues with opportunities to exploit ethnic issues and animosities for personal gain, and in the postcommunist world, where the sudden collapse of communism gave politicians in multinational states an open political field in which to organize parties on an ethnonational basis and/or to play on minority grievances.

Because the focal point of this study is the interaction between the ethnic factor and public policy, we are less focused on theories involving the origin and durability of the ethnic factor than on the way in which ethnic communities become mobilized and how different types of ethnopolitical issues unfold in policy-making processes. Here, the structuralist approach can be especially useful, but it is best perceived as only one of several means of explaining the mobilization of and conflict involving ethnic communities. Others lie along a broad continuum bounded at one end by "spontaneous combustion" explanations of ethnic conflict and at the other end by the "manually operated" (structuralist) explanations, with the middle occupied by a wide spectrum of conditions- and circumstances-based explanations of ethnic conflict. Experience, and the case studies in this volume, indicates that each approach not only has merit, but a goodly number of examples to support it.

At the manually operated end are those conflicts explicable in terms of leaders willfully using the ethnic factor to advance their personal agendas. Some of these conflicts have been highly toxic: for example, the ethnic cleansing campaigns associated with the breakup of Yugoslavia and widely attributed to the influence of Croatian and Serbian leaders. Nor is the attractiveness of this approach limited to its compatibility with structuralist explanations of ethnic conflict. It also has a certain prescriptive appeal, which possibly accounts for its popularity among the governmental, inter-governmental, and nongovernmental officials involved in postconflict insti-tution-building in war torn areas. If ethnic conflicts are the result of the activities of an unscrupulous few, then the rebuilding of post–civil war societies becomes easier. It is a matter of punishing the evil and erecting new, cross-communal institutions for the basically good members of the various communities who only recently fought one another. Unfortunately, this approach to explaining ethnic conflict also begs the question of why the few leaders were able to provoke such violence. It is one thing to incite a brief racial riot; quite another to persuade people to nail their neighbors to the doors of their houses and torch the premises.[13]

In contrast, spontaneous theories of ethnic conflict, compatible with both the narrow and expansive definitions of ethnicity and with primordial and constructionist explanations of its durability, generally explain manifes-tations of ethnic conflict in one of two ways. They are either (1) the result of tensions between two or more self-defining ethnic communities mount-ing until they explode into open conflict ("spontaneous combustion"), or—more frequently—(2) the result of a catalyst igniting simmering interethnic grievances: for example, the 1992 race riot in Los Angeles following the acquittal of white police officers accused of beating a black suspect, in which much of the violence was between a property-renting African American community and Asian immigrants owning and residing in the commercial establishments in their neighborhood.

Between these two poles lie the majority of explanations for the salience of ethnic conflict. Many of these focus on predominantly political causes of ethnic conflict: competition for scarce resources, conflicting claims to the same territory, the trauma of democratization, the inability of weak political institutions to control communal rivalries, and the like. Another set of explanations—the greater number in constructionist theory—involves economic change: for example, the dislocating influence of economic modernization, and the impact of postindustrialism and globalization on ethnic identity.[14] In these theories, individuals may play key roles in bridging the gap between ethnopolitical sentiment and its mobilization; however, they are not the provocateurs of that conflict.

Ethnopolitical Conflict: A Schematic for
Comparative Analysis

Our study of ethnic politics is organized around and proceeds on the basis of four propositions:

(1) That however it emerges ethnicity is not just a persistent issue n the political processes of the modern world, but that ethnic conflict presents particularly complex and difficult challenges to policy makers. As William Zartman has summarized, the concern of ethnopolitical communities with perceived injustices and other highly charged issues significantly reduces the prospect for compromise in ethnopolitical bargaining, the context is usually a hostile one in which at least one of the contending parties is not interested in bargaining, spokesmen capable of authoritatively negotiating solutions are often lacking, and third party mediators are usually unwanted or perceived as meddlers. Moreover, the continued importance of some of the players usually depends on the conflict continuing.[15] At the same time, the ethnic factor can also provide an intensity and durability to political demands, which enhances their likelihood of being addressed. Thus, as Milton Esman has noted, "so compelling are the normative claims of *ethnic* self-determination that nowhere in contemporary Europe have regional grievances been successfully politicized except where they enjoy an ethnic base."[16]

(2) That understanding the manner in which ethnic conflict arises is an important element in understanding its impact on the policy process—a fact of ethnopolitical life that Newman has frequently documented.[17] Hence the importance of understanding the origin of ethnic identity in a particular case as the first step in understanding both the manner in which ethnopolitical communities are mobilized and their ability to achieve their objectives and survive in changing environments.[18]

(3) That the treatment of ethnic demands in the policy process is itself a major element in shaping ethnopolitics, not merely the end product of responding to those demands. Here, we view the political process as an ongoing linkage between ethnically self-defining communities and the generation of new rounds of ethnopolitical demands.[19]

(4) That ethnicity is most salient politically when combined with and, reinforced by one or more of the other major sources of cleavage that form the basis of politics in the contemporary world.

Territory, Class, and Culture: Constructing an Analytical Model

The framework we have found useful in overcoming some of the difficulties in the existing literature while keeping a firm eye on these propositions is heavily based on an early work by Aristides Zolberg. In a paper he presented at the 1976 International Political Science Association World

Congress, Professor Zolberg argued that societies tend to have three primary sets of segmentation: cultural, territorial, and class-based.[20] Within this framework, he schematically placed ethnicity within the (broader) domain of cultural segmentation. He then proceeded to discuss generally various types of ethnicity and the factors that tended to stimulate their political saliency, including the intersection of ethnocultural cleavages with class and territorial bases for societal segmentation. In doing so, he noted the dynamic nature of ethnic identity. Under some circumstances, a group's ethnicity might have little or no political saliency whereas in others it would become significant. Moreover, the degree of saliency attached to ethnic identification can change, not only from setting to setting but over time as well.

Zolberg's scheme illustrates the essence of ethnicity as a category of cultural distinctions resting at least in part on such traditional bases for political association as culture, language, shared history, and territorial origin, rather than on class or functional interests. Using Zolberg's scheme as a building block, we can extend it to classify ethnopolitical phenomena in a fourfold manner.[21] Additionally, if the bases of segmentation are considered as different bases of identity *and as types of public policy issues*, different manifestations of ethnicity can be placed within the areas of intersection. This conceptualization, in turn, suggests interrelationships between both the categories of ethnicity and other forms of social organization, and provides a means of comparing the different policies adopted by governments to deal with such conflicts.

Ethnicity can be located as a type of cultural segmentation that may also intersect class and territorial segmentation and thereby generate a differing set of issues precisely because these intersections involve overlapping identities, which may reinforce one another. The basic types of ethnicity can, likewise, be categorized by the various intersections among ethnic, cultural, class, and territorial segmentation. The first type involves *ethnocultural segmentation*; that is, those aspects of differentiation based solely on cultural differences existing between the ethnic group and the dominant population, and /or among ethnic groups in the population. Examples of ethnocultural conflict would include the past controversy in Britain over the refusal of some Sikhs to wear a helmet rather than their turban while riding a motorcycle, and the demands of Latino Americans for Spanish-instruction public schools in some sections of the southwestern United States. Unreinforced by other lines of cleavage, the issues generated by ethno-cultural differences have typically been resolvable within the legal systems or only minimally disruptive to the political process of developed polities.

The second type of ethnicity, *ethnoclass segmentation*, is distinguishable by substantial differences in social-class status separating one ethnic group from others (or the majority) in society. Frequently the ethnic group will be, or will perceive itself to be, of a lower status because of the past or present actions of the dominant group(s). Also frequently, this category involves ethnic groups with an identifiable geographic origin that differentiates them from the remainder of society. Issues typical of this category would include questions involving the right of foreign workers to receive the same civil and economic liberties as citizens. In addition to African Americans, groups falling into this class would include Native Americans and Mexican Americans in the United States, Asians in Britain, the guest workers of Western Europe, and the Romany (gypsies) throughout Central and Eastern Europe.

The third variety of ethnicity is found in the lines of intersection between ethnocultural and territorial segmentation. Characteristic of this *ethnoterritorial segmentation* is a very high concentration of an ethnic group's members in a territory commonly perceived as their own. Typifying this area would be those groups in Western Europe and Canada who, voluntarily or involuntarily, were incorporated into larger political systems during the state-making phase of their respective countries.

These groups frequently possess a distinct set of historical and cultural customs, language, and religion, and the issues generated by the ethnoterritorial cleavage typically involve the efforts of the ethnoterritorial community to preserve its cultural distinctiveness, to obtain a fair share of the broader society's resources, and/or to achieve a greater control over its own political life. Examples include the Scots and Welsh in Britain, the Flemish and Walloons in Belgium, the *Québécois* in Canada, the Corsicans in France, the Basques in Spain, and the Hungarian minority in the current Slovak Republic.

Finally, there is that type of ethnic segmentation that involves the intersection of highly salient ethnic, class, and territorial consciousness—what we somewhat awkwardly label *ethnoclass-territorial segmentation*. The resultant social stratification tends to disadvantage an ethnic group both in terms of a distinctly lower social-class status and territorial serration. Issues typical of this category would thus tend to reflect a pattern of reinforcing cleavages, not the cross-cutting ones so useful in managing all societal cleavages in modern, normally pluralistic political systems. Perhaps the best example of this typology in the developed democratic world is the protracted conflict in Northern Ireland, where the numerical minority "Catholics" have been historically discriminated against politically and economically, while also having been forced into largely segregated living areas.

Further differentiations among ethnopolitical groups can and should be made within many of these categories. The world of ethnoterritorial conflicts, for example, is a broad one, ranging from local turf battles between rival ethnic and/or immigrant communities for control over neighborhoods or local governments to genuine separatist movements. Within this framework the most important distinction is perhaps the division between ethno*regional* and ethno*national* groups. Ethnonational loyalties usually lead to demands for self-determination. By contrast, ethnoregional groups such as the *breton* and Flemish in France normally do not seek the separatist goal of full self-government. For such actors, the symbols of (here) France are generally stronger than those of the region, though the hold of the latter on the regional population may be by no means trivial and might evolve into a nationalist feeling over time.

In a similar manner, it is possible to distinguish several broad sets of politically salient ethnoclass groupings. Indigenous, nonspatially concentrated minorities may differ in the proximity of their culture to that of the dominant population: for example, in the United States, the racial minorities may be considered as analytically distinct from the migrant peoples who share the dominant population's basic physiological characteristics (primarily skin color). Nor are all ethnoclass groups necessarily to be found at the bottom of the economic ladder. Ethnic minorities whose wealth is greater than that of society as a whole can also become a political issue where envy rather than an indigenous sense of superiority feeds a dislike for the "other," as in case of anti-Semitic sentiment and politics in the Western world and the discrimination that the overseas Chinese often face in Asia.

Finally, ethnoclass-territorial groups, like ethnoterritorial groups in general, may be meaningfully classified on the basis of whether their boundaries occur solely within a polity, or transcend state boundaries, giving rise to both irredentist politics and a multiplication of state actors involved in or affected by their interests.

Case studies are essential to refine these and other subclassifications involving the ethnocultural, ethnoclass, ethnoterritorial, and ethnoclass-territorial groups composing the broad world of ethnopolitics, and to elucidate the connection between the different modes of ethnopolitical conflict and the various challenges it presents to political systems in the modern world. There is, however, at the least a threefold heuristic value of the framework we are using, which should not be ignored. First, it provides the hitherto noted tool for comparing various types of ethnopolitical phenomena to one another across geographical and societal lines and across time. Second, it relates ethnicity to other forms of stratification, identification, and conflict in political communities. Third, it provides a means of classifying ethnopolitical groups and movements *as they show up in political processes*, thereby facilitating our understanding of ethnopolitical conflicts and the tasks of policy makers seeking to manage them.

Ethnopolitics and Public Policy:
Preliminary Observations

Conclusions concerning specific types of ethnopolitical conflicts, unfolding in different contexts, can only be approached at the end of our comparative examination of a series of case studies of, principally, ethnoterritorial and ethnoclass conflict in the contemporary world. Prefatory to that examination, however, several general observations concerning the nature of ethnopolitics and the objectives of ethnopolitical actors in the policy-making process are in order.

Ethnopolitics as Context Politics

In ethnopolitics, as elsewhere, physical, historical, and societal context influences the emergence, direction, and success of political activity. Compared to such perennial macro policy issues as the economy and foreign affairs, ethnopolitics is an especially circumstances- and leadership-sensitive policy area.

The systematic study of a variety of similar ethnopolitical conflicts enables analysts to identify not only the idiosyncratic factors influencing political action and outcomes in a particular time and place, but also recurrent elements, themes, and patterns involving the mobilization of ethnopolitical communities, the demands of ethnopolitical groups, and their impact on the political processes in which they operate. Thus, for example, in the arena of ethnoterritorial politics, the excellent pool of case studies treating ethnoterritorial movements in the post–World War II, developed democratic world suggests several common, contributive factors that have affected the recent ebb, flow, and manageability of these movements, including the role of regionally educated political leadership in mobilizing these communities, and the threat to esteemed regional ways of life as coalescing forces.[22] Conversely, the global stagflation of the 1980s had a suffocating effect on their activity, insofar as regional self-rule held no answers for a worldwide recession.

In a similar manner, the more historical studies of individual regional movements—for example, of the endurance of Basque nationalism from the Industrial Revolution to the present—have allowed many commentators to characterize several of the late-twentieth-century ethnoterritorial movements in the Western world as constituting a revival (or resurgence) of ethnoterritorial politics rather than the emergence of it in developed world. Contextual studies likewise provide the needed detail on the similarities and differences affecting the rise and quite different fortunes of civil rights movements among ethnoclass minorities in the United States and Northern Ireland during the 1950s and 1960s. Indeed, it is only because of these studies that comparative analyses beyond the most vapid macro-theorizing on the nature of ethnopolitics are possible.

Ethnopolitics as Group Politics

Ethnic groups are typically described as having three distinguishing characteristics: they are "largely biologically self-perpetuating"; "they share *clusters* of beliefs and values"; and they "have internal differentiations . . . [which affect] the community's political capacity to deal with outside pressures."[23] The first two elements are normally visibly apparent to anyone researching and writing in the area of ethnopolitics; often the third only becomes apparent in the context of a case study.

Comparativists necessarily classify on the basis of broadly held differences: for example, the racial divide between white and black citizens in the United States. A case study of the history of immigration and race in the United States quickly unearths other divisions in both communities. In some instances, the European immigrants carried their rivalries with them—for example, the Irish Americans' anti-England biases. In other instances, competition in the new world created new rivalries: for example, between the Irish and Italian immigrants in Boston. Only over generations did these rivalries diminish (as late as World War I lobbyists representing Irish American associations were urging the United States to intervene against Britain on the side of Germany), and even then often these rivalries still played significant roles in local politics in the country's multiethnic cities. Case studies of the African Americans likewise indicate both historic and currently significant lines of internal cleavage; most notably on the basis of class and color. Civil rights gains in the areas of educational opportunity, economic opportunity, and voting rights have produced an upper middle class of African American professionals in the arts, the economy, and politics. Many are now defining their interests more in class terms. Two of the most widely known of these in the political world—Justice Clarence Thomas on the Supreme Court and former House of Representative member J.C. Watts in Congress—have even gone so far as to signal a hostility to the continuation of affirmative action programs, thereby incurring the wrath of other black leaders. Even speeches by Justice Thomas to black high schools have been opposed when proposed, and picketed when delivered.

The phenomenon of U.S. ethnic minorities moving from the city to the suburbs and from the working-class bosom of the Democratic Party to the more propertied-oriented Republican Party is not new. Many of the sons and daughters of the country's European-born immigrants traveled that trail in post–World War II America. On the other hand, the African American community traditionally showed greater internal cohesiveness than the country's Euro-minorities, and even today public opinion polls continue to suggest higher group solidarity among African Americans than other non-European ethnic minorities in the United States.

Class is not the only division separating African Americans. A far older, though less publicized division has operated on color lines. In cities such as New Orleans and Savannah, social organizations composed of light-skinned Negroes have for generations excluded darker-skinned African Americans from membership. Nor is the division purely historical or social. In returning to office in the mid-1990s, Washington, D.C., mayor Marion Barry successfully ran a heavily race-tinged campaign against his fellow Democrat, Sharon Pratt Kelly, the light-skinned African American who had replaced him for a term while he was served a short jail sentence for violating federal drug laws.

As for the U.S. Native American and other non- and quasi-European minorities, not only class (the better-educated Cubans versus the Puerto Ricans, for example) but also national-origin internally divide tribal American and the Asian, Latinos, and Middle Eastern communities in the

United States, just as they do the foreign workers throughout the continent of Europe.[24]

In short, minorities that appear so cohesive when viewed through the eyes of macro-theory inevitably contain, when examined more closely, fractures and factions that can significantly undermine their effectiveness in the political process.

Ethnopolitics as Bargaining Politics

The Bipolar Nature of Ethnopolitical Bargaining

Intracommunal cohesiveness can be especially important in the area of ethnopolitics because of its "movement" nature and the frequently bipolar nature of the bargaining process it generates. To be sure, a variety of ethnic spokesmen and an assortment of "minority" groups may be involved in a particular issue, as occurred in the United States during the 1960s when several different ethnic minorities (African American, Hispanic, Native Americans) joined with other traditionally politically underrepresented groups (such as women) to press a shared civil rights agenda. Similarly, coalitions can alter over time, as when differing views toward affirmative action programs drove a wedge between African American and Jewish American civil rights groups, which had long collaborated in their struggle against discrimination.[25] Nonetheless, ethnic conflicts frequently break down into the demands of minorities and majorities, with the central government usually the third party, operating either as the referee or arbiter to the dispute, or the actor addressed by the one for policies aimed at the other.

Because cross-group bargaining is so intrinsic to the nature of ethnopolitics, focusing on the bargaining element allows us to explore ethnopolitical conflict across its various categories (ethnoterritorial, ethnoclass), space (Scot nationalism, Slovak Nationalism), and time (the Basque movement circa 1890 and 1990), and provides a basis for examining its impact on and in the policy process. Case studies such as those offered in this volume allow us to discern the changing concerns of these bargaining processes, the willingness of ethnopolitical groups and their spokesmen to compromise, and the different roles that the majority group, the minority group, and central leadership play in the various categories of ethnic conflict.

Ethnopolitical Objectives

As John Wildgen has suggested, ethnopolitical goals can be conveniently grouped under four basic rubrics: output goals, authority goals, regime goals, and community goals.[26] The most easily accommodated are the *output* goals or demands, which typically involve enhancing the ethnopolitical community's access to and share of the resources of the state. Examples of these would include government transfers to support education and health services on Native American reservations, and adequate funding for immigrant settlement programs. The demands of nonspatial minorities for civil rights protection and the demands of anti-immigrant groups to close the borders and rescind the temporary visas of foreign workers also fall under this heading.

The other three categories of goals are much less easily accommodated because they require the political leaders to cede meaningful degrees of their own power to the minority groups. Those pursuing *authority* demands seek to advance the status of their community inside the state. The demand of Flemish nationalists in Belgium for parity with the country's French-speaking leadership in the Cabinet falls under this rubric. So, too, do affirmative action programs designed to shatter the "glass ceilings" of ingrained prejudices, which arguably prevent minorities from achieving social, economic, and political empowerment.

Regime goals involve reshaping the state's decision-making structure to give a group greater say in the decision-making process. These devices can be convoluted: for example, a concurrent majority system requiring that a majority of the representatives of minority groups support a measure in addition to the requirement of an overall majority in order for bills to become a laws in specified sensitive areas. The "warning bell system" in Belgium's 1971 Constitution fits into this category, as do most of the pro-posals for ending London-rule of Northern Ireland. Typically, however, regime demands focus on reforming the state to give spatially concentrated minorities greater autonomy through decentralization, devolution, region-alization, and federalization schemes.

Finally, some groups challenge the existence of the state system (the "*political community*") in which they find themselves, seeking self-determination and the breakup of the state. These demands can be expressed peacefully, as in the Scot Nationalists' campaign for votes on the issue of an independent Scotland, or violently via attempts at secession (Croatia's withdrawal from Yugoslavia), or irredentist movements seeking to redraw the boundaries of more than one state (e.g., the militant Basque nationalists seeking to carve an independent Basque state out of the Basque regions of France and Spain).

Only ethnoterritorial groups normally have the luxury of pressing for some form of territorial self-rule. Reciprocally, a territorial base is essential if a group is to pursue the ethnonationalist goal of national self-determination. Consequently, the goals pursued by ethnoterritorial and ethnoclass-territorial groups tend to differ significantly from those pursued by ethnoclass groups. Ethnoterritorial groups can pursue all four types of objectives, whereas ethnoclass minorities necessarily concentrate on output and authority demands. Regime and extra-community pursuits are generally foreclosed to nonterritorial minorities, except in the arena of local government where con-centrations may make the national minority a local majority and hence enhance the attractiveness of financial and programmic devolution schemes.

The Prospects for Accommodation

The goals adopted by the ethnopolitical communities, in turn, greatly affect the willingness of the central government and other ethnopolitical communities to accommodate their demands. Few political systems will peacefully choose to accede to demands challenging the existence of the political community. Certainly the author cannot think of another instance like the Czechoslovakia case treated in this volume, where the leadership of the majority community collaborated with an ethnoterritorial minority to split the state peacefully into two independent countries. Few governments, for that matter, have looked favorably at first upon the demands of territorialized minorities for some form of home rule in a unitary state. Rejectionist responses have been much more common: for example, the deaf ear that Slovak leaders have turned since independence to the demands for autonomy of the Hungarian minority in eastern Slovakia.

The inclination to bargain, compromise, or accommodate is not just related to the demands of ethnopolitical communities. It also reflects the broad psychology of the group vis-à-vis its status in a multiethnic polity. A considerable body of literature, predominantly written by sociologists, exists on the reaction of ethnic minorities to their minority condition. As Brewton Berry and Henry Tischler summarize in their text on *Race and Ethnic Relations*, virtually all ethnic minorities initially experience disorganization and demoralization when confronted with a different and dominant culture. Only thereafter do minorities more permanently adjust by adopting one (or combinations) of a variety of modes of behavior, depending on the period and degree of dominance, ranging from docile servility to acceptance of minority status to efforts to assimilate into the broader culture to protesting their minority status to aggressive resistance to being subordinated by a dominant culture and/or political process.[27] By contrast, substantially less work has been done on the willingness of majorities or dominant ethnic groups to compromise or the factors (prior exposure to ethnic diversity, view of the territorial integrity of the state, commitment to the concept of equality, and so on) likely to influence them to accommodate the demands of ethnopolitical minorities. In the long run, however, conflict management is only possible when the minority community has adopted a set of demands negotiable within the existing political system, and the majority community—or at least its leadership—is prepared to accommodate to some degree the demands of its ethnopolitical minorities.

Patterns of Ethnopolitical Bargaining

Finally, where bargaining does occur, the principal actors tend to assume substantially different roles in the different facets of ethnoconflict. In *ethnoterritorial politics*, the primary actors tend to be the spokesmen for the ethnoterritorial communities, with the government initially being placed in the secondary role of respondent to their demands. The remainder of the population is apt to remain in the tertiary role of observer unless the demands of the regionalized community affect their hold on significant economic resources (the Scottish Nationalists demand for control over Britain's North Sea oil wealth) or political power at the center (the demand of Belgium's majority Flemish community for their fair [majority] share of power in governing a Belgian state long dominated by its French-speaking minority). *Ethnoclass politics*, by contrast, tend to revolve around two different configurations. Issues involving foreign workers/immigrants have largely been launched by (often self-proclaimed) spokesmen for the majority community, addressed to the government, and aimed at reducing the presence and/or rights of these minorities in their host countries. Here, where the surfacing of a large, ethnically distinct minority in the midst of a culture inexperienced with diversity can produce a cultural shock in both the majority and minority communities, the foreign workers and/or (legal and illegal) immigrants are normally the unwilling subject of the majority's action. By contrast, issues involving the status of indigenous minorities tend to be raised by the minorities, responded to by spokesmen for the majorities, and mediated or resolved by the central government.

Whatever their origin and nature, as the following case studies document, ethnopolitical issues remain persistent, often divisive, and frequently extraordinarily significant components of politics throughout much of the world in these early days of the twenty-first century.

PART 1

France: Ethnopolitics in the Developed West

CHAPTER TWO
_____

The Setting of Politics in the Advanced Democratic World

Ethnopolitics, like all politics, occurs in an identifiable environment, which to varying degrees affects the mobilization, goals, and outlook of ethnopolitical communities and the manageability of ethnic conflict in the political processes confronting it. In general, the environment of ethnic conflict in the advanced democratic world has made it easier for states such as the United States, Belgium, the United Kingdom, and France to cope with the ethnoterritorial and ethnoclass conflicts confronting them, compared to the more tumultuous world of ethnic politics in both the still politically and economically developing states of Asia and Africa, and the economically developed countries of postcommunist Europe. Yet, even in well-established Western democracies, the intensity of conflict can be high and its duration long, as witnessed by the still unresolved, protracted conflict in Northern Ireland.

The Political Context: Old, Rich, and Established Democratic States

When we speak of advanced democracies we are discussing states that tend to be both older than the countries created in Central Europe after World War I and the Third World states that, in general, acquired their independence only after World War II, and more economically and politically advanced than either. For the most part, they also tend to be liberal democracies that democratized *earlier* than most states in the contemporary world, and are among the world's earlier industrializers, with economies now dominated by the service sector.[1] In addition, their societies are normally composed of citizens who have developed at least some identity with their political processes and widely participate in them. Finally, their decision-making processes have generally acquired a sense of legitimacy and the capacity to enforce their policies effectively, and they have economies capable of satisfying the material needs and economic wants of the governed.[2]

Constitutional Government and Politicized Ethnicity

At the heart of liberal democratic systems lie both "a basic set of institutions for participation, competition, and individual liberties"[3] and a commitment to individual rights and limited government defined in terms of a companion commitment to the rule of law and the regularized restraints on the power of government which Carl Friedrich labeled "constitutional government."[4] In practice, during the 20th century it also came to mean, in the United States, Britain and a growing number of democracies in Western Europe, a dedication to the inclusiveness of all citizens in the political process, universal suffrage and free elections, and equality in the distribution of individual rights and liberties.[5]

As a consequence of their citizens' inclusion in and identification with their political processes, the governments of advanced democracies enjoy advantages in confronting ethnopolitical demands that are not normally present in either post-Communist Europe or the politically and economically developing world. Their long histories may even mean that their ethnoterritorial minorities also identify with the broader political communities of which they are a part: seeing themselves, for instance, as both Welsh and British. At the same time, because of the rights they confer on their citizens, these states must also concede organizational advantages to the ethnopolitical organizations confronting them even when the latter are peacefully demanding the dismemberment of the state. Likewise, specific rules of the game can work to the advantage as well as disadvantage of ethnopolitical organizations. Broadly defined laws against seditious utterances or hate speech, for example, can make it difficult for ethnoterritorial organizations to manage the line separating legitimate calls for regional self-determination from seditious utterances, just as proscriptions against hate speech can handicap the rhetoric of anti-immigrant and/or anti-Jewish political associations.

Specific electoral arrangements can exert an even greater influence on the fortunes of ethnopolitical organizations. As a rule, it is far more difficult for new parties to gain political representation in countries using the single-member district, winner by plurality system (SMD) than in countries committed to proportional representation (PR) systems in which parties gain a share of assembly seats proportional to their share of the popular vote. Thus, because Britain and France have customarily employed some variation of the SMD model, the Scottish Nationalists and Le Pen's anti-immigrant National Front party in France have persistently won a far smaller share of parliamentary seats than their share of the popular vote. Conversely, the PR systems of Belgium and Austria have facilitated the rise of ethnoterritorial and anti-immigrant parties.

Party Politics and the Ethnic Factor

At least as important a variable affecting the fortunes of ethnopolitical organizations as electoral arrangements is the nature of the prevailing party system. Unlike in multinational Third World countries, where parties tended to form along ethnonational and/or ethnolinguistic lines during the latter days of colonialism, or in postcommunist Europe, where the collapse of the communist party in single party states meant that formative ethnopolitical organizations did not have to compete for votes against established parties, the ethnonational parties that have emerged or revitalized themselves in the advanced democratic world since World War II have had to competed against established, system-wide parties with long track records of governing experience. It has been an obstacle to the growth of both ethnoterritorial parties and ethnoclass-focused organizations such as Western Europe's anti-immigrant parties.

The story, however, is hardly one-sided. Recent changes in the existing patterns of participation in the established political processes and the traditionally supportive orientation of their citizens toward government in the advanced democratic world have created new opportunities for ethnopolitical organization. The party systems erected during the twentieth century on class-based societal cleavages have had a difficult time in sustaining themselves in the increasingly mobile and affluent societies of the contemporary advanced democratic world.[6] In most instances, voters have been less inclined to realign with other political parties than to detach themselves from the parties for which they traditionally voted; however, this dealignment process has provided electoral opportunities, which ethnoterritorial and anti-immigrant parties have frequently exploited to their advantage.

Social Pluralism and the Ethnic Factor

The pluralistic nature of social identity in the advanced democratic world has been another obstacle to the success of ethnoterritorial movements in Western Europe and North America. In most countries, party systems still reflect the ethnically cross-cutting, social-class basis of political alignment, which developed in the late nineteenth and early twentieth centuries, with conservative parties being pitted against leftist, working-class–based parties, which today wear such labels as the Labour Party in Britain, the Social Democrats in Germany, and the Socialist Party of France.

Class is not the only important crosscutting cleavage that dilutes the political salience of ethnicity in advanced democracies. Age can provide a powerful bond between members of a multiethnic political community that has faced monumental challenges. At the same time, not all cleavages are necessarily crosscutting. Many of Europe's ethnoterritorial communities are often poorer economically than their countries as a whole. As a result, economic differences reinforce the ethnic divide in separating the majority and minority communities in many areas of Britain, Canada, France, and other advanced democratic states.[7] Still, in general, such politically salient cleavages as class, gender, and generation tend to cross-cut and dilute the importance of ethnic cleavages far more frequently in the developed democratic world than in Third World states; this factor too has played an important role in making ethnic conflicts tractable in the developed world.

The Ethnic Mosaic of the Advanced
Democratic World

Although "New World" states such as the United States, Australia, Canada, and New Zealand are old compared to both those countries of Central Europe created at the Paris Peace Conference after World War I and the vast majority of the countries in Africa and Asia, the distinction between the Old World countries of Western Europe and their New World colonies in North America and the Pacific remains a useful one for broadly sorting through the origins and nature of ethnopolitical issues in the states of the advanced democratic world. In both the New and Old Worlds, ethnic diversity was greatly increased by immigration during the second half of the twentieth century; however, the state-making eras varied greatly between the two, and ethnic politics in both areas still reflects that difference.

State-Making and the Regions of Europe

The lengthy era of state-making in Western Europe is credited with having created a large number of nation-states, but it also resulted in a large number of multinational states with territorialized, ethnically distinct regions—a not illogical outcome given the nature of the state-making process.

The dominant state-making model consisted of a centralizing and expansionist regime at the center (e.g., the capitals of most of these countries today), first consolidating its control over those areas initially tied to it through the fiefdom system of feudal Europe and then pushing its realm to either its natural limits—and sometimes even beyond its coast to offshore islands—or until it met a resistance powerful enough to dissuade if from further expansion. There are notable exceptions, of course. Belgium was born with the union of its Flemish-speaking north and its French-speaking south when these regions, under the leadership of a dissident French-speaking elite, seized an opportune moment and broke away from Dutch rule in the early nineteenth century. Italy acquired its German-speaking, Tyrolean north when its leaders opportunistically switched sides during World War I to fight on the side of the French, British, and American soldiers in return for that region, until then under the rule of an Austria about to be on the losing side in that war. Switzerland's origins are more federative than expansionary, its French-, German-, and Italian-speaking cantons coming together to escape the orbs of the powerful states around them. In general, however, the centralizing model explains the birth of most of the major states in today's Western Europe, and the manner in which their territorialized minorities were acquired.

The states resulting from these developments frequently house a number of territorialized ethnic minorities, few of which are as widely known as Great Britain's Scotland and Wales, the Basque provinces in Spain, or the Alsace-Lorraine region in France. More than two generations ago, speculating that Europe's future might eventually lie in the direction of a European federation of ethnically distinct regions, Guy Heraud identified over 30 of these zones, along with a list of organizations representing them committed to that ideal.[8] In most instances, the areas he discussed were composed of linguistic as well as ethnic minorities in the existing states of Europe.[9] By the mid-1970s many of these had joined together in founding a Bureau of Unrepresented Nationalities in Brussels to lobby the European Union (EU, then the European Community) on their behalf. In order to press their interests on the home front, most also developed ethnoregional and ethnonational parties, many of which have now also become active in the European Parliament in Strasbourg, where those elected to it have formed a European Free Alliance for collaborative action.[10]

Table 2.1, which lists the principal ethnically assertive territorial minorities within the advanced democratic world, identifies less than half of the ethnopolitical and often separatist groups Heraud identified and that remain, to a large degree, active today.[11] Among those excluded, the most notable are the ethnopolitical communities in Northern Ireland because of the broadly intermingled nature of Ulster's majority Protestant-unionist and minority

Table 2.1   Principal territorialized ethnic minorities in the advanced democratic world

Country	Ethnoterritorial minority	Geographic locale
Belgium	Flemish	Flanders, northern half of the country
	Walloons	Wallonia, southern portion of the country
	Francophone Bruxellois	Brussels enclave in Flanders
Canada	Québécois*	East central Canada
Cyprus	Turks	Northern half of the island
Denmark	Faronese*	Island group north of United Kingdom
France	Alsaciens*	Eastern France at the border with Germany
	Basques*	Southwest France's border with Spain
	Bretons*	Northwestern province of Brittany
	Corsicans*	Isle of Corsica in the Mediterranean Sea
	Occatanians*	Southern France
Italy	Sardinians	Isle of Sardinia, off Italy's west coast
	Sicilians	Isle of Sicily, off Italy's southwest tip
	South Tiroleans*	Alto Adige, at the border with Austria
Netherlands	Frisans*	Friesland, northwestern tip of country
Spain	Andalucians	South-central most tip of Spain
	Basques*	Northeastern corner of Spain
	Catalonians*	Eastern coastline of the country
	Galicians*	Northwestern most Spain
Switzerland	Jura francophones	Former Alpine zone in Bern canton
United Kingdom	Cornish*	Western England peninsula of Cornwall
	Scots	Scotland, Great Britain's north
	Welsh*	Wales, Great Britain's western region
United States	Puerto Ricans*	Island of Puerto Rico in the Caribbean Sea

* Denotes the presence of a minority language.

Catholic-nationalist communities. Territorially, each has a foot in a larger community in which Protestants (in the United Kingdom) and Catholics (in all of Ireland) constitute solid majorities. Elsewhere, omitted are offshore, already highly autonomous areas such as Gibraltar, with its separatist movement, and remote, quasi-colonial areas such as Denmark's Faeroe Islands. Finally, because of their size also excluded are the very small areas in Europe's larger states housing autonomy-to-separatist movements, including Britain's now mostly English-speaking Shetland islands, and Italy's northeastern Padania region, the stronghold of the Italian Northern League party.

In terms of salience, most of the separatist movements in the advanced democratic world pose, at most, a challenge only to domestic policy makers.[12] Neither North America nor Western Europe holds an irredentist nationalist movement comparable to the long struggle of the Kurds for a homeland in the Middle East. Even at its height, the most publicized of Europe's movements, the Basques,' confined its violent operations to Franco's Spain. On the other hand, autonomy-to-separatist movements do exist in virtually all Western European countries as well as in Canada and Puerto Rico in North America, and at least two of these movements—that of the Sami of northern Finland, Sweden, Norway, and Russia, and the Istria movement spanning Italy, Croatia, and Slovenia—link Western Europe to the post-communist world to its east.

Adding Diversity: Empire, Immigration, and Ethnoclass
Conflict in the Old and New Worlds

The emergence of the modern territorial state system in Europe, beginning with the consolidation of all of Great Britain under a single king by 1607, substantially paralleled the early stages of European empire-building and colonization: for example, the founding of Jamestown that same year. Similarly, the later stages of European state-making (the birth of modern Germany and Italy in 1870–71) coincided with the final stages of European empire-building, when Britain, France, and others availed themselves of recent developments in the areas of weaponry, transportation, communications, and medicine to bring over 80 percent of the world's landmass under European control.[13]

With the establishment of Western Europe's modern state structure and stabilization of borders on the continent, the movement of peoples from one state to another largely ceased except for the migration of Europe's stateless communities (Jews and Romany) and those occasional migrations resulting from a great political upheaval in one of the established states, such as the Russian revolution in 1917. It was not until after World War II that European states as a group began to *receive* very large numbers of outsiders. Even then, it was not from other European states but in the form of the sons and, much less frequently, daughters of their overseas empires, whose labor they recruited to help rebuild their countries after the war.

In the meantime, Europe's established states became major exporters of ethnic diversity as they constructed their colonies in North and South America and in the far Pacific region of Australia and New Zealand. The flow varied over time depending on the intensity with which the colonizer pushed its peoples abroad, their desire to start a new life abroad, the immigrant policies of the former colonies once they became self-governing, and the conditions in Europe encouraging immigration: for example, Ireland's potato famine in the mid-nineteenth century. The resultant degree of diversity also varied. Australia and New Zealand, already remote from Europe, kept a relatively tight rein on immigration with the result that their European elements remained largely of British extraction. The United States, with essentially an open door to immigrants from the 1840s until World War I, drew immigrants from throughout Europe, and the ethnic roots of its citizens today still reflect that diversity as well as the fact that many of its early immigrants came involuntarily during the years when slavery was legal. Given these waves of immigrants following the early settlement of North America, the large slave population living in the United States until its civil war (1861–65), the turf battles between the European immigrants in the older American cities, and U.S. qualified openness to Asian immigration, there is scarcely an era in the country's history devoid of ethnic and racial issues and conflict (see table 2.2). The majority of that conflict involved an ethnoclass dimension resulting from the discrimination faced by those groups arriving later or further removed from the developing White Anglo Saxon Protestant prototype of the original settlers, and their need to settle initially for jobs at the bottom of the economic ladder unless they were willing to move westward, where the frontier offered vertical mobility in the form of free land.[14]

Ethnoclass divisions also emerged in the multiethnic states of Western Europe during this period, but essentially on an "in house" basis. Where peripheral ethnoterritorial groups were disproportionately left out of the economic modernization process, their members would move toward the center, where opportunity and the dominant community lived and where they too usually had to settle for menial jobs. Nevertheless, the major ethnoclass divisions in Western Europe developed only after World War II with the mounting numbers entering Northern Europe from Southern Europe, North and Sub-Sahara Africa, and Asia, and taking their place in these countries most often at the bottom of the prevailing social and economic order.

The New World too was not bereft of ethnoclass conflicts before the arrival of the Europeans. The great indigenous empires of the Americas—those of the Mayas, Incas, and Aztecs—all practiced the most egregious form of ethnoclass discrimination: the enslavement of the tribes they conquered. With the arrival of their European conquerors, however, these and lesser empires vanished and the shape of New World politics lost most of its pre-European, ethnoterritorial layout.

Table 2.2   Selected significant dates in U.S. ethnopolitical history, 1619–1992

1619	Origins of slavery in British North America
1654	First Jewish immigrants arrive (New Amsterdam)
1664	Miscegenation laws are enacted in New England and Chesapeake
1680–1730	Indian slave trade supports economy (Carolina)
1712	First major slave revolt (New York City)
1759–61	Cherokee Wars
1777	Northeast states abolish slavery
1787–89	U.S. constitution allows southerners to retain their "peculiar institution" of slavery
1804	Ohio limits rights of blacks in north
1807	Congress prohibits further importation of African slaves
1808	Tecumseh founds Prophetstown
1810	Underground Railroad founded
1818	First Seminole War (also in 1835 and 1855)
1820	Missouri Compromise overcomes division on slavery issue
1830	Indian Removal Act passed in Congress
1831	Nat Turner's slave insurrection
1836	Trail of Tears removals begin
1840–50s	German and Irish immigration wave
1844	Philadelphia riots target Catholic immigrants
1850	Great Compromise sidesteps division on slavery issue; Second Fugitive Slave Law enacted
1855–58	Slavery issue leads to Bleeding Kansas
1861–65	Stand Watie leads Cherokee regiment for South in Civil War
1861–86	Apache Wars
1863	Emancipation proclamation
1865	Civil War ends; Ku Klux Klan founded
1866	Red Cloud's War of the Bozeman Trail; race riots in Memphis and New Orleans
1871	Indian Appropriation Act passed; Ku Klux Klan act permits federal action in race crimes
1890	Battle of Wounded Knee
1892	New wave of immigration; Ellis Island established
1898	Supreme Court affirms citizenship of U.S.-born Chinese
1898	Spanish American War gives U.S. Puerto Rico and Hawaii
1899	Yellow peril campaign against Japanese immigrants begins
1903–06	Race riots in Belleville, Ill., Springfield, Ohio, Brownville, Tex., and Chattanooga, Tenn.
1908–13	NAACP and Anti-Defamation League of b'nai b'rith founded
1917	Immigration Act of 1917 begins to shut door on immigrants
1919	Race riots occur in Omaha and Chicago
1920–30	Great Migration of southern blacks to the north and Midwest; 1.5 million migrate by 1930
1922	Supreme Court rules Japanese ineligible for citizenship
1924	Congress passes Indian Citizenship Act
1931	Mass deportation of Mexicans from California
1942–45	Wartime interment of Japanese Americans and (for a short period) Italian Americans
1943	Race Riots across United States
1946	President Truman desegregates the military
1952	Puerto Rico becomes a Commonwealth
1954	Supreme Court invalidates segregation in public education
1964	Civil Rights Act of 1964 passed
1967	Race riots in Detroit leads to Kerner Commission Report
1968	Assassination of Martin Luther King, Jr. leads to rioting
1968	Congress enacts American Indian Civil Rights Act
1971	Busing debate divides Americans
1972–79	Civil Rights demonstrations by Native Americans turn violent
1980	Riots erupt in Miami's Latino community
1991	Race riots in Crown Heights section of Brooklyn involving Jewish and black communities
1992	Acquittal of white officers tried for beating black suspect ignites interracial riots Los Angeles

Source: Compiled from *Great Events in North American History* (Pasadena, Calif.: Salem Press, Inc., 1997), and *Encyclopedia of Modern Ethnic Conflicts* (Westport, Conn.: Greenwood Press, 2003).

Settler Societies, State-Making, and the Decline of
Ethnoterritorial Politics in the New World

The competition between newcomers in the urban immigrant enclaves in the U.S. east coast and Midwest, where European immigrant neighborhoods still bear names such as Little Italy, Little Moscow, and Germantown, and between Asian arrivees and Canadians in the coastal cities of western Canada are not the only examples of territorialized ethnic conflict in North America. Quite to the contrary, the United States and Canada each have their own ethnolinguistic territorial minorities—the French-speaking Quebec province in the Canadian federation and the U.S. Spanish-speaking isle of Puerto Rico. Moreover, each continues to raise challenges to system maintenance in their respective political systems. They are not, however, so much the product of immigration and settler colonialism as the byproducts of colonial and imperial warfare.

Quebec

Britain acquired the former French outpost of New France when its troops won the decisive Battle of Quebec in 1759, 225 years after Jacques Cartier began his exploration of the St. Lawrence River and opened the door to French claims to the region. Instead of seeking to assimilate the region's population, the British, in the Quebec Act of 1774, opted to preserve its French civil codes and landholding laws, and leave unmolested the status of the Catholic church in the territory, despite the Church's role as a carrier of the French culture as well as Catholic faith. A North American variant of the system of 'Indirect rule," which the British were by then adopting in the Indian subcontinent, the Act provided the region's French majority with the legal authority to preserve their cultural identity. An 1837 rebellion by French activists seeking greater political autonomy led Canada's governor general in 1841 to inaugurate efforts to Anglicize Quebec, but by then it was too late. Hence, when the fear of invasion by the post–Civil War American army led to the unification of the various Canadian provinces in the 1867 British North American Act, the die was cast and Quebec remained a francophone-majority state in the emergent Canadian federation.[15]

Puerto Rico

Technically, the U.S. acquisition of Puerto Rico came as the result of an anti-imperial war, the Spanish-American War of 1898, when reports of Spanish atrocities in its Cuban possession were sufficiently hyped by a jingoist press to push the United States into a war with Spain over Cuba. Nevertheless, the result was, as the American diplomat George Kennan observed, that United States was left with a European-styled empire composed of not just Cuba but territories so geographically remote from the United States that at the time they were acquired they could hardly be considered for statehood. Eventually one of these (Hawaii) did join the union, but only after the marvels of twentieth-century developments involving transportation and communications, and only after the further settlement of Hawaii by and assimilation of its peoples to an English-speaking culture. Another, the Philippines, became independent after World War II. Liberated Cuba was almost immediately let go.

What remain as U.S. possessions today are a series of small, ethnically distinct Pacific islands deemed too tiny in area and population to be given independence and which legally enjoy self-governing status as federal territories, and Spanish-speaking Puerto Rico. From the beginning that island was near enough to the United States to be considered for statehood, but not so small as to make eventual independence entirely unthinkable.[16] In fact, some of its leaders have pushed the statehood option on occasion, but without support from Washington, which—given Canada's experience with Quebec—has had little appetite for the potential problems of adding an ethnically and linguistically different state to the Union. Rather, as a means of responding to the demands of Puerto Rican nationalists for independence and federalists for statehood, Washington has over time bestowed citizenship on the people of Puerto Rico, thus giving them access to the United States though not the right to vote in its elections, and has enacted a series of laws benefiting the Puerto Rican economy as a self-governing, commonwealth.[17]

The Native Americans—A Case Study of De-territorialization

Given the non-statehood status of U.S. extra-continental acquisitions, the only groups allowed territorial autonomy based on their ethnic origin within the United States are the country's first involuntary members, the Native American tribal communities. To be sure, it has been centuries since they constituted a large share of the continent's population given the waves of immigrants from Europe who quickly overwhelmed them numerically and often confiscated their lands. In a country with more than a quarter of a billion people today, only approximately 400,000 Native Americans still live on the reservations allotted to them. Even if the other 80,000 native Alaskans (Indians, Inuits, and Eskimos) are counted, their total is no larger than the number of illegal aliens estimated to be living in New York City.[18] Nevertheless, their story is worth examining as an example of the limits of assimilation efforts directed at even the smallest and weakest of ethnopolitical groups, and as a study of the fate of the indigenous ethnoterritorial communities in the Americas.

The struggle of these tribes to survive predated the birth of the United States. As an eminent American historian phrased it, "the English-American empire builders went first for the land cleared and cultivated by the First Americans."[19] The struggle of the Native Americans for their rights within the framework of a constitutional democracy, however, began with the ratification of the U.S. Constitution.[20]

As adopted in 1789, the United State recognized the tribes' territorial autonomy but at the same time seriously limited their right to self-rule by making Native Americans the wards of the federal government. Only within the wardship system were tribal nations to enjoy a limited right to self-government. Moreover, given their wardship status they were not entitled to either citizenship or the protection of the Bill of Rights or other constitutional guarantees of individual rights and liberties.

In practice, the policies adopted toward the Native Americans built more on the pattern of relations with the tribes established by Europeans prior to the ratification of the Constitution than on the benevolent guardianship role implied by the wardship system. For hundreds of years, the French, Portuguese, Spanish, English, and Dutch militarily subdued the tribes they encountered, denigrated their cultures, and confiscated their lands and wealth. Consequently, it was not a large leap for the founding fathers to continue to look upon the tribes as primitive, if not savage, obstacles to building a country, and to brush aside their right to self-government when it conflicted with the settlement of the continent.

By the 1830s the obstacle to further settlement that various east coast tribes constituted led President Andrew Jackson to implement a removal policy based on the rationale of "Indian Territory." In theory, the tribes were to be pushed westward to lands physically remote from those of the settlers to enable them to preserve their ways of life. In practice, removal was usually at gunpoint and the journey to Indian Territory was invariably harsh; most memorably in the winter of 1838–39, when 4,000 of the 16,000 Cherokees driven from their homeland died on what has become known as "the Trail of Tears." Losing wars, periodic massacres, and forced removals thus became the dominant themes of the nineteenth-century history of the First Americans.

The removal policy forced the tribal nations away from their traditional ways of life. It also often had genocidal consequences as far as the cultures of numerous Indian nations were concerned. And it forever foreclosed the pursuit of a traditional style of ethnoterritorial politics by the Native Americans, for although it did at least temporarily leave the tribes with a territorial base for self-rule, the territory was no longer *their* historical lands. Moreover, in short order the removal policy affected virtually all of the tribes east of the Mississippi River. The traditional tribes, practicing their traditional ways, on their traditional land, in the words of the great Shawnee leader Tecumseh, "vanished before the avarice and the oppression of the white man, as snow before a summer sun."[21]

Finally, when even the more remote Indian Territory areas were opened to European immigrants, the Indian Territory policy was abandoned in favor of settling the tribes in the contained borders of reservations.[22] It was an option open to the U.S. government given the vast expanse of relatively unpopulated lands in the North American continent—the same expanse that spread out the 44 million immigrant coming to the United States between 1830 and World War I, making the United States, with few exceptions, an immigrant country, but one of widely spread out and intermingled immigrants rather than of territorialized immigrant groups.

Native Communities in Other Settler Societies

The same pattern of conquering and marginalizing the native minorities can also be found in the other major settler societies of the developed democratic world: Australia and Canada. In the former, as early as 1750, "protectionist" policies were implemented to protect the aboriginal peoples (literally "the first" or "earliest known" people) from the "harmful" effects of contact with the European settlers. The heart of these policies involved moving the Aborigines to either reservations or church-run missions, while restricting their right to move freely on the island continent that was once theirs. When exceptions were made to these restrictions it was normally to provide the incoming settlers with cheap local labor. As in the United States, the vast amount of land and the relative sparseness of the approximately 600 aboriginal groups made the continent appear open for settlement. Indeed, the colonization process was based on the assumption that Australia was a *Terre Nullium* (empty land). Consequently, and in contrast to the United States, no treaties were ever negotiated to protect the rights of the indigenous peoples, and those laws which were made toward that end during the late nineteenth century were nearly impossible to enforce once the settlers moved from their initial, coastal colonies into the Outback. Moreover, the gist of those laws reinforced the initial relocation policies by prohibiting the Aborigines from leaving the reservations without permits. Finally, and as in the United States, a variety of confiscation laws were enacted, which not only deprived the Natives of their property but permitted the taking of their children for Christian rearing until the 1970s.[23]

As for Canada, although Native Americans in the United States have yet to be fully accorded the rights of other citizens, native groups in Canada are still seeking from the Canadian government the benefits that tribal groups do possess in the United States. Responding to tribal and other testimony, Canada's Royal Commission on Aboriginal People, for example, concluded in 1996 that Canada's existing system of federal paternalism had failed, and that as many as 80 tribes should be accorded some form of territorial self-rule as a first step toward restoring their dignity.[24]

The Setting of Ethnopolitics in France

France serves as our case study from the advanced democratic world because its history and contemporary politics illustrate numerous aspects of ethnopolitics in what was once called the First World. Its state-building eras left it with territorialized minorities on its periphery, including an ethnically distinct island in the Mediterranean. It was both a settler state and imperial power abroad, though it lost most of its settlements in the New World in the war with Britain, which cost it Quebec, and in the early nineteenth century when Napoleon's cash flow problem in 1803 led him to sell France's gigantic Louisiana Territory in the midst of today's continental United States. Then, in the mid-twentieth century, it lost most of its colonial empire when its overseas holdings in Indo-China, North Africa, and sub-Sahara Africa either won violently or were peacefully granted their independence. Their independence, however, soon gave way to a new round of ethnopolitics in France itself when the citizens of these areas began to flow into France as foreign workers. Yet, in France as elsewhere, ethnopolitics have not only shaped the political environment but have been shaped by the context in which they have unfolded.

Traditionally, politics in France have had a dramatic, even flamboyant, air. Political change has often originated from below, and has more than once involved a violent revolt of the governed against authority. Constitutional systems and the heads of political leaders alike have occasionally been shed in the upheavals. As soap operas, the nature of French politics has long furnished the French with hard-to-rival daily drama. Will Louis XVI be guillotined? Will Napoleon return? Will the Fifth French Republic survive without de Gaulle? And so it has sometimes been in the area of ethnopolitics. Can France be France without a centralized, assimilationist government? Can France be France with a large Muslim population?

These contemporary concerns are, in a wider sense, only the most recent manifestations of France's long-term struggle to come to terms with its ethnic composition That struggle, in turn, has been a basic part of the country's struggle to come to terms with its own identity since the French Revolution of 1789, which ushered out the old order without ushering in a new system supported by a wide and deep consensus. Unsure of their authority, French leaders have rarely been favorably disposed toward the demands of ethnopolitical minorities for state protection and promotion of *their* identity. Certainly few developed democracies have as long or aggressively denied the presence of the ethnic factor in their domestic politics as France. Nor, recently, has any Western European state been more broadly influenced by the ethnic factor.

The Geopolitics of Diversity and State-Making

Location and the nature of the terrain contributed substantially to the emergence of France as the first state on the continent integrated under a single monarch in its modern perimeters. Five of the six sides of the French "Hexagon" are defined by mountains and seas.[25] Inside its borders, no formidable mountain ranges or other obstacles to communication separate its inhabitants. Though in area it is the largest state in Western Europe, France is physically compact (about the size of Texas) and blessed with an excellent network of natural waterways that tie the periphery to Paris.

At the same time, geography exposed the emergent state to the ethnic factor from both within and without. Rivers, seas, and mountain ranges provided natural borders, but they did not insulate the country from the national groups on the other side. The Celtic language and culture penetrated Brittany along the Atlantic coastline of northwestern France no less than the Celtic portions of Great Britain's west (Wales) and north (Scotland).

On the continent, virtually all of France's neighbors have an ethnic kinship with the peripheral, ethnoterritorial communities France acquired during its state-building eras. The Flemish-speaking people to the northeast live on both sides of the border separating France from present-day Belgium, just as, to the southwest, Basques and Catalonians spill from Spain across the Pyrenees into France. Germanic-speaking peoples can be found on both sides of the Rhine and Italian-speaking peoples inhabit southeastern France at its Mediterranean junctures with Italy, and Corsica. State-makers brought these diverse peoples under a common government via a lengthy historical process that began in the tenth century; however, the process never linguistically integrated these diverse peoples within a common tongue. Instead, by the time of the French Revolution, France had over 30 different patois, languages, and dialects, a large portion of which set apart the geographically and culturally peripheralized regional minorities from the culture and language of the country's rulers at Versailles.[26]

The failure of French monarchs to fashion a less culturally and linguistically diverse society in pre-Revolutionary France can also be traced to geographical circumstance. France's state builders found in the country's outstanding river system natural arteries for constructing national communications and transportation grids. To a great extent these rivers radiate outward from France's center to its periphery like the spokes of a wheel running from hub to rim, and thus connected Paris effectively with the provinces and abetted the political integration of the realm under a single, centralized political and administrative structure. At the same time, they rarely connected the peoples in France's diverse provinces with one another. The resultant, centralized political system assured that the state's dominant culture would overshadow all others, but it never completely overwhelmed those of the periphery.

Finally, France's coastal borders have at least indirectly contributed to the recent growth in the country's multiethnic composition from without by giving France a face on the broader world, encouraging its kings to launch exploratory missions to the New World, and its Republics to build and hold empires in Asia and Africa. North Africa, in particular, fell into France's orbit many years ago. In fact, Algeria—as close to Marseille as Marseille is to Paris—was not administratively treated as an imperial possession in Republican France, but as an overseas department as much a part of France as Corsica or any of the regions of continental France. In time, the subjects of France's empire achieved independence, and even though their quest was often bloody, after independence large numbers of these former subjects sought their livelihoods in the cities of their former master.

Political Integration and Political Culture: L'état *versus* la Patrie

History bequeathed France a mixed legacy. On the one hand, prerevolutionary French history is heavily laced with stories of the glory and grandeur of a France of Sun Kings, spacious palaces, and conquests. French political leaders long dictated the trade routes in Europe. French universities educated the political elites of Europe. French diplomats wrote the rules of modern diplomacy by which states continue to live.[27] Yet mixed with the legacy of grandeur is another theme, largely dating from the French revolution: a history of political instability that made difficult both the complete political integration of the state and the creation of national party structures even after 1871, when popular sovereignty and parliamentary republics established the framework for French politics.

More than one commentator has identified political change as the dominant characteristic of French politics between the collapse of the old order in 1789 and the advent of the Fifth French Republic in 1958. The Revolution of 1789 represented a multiple assault on the *ancien regime*. It directly challenged the absolute power of the king with the doctrine of popular sovereignty and attacked the alliance between the church and state upon which the monarchy's divine right-absolute power had once rested. Indirectly, it also challenged the people's traditional passivity and parochialism with the concept that the people, as custodians of the nation's sovereignty, should actively exercise it. Yet the Revolution did not produce any broad-based agreement concerning the proper form of government for the new France. Instead, it heralded more than a century of intermittent crises and political change as the French began their search for a new political consensus, with many of the highly inflammable political issues resolved in Britain by the late seventeenth century continuing to trouble French politics into the twentieth century (e.g., the proper relationship between the church and state). Often, the political debates took tumultuous turns, as indicated by the wide swings in the constitutional designs adopted by the French between 1789 and 1870.

When Republicanism was accepted as the basic form for the state in 1871, the regime instability of the first three-quarters of the nineteenth century was replaced with chronic cabinet instability during the Third and Fourth French Republics and, hence, chronically weak parliamentary government. The absence of political consensus in late-nineteenth-century France was reflected in the numerous small parties pursuing their individual, often uncompromising political agendas.[28] With parliaments routinely containing a score of parties, coalition cabinets composed of a large number of mutually suspicious members became the rule. So, too, did governments with a short life-expectancy. During the last decades of the Third Republic (1871–1940), cabinets had an average span of eight months, approximately the same life cycle as those governing the Fourth French Republic between 1946 and 1958.

This chronic pattern of political change both contributed to and resulted from the lack of political consensus and civic consciousness in French society. Prior to the Third Republic, constitutional systems scarcely existed long enough to attract strong ties between the individual and the state. By the time of the Third Republic, political instability had become so much a part of the political landscape that the instability of past regimes created uncertainties concerning the survival potential of the existing one. In turn, expectations that the existing system too might pass away worked against the development of the type of affective ties, linkage mechanisms, and positive attitudes toward political participation and compromise-oriented politics that might have placed the Third and Fourth Republics on firmer foundations.

Moreover, whereas groups throughout France often developed (or retained) strong attachments toward their country (*la Patrie*) in post-Revolutionary France, the French state (*l'état*) seldom profited from this loyalty given the frequent changes of its governments. Napoleon enjoyed considerable support in life and a nostalgic glow in death; *he* had brought France a moment of great glory. By contrast, the Third Republic, which spread the French empire across Africa and Asia, received little respect for the imperial glory it brought France. This disconnection between France and its government, which significantly affected the development of a national political culture throughout France, seriously handicapped the assimilationist efforts of Third Republic leaders vis-à-vis the regionalized communities that did not even share the culture or language of the majority in *la Patrie*. Simply put, they lacked the legitimacy they would have possessed had the French state *and France* been more closely linked in the public mind. In this setting, allegiances to France *and* the local ethnopolitical communities flourished

Cultural Diversity and Political Incivisme

The emergence of a presidential-centered political process and national political parties after 1958 profoundly altered the environment in which ethnoregional and "anti-foreigner" parties could operate in Fifth Republic France (1958–present). Though regimes came and went during the nineteenth century, there was little popular sovereignty available to French citizens, regionalists or otherwise, and the dominant relationship between the center and the periphery remained one of the former's tight, centralized control over the latter. Republics governed France only for a short time during the more than four generations between the French revolution and the inauguration of the Third Republic, and the First Republic was under the control of Robespierre and his terrorism-practicing Committee on Public Safety for nearly half of its existence. Furthermore, until very recently all of France's constitutional designs involved highly centralized unitary systems erected upon the administrative system established by Napoleon, which organized France tightly under Paris' direction into a series of small administrative districts whose units, except for Corsica, only loosely corresponded with France's ethnoterritorial divisions.

Further, the judiciary did not offer France's ethnoregional and other minorities political options. In contrast to the U.S. separation of powers system, with its independent judiciary charged with enforcing constitutional rights, even during its republican eras France has normally placed its judiciary under the Ministry of Justice inside the executive branch. Comparatively few French citizens and even fewer minorities have viewed such courts, presided over by judges appointed by Paris and dependent upon their masters in the cabinet, as a source of relief from the heavy hand of Paris.

Much more important to the nature of pre–Fifth Republic ethnopolitics than institutional arrangements was the broader sociopolitical environment in which ethnoregionalists functioned. Especially during democratic regimes, French politics has been historically shaped by the vast number of political associations that have divided French society horizontally (provincialism) and vertically (class, religion, ideological differences) into small and politically unproductive subcultures. Thus France has often served as the model for the "continental" style of politics—a form involving a highly segmented society, a fragmented set of political values, and a tendency for a high level of conflict within the framework of a very general political consensus.

Given this hyper-pluralism, it might be expected that ethnopolitics in France would, like the ethnic factor throughout much of U.S. history, have been subjected to and moderated by crosscutting cleavages. At first sight, there is even some recent evidence to support that conclusion. Except for the ethnoterritorial parties of Corsica, for example, ethnoregional organizations in postwar France have never approximated the more than 30 percent of the regional vote mobilized during the 1970s by the ethnopolitical parties of Scotland, Brussels, Basque Spain, and Quebec. Yet, in France, this pattern appears to have resulted not so much from ethnopolitical agendas being subjected to cross pressures as from the tendency of ethnoterritorial parties to cleave themselves into ever-smaller political organizations on the basis of non-ethnoregional criteria.

In stark contrast to the coalition nature of parties and politics in the United States and Britain, French associations have been repeatedly split by other political considerations. Thus, the ethnoregional banner has frequently been borne in France not by a single ethnopolitical party (as in Wales, Scotland, French-speaking Brussels, Flanders, and Quebec) but by several ethnoregional parties competing against one another on the basis of ideological differences. Nor is this phenomenon limited to ethnopolitical groups in France. Prior to the 1960s emergence of the French Socialist Party as a single national party, the French Left similarly suffered at the ballot box from internal fragmentation on the basis of the ideological and regional differences dividing the country's socialist-espousing political parties.

The Politics of Being French

The French electorate's traditional tendency to fragment rather than collaborate to influence the political process has been broadly explained in terms of the inclination of French voters to distrust politics and the political process, inject ideological rigidity into politics, and compete in the political system not as interest groups but as narrowly focused, uncompromising political "chapels."[29] In turn, this inclination to split ideological hairs, engage in the often violent politics of protest and streetism, and the eschew political cooperation and compromise—what Frank Wilson once categorized as a "delinquent" political culture[30]—has been attributed to a variety of factors. These included the traditionally authoritarian nature of father-dominated French households (where the young learned to distrust the neighbors on the other side of the foyer), the low attention accorded civic education in French schools, the "consequence of nonparticipation in groups and lack of exercise of responsibility within them," and a history intermingling instances of political excess with instances of political paralysis.[31] Collectively, these factors have reinforced the distinction between *la Patrie* and the state. As one analyst summarized, "There is a fairly general and early commitment of the children to the national community and its symbols. . . . [But] The political world is regarded as something cold and divisive."

At the same time, political cultures are complex entities, and it is possible to push the *incivisme* and "delinquent" culture arguments too far in explaining political behavior in France. Likewise, the gulf between the French love of country and disconnection from their state has been narrowing since the Third French Republic and certainly at an increased rate during the Fifth French Republic, which has now been in place for more than two generations. France consistently rates high on most indices of social satisfaction, and to the extent voter turnout is a measurement of identity with the political process, France compares favorably with most European countries and is well ahead of the United States. Thus, as Kay Lawson has commented, the French people admire their state even as they may still distrust it, and what often appears as a lack of civility is a forceful French expression of angry concern over the direction *their* state is currently taking.[32]

Still, historically France's traditionally fragmented, nonparticipatory political culture explains much of the traditional political weakness of France's ethnopolitical minorities. Ethnopolitical communities, like all political groups, were hard-pressed to mobilize for action in this setting. In addition, ethnopolitical spokesmen in France customarily faced another obstacle in seeking to mobilize their constitutes—one not besetting those attempting to rally their fellow citizens around economic and ideological banners. In stressing the ethnically defined entitlements of their communities, they had to confront the momentum built up over generations by a French state, which, whatever its form, systematically emphasized the value of being French, speaking French, assimilating to the French culture, and taking pride in the accomplishments of France and the French. The message has been louder on some occasions than others, and has been pushed more aggressively by some governments than by others.[33] Nevertheless, through such instruments as the *national* education system, universal male military service, and the country's imperial system (which offered assimilation and French citizenship to its subjects, not the promise of home rule), the message has never been diluted by a lack of certainty at the center as to its fundamental correctness. *Au contraire*, the message has been daily reaffirmed by the leaders of the state and, during the last half of the twentieth century, by the centralized role of the state in every citizen's life.[34]

Further, the state's subunits are not equipped to challenge the center's message. Regional Councils, for instance, were not created until the political Left came to power in the 1980s, and the type of locally elected or appointed school boards in charge of public education in the United States have never existed in France. France's ethnoterritorial movements have thus, with the exception of Corsica's, tended to cast their platforms in a regionalist rather than nationalist hue, demanding the right to teach the regional tongue in school systems rather than independence, as befits a country where nearly all native-born citizens have, throughout the twentieth century, seen themselves as either French only or French first, and *Breton* or Alsatian second.

Ironically, the very factors that have united the French and have historically worked against ethnoterritorial politics inside France—the history and culture of France, the role of Paris as the country's economic, political, and cultural center—have widened the gap between the indigenous French and those immigrating to France from culturally remote areas. Consequently, for their part the spokesmen for the country's most recently arrived foreign residents have often been reduced to lobbying for their right to choose their respective degrees of assimilation, not whether to assimilate. And on occasion, their efforts have been reduced to lobbying for their right to stay in France.

CHAPTER THREE

Ethnoterritorial Politics in France

Despite the image of cultural and linguistic homogeneity that France has long sought to project to the world, France remains one of the most ethnically diverse and linguistically pluralistic states of Western Europe. Its ethnolinguistic diversity continues to grow with the rising numbers of nonassimilated immigrants and foreign workers living within its economy and borders. Diversity also characterizes the country even when the focus is on its indigenous, ethnic, and linguistic territorial minorities.[1] Absorbed early into the state, these minorities persist despite more than two centuries of political efforts to marginalize, assimilate, and/or dissolve them.

The Ethnoterritorial Element in French Politics

The Territorial Minorities and the Ancien Regime

As chapter two noted, the state-making process in France joined together, often forcibly, numerous regions in which the language and culture of Paris were neither spoken nor familiar. French kings were more concerned with expanding the realm, insuring their military control over newly acquired territories, and improving their administrative dominance within their domain than with homogenizing the cultures it contained.[2] To be sure, local cultures were not ignored. The creation of state-controlled enterprises and a centralized taxation system not only entailed the elimination of conflicting local laws, regional armies, and toll systems, but the denigration of local languages and customs and the co-optation of educated local elites. Thus, in 1635 the *Academe francaise* was established to publish a standardized French dictionary and monitor developments affecting the language—a role it continues to perform.[3] Nonetheless, by the time of the French Revolution, seven significant ethnic and linguistically diverse regions still could be found within *le Hexagon*. These were: (1) Occitania, in southern and central France, the largest and most internally diverse (its Romance languages and dialects include Provencal, Languedocien, and Limousin); (2) the Flemish region near the city of Lille along France's northern border with Belgium; (3) the German dialect–speaking areas of Alsace-Lorraine along the eastern border with Germany; (4) Brittany, an independent duchy for centuries prior to its conquest by France, whose citizens speak the Celtic tongue of *Breton* and have ancient ties with the Welsh and Cornish peoples across the English Channel in Britain; (5) the French Basque region in the northern Pyrenees at the Spanish border, speaking a language unlike that of any group in Europe and said by some to have originated in the Stone Age as the original Indo-European language; (6) French Catalonia, at France's southwestern most border; and (7) Corsica, with its Italian dialect directly derived from Latin, an island that is part of metropolitan France located in the Mediterranean and technically the southern most part of France.

Charting these regions has always been easier than quantifying the number of practitioners of the tongues they contain, principally because throughout much of the twentieth century Paris officially denied the existence of territorial minorities in France. In fact, as late as 1980, France's official censuses contained *no* questions on language use. As a result even reliable estimates of the numbers speaking the minority languages fluctuate widely. Still, the bottom line is clear. The number of French citizens speaking a language other than French as their mother tongue was, at the time of the Revolution, formidable, and the numbers remain substantial today, if considerably lower and still declining. Drawing on available official sources, James Jacob and David Gordon estimated that the numbers speaking France's minority languages in the mid-1980s still ranged in the millions, despite both policies designed to discourage their use and the shrinking populations in many of France's peripheral regions during the twentieth century. Table 3.1 lists the most important of these regional tongues, and the numbers currently estimated to be speaking them.[4]

The chronology involving the physical absorption of these languages and peoples into the Hexagon can be quickly summarized. It began as early as the tenth century when the kings of the Ile de France—where the language spoken was the *langue d'oil* dominant in the northern two-thirds of France—began to spread their empire southward into the Langue d'Oc region now known as Occitania.[5] The people of Languedoc were subsumed into France in 1270; those of Provencal in 1482. Brittany was added in

Table 3.1 The languages of regional France

Language	Region	Numbers currently speaking
Allemannish	Alsace-Lorraine	1,500,000
Breton	Brittany	500,000–1,000,000+
Basque	Basque Provinces	80,000–130,000
Catalan	Catalonian France	100,000–200,000
Corsu	Corsica	281,000
Dutch	Flemish France	80,000–100,000
Occitanian	Occitania	9,500,000–12,000,000*

* Depending on the extent to which the various dialects are treated as separate tongues.

1532, only seven years before Francois I proclaimed the "oïl" dialect of Paris as the official language of the realm. Alsace was acquired in 1648, the Basque provinces three quarters of a century later (in 1607 and 1620), neighboring Catalonia in 1659, and Lorraine in 1766. In 1768, Corsica became the last of the major regions to be added to metropolitan France. Except for the German occupation of Alsace-Lorraine during the 1870–1918 period and again from 1940 to 1945, and the Italian control of Corsica between 1942 and 1945, all have remained a part of the country since their acquisition.

The old order largely succeeded in imposing uniform political institutions throughout France, bringing local affairs under the control of central bureaucrats and establishing the agents of Paris as the realm's exclusive tax collectors and dispensers of justice. Prior to the Revolution of 1789, however, this centralization process was much more administrative and political than cultural in character. Moreover, it was incomplete in its accomplishments in France's more rural and peripheral areas. There, the royal courts were generally indifferent to the languages of their subjects until the sixteenth century. It was not until 1532 that the Crown's local agents were required to use French rather than Latin in all tribunals, and then the emphasis was not on making spoken French into the country's daily lingua franca, but merely to ensure that the ruled understood French as the link language between the state and its subjects in political affairs. Paris had little interest in the culture of the periphery and no national integration policy toward the "backward," non-French speaking peoples inhabiting these areas. Their rustic ways were often served up in plays and marionette form for the amusement of Parisians, a practice that continued throughout the nineteenth century, but no effort was made to suppress the regional *patois*. Nor was the state's administrative apparatus dense enough to impose the Parisian culture and language on them. Thus, although by the Revolution Parisian French had become the language of the nobility, bourgeoisie and the upwardly mobile in France, and of much of continental Europe's educated and ruling classes, it still lacked a hold on France's own peripheral peoples when the Bastille and the *ancien regime* fell on July 14, 1789.[6]

Revolutionary France and the Ethnoterritorial Minorities

France's nation-building activities have been concentrated in two periods: the burst of activity involving minority languages shortly after the Revolution; and the assimilationist period engulfing the first two decades of the Third French Republic (1870–1940). To the centralists who seized power in 1789, the de facto autonomy that the periphery enjoyed under the kings and which permitted local cultures and tongues to persist were obstacles to the remolding of France. The existing historic provinces were thus summarily displaced as administrative units by approximately 90 small *departements*, which rarely coincided with France's older provincial boundaries and usually divided them into numerous units.

Also in the name of the principles of the Revolution, the local tongues had to be displaced. Less than a month after the Revolution, the Constituent Assembly governing France decreed that the French people would be subject to one and only one uniform set of laws applied nationally. It soon became apparent that these laws would be uniformly promulgated only in French, the language of the Revolution. Reality, however, could not be so easily legislated away. Given the polyglot confronting Paris, in November, 1792, the same Assembly found it necessary to order the translation of laws into German, Italian, Catalan, Basque, and Breton in order to render them knowable and enforceable. In a study presented to the Convention, which had assumed control over France by 1794, Abbe Gregoire concluded that nearly a quarter of the country in 1790–91 had *no* knowledge of the French language, that another quarter could not conduct a conversation in it, and that probably only one in ten or twelve could speak and write it fluently. At the same time, French was indisputably the link language in what Gregoire described as a "linguistic tower of Babel."[7] For France to be governable, something had to be done to spread it.

For his part, Gregoire would have been content with a policy of bilingualism; that is, teaching French to everyone while allowing provincial languages to continue. By the time Gregoire tendered his Report, though, the Jacobin centralists controlling the state had already embraced assimilation. Toward that end, on January 27, 1794, a centralized, national education system was created. A teacher of French was to be dispatched to each commune on the periphery to propagate the French language. The regional tongues could persist, though the Jacobins increasingly viewed them as a threat to the Revolution; however, the center was committed to altering the linguistic mix of the people, if only indirectly. It was believed by many that the local dialects would fade away under the influence of French. In the meantime, these acts were to give the government greater control over its subjects by ensuring that the latter would be able to speak the language of France's Revolution as well as comprehend its laws.

Ethnoregionalism and the Assimilationist State: Nation-Building in the Third French Republic

Three generations later, and despite the further growth of Paris' control over the country via the prefect system, centralized bureaucracy, and uniform legal system created under Napoleon, France remained multicultural and multilingual. In nearly a quarter of the country's 37,510 communes, French was still not spoken at all, despite an 1830 law requiring knowledge of written French for a position in the bureaucracy. Even in the country's school system, nearly one child in ten could not speak French and one in four could not write it. Compared to the figures of 1790, headway had been made; however, measured by the Jacobin expectations of the 1790s of one state, one culture, and one language, French-language policy was a conspicuous failure.[8] It was time for a nation-building process—or, to use Walker Connor's terms, a nation-*destroying* process as far as the peripheral communities were concerned—to begin in earnest.[9]

Regional languages rather than a lack of access to French were now seen as the problem. The tongues not only refused to die but represented, especially the "Germanic tongues" (Alsatian, Flemish, and at times even Breton was thrust into this category) a potential threat to the state at a time when Germany was unifying into a dangerous foe on France's eastern border. The cure was believed to be more education, packaged this time in a much less tolerant educational system.

The government of the Third French Republic, itself born amid the national humiliation of France's defeat by Germany in the Franco-Prussian war and loss of Alsace and Lorraine for nearly a half century (1870–1918), essentially declared war on the minority cultures with the Fundamental Laws (or Ferry Laws) decreed between 1881 and 1884 at the instigation of Jules Ferry, who simultaneously served as France's premier and minister of education. Free and compulsory primary school education in French was mandated for all children between 7 and 13 years of age. Furthermore, that education was to be offered through a system of public schools, not the Catholic schools so closely attuned to the regional cultures in areas such as Brittany and hence reluctant to teach French, the language of the self-consciously secular, often militantly anticlerical governments of post-Revolutionary France and the early Third French Republic.

The political battle between the center and ethnoterritorial groups essentially revolved around four strong, reinforcing cleavages: the geographical one between the center and periphery; the ethnolinguistic one; the economic one between Paris and the generally, economically backward periphery; and the religious one between the modernizing, secular elites in Paris and the often heavily Catholic communities in outlying departments. In a multifaceted assault on the regional cultures that led to the birth of the first nationalist parties in many of the targeted regions between 1893 and 1928, the Ferry Laws were quickly followed by additional reforms designed to supplement the schools in assimilating the linguistic and ethnic minorities into the French nation.

The second wave of polices involved economic and commercial centralization and the development of an infrastructure capable of bringing the most remote economic and cultural backwater into the national system. The rail lines, roadways, and communication lines to be constructed would also bring the French culture to the regions. The process worked, but also only to a degree. At another level, the administrative centralization created in Paris combined with the infrastructure developed during the nineteenth century (essentially a railroad and road system in which all paths led to Paris) to concentrate the vast preponderance of industrialization in the Paris region, thus widening the economic disparity between the citizens of Paris and northeast France, and those of the vast south and west, which were inhabited largely though not entirely by France's ethnic and linguistic minorities.[10]

More successful was the third set of nation-building efforts, which stressed participation *in* the French nation. Particularly important was the inauguration of a system of compulsory military service for the country's young men. Enacted in the face of the German threat, the conscription system provided a powerful tool of national integration in its own right, especially given the polylingual nature of the regional recruits and therefore the need to use French for communication among even the lowest echelons of servicemen. By the 1920s, the number of bilinguals in France had soared, and the majority of these began to favor French rather than their regional dialects in their daily lives.[11]

In a like manner, World War I, which pitted France against Germany, was a unifying experience for all of France, not just those in service. It had, however, some curious side effects on minority policy in twentieth-century France. Possibly because of the declining importance of the regional *patois*, spokesmen for some minority regions petitioned U.S. President Woodrow Wilson at Versailles to defend *their* right to self-determination, along with the rights of those communities to the east just liberated from Hungarian, Austrian, and German rule. France's political leaders responded to these developments by denying the presence of any territorial minorities in France even as they began to repress demands for autonomy in Alsace-Lorraine by closing down the autonomist presses there, occasionally placing on trial the leadership of fringe groups promoting separatism, and making French the exclusive language of instruction at the University of Strasbourg.

Even when the coercive machinery of the state's legal system was not involved, the assimilationist policies were at times severe. The depreciation of regional cultures was intentionally humiliating. Children caught speaking their dialect at school, for example, were forced to wear around their necks such items as wooden shoes with holes in them. Yet it should be noted that such policies were not limited to France, even during this period. The United States launched an often brutal policy of assimilation targeting its Indian minorities at approximately the same time.[12]

Belgian history likewise contains abundant stories of late-nineteenth-century injustices: for example, of Flemish prisoners tried and sentenced, even to death, in proceedings conducted exclusively in the French language in which the accused were incapable of explaining themselves. France's Jacobin policies of centralization and nation-building also found imitation in Spain and Italy, and in neither of them did the policies end with the nineteenth century.[13] As late as the 1920s, Mussolini's minions were nightly busy Italianizing the German names in the cemeteries of the German-speaking Alto Adige region (the southern Tirols) Italy acquired from Austria as its prize for switching sides during World War I. Likewise, until his death in 1975, Francisco Franco refused to concede the linguistic and regional rights that his country's Basque and Catalan minorities had historically enjoyed.

As for the ethnoterritorial minorities in nineteenth-century France, so resistant to change and so de facto institutionalized in the local power

realities were the ethnocultural characters of these groups that Paris' assimilationist policies had little success initially. Even the administrative links
that Paris maintained with the provinces still depended significantly on
contacts with *regional* elites. The prefects appointed by Paris to administer
the country spoke French; the local mayors in the communes often did not,
though they were frequently willing to cooperate with Paris for sufficient
personal advantage.[14]

Gradually, however, and assisted considerably by the development of a
modern internal transportation and communication grid, a national economy, and the emergence of France as one of the world's great imperial
powers during the nineteenth century, the center's policies succeeded in
demoting the relative status of the local cultures. To be sure, in some
regions these policies led to the formation of defensive associations opposed
to forced Frenchification. In general, though, the most regionally oriented
communities gradually bent under the assimilation pressures confronting
them, accepted the need to learn French, and became imbued from their
studies in the national school system with a commitment to
Republicanism, secularism, and other principles of the Revolution. As
William Safran has summarized, "[by] the mid-twentieth century, the
debate on national unity had [thus] receded, because a congruence between
state and nation appeared to have been achieved."[15]

Ethnoregional and Ethnonational Politics
in Modern France

Ethnoterritorial Minorities in Postwar France

As the number of bilinguals in France's minority regions grew and the
numbers monolingual in their regional *patois* diminished, Paris' aggressive
promotion of the French language and attacks on regional tongues seemed
ever less necessary. Equally important in postwar France, the challenges to
the French language and culture were increasingly external. Subjects in the
French empire were rebelling, demanding not autonomy but independence. Equally daunting, with the rise of the United States to superpower
status and the growing linguistic dominance of English in virtually all professional fields, France had to struggle to preserve the international status of
its tongue (securing its adoption as the other official language of the United
Nations (UN) by a single vote),[16] and continuously rush to the battlements
to halt the seepage of English terms into common usage in France itself.

Policies gradually emerged to reflect these changes. Wars were expensively
and futilely fought to preserve France's empire, first in Indo-China
(1947–54) and then in an overseas department of France itself, Algeria
(1954–58). Shortly after the shock waves of losing Algeria settled, the
government began to articulate policies (1963) and later enact laws to protect
French from English, most notably the *Loi Bas-Lauriol*. Passed on the last

day of 1975, the act extended the government's 1972 ban on the use of English in all government publications to the communications of businesses operating in France. In the meantime, with the landmark 1951 Loi Deixonne, the government began to relax its policies toward regional languages and permit their study in Brittany, the Basque lands, French Catalonia, and Occitania.

Ethnoregional Politics in the Fifth French Republic:
The Politics of Denial and Accommodation

As progressive as the Deixonne Law was compared to previous French-language policies, it fell far short of satisfying the demands of the state's ethnoterritorial minorities. Areas speaking "allogenous" [other] languages—including Corsican, Alsatian, and Flemish dialects—were initially excluded from the Law's provisions on the grounds that they were variations of foreign languages. It was not until 1974, when Corsican was belatedly added to the list, that these tongues began to benefit from the law. Further, its implementation did not fulfill the expectations it generated. French remained the sole language for radio and television broadcasting, public proceedings, and governmental documents. Furthermore, in as much as the central government remained controlled by the parties of the Right for the first 20 years of the Fifth French Republic, and by President Charles de Gaulle himself for more than half of that time, the de facto ideology of the government remained that of a centralized state, still officially denying the presence of any indigenous ethnic minority (as opposed to linguistic groups) in France. As President Valery Giscard d'Estaing phrased it as late as 1979, the state's commitment to a strong center remained largely unchanged from the days of the Revolution. "The national unity," he wrote, "which was the source of France's strength from the fifteenth century to the Empire, must be preserved if France is to play an advantageous part in a European Confederation (e.g., the current European Union)."[17] It was not until the Socialists achieved power in 1979–80 that official policies aimed at de-concentrating the state began to benefit the regions.[18]

Moreover, the Deixonne law did not open the floodgates for the study of the initially covered languages. It *authorized* the optional study of those languages for a maximum of one hour per week (extended in 1975 to three hours per week for senior high school students); however, the Ministry of National Education charged with its implementation frequently failed to provide the necessary teachers and texts. Only in 1976 were academic institutions outside of the minority regions permitted to teach minority languages, and students permitted to pursue studies in such ancillary areas as the history, geography, and literature of France's territorialized minorities. Consequently, even in the affected regions the numbers availing themselves of the law remained almost negligible. At the same time, the modest encouragement of regional languages that occurred as a result of the

Deixonne Act was frequently offset by the policies implemented to combat the spread of English, since the promulgations against using any tongue other than French for government or business communications also applied to the public use of the regional tongues. Only the languages of the foreign populations were exempted.

Meanwhile, the fact that the government did move gradually if grudgingly toward recognizing the regional languages forced the culture-focused, ethnoregional organizations of Brittany, Alsace, Corsica, Basque France, and Occitania to adopt broader programs in pressing for ethnoregional empowerment. Hence, one of the most pronounced developments in ethnoterritorial politics during the early years of the Fifth Republic was the shift on the part of the ethnoregional organizations from the Right, where they had formerly been rooted in the clergy's use of regional tongues to combat the secularist policies of Paris, to the Left, with a newly discovered stress on the economic exploitation and/or decline of their respective regions under Parisian (mis)management. At the same time, the reluctance of Paris to extend even the Deixonne reforms to Corsica, Alsace, and Flemish France, and its failure to fulfill the promise of the law in areas such as Brittany, kept the cultural issues alive *and* led to a second element characterizing the ethnopolitical struggle of these regions in the 1970s: an increasing inclination to use political violence. Clandestine, quasi-terrorist organizations thus multiplied in France at approximately the time that parties and interest groups were the options being selected by ethnoterritorial organizations in Wallonia, Flanders, Scotland, and Wales, where regionalized minorities were dealing with governments willing to negotiate and compromise on a definable range of issues.

Especially among France's ABC minorities—Alsatians, Bretons, and Corsicans—ethnoterritorial politics often centered on the activities of extremist, sometimes separatist groups during this period. The term "extremist," however, needs to be qualified. In general the Corsican organizations tended to be the most aggressive, and the Alsatian groups the least predisposed toward political violence. For the most part, none of the organizations pursued human targets in the manner of the extremist spokesmen for the Protestant and the Catholic communities of Northern Ireland and the Basques in Franco's Spain. Rather, their targets tended to be the physical symbols of the centralized French state: national banks; the towers of the national radio and television stations; and, the most famous instance of all, the 1978 bombing by Breton terrorists of the home of French kings, the palace of Versailles.

With the possible exception of the Corsicans, France's territorialized minorities generally view themselves in a dualistic sense—that is, as *Breton* and (usually primarily) French. Certainly, they no longer see themselves in the nationalist sense of constituting distinct nations in a multinational state, and their spokesmen have had to mute their political demands accordingly. Thus, they have focused on achieving economic assistance for sagging regional economies, and/or the official recognition of their regional tongues and the right to teach them in public schools. Outside of Corsica, demands for independence have been exceedingly rare. Support for Basque irredentism has been noticeably weak on the French side of the Pyrenees, and France's "Alsace problem" has historically been and remains one of French particularism, not German irredentism.[19] Perhaps for this reason, the average citizen in Alsace, Brittany, and the other principal ethnoregional communities inside continental France have rarely rushed to avail themselves of those concessions to regional cultures pried from Paris. In Brittany, for example, interest in the study of the Breton language actually declined after these classes were integrated into the regular course curriculums. The classes had ceased to be "fun" electives.[20]

In any event, as Table 3.2 indicates, gradually the French government did move away from the denial policies of the early Fifth Republic to more accommodative policies toward the regionalized minorities. Yet, during the 1970s the new approach tended to be a double-edged sword. As Jacob and Gordon have phrased it, "What was once anathema—concessions on language use— . . . [became] a deliberate strategy of minimal concessions designed to undercut the more radical ethnic militants from their constituents and thus avoid more fundamental concessions to political power."[21] The Deixonne law was extended to Corsica in January, 1974, and radio news broadcasts in Breton were increased to 20 minutes of programming per day in Brittany by 1975, the same year that a "cultural charter" was signed between Paris and Alsace. This "charter" committed the government to supporting limited broadcasting of Alsatian cultural themes on the regional television channel in Strasbourg. Two years later, Brittany received a similar charter.[22] At the same time, these concessions not only continued to be watered down when put into practice, but were frequently accompanied by a crackdown on the more visible, "extremist" organizations. The Pompidou government's pledge to add Corsican to the languages covered by the Deixonne Law, for example, was followed by the government's late January dissolution of ethnopolitical movements in Corsica, Brittany, and Basque France on the grounds that they threatened France's territorial integrity. A similar carrot–club approach followed during Giscard d'Estaing's presidency (1974–81).

Matters temporarily improved significantly in the early 1980s. In campaigning for office in 1981, the Socialist Party pledged both linguistic and administrative reforms for the benefit of France's minorities. In 1982 the Socialist government began to implement that platform. The Giordan Report issued that February explicitly recognized the existence of "regional and minority (e.g., immigrant) cultures" and recommended that the government subsidize and promote the preservation of those cultures. By the end of the year, Paris had committed itself to supporting more than a hundred projects involving France's cultural minorities. Equally far-reaching, the government of Francois Mitterrand agreed to increase the airspace

Table 3.2   Ethnoterritorial politics and policies in France

900	Building of modern, multilingual France begins with the annexation of Occitania
13th c.	France acquires additional southern territory from the counts of Toulouse
1532	France acquires Brittany through royal marriages
1635	French Academy (*Academie francaise*) established
1648	Alsace transferred to France in Treaty of Westphalia
1729	Rebellion against Genoa rule begins in Corsica
1752	Corsica acquires nominal independence but remains officially a possession of Genoa
1768	Genoa cedes Corsica to France, concluding state-building process of modern France
1789	French Revolution ends old order in the name of popular sovereignty
1794–96	Disorder sweeps post-Revolution France, Corsica enjoys semi-independence
1871–1918	France's defeat in the Franco-Prussian War leaves Alsace under German rule
1881–84	Ferry Laws require all children under 14 be educated in French in public schools
1950s	Regional cultural associations throughout France demand regional linguistic autonomy
1951	Deixonne Law permits limited teaching in regional tongues in some public schools
1960s	Formative period for the development of modern ethnoregional political associations in France
1962	Algeria achieves independence; many Algerian French immigrate to Corsica
1963	Paris, though suppressing autonomists, creates Regional Economic Development committees
1965–67	Principal ethnoregional political organizations in Corsica established
1969	Referendum on administrative centralization fails,but carries in Corsica and other minority regions
1970s	Regionalists broaden demands, Paris adopts a more accommodative approach toward the regions
1981–86	Socialists create regional council system and promote "regional and minority cultures"
1982	By special statute, Paris establishes a Corsican Assembly
1992	European Charter of Regional Languages proposes safeguards for Europe's minority tongues
1993	Further administrative authority decentralized to Corsica
1999	France debates aligning its constitution with Charter of Regional Languages' requirements
2002	Negotiations begin on the devolution of additional authority to Corsican institutions
2003	Corsicans reject proposed autonomy statute

accorded to regional tongues in existing radio and television stations and to create independent, regional radio stations.

The Socialists soon proved to be as adroit as their predecessors at the politics of give and take. Once in office they slowed the timetable for the "new status" for Corsica promised in the 1981 campaigns, and retreated from their pledge to create a separate department for Basque France.[23] Even more revealing, the minority organizations receiving public subsidies were only those that the government chose to recognize as official spokesmen for the covered groups. The credible if militantly anti-Paris spokesmen for ethnoterritorialism in France rarely benefited from the program. To the contrary, in a process that William Safran labels "cultural tutelage," the Socialists' program led simultaneously to the proliferation and co-optation of ethnocultural associations; some of which represented ethnoterritorial minorities. Others spoke for the Gypsies and immigrant communities living in France.[24] For all recipients, there was "a plethora of regulations aimed at ensuring that the national or subcultural agencies concerned with culture and the arts did not go far afield from national [e.g., French] responsibilities and orientations."[25]

Administrative changes were slightly more revolutionary. Though committed to extending the country's *étatist* tradition by nationalizing new sectors, increasing employment in the public sector, and expanding welfare services, the Socialists embarked on a major program of administrative decentralization. The prefect system was dismantled, regional councils were created, and territorial decentralization was inaugurated for the first time since the Revolution. Nor were these shifts reversed when the neo-Gaullists returned to power in the Assembly in 1986 and later reclaimed the presidency. Rather, with regional tongues still declining in daily use in most of the country, governments of the Right and Left have followed a model of "guarded accommodation" toward these groups since the late 1980s. Political decentralization and economic development plans have been consistently proffered to accommodate ethnoregional grievances focusing on the perceived insensitivity of Paris to the lagging economies and endangered cultures of the ethnolinguistic minorities on France's periphery. Those living in these regions have been permitted to teach their minority tongues in French public schools and given subsidies to preserve their distinctive traditions. At the same time, and despite the apparent, general success of this strategy in muting ethnopolitical sentiment, the French Right in particular has continued to view regional tongues as a threat to the unity of the state. Thus, when France belatedly signed the 1992 European Charter on Regional Languages in 1999 and its government debated giving France's regional minorities the constitutional protection that the Charter requires, the old arguments against "Balkanizing" France and undermining its unity resounded. Joining the successful charge against ratifying the Charter, *Le Figaro* editorialized that such an act would threaten France's "incomparable language at a time when it is being bastardized by Anglo-Saxon words."[26]

Corsica: Ethnonationalism in Contemporary France

For the past quarter century, the French government has tried to control the political opposition in Corsica with the same formula of cultural autonomy, economic development projects, and political decentralization that has worked elsewhere in France. It has had notably less success in Corsica, however, even though Paris has been willing to give the island's people a level of home rule never offered to the other ethnoterritorial communities.

Historically, Corsica was the last part of contemporary France to be added to the realm. Moreover, when purchased in 1768 from Genoa, which had exercised nominal control over the island for five centuries, Corsica was enjoying a moment of de facto independence—the result of a series of rebellions against Genoa, which had begun in 1729 and culminated in the early 1750s with the collapse of Genoa's rule and the emergence of Pasquale Paoli as the general-in-chief of the Coracan Nation. After initially offering the island protectorate status, which Paoli refused, France dispatched its forces to the island and established a control over Corsica which has subsequently been interrupted only twice: once in the political chaos that temporarily followed the French Revolution, and again during World War II, when Italian and German troops occupied the island. The historical memory of those eighteenth-century days of independence and great power perfidy have been carefully cultivated by the island's contemporary ethnonationalists and woven into Corsica's demands for freedom from Paris' rule.[27]

Even greater obstacles to Paris' efforts to establish a tranquil means of controlling Corsica have been the island's distance from continental France, its unique Italianate language (which continues to be spoken by over 70 percent of the island's population), and its ethnocultural social structure, which is rooted in an extended-family clan system and interwoven with "strongly-differentiated gender roles, codes of honor and the vendetta, and occultism."[28] Furthermore, the economic development packages extended to the island since the 1960s have not succeeded in undercutting Corsican nationalism or moderating the acts of political violence that its clandestine nationalist organizations have frequently committed. As in the case of most of France's peripheral minority regions, twentieth-century economic changes reinforced the ethnolinguistic cleavage separating predominantly rural and relatively poorer Corsica from Paris and those provinces benefiting from modernization. The economic assistance given to Corsica during the 1960s was meant to blunt this development; however, whatever benefit Paris might have reaped from the programs was neutralized by Algeria's successful war for independence, and the subsequent immigration of many of the French settlers in Algeria to the island. On balance, these immigrants benefited the most from these economic plans, even as their growing presence as outsiders further increased Corsican resentment of its overall treatment by Paris.

By the 1970s the combination of the island's unique culture, relative economic deprivation, and the pervasive perception of Paris' insensitivity to its special character and needs had produced a strong home rule movement on the island spearheaded by two popular ethnoterritorial parties and backed by a level of popular political mobilization that far exceeded that of France's other regionalized minorities. In turn, Corsican politicians affiliated with France's major parties began to incorporate nationalist objectives into *their* platforms. Nevertheless, support for the nationalist cause continued to grow—peaking at 28 percent of the vote before splintering during the 1980s across nearly a dozen different parties competing to represent

Corsica's cause. Meanwhile, incidences of bombings and machine-gun bursts targeting public buildings and other symbols of France on the island continued to mount.

As the number of Corsican autonomist-to-separatist parties and extremist organizations and instances of political violence grew during the late 1960s and 1970s, the French government was forced to reconsider both the politics of control and the accommodation policies that it had largely unsuccessfully employed over the decades to control Corsica. Thus, in the 1980s, for the special problems posed by "Corsican specificity," Paris elevated Corsica to a special status in the unitary French state and began a three-step process of devolving authority to institutions on the isle well beyond the decentralization and regionalization process the Socialists inaugurated elsewhere in France during that decade.

The first step was taken in 1982 with the establishment of Corsica's first directly elected Assembly, and the delegation to it of executive (i.e., primarily administrative) decision-making authority in a wide range of areas, including education, economic development, agriculture, and housing. In addition, in deference to Corsican history, a new university was to be created in Corsica, to be named for Pasquale Paoli, and the house that had served as the seat of his government was to become a Center for Corsican Studies.[29]

The second round came in the early 1990s, beginning with the citizens of Corsica being, in April, 1991, officially recognized as a distinct "people" inside France. The process expanded in 1993 with a set of institutional reforms which augmented the Corsican Assembly's authority and created a second Corsican executive—this one directly elected by the island's councilors. The round culminated in 1999 with promises by both Paris and the EU to launch massive regional development programs in Corsica in order to close the economic gap separating Corsicans from most French citizens. Still, political turbulence continued on the island, albeit with Corsica's clandestine nationalist organizations functioning—for the most part—more like lobbying groups than guerrilla separatist movements such as those of Basque extremists in Spain. Then, despite the economic and political concessions that Corsica had received and the promises of more to come, the level of political violence escalated sharply, most notably with the 1998 assassination of Claude Erignac, the island's Paris-appointed governor, while he was attending a concert in Ajaccio with this wife.

In spite of this development, in 2000, Paris embarked on the third step of its planned decentralization of political authority to Corsica. Socialist Premier Lionel Jospin launched the process by concluding an accord designed to merge executive authority on the island into a single office, further expand the Assembly's power, widen the opportunities for women to hold public office by introducing a quota system, and mandate the teaching of the Corsican language in the island's public schools. Although the Corsican Assembly overwhelmingly ratified the agreement, its implementation first required the approval of Corsican voters in a nonbinding referendum and then its passage by the French Assembly. The latter, however, appeared to be a given insofar as the proposal originated under a Socialist government but had the full support of Gaullist President Jacque Chirac's interior minister, Nicolas Sarkozy, who personally campaigned in Corsica in support of the referendum.[30]

Public opinion polls on the island indicated that the vote on the referendum would be close but were generally encouraging. The principal opposition consisted of the island's councilors and other established, conservative elites, who were suspicious of any scheme that might encroach on their power. The nationalists were suspicious of, and in part divided over, whether to support the accord, but the majority leaned toward the position of the island's principal nationalist party, the Corsica Nazione, which supported the referendum as a positive step toward Corsica's eventual independence.[31] Then, in the last days of the campaign the nationalist vote swung against the referendum when a special unit of French police suddenly arrested a well-known Corsican nationalist and charged him with the 1998 murder of the island's governor. The action was widely interpreted by the nationalists as a ploy by Paris to bolster the "Yes" vote. In fact, it indisputably increased the 'No" vote when large numbers of nationalists voted against the accord, along with the referendum's conservative opponents and those on the island generally distrustful of Paris, confused by the proposal, and/or fearing that a "Yes" vote would jeopardize their access to welfare services. When the final vote was tabulated, the proposal was narrowly defeated with 57,180 voting against it and 54,990 supporting it.[32] Nearly 40 percent of the island's eligible voters stayed home, making the referendum an even greater public relations disaster for the French government, which had supported it as, in Chirac's words, "the best way . . . [for Corsicans] to affirm their attachment to France and the Republic."[33] The failure of the referendum led the French government shortly thereafter to promise a renewed hardline toward the island, though similar policies had failed in the past. France's other ethnoterritorial minorities are also not likely to witness a revival of the regional decentralization program and celebration of France's cultural and linguistic diversity that the Socialists initiated in the 1980s. These programs have been noticeably shelved since that time as the state's broader ethnopolitical agenda has increasingly focused on the assimilationist challenge posed to France by the growing number of non-Western, nonassimilating peoples now living in it.

CHAPTER FOUR

Ethnoclass Politics in France: Multiculturalism in an Assimilationist Republic

Just as France officially denied the existence of ethnoterritorial minorities for nearly 200 years, so the French have rarely thought of themselves as an immigrant society. Contrary to Americans, who have tended to exaggerate the integrative, "melting pot" nature of U.S. society, the French have clung to the image of France as a culturally homogeneous country composed of an indigenous Gaul community.[1] Significantly, it is this perception rather than reality that continues to influence policy in today's increasingly multicultural France.

The Multicultural Fifth French Republic

In one of his last works, a study of global immigration, Myron Weiner identified five distinct eras of immigration since the Renaissance.[2] France has been centrally featured in each. During the first two, France joined with neighboring "donor" states from the seventeenth century until World War I in deploying Europeans to other parts of the world and in shaping the flow of non-Europeans to distant regions, most aggressively through the slave trade. During the three twentieth-century waves, France itself has been shaped by immigrant flows. It opened its doors to the refugees produced by the 1917 Russian revolution and the new states created after World War I, which often employed forced emigration to create more homogeneous populations. Later, France absorbed a share of the migrants created by such post–World War II dislocations as the partition of Germany, the Sovietization of Eastern Europe, and the early stages of postwar decolonization. Finally, to obtain the work force necessary to rebuild its economy, postwar France opened its gates to still more of its former colonial subjects.

The Empire Comes Home: The Surfacing of the Ethnic Factor

Both the unwillingness of the French to revise their image of the French nation in light of the numerous outsiders entering their country during the first half of the twentieth century and the low saliency of the "foreigner" issue prior to 1968 can be explained in terms of the nature, numbers, and areas of diffusion of the earlier immigrant groups. Before World War II, immigrants were overwhelmingly white Europeans and frequently Catholic as well, who arrived in relatively small numbers compared to postwar arrivees. They were willing to assimilate to the majoritarian culture and tended to settle in the largest and most cosmopolitan of France's cities, Paris. By contrast, the million immigrants entering France between 1946 and 1974 came largely from non-European areas, dispersed more widely throughout France, and—except for the Vietnamese—have been slow or unwilling to assimilate. All of these elements have affected the evolution of the foreigner issue in French politics.

Becoming Multicultural
By the end of the twentieth century, when the long hovering specter of a significant antiforeigner vote had become a reality in French politics, France's population was officially estimated at 58,518.748, with 16.4 percent living in the Paris region.[3] Of these nearly 60 million people, 7.37 percent (approximately 4,310,000 in 1990) were listed as foreign residents, substantially larger than the estimated 6.5 percent in 1990;[4] however, even this figure is somewhat misleading on at least three counts.

First, the numbers include neither the illegal aliens who have been given the opportunity to legalize their status (officially numbering, in the mid-1990s, 130,000 foreign workers, but the figure is thought to be much higher), nor those citizens who continue to be perceived as "foreign" despite having naturalized or been born in France of foreign parents.[5] In 1999, the latter two categories of French citizens totaled another 1,310,000 people. When the list is widened to include the second-generation grandchildren of the foreign-born, the number of legal and illegal "foreigners" jumps to nearly 20 percent of the population of metropolitan France.[6]

Second, whereas a generation before more than half of France's foreign residents came from other European states, by 1990 EU countries only accounted for slightly over a third (36.3 percent) of them. Meanwhile, the Muslim North African contingent had grown from 34.6 percent of the foreign residents in 1975 to 45.8 percent by 1990. The remainder was mostly from sub-Sahara Africa, the Middle East, and Southeast Asia—groups whose ranks continued to swell during the 1990s.[7] These foreigners have a decidedly un-European flavor and pose a much greater challenge to the state's traditional, assimilationist approach toward emigres than their predecessors.

Third, these "new" foreigners' share of the population is likely to increase even if France successfully seals its borders. Although accounting for only a little more than 6 percent of the population, by the mid-1990s foreign residents were responsible for 12.7 percent of the births being registered in France.[8] This disparity continues to grow.

The newest immigrants stand out in the population culturally, and hence visibly, as well as statistically. Even if the government's conservative figures are used, one-third of France's foreign residents in 1990 came from either Algeria (619,900) or Morocco (584,700), and another 207,500 came from Tunisia.[9] Unlike the European immigrants who preceded them, these arrivees differ from the French in terms of religion (in a state where anti-Semitism against the Jews, constituting 1 percent of the population, still produces an occasional headline), ethnicity, history (they were once subject peoples), and race. The fact that many arrived through the backdoor with temporary work visas and not as immigrants expected to become permanent residents has exacerbated the matter.

The arrival of the North Africans began before France relinquished its empire. In a futile, 1954 effort to undercut the independence movement in Algeria, France offered Algerians citizenship and the right to settle in France. Eight years later, when France was forced to accept Algeria's independence, 300,000 Algerians were already living in France.[10]

By 1974, when France suspended further migration except in such special cases as family reunification programs, this Algerian nucleus had evolved into a large, Muslim-practicing, Arab-speaking population. It continued to grow. Again using only the state's conservative calculations, by 1990 Muslim North Africans accounted for approximately half of France's legal, noncitizen population.[11] Unofficially, North Africans were also estimated to account for 90 percent of France's 500,000 to 1,000,000 illegal residents.[12] Collectively, the number of Muslims in France is conservatively estimated as at least 5 million, far more than in any other EU state.

The Assimilation Issue

France did not adopt a *jus soli* (place of birth) basis for citizenship until 1889, and only did so then because it needed to draft the aliens then living in France. The philosophical justification for the policy shift was the belief that foreigners born in France could be assimilated into the French culture via the state's secular school system and military service, much like the ethnoregional minorities. The idea that they might *not* assimilate was scarcely considered given the prevailing belief in the strength as well as the size of the French culture enfolding the foreign communities. In fact, because most the foreigners were at that time from Belgium and Italy—that is, Catholic and often francophones—nineteenth- and early-twentieth-century experience seemed to validate this assumption.[13]

So too did France's experience in assimilating its interwar immigrants and, to a lesser degree, arrivees from Indo-China after World War II. The Vietnamese spoke French, practiced the Catholic faith, contributed to the economy, did not place heavy demands on state resources, generally kept a low profile, and overall tried to assimilate as far as their racial origins would permit.[14]

The story has been considerably different with respect to France's Arab-Muslim population, despite a few recent, encouraging signs: a slightly upward trend in mixed marriages (which extremists view as miscegenation) and a decline in Mosque attendance among second- and third-generation

North Africans in France. As a group, however, North Africans continue to dress in traditional wear and in the minds of many French, thereby demonstrate daily their unwillingness to assimilate to the French way of life. They have also raised ethnocultural issues in the public school system and have been exceedingly slow to naturalize even when encouraged by the state to do so.[15]

Their reluctance to renounce their overseas citizenship has in part resulted from the pressure placed on them by their countries of origin. North African states, adhering to the doctrine of *jus sanguinis*, have treated their sons and daughters in France as the nationals temporarily working abroad, who the French once thought they were importing. They have therefore discouraged them from adopting French citizenship, and have subsidized organizations assisting them in retaining their culture while living abroad.[16] Also under pressure from their parents to adhere to traditional ways, and frequently the target of overt discrimination by the host population, North Africans have been slow to naturalize because it would mean renouncing their former citizenship. France does not subscribe to the doctrine of dual citizenship. Nonetheless, the North Africans' reluctance to accept French citizenship has been widely cited by antiforeigner organizations as evidence of their unwillingness to assimilate, as have the wildcat strikes and general protests by North Africans of their work and living conditions, which have occasionally turned into nasty confrontations with the authorities. Above all, there is the Arab population's continued commitment to Islam. Numerous observers stress the inseparability of Catholicism from the French national culture; those not embracing it have always been suspect, be they Jewish or Protestant Huguenots.[17] The adherence of second- and third-generation residents to a non-European religion, which purports to be an overall code of conduct for life, is widely interpreted as illustrative of the Arab community's inability to integrate fully into a country whose people are preponderantly Catholic and whose state is self-consciously secular.

Economic Stagflation and Ethnoclass Consciousness

The economic modernization program launched during the Fourth French Republic and the subsequent, nearly 30-year period of high economic growth that followed (the *Trente Glorieuses*) forced a succession of governments to recruit workers from the Empire to labor in France. The goal was easily accomplished. The lure of better-paying jobs drew hundreds of thousands from Algeria, Morocco, and Tunisia. For a long time their migration was widely accepted by a country in need of manpower to sustain its economic boom; however, as their numbers increased so did tensions between the foreign workers and their hosts. Then came the energy crises of 1973 and 1979, and the global economic downturn. Unemployment rates soared in France as elsewhere, from less than 7 percent of the French work force in 1973 to 15 percent in 1980. The recession did not end there. By 1993, France's number of unemployed had doubled to over 3 million. Economic concerns began to reinforce the foreigner issue, especially among the young just entering the job market. For women under the age of 25 unemployment in the early 1990s persistently hovered in the 30 percent range; for men of the same age it increased sharply from 19.6 percent in 1984 to 24.2 percent a decade later. The overall picture was not much brighter. From the first oil crisis until relatively recently, France consistently had the second highest unemployment rate of any developed Western country, even though the French government employs a larger percentage of the workforce than any other advanced democracy (24.6 percent versus, for example, 15.3 percent in the public sector in the United States in the mid-1990s).[18]

The presence of increasing numbers of legal and illegal North Africans at a time of growing unemployment made the foreign workers easy targets for blame. The facts, however, hardly support the conclusion that foreigners took available jobs from the French, capsulized in one of the favorite slogan's of the *Front National* (FN) anti-immigrant party: "two million unemployed equals two million immigrants too many."[19] France's non-European workers were, and continue to be, concentrated in the menial jobs that the French associate with foreigners and that the French refuse to perform at the wages being offered. Moreover, the foreign workers suffered disproportionately in the era of high unemployment when, constituting only 6 percent of the work force, they routinely accounted for nearly 20 percent of the unemployed. On the other hand, high unemployment among foreign workers *did* contribute to a growth in delinquency and other antisocial to criminal acts within the immigrant communities, giving the French another grievance against this large, multicultural segment of the population.[20]

France's participation in the European Community further elevated French fears of a foreign invasion, especially during the 1980s. Even before the Maastricht concept of a "Europe without borders," the free movement of labor guaranteed to the citizens of member states stripped France of the ability to protect its domestic work force from laborers coming from an expanding number of EU states, including Portugal and Spain in the 1970s. The implementation of the Maastricht Accord during the 1990s forced France to rely on other EU states to keep out unwanted job-seekers originating outside the EU; once inside, they are free to enter France. Even the fall of communism heightened anxieties by producing a new tide of emigres seeking entry into the EU, and potentially France.

The National Front: Exploiting the "Foreigner" Issue

The principal political beneficiary of the increase in anti-immigrant sentiment was the National Front (*Front National* or FN). Ronald Tiersky describes it as a combination of the worst of French protest politics—"racial and religious prejudice, anti-establishment rhetoric, populism, [and] know-nothingism."[21] Yet in tapping into such broader issues as assimilationism-versus-multiculturalism, the FN does more than preach to the faithful or even, as Le Pen asserts, say "aloud what many French people say under their breath."[22]

Electoral Growth

Founded as a right-wing, nationalist party by Jean-Marie Le Pen and other members of the postwar neofascist *Ordre Nouveau* (New Order) in 1972, the FN showed little strength during its first decade, when the Gaullists and their Center–Right allies dominated the vote of the French Right. Its ability to attack government immigration policy improved in the 1980s when the Left took control of political power at the same time that rising unemployment was giving the FN's message resonance. Its breakthrough came in the local elections of 1983, when it captured nearly 10 percent of the vote, and in the European Parliament elections the following year, when it gained ten seats. Next came the 1986 parliamentary elections, when the governing Socialists, facing an electoral disaster, hastily adopted a PR system to limit their loss of seats in the French assembly. The tactic worked, but it also benefited the smaller parties. The FN's 9.7 percent of the vote gave it 35 Chamber of Deputies seats and the veneer of political legitimacy that the press had previously denied it. Le Pen used that image in the 1988 presidential election to capture nearly 15 percent of the first ballot vote, a feat he repeated in 1995. As for the FN, it continued to capture the anti-immigrant vote and finish in double digits in France's parliamentary elections of 1988, 1993, and 1997.

The party's persistent ability to attract 10–15 percent of the vote between 1984 and 1999, and 25 percent in cities with large North African populations, can be partially explained in terms of the French electoral system. The prevailing (non-PR) model has been a two ballot-runoff system in which voters often use the first round to cast a protest vote against the established parties. On the other hand, given France's multiparty system, 15 percent of the first round vote *is* impressive; in 1997 it brought the FN within an eyelash of finishing second among all French parties in the first round vote. Also impressive has been the durability of the political message being sent when FN support is viewed as an ongoing gauge of the public's frustration with government policy on the foreigner issue.[23]

Equally disconcerting to the FN's critics was the party's success in expanding its voter base during the 1980s. Geographically FN voters continue to live disproportionately in south and southeast France, where the French returnees from postcolonial Algeria (approximately 300,000 today) and large numbers of North Africans settled. The FN's appeal today, however, is much wider both in terms of class support (it draws support from all socioeconomic classes) and geography (with solid support in all but the country's western and southwestern departments).

The FN's inroads into other voting constituencies has been attributed to the growing importance of the foreigner issue, French willingness to ascribe rising unemployment and crime rates to the foreign element,[24] and—more recently—to the perceived threat to the French way of life posed by the unwillingness of Muslim North Africans to assimilate into the secular French state. FN voters thus became younger and more working class during the 1980s, when the party sharply benefited from worsening economic conditions as well as Le Pen's organizational and rhetorical skills in appealing to disillusioned Communist Party supporters and newer voters, including the French "skinhead" contingent.[25]

Individuals and Public Policy: The Le Pen Factor
The relationship among French ethnopolitics, the FN, and its founder has been complex. Conventional wisdom holds that a vast majority in the electorate regards Le Pen as an unsuitable national leader, and that his presence is one of the reasons why the FN has not further enlarged its base of support.[26] At the same time, Le Pen is generally credited with building the FN into an influential player in French politics, and the party's future is uncertain without him at its helm. He has not, however, been the party's only influential member.

During the 1990s, the FN's message became more specific when its then second in command, Bruno Megret, offered 50 proposals for treating the immigrant problem. These included: (1) limiting the property rights of immigrants; (2) terminating all public support of foreigner organizations; (3) establishing *jus sanguinis* as the sole basis for French nationality; (4) banning multicultural curriculums from classrooms; (5) enlarging the list of reasons for revoking nationality; and (6) giving preference to the indigenous French in hiring and in access to public housing and other social services.[27]

Few of these proposals had any chance of being enacted but they continue to find receptive audiences. In fact, the FN's performance since 1990 has, overall, been in stark contrast to the shrinking electoral strength of several of the parties that influenced the first three decades of the Fifth Republic (1958–present). In the 1993 parliamentary elections, for example, the FN outpaced the Communist Party in the first round vote (12.4 to 9.2 percent); its greater success in the 1997 parliamentary election has already been noted. Perhaps most indicative of its consolidating strength, Le Pen won 20 percent of the urban vote in the May 1995 presidential election and the FN secured control of Nice, Toulon, and two other southern French cities in the municipal elections the following month.[28] Thus far, French elections in the twenty-first century have confirmed its ability to draw double-digit support, whether the election is for the presidency, Chamber of Deputies, regional councils, or European Parliament.

The FN and Politics in France
More important than the FN's success in attracting voters has been its impact on the broader political process. Its success in mobilizing a segment of the electorate around an anti-immigrant program has caused mainstream politicians to adopt its rhetoric and co-opt portions of its program. In summer, 1991, for example, now French president Jacques Chirac stated in a

newspaper interview that he understood why the French had trouble coping with the "noises and odors" of foreigners "surviving on welfare." Then his party's leader, Chirac demanded an end to the family-reunification programs under which North Africans were still entering France. His popularity jumped five points in public opinion polls.

Thereafter anti-immigrant rhetoric became the norm. Former president and titular leader of France's then other major party of the Right, Valery Giscard d'Estaing, called the immigrant presence an "invasion," equated it with the Nazi Occupation, and advocated the expulsion of unemployed foreign workers and preferential hiring of French nationals in filling rosters.[29] Meanwhile on the Left, France's Socialist president Francois Mitterand joined the chorus by noting that the French were approaching a "threshold of tolerance" beyond which they would not go.[30] He then abandoned his proposal to give immigrants the right to vote in local elections. Indeed, more often than not, such inflammatory rhetoric by French leaders has been followed by restrictive legislation aimed at France's North African, Muslim community, although the legislation has usually been crafted in terms of interdicting all illegal immigrants or denying access to social services to all noncitizens (see table 4.1).

Finally, there has been the FN's destabilizing effect on France's mainstream parties, although occasionally this success has been costly to the FN as well. Thus, a major drama commenced when the FN won 15.5 percent of the national vote in France's 1998 regional elections, which then utilized a PR system in allocating regional council seats. Because the parties of the Left and Right each won approximately 35 percent of the vote, the FN became the kingmaker in its southeast France stronghold when the time came to elect the regional presidents. In five regions local leaders courted FN support over the opposition of their national leadership. In some instances, the deals they negotiated led to their expulsion from their parties, but they also allowed Bruno Megret to trumpet the FN as having become "a party of government."[31]

The FN's enhanced status soon became a mixed blessing for the party, the consequences of which are still being measured. Its achievement in becoming a part of the ruling bloc in several regions meant that national political leaders could no longer dismiss it as an extremist voice best ignored, and almost immediately thereafter President Chirac proposed changing the electoral system for regional elections from the PR framework so favorable to smaller parties. Demonstrations were organized against the FN and local collaborators in numerous French cities, and—initiating a chain of events that six months later produced a split in the FN—in April 1998 a French court banned Le Pen from seeking reelection to the European Parliament in 1999.[32]

Le Pen's case began in 1997 when he accosted a political opponent during the parliamentary campaign. Assault charges were filed and although the case was pursued as a criminal action the penalty levied on Le Pen shortly after the FN's success in the 1998 regional elections was political: a two-year

Table 4.1 The "Foreigner" Issue in French politics

1945	World War II ends; France begins to recruit foreign workers
1947	War for independence begins in French Indo-China
1954	Indo-China War ends and France withdraws; Algerian war for independence begins; the number of Indo-China refugees increases in France
1968	Government begins to explore ways to limit high number of immigrants and foreign workers
1972	*Front National* (FN) anti-immigrant party founded
1973	Violence against Algerians grows in France; Algeria bans further immigration
1974	Recession prompts France to halt "temporarily" immigration from non-EC states while enacting a broad program to improve living conditions of existing workers.
1977	Government offers tickets home and cash bonus to unemployed foreign workers willing to depart
1981–6	Socialists gain control of Assembly and Presidency; France "redefined" as a "multicultural society." Foreign workers get same rights as the French; naturalization laws are liberalized
1986	Control of Parliament reverts to the parties of the Right; sponsorship of foreign associations reduced
1989	National furor occurs when three North African students in Paris refuse to remove traditional Muslim head coverings; government announces tighter control of borders and immigrants in France
1990	Constitutional Counsel refuses to rule that all forms of discrimination are unconstitutional; immigrants riot in Lyons, attacking police and looting shops
1993	New laws, including a constitutional amendment, enacted to reduce numbers of illegal immigrants
1995	Jacque Chirac elected president on platform stressing a new toughness toward illegal aliens
1996	UN Human Rights Commission denounces "wave of xenophobia and racism" in France. A week later France adopts new restrictions on entry into France and the access of legal immigrants to health care, education, and other services
1997	Socialists regain control of French Assembly, grant automatic citizenship to children born in France of foreign parents when they reach 18, and liberalize immigration laws for highly skilled
1998	FN wins 15% of vote in regional elections; Center–Right parties form alliances with the FN as a "party of governance" in three regions
2002	May–June: Socialist leader and premier of France Jospin places third in first round of balloting for French presidency; FN leader Le Pen finishes second but is routed by Chirac in runoff
	December: government creates Muslim Council to advise it on issues concerning French Muslims
2004	In defense of secular French state, parliament bans Muslim headdress from public schools
	Parliament authorizes deportation of noncitizens advocating violence against any group
2005	Accidental death of two Muslim teenagers fleeing police in depressed area north of Paris ignites nearly two weeks of arson and rioting by Muslim youth, affecting 300 French towns

ban on participating in politics, which left Le Pen unable to head his party's list in the European Parliament's 1999 elections. Le Pen's response was to protect his seat by inserting his wife's name at the top of the FN's list, not that of his lieutenant, Bruno Megret. Megret retaliated by naming himself as acting party leader. When the fallout settled, the FN had split into two factions: Le Pen's National Front and Megret's National Front-National Movement. Both offered lists in the European Parliament elections. Not surprisingly, the in-fighting resulted in a combined vote for the two lists which was far poorer than the FN's showing five years previously. The FN gained only 5.7 percent of the vote and five of its former twelve seats; Megret's National Movement won only 3.3 percent of the vote and no seats. Two years later, Megret's party was allied with the FN in the 2004 regional elections in which the FN drew approximately 16.5 percent of the vote, but the partnership with Le Pen remains tense.

Public Policy and "Les Étrangers"

"Les Étrangers" in France

The foreign workers' preparation for life in France varied significantly depending on their points of origin. Algerians were much more likely to have a pre-arrival ability to speak French than the Senegalese and others from sub-Sahara Africa. All, however, initially tended to be young, of peasant background, and unemployed on arrival.[33] Most also had to spend months job hunting before finding employment. Opportunities were limited by their skills and French law, which permitted employers to hire migrants only in industrial sectors, where there was a shortage of French workers. As a result, when secured, employment was usually as wage labor in "the dirtiest, most painful, and risky occupation positions."[34]

Housing opportunities were likewise limited and France's social services system provided little assistance to the arriving workers. North Africans frequently relied on the members of their family or villages already in France to house them temporarily. Also frequently those temporary, over-crowded arrangements became permanent as the Maghreb work force gradually settled into industrial suburban ghettos in the substandard housing available to them.[35]

Nearly two generations have passed since those days. French governments have permitted the non-European population to continue to grow through family unification programs and, most recently, special status immigration laws favoring well-educated applicants with skills currently needed in France. France now contains at least five million Muslims, many of whom are beyond easy deportation because they were born in or have become naturalized citizens of France. Yet, few of the postwar arrivees from North Africa have become more integrated into French society. Most continue to find employment in relatively low-paying jobs, often in declining industries. Career mobility has continued to be blocked by the discrimination they have faced, their underdeveloped linguistic skills, and their generally unskilled status.[36] French law has also played an important role in restricting their mobility. Not only are public service jobs limited to French citizens but typically numerous positions in the private sector have been reserved for the French.[37]

The housing of North Africans has also remained substandard, usually in Arab ghettos. To the extent that North African communities have achieved a more normal lifestyle, it is because of the family unification programs, which have enabled the workers to have a family-oriented lifestyle, albeit apart from typical French family neighborhoods.

Because of their semi-outcast status, the psychological condition of these workers continues to be described as "demoralized" compared to such groups as the Latino population in the United States.[38] It is a collective mindset that encourages them to turn ever more inward. As a Muslim worker recently phrased it, "I have never felt French . . . . [In an Arab community] I feel safe because everyone is Arab. But the France outside is a France of racism, and the racism has gotten worse since September 11."[39]

It should not be overlooked that those who have foregone naturalization have also foregone full participation in the political process, thereby weakening the bargaining position they would have as a voting bloc. The protection of their interests thus continues to depend on the French government, and the oversight lobbying efforts of the Arab governments monitoring the living conditions of their nationals abroad. Meanwhile, given the French perception of the immigrant population as unwilling to assimilate, the nature of the economy, and the success of the FN in keeping the foreigner question salient, it is not surprising that political debate on the "foreigner" issue has remained predominantly one sided. It has been preoccupied with the impact of the "outsiders" on France, not the living conditions of the foreign communities in France.

Public Policy and the Foreigner Issue

With one notable exception, since 1945 France's policies toward the foreign communities have reflected the changing patterns of interaction between the incoming foreigners and their French hosts. As that relationship has altered, so has public policy. To date, those changing patterns have produced five distinct periods of policy making: a *buildup* period during which the foreigners arrived without discernible public reaction; an *issue emergence* phase; an *issue intensification* period largely attributable to the declining economic conditions and rising unemployment rates; a period of *issue exploitation and public mobilization* against the foreign presence, and the now long-term, current era of *mainstreaming,* or *issue legitimization,* in which leading national politicians have exploited the foreigner issue for partisan advantage, albeit with significant new elements added in the early twenty-first century.

Buildup, 1945–68

In 1945, France established a National Immigration Office to recruit and regulate the immigration of foreign workers. If there was a how-to-do-it plan behind the Office's creation, it was quickly lost as postwar France became immersed in establishing a new constitutional order (the Fourth Republic) and maintaining its empire in Asia and North Africa. In practice, most foreign workers arrived as a result of bilateral accords concluded between their home states and the governments of the Fourth and Fifth French Republics. More importantly, with the National Immigration Office moribund, prior to 1968 France essentially adopted a *laissez faire* approach toward both the number and the social problems of the foreign workers entering France.

Issue Emergence, 1968–72

By the time the government began to consider controlling the number of foreigners entering the country, the presence of a sizeable "foreign" element had already become an issue. The French who had been forced to return to France from newly independent Algeria had personal reasons to resent the large numbers of Algerians in their homeland. More broadly, the May riots of 1968 convinced much of the populace that the postwar economic recovery was over and that the need for foreign labor may have been overfilled.

The government's sluggishness in restraining the inflow of foreigners gave Le Pen an open field when he founded the FN in 1972 as an avowedly anti-immigrant party. Shortly thereafter, the government distributed to French businesses a circular indicating a new toughness toward those workers already in the country. Loss of job would henceforth result in an immediate withdrawal of work permits, and the length of future work permits was to depend on the workers providing evidence that they had acquired adequate housing.

Issue Intensification, 1973–81

The distribution of the circular, it should be noted, preceded France's general economic downturn following the oil crises of 1973, as did the founding of the FN and the onset of occasional acts of violence aimed at North African workers. Therefore, neither the 1972 immigration policy, nor the National Front, nor French antiforeigner sentiments can be explained entirely in terms of economic concerns. Still, prior to the first oil crisis the attacks on the foreign workers were more verbal than physical. The oil crises intensified the foreigner issue as an increasingly unemployed host working class nodded in agreement when Le Pen blamed the foreigners for the country's soaring unemployment rate. The number of assaults on foreign workers also began to increase—to the point where the government of Algeria in 1973 banned further immigration to France.

The economic downturn came at, demographically, an extremely bad moment: when existing immigrants were being joined by family members and thereby visibly growing in number. The government responded to these developments with policies aimed at both the number of foreigners entering France and those already in the country. The first shoe dropped in

1974, when the government imposed a "temporary" stop on all immigration from outside of the European Community (now the EU). The temporary stoppage order soon became permanent.

The second policy, operational by 1977, addressed an increasingly apparent flaw in the original theory of admitting temporary laborers: the assumption that in time they would return to their homelands. To persuade part of the foreign work force to leave, the government offered a free ticket home and a 10,000-franc bonus to any unemployed foreign worker or foreign worker employed for less than five years who would be willing to depart. The goal was to reduce France's then two million foreign workers by 250,000. Only 5 percent of the country's *unemployed* foreign laborers and a minute segment of France's overall foreign work force accepted the offer.

The Politics of Mobilization, 1981–86

The continued growth of the foreign labor force and France's unemployment rate made the foreign workers a hot button issue during the recessionary years of the 1980s. As already noted, the FN contributed to this development and profited from it. Public policy, however, was uniquely out of step with public opinion during this period.

In control of both the presidency and parliament, the French Socialist Party (PSF) inaugurated a series of programs between 1981 and 1986 built upon the assumption that France conceived of itself as a "multicultural society." The process of regionalizing power to the ethnoterritorial groups was paired with policies designed to subsidize the cultural associations and activities of foreign communities in France. Immigrant workers were accorded the same rights as French workers with respect to wages, holidays, and pay. Children younger than ten were exempted from deportation regardless of reason.

These policies reflected the PSF's commitment to the equality and fraternity of the working class. They also acknowledged the reality that France's temporary foreign workers had become a permanent part of the population. Even during this period, however, the politics of inclusion were tempered by the politics of tradeoffs. Many of the PSF's inclusionary policies *were* important to the Arab community: for example, those policies permitting private radio stations to broadcast in the languages of ethnic minorities (so long as the message was not political) and those that relaxed the knowledge of French required for naturalization.[40] At the same time, the procedural obstacles standing between those born of foreign parents and full French citizenship were never fully eliminated.

Mainstreaming: 1986–Present

In 1986, the political Right regained control of the Assembly and abruptly terminated active government sponsorship of social pluralism within the foreign communities. Soon thereafter the policy agenda began to focus on the continuing presence of the "foreigners" as *the* issue—a development traceable to both the FN's growing electoral success, and to several political activities pursued by the foreign communities.

One of the most publicized of these activities involved the *foulard* dispute. It began in 1989, when North African women in public schools refused to conform to the dress requirements by removing the scarf traditionally worn to cover the head of a Muslim woman. The incident would have gone largely unnoticed had not school administrators overreacted by expelling the girls. In turn, Arabs throughout France protested in support of the students. Although school administrators eventually relented, the protest was widely viewed as a rebellion against assimilation, the cornerstone of French immigration policy. The government responded by declaring that France "can no longer be a land of immigration," and announcing a new set of strict border controls and statutes aimed at the aliens already in the country. Significantly, when several of these regulations were challenged as discriminatory before the Constitutional Counsel, even as it granted partial relief the Counsel refused to rule that all forms of ethnic-based discrimination would be unconstitutional.

The following year another protest by the immigrant community generated largely counterproductive consequences. Much like the prolonged, April 1992 rioting in Los Angeles following a white jury's acquittal of white police officers charged with beating a black suspect, a minor event in 1990 led to rioting by discontented immigrants living in a "model" redevelopment area in Lyons, with demonstrators attacking police and looting shops. The government reacted with words of moderation, citing the riots as evidence of the need to integrate the foreign population better into French society. Nevertheless, the policies that have followed have been far more restrictive than integrative, although the degree of restrictiveness has depended on which parties have controlled the National Assembly and presidency.

The differences between the mainstream parties on the "foreigner" issue were highlighted at an April, 1992, all-party conference. The Socialists wanted to temper a generally hardline approach toward the foreign communities with public awareness campaigns and laws allowing residents to sue over racist remarks. The Gaullists and their allies on the Right stressed limiting immigrant access to welfare and ending illegal immigration. Consequently, when the Right regained control of the Assembly in 1993, legislation focused on limiting political asylum, accelerating the deportation of illegal immigrants, and procedurally restricting the acquisition of *jus soli* citizenship. A key portion entitled police to make identity checks of people whose behavior—for example, reading a foreign newspaper—indicated that the person was possibly an alien.[41]

The politics of restrictionism received a further boost in 1995 when Neo-Gaullist Jacques Chirac was elected president on a platform promising still greater toughness toward illegal immigrants. The following year, only a week after the United Nations Human Rights Commission denounced the "wave of xenophobia and racism" in France, Chirac's government proposed laws to: deny asylum to anyone without identity papers; require the fingerprinting of visa applicants from "high immigration risk countries"; impose heavy fines on those employing illegal immigrants; and restrict the access of noncitizens to health care, education, and other services.[42] Most of the proposals passed. Meanwhile, and at approximately the same time, French police stormed a church in Paris to arrest Africans protesting the speedy deportation proceedings newly inaugurated to evict even those illegal immigrants who had lived for years in France.

The Socialists regained control of the Assembly that December and eased naturalization laws to grant citizenship automatically to children born in France of foreign parents once they reached 18. Insofar as candidates for naturalization had only to declare their intention to accept French citizenship before reaching 18, the law was basically a symbolic gesture. Nonetheless, public opinion polls in November 1997 showed 75 percent of the French opposed to it.

Even more inflammatory, the Socialists also eased the immigration laws passed in the early 1990s to permit the special status entry into France of foreign professionals, highly skilled workers, and foreign students. Objectively the action, recommended by a panel of government and out-side experts, made sense. France's unemployment rate had dropped below 10 percent and the country was experiencing manpower shortages in the areas earmarked for special status immigration. In terms of popular reaction, however, liberalizing immigration laws was a loser. By the late 1990s the impact of foreign workers on unemployment rates was no longer the public's main concern. Rather, the issue had now become the threat posed to the secular French state and French culture by the large and growing presence of Muslim non-Europeans unwilling to assimilate to the French way of life. The Socialists' policies resulted in the number of work visas issued to Algerians increasing from 57,000 in 1997 to 275,000 in 2001,[43] and in the party's electoral fortunes sharply decreasing, first in the 1998 regional elections, held shortly after the liberalization of citizenship requirements, and then in an embarrassing manner in France's 2002 presidential and National Assembly elections.

The impact of the public's mood is not limited to the political scene in Paris. It also encompasses day-to-day politics at the local level. There, even when Paris is emphasizing nondiscriminatory policies, local administrators have frequently been able to find creative means of placating public opinion. For example, although it is illegal to refuse to allocate public housing to foreigners, local housing directors have long justified such action on the tortured reasoning that, by excluding foreigners, they are actually working against racism by avoiding those ethnic concentrations likely to produce racial tensions.[44]

The Limited Range of Options

France's foreigner "problem" is, ultimately, a multidimensional issue involving legals and illegals, French born and naturalized citizens (who still "look Arab") and noncitizens, immigrants, and temporary workers and refugees, and French discriminators and those discriminated against. Its complexity defies sweeping policy responses.

Large-scale immigration essentially ended in 1974. Except under family reunification programs, residence visas have been too limited in duration to permit travelers, students, or the more recent special status workers to qualify for naturalization. Nor would focusing on the reunification programs be of much avail. Compared to the overall number of North Africans in France, the number annually entering under these programs has been proportionately small; on the average, less than 1–2 percent of the foreign residents in the country.

Illegal immigration is, well, illegal, and there are limits to how aggressively a democracy concerned with basic rights can enforce existing laws, however loud the clamor of public opinion. On the other hand, even Socialist governments have been aggressive in cracking down on illegal residents *and* legal immigrants deemed a threat to the public order. Under the provisions of the 1993 law enacted by the Socialist Balladur government authorizing random checks of identity papers based on suspicious behavior, officials were empowered not only to deport illegal residents but to deny health benefits to legal residents whose papers were not entirely in order. Furthermore, even if illegal immigration were to continue at the level of the past decade (between 35,000 and 100,000 per year for all groups) the number of illegals would remain small compared to the French population. At the most, only a little over 0.5 percent of the population slips into the country each year,[45] and the cumulative buildup is significantly blunted by the eventual apprehension of many.

Lastly, naturalized immigrants *are* French citizens. William Safran's figures indicate that by 1990, as many as 1.5 million of the 4 million immigrants then in France already fell into this category.[46] From the viewpoint of the general public, the central problem may lie here, among those who have made the transition from foreign worker to citizen, or who achieved citizenship by being born in France, but who have retained their culture and openly practice their "foreign-ness" by shopping in "Arab markets" and erecting mosques. Nonetheless, they are entitled to the rights and privileges of other citizens. Short of implementing the FN's program of immediately expelling non-naturalized residents, rescinding naturalization wherever possible and then expelling the newly de-naturalized, the government has limited options in dealing with this situation.

The "Foreigner" Issue in Post-9/11 France: Walking the Line

The terrorist attack on New York and Washington on September 11, 2001, and the U.S. military action against Iraq in the spring of 2003 did not discernibly alter French attitudes toward the large Muslim community in France, although perhaps only because antiforeigner opinion was already well established on a wide range of issues. The events did, however, cause the French government to reexamine its policy options in terms of the security issues involved in hosting a large, partially alienated Islamic community in an era of transnational terrorism aimed at Western culture and institutions. The government subsequently intensified its efforts to find policies capable of both courting the Muslim population and appeasing antiforeigner sentiment in France without strengthening the militant Islamic factions inside the country.

The 9/11 Factor

As discussed elsewhere, France has had intermittent experience with terrorism from both within and without.[47] Extremists in the Breton and Corsican nationalist camps have resorted to nonlethal violence against the property of the French government (banks, radio antennae, power lines), and Jewish synagogues and cemeteries continue to be desecrated by anti-Semitic groups within France. Transnational terrorism made its appearance in France in January, 1975, when an anti-Israel Arab cell struck at Paris' Orly airport, taking ten hostages and successfully demanding to be flown to safety in Baghdad. It continues to recur from time to time, most violently in August of 1975, when a bomb detonated at one of Paris' busiest metro stations and killed or injured nearly 100 people.[48] Like that bombing, most of the attacks attributed to outside interests have been blamed on radical Algerians opposing the French government's support of the regime in Algiers, and hence seen as episodic in nature and involving only a faction of one of the country's Muslim communities.

The 2001 attack on the United States by al-Qaeda operatives, and the 2004 terrorist assault on commuter trains in Madrid attributed to Moroccan terrorists changed the equation and gave new impetus to the French government's already ongoing campaign against radical Islamic fundamentalists in France. A global terrorist organization seeking recruits in any Muslim community in any Western country poses a different threat than the occasional assaults of disgruntled Algerian extremists. It is a fact of twenty-first-century political life not lost on the government, especially given the obvious differences of opinion between France's Muslim community and the rest of the country revealed by the public opinion polls measuring reactions to the U.S. invasion of Iraq in 2003. The Paris daily *Le Figaro*, for example, found during the week of the invasion that 94 percent of French Muslim respondents were opposed to the war and 72 percent wanted Saddam Hussein to win, in contrast to only a third in the rest of the population who did not want to see the U.S.-led "coalition of the willing" to succeed.[49]

The French response to the safety issues involved in being a multicultural state in today's Europe has been a carrot-and-stick approach toward the Muslim communities, which relies on two policies that were already in progress on 9/11. The carrot part of the package was the creation of a French Council for the Muslim Religion composed of members drawn from France's main Islamic organizations and designed to formalize a relationship between France's Muslims and public officials. The idea of such an advisory body, similar to the one created for France's Jews two centuries ago and the already existing Muslim Council in the United Kingdom, had been discussed for several years. The 9/11 attack on the United States gave new importance to creating it, and in December, 2002, it became a reality when the leaders of three of France's leading Islamic groups agreed to join.[50]

Meanwhile, France has expanded its efforts to curb radical Muslim clerics who use their religious positions as political forums,[51] even when it means expelling clerics who have resided in France for decades. Based on a 2004 law enabling deportation of noncitizens who incite "discrimination, hatred or violence" against any group, the expulsion option has also been used when radical clerics have counseled nonpolitical violence, as in October, 2004, when an Algerian-born Islamic cleric condoned wife-beating.[52] Elsewhere, operating with the strictest antiterrorist laws on the continent, and backed fully by French public opinion, government action had expanded by the end of 2004 to aggressively raiding the headquarters of suspected terrorist cells and closing down the television station of the Lebanon-based militant Islamic organization Hezbollah for posing a danger to the public order.[53]

The Scarf Issue Revisited

The Chirac government also favored the banning of all religious symbols from public schools as an essential step toward preserving the secular nature of the French state, including the wearing of scarves by women when posing for identity card pictures. Until 9/11, however, such sweeping proposals remained trial balloons, even thought the headscarf issue had remained a sensitive issue since surfacing in Paris in 1989. The compromise at that time, that religious apparel was permissible as long as it did not involve efforts to spread the faith, had never satisfied the uncompromisingly secular strand of the French electorate, and the FN in particular had kept it alive as a vote getter. In post-9/11 France, the consensus outside the Muslim community was that it was past time to clarify the matter. In early 2004, the government did precisely that. Framing the issue in the statute's preamble in terms of the state's commitment to secularism and the central role of French public schools in teaching the ideals of republicanism, the French government banned the headscarves from all public schools, along with such other conspicuous religious symbols as Jewish skullcaps and *large* Christian crosses.

The "Foreigner" Issue and the "Foreigners"

In the half century that has passed since young, poor, and often unskilled North Africans began arriving in France, the Muslim community has changed. Quite apart from the fact that it now contains substantial numbers of naturalized and native-born French citizens, though still an underclass as a whole it has gradually become more middle class in income and housing, and more highly skilled-to-professional in its employment profile. Its newer members have also developed greater expectations in terms of acceptance by French society, and have, therefore, for the greater part, reacted differently to the discrimination they have faced than the first generation of Muslim workers entering France.[54] Resentment now flows both ways—the native French resenting the not-so-creeping multiculturalism affecting their country; the Muslims resenting the government's targeting of their leaders, culture, and practices for political gain. Two cultures now inhabit France: both perceptible by appearance, both defined in ethnoreligious terms, and each seeing events and the other through the prisms of its own culture and experience. Thus, even the creation of the Muslim Council struck negative chords in those Muslim communities where it was seen as an unrepresentative body because of the dominance of North Africans on the Council and the absence of representatives from many of France's more conservative Muslim associations. Ironically, the Council has also been criticized because of the diverse outlooks of the three groups originally appointed by it: the Union of French Islamic Organization, with its fundamentalist bent; the Moroccan-oriented National Federation of French Muslims; and the Algeria-backed, Westernized Paris Mosque. As for the banning of scarves from public schools, what the government framed in terms of preserving the secular nature of the Republic, Muslims often saw as another policy designed to separate them from French society as a whole.[55] And above all, the poverty and unemployment that still defines so many French-born Muslims creates a seething resentment capable of exploding into political violence, as when the accidental death of two Muslim teenagers fleeing the police in the fall of 2005 triggered nearly two weeks of arson attacks and rioting by Muslim youth throughout France.

The Secular State and the Politics of Ambivalence

French political leaders continue to talk in absolutes of the need to maintain the secular nature of the Republic. In urging the ban on headscarves in French schools, President Chirac argued simply, "Secularism is not negotiable."[56] On this highly charged matter, the parties of the Center–Left and Center–Right were joined. The vote on the headscarf issue passed the French Assembly with 494 votes in favor of the ban and only 36 opposed, and the Senate by a similar majority.[57] Yet, for the foreseeable future, ambiguity and a considerable amount of tight rope walking and waffling are essential on the part of the government and the Muslims alike if ethnic conflict involving the various shapes of the "foreigner issue" in the avowedly secular French state is to be managed.

The problems for those governing France begin with the broader practical and legal obligations placed on them by virtue of their desire to be reelected in a country where limiting the display of the Muslim faith can translate into votes, their ideology (e.g., the Socialist Party's universal commitment to workers' rights) and, most importantly, France's membership in the EU and other European associations committed to human rights.

The "Europe without borders" now exists; it would be difficult-to-impossible for France to reestablish internal border controls on people entering France from other EU states. Moreover, when the countries to the east and south admitted to the EU in 2004 acquire full access to this Europe, France can expect its nonnative population to continue to grow. Most will be European, but their numbers will keep the "foreigner" issue salient, even though its focus will likely remain the North African Muslims population.

France's economic needs also restrict options. Neither guilt over the treatment of its former subjects during the days of empire nor international altruism prompted France to admit foreign workers in large numbers prior to 1974. It was the need for cheap labor and skills that the French labor force lacked. That need in 1972 prompted Paris to enact antidiscrimination statutes to protect its foreign workers and, two years later, a 25-point program to improve the living conditions of existing workers even as it was halting further immigration from non-EC states.

The need for cheap and/or specialized labor is not over. Birthrates in the host population have slowed to below replacement levels. The French economy, like most aging industrial economies, still requires the performance of tasks that few native workers will do at existing levels of pay. The choice may thus be among accepting more immigrants (legally or illegally) from North Africa and other Third World areas, actively seeking such workers in the EU's new member states of Eastern Europe (whose citizens are visibly and culturally less foreign than the North Africans), and/or raising wages to attract French workers at the cost of potentially inflating the economy. No choice is easy or cost free.

There is also the more difficult problem of finding means of periodically placating domestic opinion against "foreigners" without further estranging the foreign communities. The centerpiece of the Gaullist agenda in the early years of this century has been to foster the development of a "Euro" form of Islam—moderate rather than fundamentalist in nature, and stripped of its political content in the secular Fifth French Republic. It is the pursuit of this goal that links recent French politics involving the creation of a Muslim Council (to strengthen the voice of moderate Muslim spokesmen), the deportation of fundamentalist clerics espousing extremist views, and the banning of overt displays of Muslim religious attire from French public schools. Such policies must be pursued cautiously if they are to work, and they have often been qualified in practice to minimize adverse reactions in the Muslim communities. The ban on religious symbols in schools illustrates this point. It became official French policy in March, 2004, but its implementation was delayed until that fall. Moreover, when enacted it was due to be reviewed after a year, it only applied to public schools, and the government allowed local school administrators considerable leeway in deciding how to implement it. On the other hand, the open defiance of this law by the Muslim community could not be tolerated, so when initial compliance with the ban was challenged by more than 100 French school girls, school expulsions followed and a new round of behind-the-scene administrative negotiations were necessary to restore calm.

Finally, there are France's Muslims. It is not so much that they must adopt an ambiguous course of action as that they are in an ambiguous position. The vast majority may be, as the government's concept of an Islam for France assumes, law abiding, mainstream in political thought, residents if not citizens of the Republic. Nonetheless, on the one hand they live in an assertively secular state; on the other hand, their religion offers a comprehensive guide to life that does not include the Western concept of separation of church and state, however it has evolved in practice. In a sense, for them life is a zero – sum game. The more they retain their religion and wear it on their heads and body in public, the more they separate themselves from French society. The more they succumb to the state's pressure to assimilate into a French society still none-too-hospitable toward them, the more they have reason to question their commitment to their faith.

CHAPTER FIVE

Ethnopolitics in France in a Comparative Perspective

Few countries in the advanced democratic world have as many mobilized territorialized minorities as France or as large a Muslim community and highly visible anti-immigrant party. In this sense, France is hardly a prototypical, advanced democratic state. Yet, within the wide spectrum of ethnoterritorial politics in France are to be found examples of most forms of ethnoterritorial politics in the advanced democratic world. Likewise, with Europe's nonassimilating foreign underclass growing in size, and threads of it increasingly linked to international terrorist organizations, the pattern of ethnoclass politics that has emerged in France vis-à-vis its North African communities can be discerned emerging in the policies of other Western democracies, especially in the post-9/11 world.

Ethnoterritorial Politics in the Advanced Democratic World

Political Goals of Ethnoterritorial Politics

As noted at this volume's outset, territorially concentrated ethnopolitical communities can frame their goals across a wide spectrum of objectives. They can demand a greater share of the state's resources (*output* goals), greater participation for their representatives in their states' decision-making arrangements (*authority* goals such as proportionality in the civil service and cabinet); a restructuring of the state along federal lines (goals affecting the nature of the *regime*), or separatist, secessionist, or irredentist objectives, which challenge the legitimacy of the state's existing boundaries.[1]

It is not always easy to identify their actual goals with precision at any given moment. Groups often articulate demands greater than they actually expect to achieve as bargaining positions from which they can retreat to their true objectives. Goals can change as gains stimulate demands for still more, or as frustration produces an escalation in demands. Their goals will also be heavily conditioned by the response they receive by the government to which they are addressed. Output goals are the most easily accommodated because they do not threaten the existing state's distribution of decision-making power; whereas authority and regime demands undercut the power of the political "haves" and are therefore likely to be resisted more tenaciously. Thus, as Robert Thompson once noted, negotiations between governments and ethnoterritorial spokesmen often begin with a certain amount of ambiguity on both sides.[2] Nonetheless, most groups over time can be categorized as fundamentally concerning themselves with one or more of these four general categories, and measured by these goals, there is still a diverse lot of ethnoterritorial political activity in the Western world. It ranges from communities whose levels of mobilization have progressed little beyond a collective sense of self, to groups such as the Welsh Language Society peacefully lobbying for essentially output concessions, to large numbers of federalist-oriented parties (the Basque National Party, the *Parti Québécois*), to the separatist and irredentist organizations to be found in Corsica and among the diehard Irish nationalists in Ulster and Basques in Spain.

Excluding Corsica, where there are both autonomists and federalists who wish to redefine the structure of the regime, and separatists who want to restructure the political community, most groups in France operate at the output-oriented end of the spectrum, seeking cultural and/or economic concessions rather than federalist autonomy from Paris. The goals of the Bretons and Alsaciens, in particular, have historically revolved around the use and promotion of their language. The economic underdevelopment and marginality of Brittany, Occitania, and Basque France have given their demands an economic edge as well. As a consequence, most of their movements have been susceptible to accommodation by concessions involving policy outputs (access to radio and television broadcasting in the regional tongue; economic subsidies), or a degree of administrative autonomy. Separatism has found little support outside of Corsica, and even there the hard-core advocates of independence have rarely exceeded 15 percent of those polled.

Causes of the Postwar Mobilization of the Ethnoterritorial Cleavage

A comprehensive listing of those factors that contributed to the growth in ethnoterritorial activity in the developed Western world would include, at a minimum: the increasing encroachment of the dominant culture on the minority culture; the region's enhanced awareness of its relative economic and cultural deprivation; the declining prestige of central governments forced to withdraw from their overseas empires; the steadily increasing bureaucratization, centralization, and impersonalization of postwar governments in capitals already viewed as insensitive toward the concerns of their peripheral minorities; and the initial unwillingness of state leaders to acknowledge the growing importance of ethnopolitical sentiment in their states and the resultant further politicization of the ethnic factor in their culturally distinct regions.

The mix of these elements and the importance of that mix in the development of ethnoterritorial politics has varied from country to country, and often within the same country from one region to another, depending on not just the objective conditions present (declining use of regional tongues, relative economic deprivation), but also on the presence of regional political entrepreneurs able to capitalize on these developments and politicize ethnic identities to the point where they displace other issues.[3] Indeed, one common explanation for the revival, resurgence, and/or emergence of ethnoterritorial politics in the Western world is the skill of ethnopolitical leaders in turning the economic argument to their advantage in both countries where the ethnoregional economies have fared worse than the country as a whole (e.g., Scotland and Wales, the South Tirols, Brittany) *and* in countries whose minority regions have done better than their country as a whole (e.g., Flanders in Belgium, the Basque and Catalonian regions in Spain). In each instance, the argument has been the same: the region is worse off having decisions made for it by the center than it would be with control over its own affairs.

Ethnoterritorial Parties and Ethnoterritorial Politics

It is also intriguing to consider those elements present in the more successful ethnopolitical movements in the developed world during the last quarter century that are missing in France. Two of these stand out: the absence of strong ethnoregional parties as the principal carriers of ethnoregional politics in continental France; and the failure of a generally successful, ethnoregional political class to emerge in postwar France.

Unlike in Britain, Spain, Belgium, Tirolean Italy, and Quebec, where strong ethnonational parties emerged to garner 20 to 30 percent or more of the regional vote consistently during the 1970s, the primary spokesmen for ethnoterritorial interests in continental France have remained cultural associations with an interest group hue, not political parties. Several factors converged to produce this result. Perhaps most obviously, the rejectionist and nonaccommodative nature of Paris vis-à-vis its territorial minorities until the late 1950s discouraged French regionalists from pursuing system-participatory political linkages.

The electoral system of the Fifth Republic has also been less than encouraging to would-be party builders even in those periods when the French government has been willing to consider accommodative policies. As noted previously, in its parliamentary elections, the Fifth Republic has generally shunned the PR system so generous to the chances of smaller parties achieving parliamentary representation. Instead, it has favored a two-step variation of the first-past-the post, winner-by-plurality, single-member district system in which those seats not won with an outright majority in the first balloting have been subject to a run-off system, which excludes parties failing to win 12.5 percent of the first-round vote. It is a system that normally favors parties with broad strength throughout the country. Hence, given the dual allegiance nature of political identity prevailing in France, in which even territorial minorities have generally defined themselves as both French, and Breton, Basque, or Alsacien, *and* given the centralized, unitary nature of government in France, which historically offered no elective local offices from which successful ethnoterritorial parties might build effective regional party organizations, it is not surprising that outside of Corsica one or more of France's system-wide parties has been able to entrench itself in the regions of France's territorial minorities.[4] Few voters have thus been easy targets for realignment and the partisan mobilization of the country's ethnoterritorial minorities remains low.[5]

Ethnoterritorial party-building was further retarded by the failure of a regionally focused, pragmatic class of political entrepreneurs to emerge in continental France's minority regions. Instead, the leadership element of the cultural-political organizations in Brittany, Alsace, and Occitania remained largely of an academic-intellectual nature, more analogous to the *Plaid Cymru* and Scottish National Party (SNP) leaders of interwar Britain than to the gifted party leaders who emerged in the SNP and elsewhere during late 1960s and early 1970s.[6]. Those few individuals in France who did devote their energies to mainstream political activities on behalf of their country's territorialized minorities often, as previously noted, bypassed France altogether and focused their efforts at the European level.[7]

Ethnoterritorial Politics in the Contemporary Western World

Ethnoterritorial politics in the Western world in general, as in France, have evolved considerably since the late 1960s, when Paris was still reluctant to move beyond (minimalist) output concessions in seeking to accommodate the demands of its territorialized minority communities and when outside of France, ethnonational parties were becoming increasingly successful at the ballot box. To be sure, as table 5.1 indicates, ethnoterritorial actors and politics remain very much a part of politics in developed democracies; however, their changing nature tells us much about not just ethnoterritorial politics in our time but also the manner in which it has been handled in the advanced democratic world over the last 30–40 years.

The Changing Face of Ethnonationalism

As Walker Connor reminds us, although ethnic identity and conflict have been parts of the political world for centuries, specific ethnic issues and actors have been more transitory. Some players have been virtually erased: for example, many of the tribes of Native Americans who encountered the arms and diseases of North America's early settlers. Some issues have acquired salience as a result of external and internal political dynamics: for

Table 5.1 Recent developments in ethnoterritorial politics in the developed Western world

Output-related developments

1993	Welsh Language Act places English and Welsh on equal footing for public business in Wales
1996	Separatist Corsican National Liberation Front demands economic concessions from Paris for Corsica in extending its moratorium on clandestine operations for another three weeks
1997	Basque ETA separatists demand that Spain transfer 500 ETA inmates in jail elsewhere in Spain to prisons in the autonomous Basque region
1997	Quebec's French Language Office demands that all companies operating in Quebec post their Internet pages first in French and only secondarily in other languages
2001	70% on the Puerto Rico isle of Vieques vote against the continued presence of a U.S. Naval base on the island; President Bush agrees to close the base within two years

Authority-related developments

1995	Militant nationalist leaders in Catholic and Protestant camps in Northern Ireland and Sinn Fein leadership in Republic of Ireland demand right to participate in the British-led discussions on the future of Ulster
1998	Good Friday Agreement calls for restoration of self-government in Ulster via a power-sharing plan
2002	Northern Ireland Assembly elected under Good Friday Agreement suspended
2003	Assembly elections strengthen both Protestant and Catholic hardliners in Northern Ireland; full implementation of Good Friday agreement still stalled on disarmament of militias issue
2004	Canadian parliamentary election results in minority Liberal government depending on *Bloc quebecois* support to govern

Regime-related developments

1990	Failure to enact Lake Meech Accord designed to accommodate Quebec nationalists by giving Quebec special status among the provinces forming the Canadian federation
1993	Referendum on statehood fails in Puerto Rico; 48.6% vote for continued commonwealth status, versus 46.3% for statehood and 4.4% for independence
1996	Dutch-speaking leaders demand greater autonomy for Flanders in the already regionalized Belgian state.
1997	Scottish and Welsh nationalists demand that Labour create promised assemblies for Scotland and Wales
1997	Referendums on devolving power to assemblies in Scotland and Wales pass by 50.3% in Wales and 74% in Scotland
1998	The United Kingdom amends constitution to create assemblies for Scotland and Wales; powers formally transferred to these bodies on July 1, 1999
2003	Basque Nationalist Party controlling Basque region proposes power-sharing with Madrid in areas now under central control; Madrid rejects proposal
2004	In a close vote, presidential candidate favoring continued commonwealth status for Puerto Rico defeats opponent running on a statehood platform
2005	Spanish Parliament rejects ruling Basque party's demand for additional authority

Community-focused developments

1995	Referendum to permit Quebec to negotiate its withdrawal from Canada fails in Quebec 50.6% to 49.4%
1996	Leaders in French-speaking Belgium respond to the demands of ethnonationalists in Flanders by proposing that Wallonia separate from Belgium and join France
1997	National parliament in Canada debates *Bloc Québécois'* demand that Quebec be permitted to hold a new referendum on separating from Canada
2000	After briefly suspending activity, ETA separatists resume bombings to pressure Madrid into creating an independent Basque state. Violence less than in former era but sustained 2002–04

Continued

Table 5.1 Continued

2003	December elections in de facto Turkish Republic in northern Cyprus produces coalition government willing to negotiate on reunification of an island essentially partitioned since 1974
2004	April referendum on UN negotiated plan for reunification of Cyprus fails when Greek leader campaigns against it; final vote: 64.9% in Turkish north vote for reunification; 75.8% in Greek south vote "No."

example, the modern politicization of the cleavage in Cyprus between its two settler communities from antiquity can be traced, first, to the process of decolonization, then to political opportunism when the island's Greek Cypriot president tried to merge Cyprus into Greece, then to the interplay of regional politics when Greece and Turkey sought to gain controlling influence on the isle, and finally to the entry of Cyprus into the EU and the efforts of Eurocrats to unify the island under a single government. Other examples abound, such as the declining importance of extremist spokesmen for Spain's Catalonian and Basque communities after the death of Spain's long-time leader, Francisco Franco, and the decision of moderate Spanish politicians to accommodate these communities with constitutional guarantees of their autonomy.

Still elsewhere, it has been the success of ethnopolitical actors in achieving their objectives that has rendered them superfluous and led to their passing or diminished political influence—a development that has not only affected ethnocultural spokesmen such as the Welsh Language Society and their counterparts in Alsace and *Breton*-speaking France, but also ethnonational parties such as the *Rassemblement Wallon* (RW) in Belgium's French-speaking south, which has completely disappeared from the political scene even though (or perhaps because) its objective of federalizing power in Belgium into the hands of regional assemblies has been largely implemented by the leaders of Belgium's traditional parties.[8]

The Growing Prevalence of Accommodative Politics

Perhaps the primary reason why some ethnopolitical actors have recently faded thus lies in the changing willingness of governmental leaders in advanced democracies to meet some of their demands. This tendency marks a significant policy departure from the days when influential ethnonational organizations began to emerge in Belgium and other Western states. Then, responses typically involved denying their existence, evading the need to deal with them, stigmatizing them, trying to placate the communities they represented with symbolic concessions, and/or repressing them. The reaction in Britain to the nationalists electoral breakthrough in Scotland in the mid-1960s was to appoint a Royal Commission to study the matter of devolution, basically in the hope that the surge in Scottish nationalism, which sent an SNP candidate to Parliament, would abate by the time the Commission finished its work. The pro-federalism parties that emerged in Belgium were castigated as threats to Belgium's existence (*"fédéralisme = séparatisme"* in the language of the Liberal, Catholic, and Socialist parties, which then dominated Belgian politics). Ottawa responded to the emergence of nationalism in Quebec with a campaign to make Canada bilingual, when Quebec's desire was increasingly to be an officially monolingual, French-speaking province. Meanwhile, in Northern Ireland and Spain, and to a lesser degree in France before the 1970s, the nationalist spokesmen of ethnic minorities were routinely manipulated and repressed, with Northern Ireland's Protestant leadership gerrymandering Ulster to the point where Catholics could not control local councils even in Catholic majority areas and allowing paramilitary groups such as the Order of the Orange to enforce extra-legally their hold on a region in which they outnumbered Catholics two-to-one.

No single factor explains the shift away from these tactics over the last two generations to more accommodative approaches toward the demands of ethnoterritorial groups in the developed world. In part, policies changed because several of the earlier strategies were inherently flawed, such as ignoring the changing nature of ethnoregional political cultures. The strategy could even be counterproductive when time and unforeseen developments benefited the ethnoregionalist cause. During the time between the appointment of the Royal Commission to study the issue of devolution for Scotland and its report, for example, oil was discovered in the North Sea off the coast of Scotland, filling nationalist heads with dreams of petroleum wealth ("Scottish Oil for Scotland") and giving the idea of an independent Scotland an economic credibility it previously lacked.

Earlier approaches were also gradually abandoned because the cost of continuing them became prohibitively expensive in political capital. Thus, the British government finally intervened in the protracted conflict in Ulster when the growing incidences of political violence in that region made neglect untenable. Frequently, the electoral success of ethnonational parties also forced system-wide leaders to reconsider their strategies: for example, when the growth of Belgium's ethnonationalist parties began to cause the country's principal parties to fragment into their regional wings, and when the success of the Welsh and Scottish nationalist parties began to eat into the Labour Party's dominance in Celtic Britain and thereby threaten its ability to win British elections. And sometimes the change reflected the growing influence of generally conciliatory political cultures in problem-solving, or profound changes in the nature of the regime, as in post-Franco Spain when democratizing the state required giving federal autonomy to its Basques and Catalonians.

The drift toward accommodation has not, however, been universal. There are blocs in Madrid unwilling to extend further concessions to Spain's Basques lest they encourage further violence by Basque extremists. Protestants in Northern Ireland continue to prolong the process of establishing a power-sharing system in Ulster despite the pressure placed on them by both Britain and the outsiders (the Republic of Ireland and the United States) which have become parts of the institution-building process affecting that region. Most conspicuously, despite the threat of economic sanctions from the EU, the Greek Cypriots—who constitute the majority on Cyprus—have refused to accept a federalized state in which the Turkish controlled north (the self-proclaimed Turkish Republic of Northern Cyprus, or TRNC) would rejoin the country. Hence, for governmental purposes Cyprus remains a partitioned island despite the political fiction of it having joined the EU in 2004 as a single entity.

The Declining Presence of Output- and Authority-Centered Concessions

Table 5.1 is not comprehensive but it does generally illustrate developments involving the nature of ethnoterritorial politics in the West during the recent past, and the trend there away from both output- and authority-centered demands and from concessions of this nature by governments in response to ethnonational pressures.

Why has this occurred? Certainly such demands previously figured prominently in the territorial movements of France (Alsace and *Breton* demands for the right to teach their regional languages), Belgium (the Flemish demand for parity in the ranks of military officers, the Walloon demand for development funds), Britain (Scotland's demand that its members of Parliament be given a greater voice in decisions affecting Scotland; Wales' calls for protective measures to prevent the extinction of the Welsh-speaking Welshman), and Italy (demands for a German-based civil service in the German-speaking South Tirols).

Clearly the development does not reflect an across-the-board escalation in the demands of ethnoterritorial groups to the point where accommodation measures short of regime change are irrelevant. As noted, many ethnoterritorial actors of the past are no longer central players in contemporary European politics. Rather, it appears to reflect the fundamental difference between ethno*regional* and ethno*national* demands in developed democracies, and the manner in which politics involving these demands have evolved in Europe in recent decades. Both sets of demands are rooted in the concerns of ethnically self-differentiating peoples and both have played out within the same environment of cross-cutting cleavages, dualistic political identities, and established political processes. Ethnoregional demands, however, tended to center on tangible grievances—an absence of support for declining regional languages or declining regional economies being the recurrent themes—and were usually voiced by territorialized minorities whose national allegiance rested with the broader political community. The responses of the central governments to these demands sometimes resulted in requests for more of the same, but do not appear to have fed a desire for gains beyond the output variety.

In contrast, ethnonational politics revolve around the right of the regional community to have a greater control over its affairs via a government of its own. Experience indicates that authority-oriented concessions are insufficient responses to it, and among the countries of the Western world none better illustrates this fact than Belgium. During the last three decades of the twentieth century its government employed an extraordinary wide range of options in response to the ethnoterritorial demands confronting it, including concessions involving the authority issue of *who* makes decisions. Its story is thus instructive.

Straddling a centuries old line that has run east–west across the center of Belgium since the days of Charlemagne, since its 1830 birth under the guiding hands of a French-speaking elite its government has frequently confronted nationalistic demands from the Dutch-speaking Flemish community lying north of that line in Flanders. Though always a majority of the country's population, the Flemish were denied the right to use their own language for official purposes in their own region until the second half of the nineteenth century, when the essentially output-structured demands of early Flemish nationalists produced a series of concessions, including the right to conduct official business in Flemish in administrative and criminal proceedings, and to establish public schools conducted in their own tongue. As a result of these concessions, Flanders eventually evolved into a monolingual, Dutch-speaking region in the officially bilingual Belgium of the twentieth century.

Ethnonational sentiment developed later in the French-speaking Walloon south, in part because its language was the ruling elite's language but also because Wallonia was the birthplace of Belgium's industrial revolution and enjoyed a vibrant economy until the twentieth century. Likewise, though the overwhelmingly French-speaking capital area of Brussels is located north of the linguistic frontier, its status remained uncontroversial until the 1960s, when its spread into the surrounding Flemish countryside began to affect the language of instruction in once Flemish-speaking majority areas. In the meantime, Belgium developed three system-wide parties (Socialist, Liberal, and Catholic) and the managerial system of interparty collaboration that Arend Lijphart has designated "consociational democracy"; that is, a "government by elite cartel designed to turn a democracy with a fragmented political culture into a stable democracy."[9] Because all three of the major parties had wings in French- and Flemish-speaking Belgium, their leaders had a vested interest in containing Belgium's ethnolinguistic cleavage.

They succeeded in doing so for more than a century. Then, two post–World War II developments undermined their efforts. First, during the 1950s Flanders benefited disproportionately from postwar foreign investment in Belgium while Wallonia's aging, metallurgy-based industry was declining. By the decade's end, the Flemish constituted the country's economic as well as numerical majority. Their minority status in their state's highly centralized, unitary political process was no longer acceptable, and the Flemish nationalist party *Volksunie*—with its demand for federal autonomy—began to draw votes away from Flanders' established parties. Meanwhile, having granted its African colony, the Belgian Congo, independence in 1960, Belgium's government was forced to adopt an austerity program whose effects were disproportionately felt by Wallonia's already declining economy. Shortly thereafter an ethnonationalist party emerged in

Wallonia, and—in response to the *Volksunie*'s growing influence—in French-speaking Brussels as well.

Within a decade these three parties were polling between 20 and 35 percent of the vote in their respective regions, had forced the regional wings of the established parties to adopt their nationalist rhetoric in order to protect their electoral flanks, and had pushed the accommodation process beyond the proffering of symbolic and output-oriented concessions in response to their demands for regional autonomy. During the 1970s the leaders of Belgium's fragmenting, once system-wide parities undertook a series of authority/power-sharing moves designed to undercut these ethnonational organizations. Accommodation devices shifted to parity formulas involving the composition of the Cabinet and military command. On occasion, the leaders of the ethnonational parties became parts of the governing coalitions at the center, where vain efforts were made to retain the consociational nature of the decision-making process. In sensitive issue areas, the constitution was modified in 1970 to include concurrent majority provisions whereby the passage of legislation would require a majority in each community *and* a two-third majority overall.

In the end, none of these devices satisfied regional appetites for autonomy or dampened the nationalist rhetoric of the ethnonational parties representing Flanders, Wallonia, and French-speaking Brussels; nor could they have done so. The consociational approach was doomed once the ethnoterritorial communities were mobilized by ethnonational parties. By their very nature, consociational politics and ethnonational parties do not mix. Unlike the leaders of the system-wide parties, the leaders of ethnoterritorial parties have an interest in exploiting these issues. Their success at the ballot box and influence in government depends upon it. Furthermore, the nationalist desire of ethnically self-differentiating peoples for control over their own affairs is a proactive desire; warning bells and concurrent majorities are defensive mechanisms that can protect one from hostile majorities at the center but not requite that urge. Consequently, beginning in the 1971–74 period Belgium's constitution was significantly altered as regional councils and then assemblies were created for Brussels, Flanders, and Wallonia, and the process of steadily transferring power from the center to them began in earnest in an effort to keep the state together.

The Centrality of Regime-Centered Politics and the Institutionalization of Ethnoregional Cleavages

In Belgium, then, as elsewhere, the mechanism of choice for accommodative politics has become institutional reform of the regionalized home rule variety. (see table 5.1). Where unitary states once existed, changes range from the transfer of limited decision-making authority from Westminster to assemblies in Scotland and Wales to the dismemberment of the old system and establishment of a highly peripheral form of federalism, as in Belgium. Where federal systems already existed, changes have involved carving new units out of existing federal ones (the creation of the French-speaking Jura canton in Switzerland), and transferring additional authority to the existing units (the Quebec case).

The federalist approach, it should be noted, has not always worked to preserve union. It has yet to pay dividends in Cyprus, and Denmark was obliged to give Greenland its independence when Copenhagen decided to join the European Communities in the early 1970s but Greenland voted to stay out. In general, however, reliance on some variation of federalism has been an accommodation strategy in the Western world for nearly 40 years. Thus, to those reforms that institutionalized ethnoterritorial sentiment during the 1970s in Switzerland, Italy (which gave its northern, German-speaking area around Bolzano a measure of autonomy), and post-Franco Spain can be added the more recent, successful and unsuccessful efforts to accommodate through home rule measures regional sentiment in Scotland, Wales, Corsica, and a federalized Cyprus.

The Declining Salience of Separatist Politics

The principal casualties of the politics of compromise during recent decades have been the separatist organizations in Western democracies, especially those practicing political violence. As Raphael Zariski has summarized, extremist nationalist movements thrive in environments in which ethnoregional minorities feel economically exploited, demographically weak, and culturally undervalued, and/or are the victims of state violence, state repression, and official discrimination. They lose their legitimacy when the center is willing to negotiate on a wide range of issues, including regional autonomy.[10] Once decision makers moved in this direction in post-Franco Spain and Ulster under London-rule, the extremist wings of the Basque and Catholic nationalist organizations began to lose their leverage, displaced by their political arms and other moderate nationalist spokesmen invited into the bargaining process. The IRA's Provisional Wing still operates, as do the highly toxic remnants of the ETA separatist-irredentist organization in Spain; however, they primarily function as "rejectionist" elements today—splinter groups with the ability to delay and perhaps sabotage compromises between Madrid and the Basque region and the moderate Catholic and Protestant leadership in Ulster. They can no longer pose as legitimate spokesmen for their communities.[11]

Referendums as Increasingly Common "Decision-Making" Processes

The major blemish on this otherwise rosy picture of the triumph of accommodative politics over separatism and political violence—as well as a factor that explains why many of the recent attempts to resolve ethnic conflicts through regime modification have failed—is the increasing use of referendums as part of the decision-making process in place of definitive elite bargaining. The referendum approach has obvious appeal: it leaves decisions in the hands of the people who will be most affected by them. It also seems a feasible approach because moderate ethnoregional spokesmen and the leaders of the major system-wide parties alike have little fear that the voters will choose independence given such factors as both their dual identities and the track record of prior referendums in the West, where voters have generally demonstrated an ability to engage in cost–benefit analysis and have eschewed radical options. Even controversial outcomes— for example, when the bloc voting against separation by the English-speaking minority in Quebec produced an overall "No" vote in the Quebec 1995 referendum on that issue—have not resulted in new surges of separatist sentiment.

The referendum approach nonetheless has its drawbacks. A prolonged public debate of the autonomy option can be educational, but when referendums are used as preliminary steps toward policy outcomes rather than as means of legitimatizing agreed upon policies, the debate over what is being authorized and what the future will hold is apt to be as confusing as enlightening, as when the autonomy issue was put before Corsican voters in 2003. The standard indictment against the use of referendums as policy-making devices still applies: they "force a decision, not forge a consensus."[12] Indeed, this criticism is particularly applicable to their limitations as devices for managing ethnopolitical conflicts, where they can become one more means of mobilizing ethnoterritorial sentiment against "outsiders," be they described as insensitive central governments or—as in the case of the recent referendum on unification in Cyprus organized by the UN with EU encouragement—intrusive international organizations.

Ethnoclass Politics: The "Foreigner" Issue in a Comparative Perspective

At approximately the same time as the FN's success in France's 1998 regional elections the ultra right-wing, antiforeigner German People's Union won 13 percent of the vote in the eastern Germany state of Saxony-Anthalt,[13] and, at the other end of the earth, the year-old, anti-Asian, One Nation Party garnered 23 percent of the vote in the state elections in Queenlands, Australia.[14] Only a few months previously, in March, 1998, following unexpectedly severe setbacks at the hands of parties capitalizing on antiforeigner sentiment in state elections, Chancellor Helmut Kohl's Christian Democrat government voted down a proposed revision of Germany's laws, which would have made third-generation, German-born children of foreign workers eligible for German citizenship.[15] Three months later on the other side of the Atlantic, Californians voted overwhelmingly to abolish bilingual education in the largest state of the United States.[16] As table 5.2 indicates, developments of this nature became commonplace during the last days of the twentieth century as antiforeigner issues, and sometimes political violence aimed at the perceived "outsiders," penetrated political processes throughout the developed world.

Table 5.2 The "foreigner" issue in the advanced democratic world, selected news stories, 1989–2001

1989	Japan: rising number of immigrants prompts national debate on value of taking in foreigners
1991	Austria: underground Austrian video game discovered targeting Jews and Turks; players portray death camp guards
	Switzerland: Adoption of laws restricting the employment of immigrants
1992	Swiss voters narrowly reject adding an anti-immigrant clause to Switzerland's Constitution
1993	Germany enacts legislation effectively denying refugees the ability to enter country by land; courts uphold act in 1996
1994	Britain abolishes trailer camping parks in move to discourage Romany from settling in Great Britain
	Canada adopts laws restricting access to Canada of immigrants and refugees, including screening of applicants for skills
	Greece deports hundreds of foreigners to ease public fear over soaring crime rates
	U.S.: Californians pass Proposition 187, denying illegal immigrants public services and public schools to their children
1995	Britain: race riots in Brixton follow death of "coloured Commonwealth" suspect while being arrested by police
	Italy: "Italians Across the Political Spectrum Seek Curbs on Immigrants"
	U.S. House of Representatives opens debates on making English the official language in the United States
1996	Germany: German states pressure Bosnian refugees to leave, and consider expelling those refusing to go
	U.S. Senate votes 97-3 to tighten U.S. borders; U.S. limits federal benefits available to even legal immigrants
1997	Britain: Romany asylum-seekers from Slovakia are turned away
	Europe: At Prague conference, delegates from nearly 40 states promise strong measures to halt illegal immigration
	Germany: Foreign Minister Weigel asserts that immigrants in Germany sharpen the German unemployment problem
	Germany debates a controversial law proposing dual nationality for children of immigrants born in Germany
	Italy: government gives Albanian refuges until end of August to leave or be expelled; deportations follow
	United States adopts a new "means" test, which limits ability of immigrants to bring family into county
1998	European Police chiefs from seven countries agree to tighten border control and share information about illegal immigration
	EU interior ministers agree to fingerprint refugee asylum-seekers to combat multiple applications problem
	France: Premier Jospin defends policy of denying residency rights to thousands of illegal immigrants and deporting them
	Germany: "foreigner free" zones are in effect in at least 25 east German towns
	Germany: Kohl government rejects reform law proposing dual citizenship for German-born children of foreigners
	Holland: civil rights protesters blame government's increased reluctance to admit refugees on Dutch racism
	Italy tightens immigration law to assure that illegal immigrants ordered out of the country do not reach Western Europe
	Russia: complaints of harassment rise among Africans drawn to Moscow by Russian universities
	United States: Californians vote overwhelmingly to abolish bilingual education in the state's public school system

Continued

Table 5.2 Continued

1999	Austrian antiforeigner party finishes second in Austria's parliamentary elections
	Britain: minorities targeted in London bombings; government commission concludes British society tainted by racism
	German antiforeigner party gains representation in two additional state parliaments
	Switzerland: antiforeigner party receives substantial share of vote in Switzerland's national elections
	U.S. Supreme Court sharply limits First Amendment rights of illegal immigrants
2000	Austria: anti-immigrant Freedom Party becomes part of governing coalition
	Italy: leading Italian cardinal urges limiting Muslim immigrants to preserve state's Catholic character
2001	U.K.: race riots occur in Burnley, Leeds, and Oldham during a campaign in which race and asylum-seekers are major issues

The transnational concern with the growing numbers of refugees, immigrants, and foreign workers has its roots in the postwar development of advanced industrial economies in the West. As Milton Esman has noted, high-income economies have a need for labor in high-growth periods because of the low birth rate common in developed democratic societies. Low-income countries with high population growth have chronic labor surpluses.[17] As postwar France illustrates, the result of this pull–push dynamic has been a steady flow of people from the latter to the former. Add the number of refugees tumbling out of politically unstable areas following postwar decolonization and the more recent fall of communism in Europe, and the result has been a steady flow of people into the politically stable, economically advanced democracies.

Context: The Legal and Political Environments of Antiforeigner Politics

There were profound differences in the legal and social reception that migrating peoples received upon arrival. To a substantial degree, ethnopolitics involving foreign workers, immigrants, asylum-seekers, refugees, and Romany peoples in the West continue to be shaped by those differences.

The variations in the legal environments are most vividly apparent in the policies governing their eligibility for full citizenship. Until recently France has been an "immigrant" nation in the sense that its borders and services have been open to immigrants and its citizenship laws have adhered to a *jus soli* basis of nationality. Additionally, arrivees have been entitled to the same health, education, and social security benefits as French citizens, and in some instances even foreign workers could naturalize.

At the other end of the continuum lies Germany, which once led Europe in recruiting guest workers and was extremely generous in admitting refugees and asylum-seekers until the mid-1990s. By definition, Germany is not an "immigration country" but a "destination" country for those of German descent. Even though Germany has recently bent its naturalization rules to admit a small percentage of German-born Turks to citizenship,

citizenship has remained based on a 1913 law, which ties it to the *sui generis* tests of parentage and ancestry. Overall, less than 3 percent of the more than two million Turks in Germany hold German citizenship. The vast majority are still officially guest workers, precluded from assimilating or participating in the political process and living without constitutional protection of such basic citizens' rights as the right to peaceful assembly, freedom of association, and freedom of occupation.[18]

The Unites States and Australia have traditionally been at the same end of the spectrum as France; most other European states fall toward the middle or even the German end of the spectrum in terms of their foreign populations' access to citizenship and/or the services and rights available to citizens. In virtually all Western countries, however, the postwar history and politics of the "foreigner" issue have tended to evolve in a manner paralleling the pattern in France. Only the timetable, until recently, has varied from state to state.

The Evolution of the Foreigner Issue in Western Europe

Buildup

Many of the circumstances that led postwar France to seek foreign workers also caused its neighboring states to recruit from abroad the work force they needed to rebuild their infrastructures, cities, and economies. Countries with prewar empires usually had subjects more than willing to be recruited. Others, such as Germany, turned to the more economically depressed countries of southern and Central Europe for their needs. Everywhere, unattractive economic conditions in the hunting grounds abetted their search.

Occasionally, the workers arrived with immigrant status; most notably, the members of the British Commonwealth who took advantage of their Commonwealth passports to journey to postwar Britain when British rule ended in India. On even rarer occasions, the early arrives were professionals who found employment in their professions once abroad; again, most notably in the case of the United Kingdom, which raided India's medical community for the supplemental doctors necessary to staff the National Health System created in postwar Britain. In most instances, though, the workers were unskilled or semiskilled laborers who entered as temporary workers taking low-paying jobs.

As in France the numbers subsequently grew. By the late 1960s, they had become statistically meaningful (3–6 percent) parts of the receiving states' work forces. Also as in France, public policy initially encouraged this buildup but did little either to settle the workers into their host countries or to prepare receiving societies for a possible multiculture future.

Issue Emergence

By the 1960s the presence of the foreign communities had become an issue in Germany, Holland, and other states, even though their economies were enjoying very strong growth rates. As the foreigners multiplied, cultural shocks—the phenomena of one culture confronting another—became two-sided, and not just in the workplace where nationals and foreign workers interacted. In Strasbourg, Arab women in flowing Arab robes incongruously began to appear along the city's Germanic streets. Across the Rhine, the cultures literally collided daily when Turkish guest workers took their traditional afternoon strolls on the plazas in front of metropolitan railway stations just as German workers raced to catch their commuter trains home.

The salience of the foreign worker issue varied across Western Europe, reflecting such factors as the size of the foreign workforce, the host population's previous experience with cultural diversity and/or racist tendencies,[19] and the willingness of leftist parties to defend the solidarity of the working class. In West Germany, whose guest workers by 1973 constituted nearly 12 percent of its work force, and in neighboring Holland, the foreigner issue became significant earlier than elsewhere. By 1972 their governments had halted the further entry of workers from outside the European Community area. France, Sweden, and others adopted similar action, including Belgium, the seat of Europe's evolving supranational institutions, which reacted to its economy's slowdown in 1967 by tying work permits to the immigrant's willingness to fill existing job vacancies.

Where the foreigner issue involved immigrants eligible for citizenship, policy focused on tightening laws along the lines enacted by Britain over a 20-year period beginning in 1962. The 1948 British Nationality Act, passed the year following Britain's withdrawal from the Indian subcontinent, opened the door to Britain's first significant number of nonwhite immigrants when it confirmed that the citizens of British colonies and the British Commonwealth were British subjects and therefore entitled to enter the United Kingdom. That right lasted only 14 years. By then, the numbers arriving on the basis of their subject status had become an issue and London began to whittle away at the 1948 Act. The 1962 Commonwealth Immigrants Act imposed a series of burdens on immigrants from the "Coloured Commonwealth" (i.e., the West Indies, Africa, and Asia), which were not applied to anyone arriving from Canada, Australia, or New Zealand. Further restrictions were added in the Immigration Act of 1971, which effectively halted immigration tied to jobs (as opposed to family unification programs), and again in 1981.[20]

The closing of the gate to legal immigrants and foreign workers in Europe soon produced a sharp increase in the number of illegal aliens. By 1993, that number was estimated at approximately 900,000 in Germany alone, a figure comparable to the million illegal aliens presumed to be in France and nearly double the 450,000 illegal immigrants presumed living in Spain and in Italy.[21]

Mobilization and Issue Intensification

The economic recessions following the 1973 and 1979 oil crises affected the foreigner issue throughout Europe. Rising unemployment figures provided antiforeigner politicians with a concrete issue around which to mobilize the public's vague uneasiness over the increasingly multicultural nature of their respective societies. Arguments invariably mirrored the FN's line: if the foreign workers left, there would be jobs for unemployed nationals. To this refrain other arguments were attached. The strains on welfare programs could be eased by limiting their use to nationals. Crime rates could be cut by deporting the "foreign workers," and so on.

As in France, few of these arguments could bear close scrutiny. In several instances, however, the arguments were not without foundation. Where illegal immigrants cannot find employment, a rising crime rate is likely as some turn to pickpocketing and other petty crimes to support themselves. More interesting, by the 1970s in some labor-importing states the guest workers were generating a need for further guest workers. As they became, de facto, permanent parts of work forces, it became necessary to import additional workers to erect the houses, hospitals, and schools needed by them and their growing families. Occasionally their needs outstripped those of their hosts. Given the substandard nature of their housing, for example, they were often afflicted with greater health problems than the population as a whole.

The lines separating the valid, quasi-valid, and invalid arguments against the foreign communities rarely received close examination. Nor did any country prudently note the problems faced by the foreign workers during this period beyond passing antidiscrimination laws, which usually suffered from weak enforcement. It is worth recalling that the Slavic word for worker is *robot*; hence West Germany's oft expressed lament during the 1970s: "We asked for workers but they send us people."

Mobilization and Issue Exploitation

As the foreigner issue became a hot topic in national political debates, single-issue parties such as France's FN began to emerge and/or gain influence, simultaneously exploiting the issue and keeping it alive. The first to develop substantial followings were the FN, Austria's Freedom Party, which reputedly has the allegiance of a quarter of the Austrian electorate and is the oldest anti-immigrant party in Europe (established 1956),[22] and Britain's National Front, which gained nearly 120,000 votes in London's 1977 local elections. Over time, these parties have found their counterparts in the National Alliance party in Italy, which gained one vote in six in that country's 1996 parliamentary elections, the Swiss People's Party, which polled 23 percent of the vote in Switzerland's 1999 parliamentary election, and in a variety of small right-wing parties in unified Germany, Sweden, Norway, Denmark, and the Netherlands, many of which have been capable of capturing double-digit followings at some point or another.[23]

The electoral breakthrough in Germany occurred in 1991 when one of its antiforeigner parties gained over 5 percent of the vote in the Hesse state elections and, for the first time, representation in a German state legislature. The potential for additional gains by such pro-German parties was obvious.

Public opinion polls showed nearly half the electorate (47 percent) opposed to having Arabs as neighbors and 39 percent that did not want Turks in their neighborhoods.[24]

The buildup of the foreign population occurred more slowly in Scandinavia. Hence, the development of antiforeigner parties has been later there but no less significant. In Norway's 1997 national elections, for example, the Progress Party campaigning on the promise to reform the country's liberal policies toward its Lapp minority, immigrants, and single mothers, finished second with 15.3 percent of the vote and became a major part of the coalition governing Norway.

Even before these parties became electorally successful, the fear that they might prompted governments throughout Europe, as already noted, to adopt policies designed to reduce the number of immigrants and foreign workers even as they were passing antidiscrimination statutes. For its part Germany followed the French model of the 1970s and offered its *gastarbeiter* incentives to return voluntarily to their homelands. Approximately one million took the incentives and departed; however, as in France most foreign workers chose to remain in the host country, where wages were decidedly higher than in the areas from which they came.[25]

The refugees and asylum-seekers who arrived in large numbers following the fall of communism in Central Europe further fueled antiforeigner sentiment. Given its front line location, generous asylum laws at the time, and willingness to subsidize refugees as well as extend social welfare services to them, Germany received the largest injection of these refugees. There, the number of asylum-seekers soared from approximately 35,000 annually before unification to 256,000 in 1991 and 438,000 in 1992, with 39 percent coming from the former Yugoslavia.[26] Throughout the EU, however, the number of refugees soon taxed the tolerance and welfare systems of the countries receiving them.[27] Instability in Asia produced a similar dynamic vis-à-vis Australia, just as instability in Central America as well as Europe and Asia increased the number of asylum-seekers arriving in the United States and Canada. In some instances, their arrival led to acts of violence against all foreign communities; sometimes with the tacit approval of local police and political leaders.[28] One of most notorious of these instances was the 1992 fire bombing of an apartment in Germany that killed two children and a grandmother, all Turks;[29] however, only a few days earlier immigrants in Madrid were fired upon by masked gunmen.[30] Similar stories involving other countries pepper the news stories from Europe throughout the 1990s.

Mainstreaming

Antiforeigner parties have also benefited from the willingness of national politicians to adopt FN-like, antiforeign rhetoric in order to protect their electoral flanks. In doing so, they gave legitimacy to antiforeigner parties and the racist sentiments on which these parties fed and grew.

When mainstream French politicians spoke of "smelly foreigners" in the mid-1990s, they were following a well-traveled path which continues to see heavy traffic. In her 1979 campaign Margaret Thatcher frequently used code phrases (e.g., "protecting the unique character of the British people") commonly associated with Enoch Powell and his antiforeigner followers in appealing to anti-immigrant sentiment in Britain. In preparing for a reelection campaign in 1998, members of Helmut Kohl's party repeatedly blamed foreign workers for Germany's unemployment rate. In the years between these campaigns, leading politicians throughout Europe moved in similar directions in both words and deeds, issuing restrictive executive orders,[31] enacting ever more restrictive immigration laws,[32] collaborating in efforts to seal their borders against illegal aliens,[33] and diluting with qualifications those laws they did enact that guaranteed specified rights to their noncitizens.[34]

This mainstreaming of the foreigner issue broadly shaped public debate on the topic. As a result, and again as in France, the "foreigners" have overwhelmingly become the *problem/subject* of political discourse, not active participants in it. Lobbying efforts by groups such as SOS Racism and the occasional, organized demonstrations against antiforeigner violence have had little impact on policy-making processes geared to public opinion polls showing large national majorities favoring anti-immigrant legislation and opposed to liberalizing citizenship laws.[35] Similarly, the advisory Muslim councils created in Britain and France remain just that: advisory.

The generally one-sided nature of the political debate has, in turn, resulted in common outcomes. Virtually everywhere, the foreign element has been locked across generations into a standard of living considerably below that of the indigenous population. Except for Britain, where integration has discernibly occurred in lower working-class areas such as London's East End and whose Labour Party has aggressively courted the immigrant population, foreign communities have likewise been politically isolated and generally consigned to culturally isolated zones in the cities housing them.

To be sure, as in France, the foreign communities have attained some gains. Given their commitment to fundamental rights, most receiving states adopted civil rights legislation to protect their minority communities, however anemic its enforcement has sometimes been. French statutes prohibiting discrimination in the leasing of public housing, for example, parallel the 1965 and 1968 Civil Rights Acts in Britain forbidding racial discrimination in housing, employment, and access to goods and services. There has also been a willingness of national politicians to criticize the racism of overtly anti-immigration parties, and to make symbolic concessions to the immigrant community. France has even permitted villages to depict as black Marianne, the 200-year-old symbol of French republicanism and liberty.[36]

On the other side of the ledger, civil rights and symbolic action have been offset by legislation closing borders, shunning bilingualism, denying noncitizens access to welfare services, moving refugees to points far from the majority populations, redefining asylum laws to limit their application, expelling refugees from civil wars immediately upon the cessation of violence, and otherwise catering to antiforeign opinion. Coupled with the willingness of national politicians to retreat from multicultural policies when confronted with strong opposition (the French Socialists in the mid-1980s, the German Socialists in the late 1990s), the mix of antiforeigner legislation and antidiscrimination statutes has at best sent an ambiguous signal to host populations when strong leadership has been needed to overcome the hostility to the foreign communities. Then came the antiforeigner politics of the world after 9/11.

Europe's Foreign Communities after 9/11

Anti-immigrant sentiment and parties in the advanced democratic world have been bolstered by outside events for more than a generation. The late 1980s agreement among Europeans to work toward a "Europe without borders" awakened fears throughout domestic labor markets of being overrun by workers from poorer European countries. The decision during the 1990s to enlarge the EU to include countries of the postcommunist world, with their skilled labor and depressed wage structure, intensified those fears. The fall of communism also had its impact, unleashing a sudden influx of immigrants from the East, including Muslim and non-Muslim refugees from the wars in the former Yugoslavia, at a time when most Western states were just recovering from the economically stagnant years of the previous decade. The collapse of communism also resulted in the arrival of a new wave of Romany peoples from Central Europe in Western countries which had never been friendly to those already inhabiting their borders.[37]

To a degree, the exploitation of security concerns by antiforeigner forces in the wake of the terrorist attacks on the United States in 2001 and the subsequent attacks on public transportation carriers in Madrid and London fits into this mold. However, unlike the specter of immigration running wild in an expanding Europe without borders, the danger of Muslim communities in the Western world harboring and/or abetting international terrorists is not hypothetical, especially to a continent that has had experience with international as well as homegrown terrorists of the Basque separatist and urban terrorist (e.g., Italy's Red Brigade, Germany's Maader–Meinhof cell) variety. The first major instance of transnational terrorism unfolded in Germany before the eyes of the world when Palestinian terrorists took Israeli athletes as hostage at the 1972 Olympics in Munich. France, too, has likewise had prior experience with international terrorism, especially Algerian terrorists opposed to French support of the secular government in Algiers. Elsewhere, Middle Eastern groups during the 1970s were responsible for major terrorist action involving, among other locales, international airports in Athens, Rome, and Vienna. And, since 9/11, Western Europe has been the scene of two ugly instances of political violence linked to Moroccans: the March, 2004, bombing of commuter trains in Madrid and the murder that fall of a Dutch filmmaker whose works were critical of the treatment of women in the Muslim world.

The full impact of recent events on anti-immigrant politics in the West and Europe's culturally foreign communities can be assessed at some future point; however, as in France, some interim patterns of political and societal responses to these events are already evident in the advanced democratic world.

An Absence of Obvious Options

In numerous countries, as in France, the "foreign" communities are citizens either by birth or naturalization, not foreign workers legally subject to deportation at the will of their hosts. Also as in France, throughout Europe legal and illegal aliens perform necessary tasks, which the host populations are unlikely to do at the wages being offered. They thus provide a standard of living subsidy to all, which governments are loath to lose.[38]

Options are also limited because whatever security danger the immigrant communities pose to Europe is rooted in the long neglect of their problems, which has, in some quarters, now resulted in a deep alienation separating these groups from the societies and governments hosting them. *They* have been expected to assimilate as much as possible and at whatever cost to ways of life they disdain while their hosts have made little effort to interact with them, even those among them in transition between their native culture and the more secular and cosmopolitan cultures of the countries where they now reside.[39] They and their hosts now literally live in two different, segmented worlds much of the time, with the immigrant communities' the distinctly poorer and more crime-ridden one. It is a physical and psychological situation that cannot be remedied overnight even where, as in Holland, the foreign communities have access to generous social welfare programs. Meanwhile, potential terrorists can emerge from the ghettos of Western Europe as well those of Casablanca.[40] Nearly a generation ago, researchers warned that, if unaddressed, the "spectacular failure rate of the children of immigrants" from the Moroccan communities in Europe's schools, and their proportionately higher rate of unemployment compared to immigrants as a whole were likely to lead to serious future problems in Europe.[41] That future has now arrived and the problems it holds are susceptible to no easy or quick cures.

Anti-Muslim Prejudice and the New Legitimacy of Antiforeign Sentiment

To the extent that post-9/11 policy making has generated new efforts to curtail immigration and deny benefits to illegal aliens, all foreign communities are being affected by recent policy developments. These include the Latino communities of the American southwest, and Latin American immigrants who have found their way to Spain; however, the primary targets have been the Muslim communities. The arrival of anti-Western, transnational terrorism has given a new legitimacy to anti-Muslim sentiment and spurred its growth in Western societies. Polls conducted in the

United States in the fall of 2004, for example, found nearly 60 percent of the respondents believing that the Muslim religion teaches hatred, and that Muslims value life less than others and teach their children to hate those of other faiths.[42] Three months later another survey found nearly 50 percent of respondents expressing the belief that the civil liberties of Muslim Americans should be curtained.[43] Similar increases in anti-Islam bias can found throughout Western Europe even before the July, 2005, suicide attacks in London.[44]

Recycling the 1990s

In a very compressed period (2002–04), and focusing on a different set of issues (national security and Muslim unwillingness to assimilate rather than unemployment and alien access to state systems), the pattern of anti-immigrant politics that emerged in the West during the 1980s and 1990s has repeated itself in the early twenty-first century. Although anti-immigrant parties in some states—notably Austria, Italy, Norway, and Switzerland—had already done well in elections prior to 9/11, since the terrorist attack on the United States the parties of the antiforeigner Right have generally grown in strength and have made gains in numerous elections in Europe since 2001, including elections at the state level (in Germany's east, for example) and elections for the European Parliament.[45] Their success, in conjunction with the real security issues confronting contemporary Western societies, has led the system-wide leaders to respond with a new series of restrictive measures aimed at the foreign communities, including security-motivated raids on Muslim neighborhoods, the deportation of Islamic clerics for inciting violence, and forced secularization measures, even at the inevitable cost of provoking a backlash among European Muslims (see table 5.3).

On several occasions, the harsher measures aimed at the 'foreigner" communities have been tempered by more moderate policies and court judgments upholding civil and procedural rights despite heightened security concerns. Germany and Belgium have tried to ban their more inflammatory right-wing parties—moves primarily designed to lower the heat of racist rhetoric, though in both instances the governing parties would have benefited from their dismantlement. Muslim Councils, as we have noted, have been erected as government advisory groups in several countries. German courts have upheld the right of Muslims to wear scarves in schools; Ontario permits its Muslim community to utilize an Islamic court to settle specified civil disputes. The British Labour Party has continued to court the immigrant vote and permit immigrants from Commonwealth communities to stand for parliamentary seats; one (Chief Secretary for Treasury, Paul Boateng) was seated in the Cabinet following Britain's 2001 general elections. Still, overall the revival of anti-immigrant parties has limited most governments' ability to reach out to their Muslim communities. Moreover, to the extent that the policy-making process is viewed as a part of the system by which attitudes are shaped in all communities, the aerosol effect of the dominance of

Table 5.3 The "foreigner" issue in the post 9/11 democratic world, selected news stories, 2002–05

2001	Australia: two main parties endorse tightening immigration and asylum laws in election campaign
	Germany: Party for a Law and Order Offensive wins 20% of vote in state elections held after 9/11
2002	Europe: at the Seville Summit, EU leaders agree on tighter controls on immigration from without
	Austria: coalition government enacts rules virtually halting non-EU area immigration into Austria
	Denmark: coalition relying on anti-immigrant Danish Peoples Party tightens immigration law
	France: FN leader makes runoff in presidential election; party scores well in parliamentary elections
	Germany: enacts first ever law to regulate immigration, tightens asylum law
	Holland: assassination of anti-immigrant Dutch populist Pim Fortuyn on eve of national elections
	Holland: Parliament limits immigration
	Holland: Ministry of Immigration and Integration created; headed by member of Fortuyn's party
	Italy: The premier calls for immediate expulsion of immigrants illegally entering country
	Norway: anti-immigrant party becomes part of governing coalition
2003	Germany: Rock singer sentenced to three years for hate songs; German teacher wins right to wear scarf
	Germany: High Court invalidates government's effort to outlaw antiforeigner, neo-Nazi party
	Italy increases its efforts to locate and deport illegal Albanian Muslims
2004	Europe: soccer games become an arena for abuse of nonwhite players in England, France, Spain, Italy
	Austria: anti-immigrant Freedom Party candidate narrowly defeated in presidential race, 52% to 48%
	Belgium: government seeks to ban Flemish Bloc party for distributing racist literature
	Britain: communal tensions rise over arrest of Muslims; Muslim Council of Britain calls for calm
	Germany: June bomb blast in Turkish part of Cologne injures nearly 20 Turks
	Germany: fearing it would be a forum to preach hate, Berlin bans September Islamic conference
	Greece: Albanian immigrants implicated in bus hijacking
	Holland: murder of critic of Islam causes violent backlash, including arson, at mosque and school
	Holland: raid on Kurdish training camp in Netherlands results in 38 arrests
	Italy: North Africans convicted of terrorist ties; 360 boat people interdicted, sent back to Libya
	Spain: May bombing of commuter trains results in crackdown on Muslim population
	Sweden: the number of foreigners an issue, freedom of movement of new EU members limited
2005	Europe: suicide bombings in London trigger security sweeps of Muslim neighborhoods on continent;
	Britain: anti-Western preaching by Muslim clerics becomes major issue in U.K. politics; Prime Minister Blair proposes tough new restrictions on Muslims in Britain
	Denmark: elections result in government committed to tightening laws on country's foreign residents
	France: rash of fires destroy apartments housing foreigners in late summer–fall

anti-immigrant rhetoric from leading political figures and the wave of recent policies targeting the foreign communities accounts in part for both the rise in anti-Muslim bias reflected in public opinion polls and the new round of violence recently directed at the foreign communities.

In summary, then, as in France political leaders throughout the Western world continue to walk a line between, on the one hand, an economic need for inexpensive labor and the ease of acquiring it from Third World countries, Central Europe, and a secular but Muslim Turkey on the edge of being admitted to the EU, and hostile public opinion, politicians willing to exploit that opinion, a deep commitment to the secular nature of their states, and security considerations on the other.[46] For this reason, as well as because of the need for a Europe-wide policy on immigration in a Europe without internal frontiers, leaders in a growing number of EU countries have urged supranational action on both immigration policy and the rights of non-EU nationals in the states of a uniting Europe.

Ethnopolitical Conflict in the Western World, an Interim Epilogue

Coping with the foreigner issue has generally been much more difficult than managing ethnoterritorial conflict in the First World. Except where ethnonational conflict has been protracted and at times violent (Northern Ireland, Basque Spain) ethnoterritorial demands have normally been subject to accommodation. The centralized state, which has been regionalized, federalized, or otherwise reshaped in order to satisfy the ethnoregional communities, has been a casualty of this accommodation process; however, the state has, in general, remained whole. The issue of how to treat the foreign communities has provoked far more heat, and the conflicts between the indigenous and foreign populations have not always been restricted to verbal sparring. What general propositions explain the contrast?

One obvious, cross-national explanation involves the sociocultural distance separating the groups involved in these political conflicts. Territorialized minorities and majorities in the West usually share a common language, much of the same history, the Christian faith, and same philosophical heritage. It is thus not too difficult for a Londoner to believe that someone can be British and Welsh, or for those in Strasbourg to consider themselves French and *Alsacien*. It is much more difficult for a Muslim, dressed in North African garb, in Nice to argue that she can be both French and Arab; a Muslim Turkish worker in Cologne has little chance of convincing his employer that he can be both a good German citizen and a Turk. The Us – Them element in the foreigner debate becomes an Either–Or factor—either you are or you are not French. The degree of minority assimilation that is a prerequisite for accommodative politics vis-à-vis foreigners is, normally, already visibly present among most ethnoterritorial minorities in developed democracies.

Equally important are those factors that customarily tend to moderate social conflict in general in the First World but which tend to intensify the foreigner issue. Ethnoregional cleavages, for example, are normally bridged by crosscutting social-class cleavages. Working-class Scots share job security concerns with the working class in England and Wales. They are all also apt to identify in common with the system–wide Labour party committed to working–class interests.

In contrast, the foreign worker issue usually manifests itself in ethnoclass terms. The foreign workers are not only foreign, their socioeconomic status tends to be at the bottom in the host societies containing them. Class differences reinforce and intensify cultural differences, not ameliorate them. Likewise, the host society has the vote, the foreign element does not except where permitted to vote in local elections or when naturalized citizens. Their presence can prompt political opportunists to found an antiforeigner party; however, in general these organizations function more like success- ful interest groups than political parties. They do not need to win seats to secure their objectives. It is enough if they keep antiforeign sentiments alive and win enough votes to force the governing parties to embrace many of their proposals.

PART 2

Czechoslovakia: Ethnopolitics in Postcommunist Europe

CHAPTER SIX
_____

The Setting of Politics in Postcommunist Europe

Even without the civil wars that destroyed the former Yugoslavia during the 1990s, politics in the postcommunist world of Central Europe would have attracted considerable attention. With little advanced warning nearly a dozen countries were confronted with a seemingly everything-at-once set of problems, headed by the twin challenges of political democratization and economic liberalization. In the short term, the latter proved the more disruptive for most states. Given the disproportionately high level of suddenly uncompetitive industries and unmarketable skills in their economies, higher unemployment and lower standards of living were the immediate consequences of simultaneously moving in a market-based direction and curtailing state subsidies in numerous areas. In the multinational states of Central Europe, however, the management of ethnic conflict soon became a central concern as minority desires for political self-determination and interethnic animosities contained under communist gathered momentum.

State-Making after the Fall of Communism

Within a decade after the fall of communism during the 1989–92 period, Central Europe's political leaders had—outside of the former Yugoslavia— succeeded in stabilizing their political processes. It was an arduous task. First, they had to detach. insofar as possible, the political difficulties of democratizing their political processes from the challenges posed by rapid economic change and, not infrequently, the need to ease tensions between the diverse communities composing their societies. Within the diverse environment of Central Europe (see table 6.1), the level of success tended to correlate with the individual country's prior experience with democracy, level of economic development (roughly reflected in per capita income), and degree of ethnic homogeneity—criteria that made Hungary, Poland, and the Czech Republic attractive candidates for early admission to the EU. In addition, Central European governments had to unbundle,

Table 6.1 Socioeconomic and National Diversity and the States of Central Europe

Country	Population	Ethnic composition	Literacy	Per capita income (US$)
Albania	3,365,000	95% Albanian	93%	1,490
Bosnia	3,483,000	40% Serb 38% Muslim 22% Croat		1,720
Bulgaria	8,195,000	85% Bulgarian 7% Turk 6% Romany	98%	4,100
Croatia	4,677,000	78% Croat	97%	5,100
Czech Republic	10,290,500	90.3% Czech 99% 3.7% Moravian 3.0% Slovak		11,300
Hungary	10,186,400	90% Hungarian 4% Romany 3% German 2% Serb 1.7% Slovak	99%	7,400
Macedonia	2,023,000	66% Macedonia		1,050
Poland	38,609,000	98% Polish	99%	6,800
Romania	22,344,300	89% Romanian 9% Hungarian	97%	4,050
Slovakia	5,396,000	85.7% Slovak 9.7% Hungarian 4.2% Romany	100%	8,300
Slovenia	1,970,000	91% Sloven 3% Croat 2% Serb 1.7% Muslim	★	10,300
Serbia and Montenegro	11,207,000	63% Serb 14% Albanian 6% Montenegrin 4% Hungarian 13% Other	★	2,300

Sources: Minton F Goldman, *Global Studies: Russia, the Eurasian Republics, and Central/Eastern Europe* (Guilford, Conn.: Dushkin/McGraw-Hill, 2001); Regular Reports 2002 at http://www.europa.eu.int/comm/enlargement/report2002/index.htm. Specific country profile at http://www.europa.eu.int/comm/enlargement/candidate.htm.

again insofar as possible, the various tasks confronting them in the democratization process: for example, detaching their states from their ideological moorings and single-party construction under communism.

The Political Setting: Creating Constitutional Government

Their labors focused on creating constitutional systems that formally institutionalize most of the rules of the game long seen as indispensable for the operation of genuine democratic government: decision-making bodies deriving their legitimacy from free and open elections; the right of the people to engage in freedom of speech, association, and of the press; and to organize political parties to contest elections, and—if successful—to participate in the governing process.[1] For their constitutional designs, state-makers generally shunned the U.S. model of separation of powers as too cumbersome, too likely to result in divided government, and too inclined toward paralysis for countries facing a myriad of challenges demanding energetic action. Instead, they broadly opted for parliamentary systems, with their promise of disciplined government based on an assembly under the control of a prime minister commanding a legislative majority. And, within the world of Western parliamentary systems, the model of choice has been the system prevailing in West Germany during *its* post–World War II period of democratization and stellar economic recovery and performance. From it, Central Europe's constitution-makers have generally extracted three elements: (1) a head of government equipped with strong constitutional authority similar to that enjoyed by Germany's chancellor; (2) constitutionally protected basic rights; and (3) threshold clauses, such as the 5 percent clause in Germany, designed to prevent the development of extreme multiparty systems by excluding from parliaments those parties failing to obtain the preestablished, threshold percentage of the national (or regional) popular vote.

Achieving Constitutional Democracy

The results of their efforts to enact democracy have been uneven. Free to organize for political activities and lacking established system-wide parties in the aftermath of the disintegration of their respective communist parties, the fragmented societies of postcommunist Europe have spawned numerous parties, especially in the multinational countries where ethnic and national identity became common organizational bases for parties and other forms of political association. Thus, although 4 percent and 5 percent threshold clauses have kept the more eccentric parties out of the democratically elected parliaments—for example, the Beer Drinker and Topless parties, each of which fielded candidates in the Slovak Republic's first national election—they have not prevented the emergence of multiparty systems composed of five or more parties in most Central European states. In turn, the emergence of these multiparty systems has necessitated coalition governments, resulting in parliamentary government more akin to that found in continental countries than the U.K. system of government based on rule by a single, internally disciplined, majority party.

More fundamentally, and as was true in early postwar West Germany, at their inception these constitutions were somewhat out of synchronization with the political personnel, attitudes and habits prevailing in much of postcommunist Europe. It is one thing to recognize the freedom of the press; it is quite another to develop a press corps willing to ask penetrating questions and report objectively in a country where the press traditionally functioned as a public relations arm of government. Nor will governments composed of former communists and their cohorts necessarily embrace the concept of a free media, as Vladimir Meciar's government quickly demonstrated in Slovakia, where partisan-based disagreements over programming limited the term of those officials in charge of the state-owned television system to under a year throughout Meciar's years in office.

In a similar manner, whereas judicial tribunals charged with protecting individual rights can be structured as independent branches of government, developing a rule of law mentality and instilling in judges and citizens alike the desire to see individual rights upheld takes a long time, especially when the beneficiaries are viewed with great contempt (e.g., gypsies). Fitting political cultures with little experience in participatory democracy to democratic institutions of governance can take decades if not generations. There is also the problem of the concept of "democratization" being subject to various interpretations, some of which bear little resemblance to its meaning in the developed West. As one commentator summarized, in most post-communist states " 'Civic Society' means uninhibited pursuit of private activities for many. 'Democratic' values seem to be of little use for them, unless democracy is identified with a system improving living standards."[2]

Citizens of established democracies occasionally forget how long it required for their countries to develop systems of constitutional government. In the United States, for example, the quest only began with the adoption of the Constitution. A generation later, the author of the Declaration of Independence, by then president, Thomas Jefferson, was threatening to impeach the members of the Supreme Court if it ruled against the White House in the 1803 case of *Marbury v. Madison*. That case grew out of the last minute appointment of a minor federal judge by Jefferson's predecessor; however, its importance escalated when Jefferson refused to honor the appointment. The independence of the federal judiciary itself was at stake by the time that Chief Justice John Marshall found a means of deciding the case in a manner that affirmed the right of federal courts to determine the constitutionality of acts of Congress but stopped short of ruling against Jefferson and challenging him to pursue his threats against the Court.[3]

The matter did not end there. Another generation later, one of the most influential senators of his time, John Calhoun, was arguing that states could nullify acts of Congress with which they disagreed, and states *were* routinely ignoring Supreme Court opinions when they knew they would not be enforced—in particular, the series of opinions in which Chief Justice Marshall sought to protect the rights of Native Americans against state abrogation.[4] Most obviously, another generation later it required a bloody civil war to establish definitively the supremacy of federal law in those areas constitutionally assigned to the central government. Even then, it was nearly another century before a civil rights movement finally resulted in African Americans attaining the same rights in practice as those enjoyed by white Americans.

The long story of the U.S. struggle to achieve a functioning constitutional democracy with political equality for all of its citizens is hardly unique Britain may have begun its march toward parliamentary democracy as early as the Magna Carta; however, it was not until the late nineteenth century that its male citizens universally acquired the right to vote and not until the eve of World War I that the popularly elected House of Commons established itself as the dominant element in Britain's Parliament. Along the way, the struggle for parliamentary supremacy over royal prerogatives not infrequently led to bloodshed, most conspicuously during the years of the Cromwell Revolution, which also offers a major study of religious intolerance in seventeenth-century Britain. Elsewhere, others—such as the leaders of the Weimar Republic of interwar Germany—failed altogether in their attempts to erect viable democracies. Thus, the success already achieved by Europe's postcommunist leaders in leaping the evolutionary distances that took generations for others to cover and moving their states bloodlessly in democratic directions well deserves the praise it has received. All the same, their work is still in its early stages.

Political Change and the Ethnic Factor

In much of multiethnic, postcommunist Europe, the decision to create parliamentary systems based on strong majoritarian rule awakened fears in territorialized and territorially intermingled minority communities alike. Even the specification of long lists of constitutional rights did little to dispel their anxiety given the absence of any experience with the rule of law in the Western sense in most areas. Meanwhile, the process of economic liberalization frequently reinforced ethnic cleavages by widening the socioeconomic status separating the more favored ethnopolitical groups (usually the majorities) from the less economically developed communities (usually such national minorities as the Slovaks in Czechoslovakia, the Hungarians in Slovakia, and the Muslim communities in Yugoslavia). Even without these developments, however, the task of molding the diverse ethnic communities contained in the states emerging from the former Soviet Union and communist Central Europe was formidable.

The Ethnic Mosaic of Postcommunist Europe

The pervasiveness of multiethnic and/or multinational societies in the postcommunist world is indicated in table 6.2. Despite the fragmentation of the Soviet Union, Yugoslavia, and Czechoslovakia along ethnoterritorial lines, it is rare to find a state without a notable minority element. In fact, taken as a whole—and excluding the immigrant element—the terrain is far more polyethnic and multinational than in the advanced democratic states of Western Europe. Yet the prevailing degree of diversity is not the only element separating the nature of ethnic politics in Central Europe from ethnopolitics in the West.

In the advanced democratic world, state-building commonly preceded the development of national consciousness. The concept of national

Table 6.2   The States of Central Europe and the former Soviet Union

Country	Dominant nationality	Principal minority/minorities
Former Soviet Union states		
Armenia	Armenians (93%)	Azerbaijani (3%)
Azerbaijan	Azerbaijani (90%)	Daghestani (3%)
Belarus	Belarussian (79%)	Russian (13%), Polish (4%)
Estonia	Estonian (62%)	Russian (30%), Ukrainian (3%)
Georgia	Georgian (70%)	Armenian (8%), Russian (6%)
Kazakhstan	Kazakh (42%)	Russian (37%), Ukrainian (5%)
Kyrgyzstan	Kirghiz (52%)	Russian (18%), Uzbek (13%)
Latvia	Latvian (52%)	Russian (34%), Belarussian (5%)
Lithuania	Lithuanian (80%)	Russian (9%), Polish (8%)
Moldova	Muldovan/ Romanian (65%)	Ukrainian (14%), Russian (13%)
Russia Federation	Russian (82%)	Tatar (4%), Ukrainian (3%)
Tajikistan	Tajik (65%)	Uzbek (25%), Russian (3%)
Turkmenistan	Turkmen (73%)	Russian (10%), Uzbek (9%)
Ukraine	Ukrainian (74%)	Russian (22%)
Uzbekistan	Uzbek (71%)	Russian (8%), Tajik (5%)
Republic of Albania	Albanian (95% Geg & Tosk)	Greek (5%)
Republic of Bulgaria	Bulgarian (85%)	Turk (9%), Romani (6%)
Czech Republic	Czech (94%)	Slovak (3%)
Hungary	Hungarian (90%)	Romani (4%), German (3%)
Poland	Polish (98%)	Other (2%)
Romania	Romanian (89%)	Hungarian (9%)
Slovakia	Slovak (86%)	Hungarian (11%)
Republics of the Former Yugoslavia (FRY)		
Bosnia-Herzegovina	Serb (40%)	Muslim (38%), Croat (22%)
Croatia	Croat (78%)	Serb (12%)
Macedonia	Macedonian (66%)	Albanian (23%), Turk (4%)
Slovenia	Slovene (91%)	Croat (3%), Serb (2%)
Serbia and Montenegro★	Serb (63%)	Albanian (14%), Montenegrin (6%)

★ The Albanian peoples live almost entirely inside Serbia's Kosovo province, which is 90% Albanian.
Source: Minton F. Goldman, *Global Studies: Russia, the Eurasian Republic, and Central Europe* (Guilford, Conn.: Dushkin/McGraw-Hill, 2001).

identity, however much it is built around ethnic identity in the more ethnically homogeneous countries and those with a strongly dominant ethnic group, developed within the boundaries of these states. The same is true of the principal settler states of the developed democratic world, where the United States provides the perhaps unique example of a multiethnic nation-state emerging within a shared territory despite the formidable nature of two different "identity barriers" that had to be overcome in the process: the historical differences separating the citizens of its original, largely British settlers (who in 1776 saw themselves primarily as Pennsylvanians, New Yorkers, Georgians, and the like) and the subsequent "hyphenated" identities (Italian Americans, German Americans, Polish Americans, and the like) based on the lines of ethnic stratification separating the approximately forty-four million who immigrated into the expanding borders of the United States between 1840 and World War I.

For much of contemporary Central Europe, the state-building process was the exact opposite. The contending sets of national consciousness that developed during the nineteenth century eventually produced twentieth-century states purportedly based on the principle [for the majority population at least] of national self-determination. The post–World War I breakup of the Austrian-Hungarian empire produced two states of this ilk supposedly rooted in Slavic nationalism: Czechoslovakia and Yugoslavia. Their postcommunist breakup into their more sharply defined ethnonational components, as well as the collapse of the Soviet Union into nearly a score of states based on ethnonational cores, furthered this development at the century's end. Moreover, throughout the region, commonality of ethnic descent rather than commonality of residence in a modern territorial state has continued to define national identity.[5] Since the collapse of the communist order, it has also driven much political conflict between the majority (or plurality) and minority ethnic communities sharing the same territory but no overarching sense of identity.

Finally, the nature of the minority communities in postcommunist Europe also differs from that of the ethnopolitical communities in the advanced Western world. In the latter, the principal minority communities tend, as we have seen, to fall into one of two categories. There are the territorialized minority populations who continue to live in regions that fell under the control of the capital during the era of state-building; and there are the usually geographically intermingled, ethnoclass minorities who have migrated to that state in relatively large numbers.

Central Europeans, by contrast, currently define themselves and others as falling within one of four different categories, each potentially the source of a different type of ethnic conflict and each category seeking a different means of protecting its rights. First, there is the "mother nation," which normally constitutes a majority and consequently has an ability to protect itself in a democratized political process based on majority rule. Second, there are the "national minorities"—the indigenous people who find themselves living in a country whose borders separate them from their national counterparts in neighboring states. The Poles, Germans, and Hungarians living in the Czech Republic fit into this category, as would the Italian minority in Slovenia and the Slovak minority in Hungary. Especially where they constitute a large territorialized minority, their security concerns can at least in theory be addressed by devolving regional decision-making autonomy into their hands in sensitive policy fields. Third, there are the "imperial remnants" — those often nonterritorialized minorities who have survived from the days in which these areas were ruled by outsiders. The large Russian population in the former Soviet republics of Estonia and Latvia and in the eastern Ukraine are examples of this category; so too are the Czechs in Slovakia and the Croats and Serbs in Slovenia. These minorities, and many of those falling into the second category, can look to outside protectors lobbying on their behalf: for example, Hungary adopting an oversight policy with respect to the treatment of Hungarians living outside of Hungary. Finally, there are the "transitional" minorities — a category that includes the internally displaced peoples (IDPs) and refugees created by the civil wars in the former Yugoslavia but which, in the context of Central Europe, more normally refers to the Romany community. Those falling into this class invariably look to outsiders for protection — the Organization for Security and Cooperation in Europe (OSCE) and NATO in the case of the refugee and IDP peoples, and increasingly the EU in the case of the millions of Romany spread across Central Europe.

Within the context of this polyethnic terrain, ethnic conflict is fueled not just by the numbers, but also by historical animosities, nationalist feelings, and combinations thereof.[6] Ill feelings often run deep, and the resultant conflicts can be disruptive even when contained in the electoral process, with ethnonationalist and class-oriented parties outbidding one another in attempting to establish themselves as, for example, the most pro-Slovak, anti-Hungarian, or anti-Romany political organization.[7]

Postcommunist Czechoslovakia

In his introductory comparative politics text, Michael J. Sodaro lists ten factors widely considered conducive to both successful democratization and the operation of durable democratic systems of government. Among the items on the list are elites committed to the democratic ideal, a sizeable middle class, national wealth, a policy agenda committed to supporting the disadvantaged of society, and an international environment supportive of the democratization process.[8]

Judged by this list, postcommunist Czechoslovakia was one of the best positioned countries of Central Europe to make the transition to democracy when, in the country's "Velvet Revolution" of 1989, the Czechoslovakia Communist Party peacefully relinquished authority to the Czech and Slovak leaders who had long struggled to liberalize the regime governing their country. Not only was Czechoslovakia one of the few countries in communist Europe with interwar experience in democratic government, but from the time of the "Prague Spring" in 1968, when the efforts of Czechoslovakia's leaders to liberalize the country's political process were crushed by Soviet military intervention, until the collapse of communist rule, the country was never without an intellectual community vigorously pressing the regime in Prague to respect individual rights. Its most famous member was the Czech dramatist Vaclav Havel, whose plays frequently contained a strong political subtext when allowed to be presented; however, the country's liberal cadre had depth as well as membership in both the Czech and Slovak lands.

Czechoslovakia was also economically more advanced than many of Europe's postcommunist states, with a solid middle-class element in both regions and a functioning, comprehensive welfare system. The Czech lands were economically more developed than Slovakia — a fact of economic life that was quickly co-opted by Slovak nationalists to advance their political agenda—but by the time communism collapsed in Czechoslovakia, western Slovakia had modernized considerably and the region contained an automotive industry and other plants attractive to outside investors. Moreover, the international environment was highly conducive to both regions drawing these outside investors, as well as the support of Western governments and nongovernment actors in their efforts to Westernize their economic, educational, and political systems.

Most important, at the time of the Velvet Revolution, if the peoples of Slovakia and of the Czech lands did not possess *en masse* a sixth element on Solberg's list, a political culture supportive of democratic decision-making arrangements, neither did they share a history of animosity. Czechs had never victimized or oppressed the Slovaks and vice versa. Given the many aspects of a shared Slavic culture uniting them, a Czecho-Slovak political divorce seemed impossible at the time of the Velvet Revolution.

Poets and Demagogues, and the Surfacing of Ethnopolitics

The first cracks in postcommunist Czechoslovakia's social and political edifice nonetheless appeared almost immediately. The arena was political leadership, an area that quickly became a problem throughout postcommunist Europe, where communist party officials were initially discredited and alternative personnel with political experience in limited supply. The men and women who had taken control of Czechoslovakia after the Velvet Revolution, at the center and in its regions, were gifted intellectuals — political philosophers, economists, journalists, and literary figures such as Havel. They were also political survivors skilled in the art of dissent; however, as a group, they lacked practical training in the area of governance. They also frequently complicated their shortage of trained manpower by investing considerable energy in seeking out communist informers and terminating the employment of experienced staff in the bureaucracies and law enforcement sectors. Meanwhile, as many were learning on the job, problems and scandals began to develop in such vital areas as health care and the privatization process even before Czechoslovakia's pivotal 1992 national and regional elections.

Matters unraveled even more seriously on the ethnopolitical front. In both the Czech and Slovak lands, rising crime rates begat violent clashes between the Czechs and Slovaks on the one side and the much despised ethnoclass Romany minority on the other. In Slovakia, tensions also mounted between Slovaks and the region's Hungarian minority. The state-threatening development, however, lay elsewhere, in the skillful mobilization of Slovak nationalism by former communist officials such as Vladimir Mechiar, who found a second political life by becoming a born-again nationalist and riding the rising tide of Slovak nationalism back into public office. By the time the federalist–minded inheritors of political power in Prague and the Slovak regional capital of Bratislava began to gauge the importance of the nationalist issue to Slovaks, a solid plurality in the Slovak electorate favored renegotiating Slovakia's relationship with Prague. Pledging to do just that, Slovak nationalists were swept into power in the country's June, 1992, vote.

CHAPTER SEVEN

Ethnoterritorial Politics in Czechoslovakia and the Creation and Dissolution of a State

Created in part by outsiders in the aftermath of World War I, Czechoslovakia enjoyed only a brief period of self-rule during its short history. Scarcely was the state in place before the Great Depression and the prelude to World War II deprived its leaders of the opportunity to build either durable political institutions or a durable political community. Then came the twin traumas of German occupation during the war and postwar Soviet control. Consequently, in a sense it was not until the peaceful overthrow of the country's communist regime in 1989 that the Czech and Slovak peoples themselves had the opportunity to decide what they wanted to do with their union. Within three years they decided to end it.

The Origins of Czechoslovakia

The partition of Czechoslovakia on January 1, 1993, into the Czech Republic and Slovak Republic can be viewed as the triumph of ethnonationalism over both linguistic affinity and economic compatibility. The more numerous Czechs living west of the Moravia River in the regions of Moravia, East Bohemia, and West Bohemia shared an alphabet and very similar Slavic tongue (Czech) with their Slovak-speaking, "Little [Slavic] Brothers" to the east in Slovakia. In addition, the two communities had intermarried for centuries, and shared a history of common rule by the Austro-Hungarian Empire for generations prior to World War I, as well as by a Soviet-backed government for more than four decades after World War II. They also possessed complimentary economies. The Czech lands were more industrialized and contained one of Europe's great capitals, historic Prague; Slovakia was extensively composed of agricultural lands, capped in the north by the Tatras, a short, imposing mountain range with its own tourist appeal. Yet, differences, also rooted in both culture and history, separated these two communities, fueling the development of two quite different nationalist movements and ultimately leading to the dismantlement of the state.

The Hungarians date the origins of their one-thousand-plus years empire from the end of the ninth century, when the leaders of the tribes of Hungary ended their internal warfare and began their conquest of adjacent territories. By A.D. 1000, the Slovak region to the north was firmly under the repressive control of the Hungarian state. Subsequently, Budapest's control of this land, which Hungary came to consider "Northern Hungary," was interrupted only twice—by the Tatar invasion in 1241 and the Turkish invasion in 1530. Thereafter Hungary reestablished exclusive control over the region, which endured until the post–World War I collapse of the Austro-Hungarian Empire (1867–1918). Meanwhile, throughout the Slovaks were persistently ruled by foreigners. They never enjoyed, even for a brief moment, self-rule, much less an empire of their own. To the contrary, more often than not they were oppressed, and remained a poor, subservient community. Thus, it was not until 1785 that serfdom was abolished in Slovakia and another 60 years passed before Slovak was legalized as a literary language. Moreover, it was not until the creation of the Austro-Hungarian Empire that the Czech and Slovak lands were joined under a single government, albeit a Dual Monarchy with dual capitals in Vienna and Budapest.

For most of this millennium, the Czech lands had a different history. Before the rise of Hungary, the Empire of Great Moravia was a major player in regional politics for nearly a century (833–907). More importantly, from the days of the Holy Roman Empire through their years of administration under the Austro-Hungarian Empire, the Czech lands enjoyed moments of either actual independence or significant political latitude under foreign rulers. In this context, Prague emerged as one of the jewel cities of Central Europe, and the Czech lands prospered economically while Slovakia remained poor and—by the standards of such imperial centers as Vienna and Budapest—culturally backward.

The contrast was particularly sharp during the half century of Austro-Hungarian rule, which immediately preceded the creation of Czechoslovakia, and during which Czech and Slovak nationalism developed separately. The Czechs were ruled indirectly by Vienna, with Austria allowing the Czech lands, already industrialized, to continue to expand economically and enjoy a substantial degree of autonomy as long as they did not challenge the permanence of Austrian rule. Slovakia, however, was under the direct rule of Budapest, whose response to the early stirring of Slovak nationalism in the late eighteenth century and the Slovak Uprising in 1848–49 was to intensify its efforts to Hungarianize Slovakia ("Magyarization"), often brutally and rarely with any respect for the cultural integrity of the Slovak language or way of life.

These differences in historical experience not only resulted in there being few political ties between the Slovaks and Czechs by the end of the nineteenth century, but in vastly different societies with quite different forms of national consciousness. The Czech lands were as developed as most of Western Europe, with nearly as many Czechs working in industry (36.2 percent of the work force) as agriculture (39.1 percent). In Slovakia, nearly five times as many Slovaks (72.3 percent of the work force) were working in agriculture as in industry (15.8 percent) as Europe stumbled toward the Great War.[1] So great were the socioeconomic differences separating the two regions that 40 years later, when the famous Czechoslovakian photographer Karola Plicky produced a two-volume study of his country, the book on Slovakia was dominated by photos of natural wonders, quaint villages, and a traditional peasant society unchanged for centuries while his volume on Prague featured the castles, cathedrals, and artistic treasures of an old, great, culturally advanced European city.[2]

Similarly, whereas those involved in the awakening of modern Czech national consciousness could stress often illustrious moments in Czech history, those speaking for Slovak nationalism most often focused on Slovakia's victimization at the hands of its foreign rulers. The Czechs thus celebrated their region's heroic figures and great political leaders—like the "Good King" Wenceslaus (tenth century), the only "King Saint" to whom an altar is dedicated at St. Peter's Cathedral in Rome, and King Wenceslaus (1361–1419), Holy Roman emperor and king of Bohemia. For their part, Slovak nationalists concentrated on ancient folk songs telling of fathers and brothers killed by the Magyars and brides carried off by the Turks, and celebrated such Slovak folk heroes as Janocik, a Robin Hood–like figure who stole from rich foreign tyrants to give to the poor and exploited Slovaks, before he was betrayed by a comrade and hung.

Based loosely on the deeds of a local outlaw (Juro Janocik, 1688–1713), the Janocik legend endured because the Slovaks could read "in the Slovak national character a heroic feature which shows that Slovaks suffer for justice."[3] Suppression can provide an odd but solid basis around which a people can erect a national identity that demands self-determination; when Slovak nationalism flowered during the nineteenth century (as did nationalism more generally among the various Slavic peoples under Hungarian rule), Slovak nationalists did precisely that. Stress was placed on the long and unique history of the Slovak people, and the survival of their distinctive folk culture even in the face of forced Hungarianization. They had earned, in the minds of Slovak nationalists, the right to a state of their own.

By contrast, Czechs frequently stressed—usually with scant historical evidence—the *commonality* of the Czech and Slovak people: their common ancestry; their shared Slavonic tongue; and their shared historical origin in approximately the sixth century, when the Slavs settled the Czecho-Slovak regions of Central Europe. To be sure, these elements were normally woven into such mainstream topics of Czech nationalism as the historical accomplishments of the Czechs even when under outside rule, the success of Czech merchants, and the grandeur of Prague.[4] Still, on balance Czech nationalism was far more pan-Slavic than Slovak nationalist thought, but with a *noblesse oblige* twist which Slovak nationalists often found galling.

The corollary to the thesis that the Czechs had done well even under adverse circumstances was that the Czech lands had an obligation, through merger, to assist their less fortunate Slovak relatives.

The Post–World War I Bargain: Making the Czechoslovakian State

Given the different vantage points and interests of Czech and Slovak nationalists, the creation of Czechoslovakia in 1918 can be viewed as an Old World marriage of convenience, resulting not so much from desire on the part of the betrothed as from the mutual advantages both could derive from the wedding. Furthermore, although the resultant state, which placed the more numerous Czechs in positions of influence, clearly fit the goals of Czech nationalists more than those advocating Slovak self-determinism, the creation was as much the result of factors outside the control of the affected communities as the product of their respective labors.

Perhaps above all else, Czechoslovakia owed its creation to the ambience spawned by the wartime rhetoric of President Woodrow Wilson, who rallied American support for the war with talk of making the world safe for democracy and creating a postwar order based on the principle of national self-determination. To be sure, Wilson never intended for that ideal to be universally implemented (it was never meant to apply, for example, to the Irish seeking independence from his wartime ally, Britain) and it found little support at the postwar conferences at Versailles, where Britain and France quickly carved up for themselves much of the Arab territory previously governed by the Ottoman Empire. Wilson did, however, intend for the idea to be applied to Austria and Hungary's Central European empire, and that fact encouraged a wave of outside lobbying by Slavic immigrants in America and Czech and Slovak exiles living in America and France; most notably, Tomas G. Masaryk and Edvard Benes on the Czech side and Milan R. Stefanik and Stefan Osusky for the Slovaks. Collectively and individually they urged the governments in Washington and Paris to unite into a single, sovereign Slavic state the Slovaks and Czechs, who for centuries had been under the rule of Vienna and Budapest. Impressed by the culture and language linking the Czech lands and Slovakia amid a sea of surrounding, non-Slavic states (Germany, Poland, the Soviet Union, Hungary, and Austria), the victors gathering at Versailles visualized a united, Czecho-Slovak state as a model of Wilsonian national self-determination.[5]

The Czechs and Slovaks in Czechoslovakia saw matters differently. Although it fell far short of the state they envisioned, a united Czech-Slovak state did have a certain geographical and mathematical appeal to both communities. For the Slovaks, it was a means of escaping the influence of Budapest. By joining with a larger, Slavic ethnic group with whom they already shared a degree of common history, Slovaks could return to their Slavic heritage after centuries of oppression. Conversely, even if they were to be offered national self-determination at Versailles, Slovak leaders recognized that there was little chance that a small Slovak state containing a large Hungarian minority and located on the northern border of Hungary would be able to establish, quickly or securely, its own identity.

For the Czechs, the mathematics of the pairing was even more important. The Czech lands near Germany had their own minority problem: a very large number of Sudenten Germans. In 1921, ethnic Germans constituted 33 percent of the population in Bohemia and 20.9 percent of the people in Moravia. To Czech nationalists a merger with the economically backward Slovaks was a means of decisively tilting the numbers inside a polyethnic Czechoslovak state in a Slavic direction.[6]

Czech–Slovak Conflict: The Formative Years

Scarcely was the union born before tensions sharpened between the Czech and Slovak communities inside the new state. Economics as well as numbers consigned the Slovaks to minority status Not only were they outnumbered two-to-one by the Czechs, but Slovakia's economy remained rooted in agriculture and in general "continued to exist on the European economic periphery."[7] Even more importantly, the Czech lands already possessed a large number of professionals and public sector workers. On the eve of World War I, 12.3 percent of the Czech work force was in these two categories. The Czech lands were thus much better prepared to assume political, economic, and bureaucratic leadership than Slovakia, where, as a result of its long, direct dominance by Budapest, less than one worker in fifty (1.9 percent) was employed either in the public sector or a professional field as late as 1910.[8] It has even been argued that the absence of a trained administrative class among the Slovaks was yet another reason why Slovak nationalists were willing to support merger with the Czechs after World War I; an independent, self-governing Slovakia was not a realistic option in 1918.[9]

A multidimensional, minority status of this nature would have been difficult for any ethnic group to have accepted, but it was particularly grating to the Slovaks. Years of subjection to Hungarianization efforts had left them with a deep sense of inferiority and aggressive defensiveness. Defensiveness boiled into anger when the chief negotiator for the Slovaks, Stefanik, was killed by Czech anti-aircraft fire on his way to Slovakia to inspect the conditions in the new state at a moment of acute difference of opinion between the Czech and Slovak leaders about the direction of the country. Whether the action was an accident or intentional remains a mystery; however, Stefanik's death gave the Slovaks a new national hero around which to rally the cause of Slovak nationalism. Consequently, when Czechoslovakia's (basically Czech) leaders in Prague [1] repeatedly rejected organizing the new state along federal lines with the type of regional autonomy for Slovakia promised in the Pittsburgh Pact signed by Slovak and Czech leaders only a few months before the founding of

Czechoslovakia, then [2] launched a Czech culture-based educational program to close the social and economic gaps between the Czech lands and Slovakia, and [3] staffed the state's bureaucracy overwhelmingly with Czechs, large numbers of Slovaks began to press for the independent Slovakia of which they dreamed but which they did not pursue in 1918.

Walker Connor once observed that ethnonationalism feeds on both "adversity and denial," which exacerbate grievances, and concessions and gains, which whet the appetite.[10] For the Slovaks, the first Czechoslovakian Republic was a little of both. It gave them a large taste of freedom compared to their prior experience with Hungarian rule, but instead of giving them even regional self-government it placed them under the rule of Prague in a state committed to building a single nation on the Czech model. By the mid-1930s, a litany of grievances had so fueled the growth of Slovak nationalism that estranged Slovak nationalists were openly negotiating with Germany, offering to support Hitler in his confrontation with Prague over the treatment of the Germans living in Bohemia in return for his promise to create an independent Slovak Republic should Germany invade Czechoslovakia. The crucial period occurred during those months between the Munich Agreement of September 29, 1938, in which France, Britain, and Italy acquiesced to Germany annexing Czechoslovakia's Sudetenland in return for "peace" in their time, and Germany's 1939 invasion of Czechoslovakia, which ended the first Czecho-Slovak Republic. During that period, the leader of the pro-autonomy Slovak People's Party, Josef Tiso, successfully persuaded Hitler to make Slovakia a separate state under German sponsorship in return for Tiso declaring Slovak independence in March, 1939. Thus was born the First Slovak Republic, with Slovakia becoming nominally independent throughout World War II (1939–45) while the Czech lands lapsed into a German "Protectorate" under German occupation.[11]

Although successful at the time, Tiso's negotiations haunted Czech–Slovak relations for years following the war. Nor was the First Slovak Republic the sovereign entity for which Tiso had negotiated. It quickly proved bogus—a Third Reich creature whose existence depended on German military support. Its existence, however, drove a wedge between the Czech and Slovak communities which would have probably made a reunified, postwar state impossible had it not been for the 1944 Slovak uprising against the Germans occupying Slovakia. Stanislav Kirschbaum is undoubtedly correct when he notes that the "fact that this action took place quite late in the war and was of very short duration [it took German forces only two months to end it] testifies . . . to the frailty of the resistance movement."[12] Nevertheless, the uprising provided a sufficient enough effort at atonement for collaboration with the Nazis for a reunited, independent Czechoslovakia to be a viable postwar option.

Czech–Slovak Relations in Communist Czechoslovakia, 1945–89

The rebuilding of the state had not progressed very far after World War II before the Red Army occupied the country and converted it into a Soviet satellite state. Moreover, neither the Slovak uprising nor the joint occupation of the Czech and Slovak lands by the Red Army ended all Czech efforts to punish Slovakia for its wartime perfidy. Expressions of Slovak national identity were severely punished by the (largely) Czech communist leaders in Prague as assertions of "Bourgeois Nationalism." Slovak political parties were either banned or enfolded into the Czech-dominated Communist Party of Czechoslovakia, and in the short term the First Slovak Republic disappeared in the communist state created in Czechoslovakia under Moscow's supervision. In the long term, though, policies enacted during Czechoslovakia's era of communist rule advanced the cause of Slovak nationalism on several fronts.

First, the Marxist answer to closing the socioeconomic gap separating the Slovaks and Czechs was not cultural assimilation but economics: the industrialization of Slovakia. The program had only limited success. The Czech lands' headstart in industrialization, their more educated population, and their forward position on the edge of Western Europe gave the Czechs a competitive advantage that could not be overcome by the relatively meager resources subsequently invested in modernizing Slovakia's economy. Nevertheless, by the time of the Velvet Revolution, Slovakia had at last developed the type of mixed (agricultural–industrial–service) economy necessary for survival in the modern world. Alternately, as one commentator summarized, "the modernization of Slovakia . . . accomplished mainly during the socialist era was a necessary . . . condition for the [subsequent] disintegration of Czechoslovakia."[13] For the first time, Slovak nationalists could realistically talk of an economically viable, independent Slovakia, complete with a modern, urbanized capital in Bratislava.

Second, Slovak nationalism profited substantially from the changes that communist rule made in the state's political structure following the 1968 mini-revolution (the Prague Spring), which Czech intellectuals and politicians launched against communist rule in an effort to establish a more democratic political process. Shortly after summarily ending the reform movement by militarily intervention, Moscow engineered several reforms of its own in order to minimize the costs of controlling Czechoslovakia.

The centerpiece of these reforms involved courting the Slovaks by restructuring the country along federalist lines, creating a Slovak regional government in Bratislava, and appointing Slovaks to important positions in the federal government in Prague. The strategy appears to have succeeded at least partially. In return for their economic and political gains, Slovaks supported their communist rulers to a far greater extent than did the Czechs. The Prague Spring had been a Czech movement, with scant echoes in Slovakia even though the political figure arrested and held responsible for the uprising, Alexander Dubcek, was a Slovak. Similarly, the Charter 77 movement, which was launched in 1977 when a petition circulated by dissidents to protest the government's continued suppression of intellectual discourse obtained more than a thousand signatures in the Czech lands but attracted only one Slovak signature.

Even the Velvet Revolution was largely a Czech phenomenon. As communism began to crumble elsewhere in Central Europe, beginning with the dramatic collapse of the regime in East Germany, hundreds of thousands filled Prague's streets on November 24, 1989, to protest the continued rule of Czechoslovakia by the communists. In Bratislava, however, only a few thousand gathered. And when the Velvet Revolution succeeded and the communist party began a two-month-long process of peacefully transferring control of the state to the coalition of opposition forces known as the Civic Forum, the arena for action was Prague. Except for Miroslav Kusy, who became President Havel's agent in Bratislava following the transfer of power and who had been the one Slovak to sign the Charter 77 petition, Slovaks again found themselves largely the observers of political events. This time, however, as Czech–Slovak tension again simmered, they lived within a federal state in which Slovakia already had an institutionalized political presence

Finally, the demographic changes that occurred in Czechoslovakia in the immediate aftermath of World War II and during the more than 40 years of communist rule sharpened the sense of Slovak identity and increasingly shifted the goal of Slovak politicians away from autonomy within a Czecho-Slovak state toward an independent Slovakia. Prior to World War II the Czechs and Slovaks were only two of the four largest ethnic communities in a polyethnic state, and each had one of the other two largest communities living in their region: the aforementioned Sudenten Germans who had inhabited portions of the Czech lands for 700 years; and the Hungarians in Slovakia. In that setting, there was ample reason to focus on the transcending Slavic identity linking Czechs and Slovaks and giving them a solid, joint majority in the country's population. Immediately after World War II, however, approximately 2.5 million Czechoslovakian Germans were accused of collaborating with the Nazis, stripped of their citizenship, and deported. With their expulsion and the freezing of Czechoslovakia's borders under communism to the point where other minority communities (Ukrainian and Polish, for example) could no longer replenish themselves by immigration, Czechoslovakia essentially became a territorialized, bi-national state with two dominant communities: the 9.8 million Czechs, who by 1988 encompassed 94.1 percent of the Czech Republic's population but only 1.2 percent of Slovakia's; and the approximately 5 million Slovaks who composed 86.7 percent of Slovakia's population but only 4 percent of those living in the Czech lands.[14]

Against this backdrop, other variables weighed more heavily than previously in dividing the Slovaks and Czechs. For one thing, only one of the country's territorialized national communities, the Slovaks, had to contend with a sizeable minority in its own region (the Hungarians, who continued to represent approximately 10 percent of Slovakia's population). For another, despite its economic growth under communism Slovakia remained a predominantly agrarian region and still lagged appreciably behind the Czech lands in economic development. Quite suddenly the links they shared as Slavs loomed less large than the fact that during the 71 years from the creation of Czechoslovakia in 1918 to the Velvet

Revolution in 1989—the longest period of direct contact between Czechs and Slovaks in the history of Czech–Slovak relations—the Slovaks had persistently been treated as the Czechs' poor country cousins and junior partner.

Czech-Slovak Conflict and the Demise of Czechoslovakia

The slow death of communism in the Soviet Union, which began during the 1980s when Soviet leader Mikhail Gorbachev began to liberalize the USSR's economic system and tolerate the discussion of political reform inside Central Europe as well as the Soviet Union, and which effectively concluded with the failed August, 1991, attempt by communist hardliners to overthrow Gorbachev, opened the door in Czechoslovakia to a quickly developing, ethnopolitical debate about that country's future. Fueled by old grievances on both sides, the debate focused as much on whether Slovakia should remain as a federally autonomous region or should secede as on the proper pathways and pace toward democratization and economic liberalization. The debate began almost immediately, when the Czech-dominated Charter 77 opposition movement became the Civic Forum and assumed control of the country.[15] Even though a Slovak, Marian Calfa, was installed as premier and the moderate Vaclev Havel was elected president by the national Parliament, tensions grew quickly enough to force the country to jettison its name, the Czechoslovak Socialist Republic, in favor of a label more reflective of its increasingly tenuous nature, the Czech and Slovak Federative Republic.

The decisive showdown between the federalists who wanted to preserve the state and Slovak nationalists campaigning to dismember it came in the June, 1992, national and regional elections in which Slovakia's relationship with Prague was *the* issue in the Slovak region and in which a nationalist coalition headed by Vladimir Meciar gained control of Slovakia's regional assembly. Throughout the campaign Meciar's rhetoric was unabashedly nationalistic and direct, even to the point of acknowledging some of the negative consequences that independence would hold for Slovakia in coveted areas such as entry into the EU. As Meciar phrased it near the end of the campaign:

> Europe is unifying. If we want to be a member of this society we have two choices. We can enter as part of Czechoslovakia. That would be quicker, but Slovakia wouldn't be treated as a state. . . . But if we enter Europe as a state we would keep our identity and we would be the equal of other states.[16]

Only on the issue of the means toward achieving independence was Meciar ambiguous, frequently endorsing the time-consuming method of putting the future of Slovakia to Slovak voters in a referendum, while on other occasions promising independence within two months of election victory.

Once the June election was over, Meciar gravitated toward the "fast track" approach. Claiming that the election provided him with a mandate to pursue the Slovaks' long-standing dream of national self-determination, Meciar immediately began negotiations with the prime minister of Czechoslovakia, Vaclav Klaus, over the future of Slovakia.

Negotiating the Disaggregation of a State

Commentators are still debating whether Meciar was singleminded in his desire for Slovak independence, or was threatening secession in order to persuade Prague to increase the scope of Slovakia's federal autonomy and pump more investment capital into his region. Even with his talk of independence, Meciar's claim to nationalist status remains somewhat dubious. A communist under the old order, his embrace of nationalism has been frequently interpreted as a born-again, opportunistic means of prolonging his political life in postcommunist Czechoslovakia. If so, it was a successful ploy.

Prior to the fall of communism, there was only the Communist Party of Czechoslovakia; after the fall of communism, the electorate in both the Czech and Slovak republics was fully available for mobilization under the banners of new political parties. Given the long-standing desire of Slovaks for their own state, the argument of Meciar's *Hnutie za demokratické Slovensko* party (HZDS, Movement for a Democratic Slovakia) that the Slovaks needed independence to pursue their destiny, struck a responsive chord.[17] So, too, did the similar platforms of the other nationalist parties, which sprung up in Slovakia after the Velvet Revolution and which also enjoyed a measure of success in the June vote. Thus, despite President Havel's warnings of the dangers of separatism, when the dust settled after that election the HZDS had won approximately 35 percent of the vote *and a plurality in every region of Slovakia.*[18] Meanwhile, the moderate, pro-federalist Civic Democratic Union, which had previously been Slovakia's leading party, failed to win a single seat in either the national or regional parliament. It was consequently the nationalist parties who collectively controlled the Slovak Assembly and, as the head of the largest of these parties, Meciar, who headed the regional government formed following the vote. He quickly appointed a cabinet filled with fellow separatists (and fellow former communists). Equally quickly, with talks on preserving the unity of the state already faltering, the newly elected Slovak National Council, on July 18, 1992, promulgated a Declaration of Sovereignty proclaiming "that the thousand years' striving of the Slovak nation for independence has been accomplished."

If Meciar intended to use this document and the separation talks as a bargaining ploy, he grievously miscalculated. The success of the nationalists in mobilizing Slovak voters around the promise of independence severely restricted Meciar's ability to back away from independence at the last moment. The support for outright independence may have been the strongest in eastern Slovakia, where resentment against the Czech rule of distant Prague was reinforced by the strong and open desire to repay the large Hungarian minority for Slovakia's centuries of abuse at Hungarian hands; however, the public opinion soundings recorded by Comenius University in the run up to the 1992 elections found a sizeable plurality throughout Slovakia in favor of going it alone. Even among the most sophisticated groups in Bratislava, who were aware that independence would bring at least short-term financial costs, significant numbers expressed the belief that it was a step Slovakia had to take if the world was ever to be aware of the Slovaks. Hence, whereas it is true that polls never found a majority in Slovakia in favor of splitting the state, given the momentum of the Slovak nationalist movement, by the summer of 1992 Czech leaders would have had to extend extremely generous concessions to Slovakia to remain a part of the state for Meciar to have been able to backtrack and accept them.

There was never any likelihood that such enticements to stay would be forthcoming. It takes two sides willing to compromise for reconciliation to occur, and at least three factors worked against the Czechs making any major concession to the Slovaks during the negotiations preceding the country's partition. At the top of this list was the fact that on the eve of the split the Slovak economy still lagged behind the Czechs in virtually every area, from its level of urbanization to per capita income ($1,222 in Slovakia versus $1,390 in the Czech Republic) and unemployment figures (10. 6 compared to 2.5 percent in the Czech lands), to life expectancy (66.5 years for men living in Slovakia, 68.1 years for men living in the Czech Republic).[19] In the minds of Czech leaders in Prague, an independent Czech Republic would be able to achieve early admission into the EU; continuing the union with Slovakia would delay that admission and force Prague to spend considerable resources on developing Slovakia, especially its very poor eastern half. In short, union with Slovakia had become an economic inconvenience at a time when Czech voters had seemingly given Klaus and his Civic Democratic Party a mandate of its own: to move swiftly in pursuing the free market economic reforms it had promised in campaigning for office. In Klaus's mind that pursuit necessitated centralized economic planning and implementation, a managerial approach incompatible with the confederate Czechoslovakia being proposed by Meciar.

Furthermore, there were no obvious political benefits apparent to the Czechs in continuing their union with the Slovaks. The German community whose presence made union with the Slovaks mathematically attractive in 1918 was gone. The Slovak counterweight was no longer needed. Likewise, after the 1992 elections there were no partisan political reasons for clinging to Slovakia given the quite different nature of the party systems in the two halves of the state. After the Velvet Revolution, the Czechs developed a system similar to that of most developed democratic states: a class-based system in which the parties primarily differed over the limits they would place on government intervention in the economy and society. By 1992, Slovakia's party system was dominated by nationalist and federalist organizations less concerned with economic policy than redefining Slovakia's political relationship with Prague. Unlike the leaders of Belgium's major political parties when strong ethnonational parties surfaced in that state during the late 1960s and whose organizations had wings in each of Belgium's ethnolinguistic regions, those governing in Prague no longer had regional wings in Slovakia to protect.

Lastly, there was a personal element at play in the Klaus–Meciar talks, which made the Czechs less than enthusiastic about compromising with Slovakia's leaders and which encouraged one former Czech leader to describe their discussions as "negotiations between two bulls."[20] The government in Prague was widely staffed by Czechs who had been in the resistance to communist rule, many spending years in jail or on state work farms. Slovakia's rulers were, overwhelmingly, former communists who had once been a part of the establishment that had jailed them.

Fortunately it also takes two irresolute sides for a civil war to occur: one side willing to fight to leave and another willing to fight to maintain the union. Whether the Slovaks would have fought to leave if Klaus had taken a hard stand against separatism makes for interesting speculation and nothing more. Pointedly, despite President Havel's pleas for a Czechoslovak Plebiscite on the future of the country, within a month neither Klaus nor Meciar had any interest in putting the issue of the union's future to a referendum vote in his region. In part, the referendum approach to dissolution doubtlessly lost appeal because polls in both Slovakia and the Czech lands near the end seemed to indicate a growing minority and perhaps even a majority opposed to partition;[21] however, there were also practical reasons to work around it. The referendum route could have taken as long as 18 months to split the country, during which economic reforms in the Czech lands would have had to be postponed. In any event, the Czechs were no more interested in fighting to keep Slovakia in the union than they were interested in bribing Slovakia into staying. By August 26, 1992, the decision to split the state had been reached. Shortly thereafter, the Klaus–Meciar negotiations concluded by setting an early date for the dissolution of the Czech–Slovak Federal Republic.[22]

Ethnoterritorial Conflict in Slovakia: An Epilogue on "Minority Rule"

The inevitably of Czechoslovakia's dissolution is still being debated, with many tracing its breakup to the unwillingness of the Czechs to embrace a territorial management of their "Slovak problem" and extend federal autonomy to Slovakia either at the inception of the state or following World War II. Certainly by the latter date, the support that the Slovaks had initially given their Germany-bequeathed First Republic should have made it clear that Slovak nationalism could, if ever, no longer be taken lightly. On the other hand, when the final split came it was a combination of factors rather than a single one that prompted the partition solution to Czech–Slovak conflict. The leadership arena was composed of a medley of political opportunists, politically inexperienced, and people with incompatible political agendas. The postcommunist political landscape was an open field cultivated in Slovakia by nationalists with an interest in moving away from union whereas the federalists in Prague were focusing on economic policies and bringing Czechoslovakia into Europe.

Inevitable or not, on January 1, 1993, less than seven months after the summer elections brought the Slovak nationalists to power, the existing state of Czechoslovakia was peacefully partitioned into the Czech and Slovak Republics—a means of managing ethnoterritorial conflict nearly unique in the annals of ethnopolitics.[23] In Slovakia, however, partition did not so much mark the end of often acrimonious ethnopolitics as clear the agenda for a new set of ethnopolitical issues. The Slovaks gained their own state, complete with its own passports, currency (despite the Klaus–Meciar agreement to retain a common currency), border posts, and territorialized, autonomy-demanding ethnic minority in the Hungarian-majority lands of southeastern Slovakia.

These and other accouterments of independence have proven to be a mixed lot for both Slovakia's people and its government. In some instances, the changes have forced painful societal adjustments. The Czechs, for example, refused to permit dual citizenship, so Slovaks along the border had to choose between carrying Czech or Slovak passports in their travels abroad.[24] For many, the disappearance of common radio and television stations and appearance of border posts between the two new Republics were likewise hard to accept, seemingly relegating Czechs and Slovaks to "little more than neighborly partners-in-trade."[25] Sometimes, developments have been both tragic and ironic: for instance, the Slovak nationalist primarily responsible for the creation of border posts literally lost his head because of them when his driver unexpectedly came upon a mile-long trail of trucks backed up at the border and in the resultant accident he was decapitated.

The post-partition relationship between Slovakia's government and its Hungarian minority is both interesting and instructive as a study in ethnoterritorial politics in areas where yesterday's minority has become today's majority. That study, however, begins not with Slovakia's independence but the Velvet Revolution, which devolved significant authority into the hands of the Slovak National Council created when Czechoslovakia's communist regime federalized the country after the Prague Spring of 1968.

Almost immediately after the Velvet Revolution, the governing coalition in Bratislava not only ignored Hungarian demands for local autonomy but enacted a series of laws prejudicial to Slovakia's Hungarian minority. The Hungarian department in the Ministry of Education, charged during communist rule with caring for schools in Hungarian minority areas, was eliminated, and laws were enacted to limit the names of newly baptized babies to those on an officially approved list, which contained negligibly few of Hungarian extraction. Efforts were even made in 1990 to bar the use of the Hungarian language in schools and the workplace before violent demonstrations caused the Slovak National Council to compromise and permit Hungarian-speaking Slovaks to use their native language in public areas where 20 percent or more of the local population is composed of Hungarians.[26]

After independence, with Slovakia's 600,000 Hungarians no longer enjoying even the nominal protection of Prague, "score settling" intensified during Meciar's tenures in office. Not only did the Meciar government reject the Hungarians' demands for local autonomy and language protection, but it instituted a series of policies deeply prejudicial to the interests of Slovakia's Hungarian minority. Road signs were posted only in Slovak even in Hungarian-majority areas, schools that had been operating only in Hungarian were replaced with bilingual schools, and Hungarians found it very difficult to gain jobs in the state's bureaucracy.

Very quickly the conflict between the Slovak government and the spokesmen for the country's Hungarian minority spilled over into Slovakia's relations with its southern neighbor, with Hungary holding up Slovakia's initial application for admission to the Council of Europe until the government in Bratislava agreed to moderate its politics toward the linguistic and economic rights of Slovakia's Hungarians. Pledges were forthcoming, and for the brief period during 1994–95 when Meciar was temporarily out of office the government did moderate its policies. Matters did not change appreciably for Slovakia's Hungarians, however, until the Meciar administration was voted out of office in 1998 and replaced with a governing coalition that included parties representing Slovakia's Hungarian constituency. Subsequently, the need to maintain the support of these parties and to court the international support necessary for Slovakia to enter NATO and join the others on the list for membership in the EU combined to produce a series of policy outputs favorable to the Hungarian community. In January, 2001, for example, the Slovak government adopted the European Charter of Regional and Minority Languages, which permits the use of ethnic minority languages in education, justice, and other areas. Two years later, Bratislava authorized the construction of a Hungarian-language university in the southern Slovakia town of Komarno. Nevertheless, the experience of Slovakia's Hungarians with their Slovak rulers and/or coalition partners does not support the proposition that former minorities are apt to be generous once in office. Quite to the contrary, like the Native Americans and recent foreign immigrants in Quebec, Hungarians in Slovakia have found it expedient to look elsewhere for protection.[27]

CHAPTER EIGHT

Ethnoclass Politics in Former
Czechoslovakia

Ethnoclass conflict in the developed democratic world has customarily involved an economically more prosperous ethnic majority and an economic and ethnic minority underclass. Typically, the latter has been composed of newly arrived immigrants or foreign workers willing to take jobs at the lower end of the economic ladder. These low-status jobs have, in turn, often been interpreted as badges of ethnosocial inferiority, especially by the indigenous, unskilled labor force feeling pressured by their presence. The shift of votes of France's unskilled laborers from the French Communist Party to Le Pen's right-wing National Front reflects this phenomenon; as did the tenacious support that unskilled and poorly educated whites in the southern United States gave the Jim Crow laws discriminating against southern blacks until the civil rights movement in the 1950s and 1960s brought the system of race-based discrimination to its legal conclusion. To French and southern American whites, the color of their skin was the major edge they held over, respectively, North Africans and African Americans willing to work for less.

Ethnicity can also be a basis for discriminating against minorities who are, on average, more economically successful than ethnic majorities. On rare occasions, anti-Romany prejudices in Central Europe fall into this category, but the anti-Semitic sentiment in pre–World War II Central Europe is the definitive example.

Ethnoclass Discrimination and Czechoslovakia's
Jewish Minority

In the United States, the term "ghetto" normally evokes images of inner city slums populated by a mix of ethnic minorities and disease-bearing rodents. In its origin and during the history of nineteenth- and twentieth-century Europe, however, its meaning is more restricted and now shrouded in tragedy and infamy—in *Webster's* words, "in certain European cities, a section to which Jews are, or were, restricted: the word also is applied, often in an unfriendly sense, to any section (of a city) in which many Jews live."[1] Often, these ghettos were anything but slums.

In Prague, the Jewish ghetto continues to testify to the affluence that the Jewish people possessed in many European capitals during the nineteenth century, when men so recently liberated from the ghetto as Kafka, Freud, and Marx played major roles in reshaping Europe's culture, social sciences, economy, and politics.[2] It is one of the most beautiful sections of one of Europe's most remarkably preserved, beautiful cities.

Postcards tinted with age indicate that Bratislava once possessed an equally beautiful, if smaller Jewish ghetto while under Hungarian rule. Today, it is gone, obliterated by a decision in the 1970s to run an intercity highway through its heart and to erect a steel and concrete bridge across the Danube at its edge. Under the bridge on the city's commercial side, a public bus station and beer and tobacco kiosks now occupy the space where the synagogue once stood. The only remaining signs of the ghetto's existence are drawings of the houses that once formed the ghetto, occasionally sketched by local graffiti artists on the bridge's lower beams.

In no part of Czechoslovakia did a sizeable Jewish minority remain when the country split apart.

Historical Background

The migration of Jews from the Middle East to Europe's southern Mediterranean edge and then into northwestern and Central Europe largely occurred between A.D. 70 and 300. By A.D. 300, estimates suggest that nearly three million Jewish immigrants were spread across all parts of the Roman Empire except the British Isles. Discrimination against them followed shortly thereafter.

In 312, Emperor Constantine decreed that Christianity was the official religion of the Roman Empire and inaugurated three centuries of discriminatory laws against Europe's Jews. Barred from holding high public offices or owning slaves, they were consigned to a second-class status by laws prohibiting their marriage to Christians and the conversion to Judaism of non-Jewish peoples. Then, in the late sixth century, the opportunity to prosper was indirectly opened to them. The era began in 591 when Pope Gregory the Great forbade the further, forced conversion of Jews to Christianity, and blossomed nearly two centuries later when Charlemagne (742–814) opened his realm to the Jews. By the time William the Conqueror did the same for England (1066), Jewish immigrants could move freely in much of modern day Italy, Germany, France, and England, albeit as outsiders to the existing feudal and guild systems. On the other hand, because Christianity then prohibited the lending of money with interest, as outsiders they were able to prosper in moneylending and trade as the "financiers of Christian Europe."[3]

Soon thereafter, the combination of the European Crusades in the Holy Land (1095–1272), which triggered a backlash against all non-Christians in

Europe, and the gradual demise of the feudal order, which opened to European Christians the economic roles previously monopolized by Jews, reversed yet again the fortunes of Europe's Jewish communities and eventually prompted their exodus into Eastern Europe. Amidst periodic massacres and the expulsion of Jews throughout the continent, an ecclesiastical council in 1215 issued orders requiring that Jews earmark themselves by wearing special dress, badges, or conical hats. By the fourteenth century, the process of confining Jews in compulsory ghettos had begun.

As the Reformation began to unfold across Europe after 1521, Jews were once again welcomed by countries from which they had previously been expelled. The development was most advanced in Western and Central Europe, where influential Jewish financiers were frequently appointed to ministerial roles ("Court Jews") to provide economic advice to the governments. Capping the trend, in 1780, Emperor Joseph II abolished the badge and permitted Jews throughout the Hapsburg areas of Austria, Hungary, Bohemia, and Moravia to leave the ghetto, attend public schools and universities, and engage in all forms of commerce. To the east, however, where the majority of Europe's Jews lived, discrimination remained the rule.

Developments in the nineteenth century further widened economic opportunities for the Jews in the Hapsburg Empire, and set the modern foundations for anti-Semitism in the current Czech and Slovak Republics. On the one hand, economic development in Europe increased the wealth and status of European Jews. In Austria "the Jews replaced the somewhat jaded Austrian aristocracy as the carriers of culture and the patrons of the arts";[4] in Hungary, whose one million Jews (5 percent of the population) were the most assimilated in Europe prior to World War I, the "Magyarized Hungarian Jews" were "indispensable for preserving Magyar hegemony in outlying areas" of the Empire.[5] On the other hand, because the jobs that they obtained were often in the service of Hapsburg rule, they often incurred great animosity among the local peoples. In the Czech lands, the fact that the Jewish businessmen spoke the language and were identified with the culture and political goals of the German administrators gave them temporary cover; however, in Slovakia and other poor, predominantly rural parts of Hungary's empire, the Jews often *were* the Hungarian administrators, and hated accordingly.[6]

With the rise of nationalism in the Czech and Slovak lands, anti-Semitism intensified. Almost a quarter century before the term "anti-Semitism" was coined in the 1870s by a German journalist, Wilhelm Marr, to describe what he felt to be the justifiable hatred of Jews on the basis of socioeconomic, political, and/or *racial* considerations rather than religion, anti-Jewish riots swept Prague in 1849. More to the point, one of the leading founders of Czech nationalism, Karel Havlicek-Borovsky, described the Jews in 1846 "as 'a separate Semitic nation which lives only incidentally in our [the Czechs'] midst and sometimes understands or speaks our language.' "[7] By the time that growing Czech nationalism had produced a series of clashes with German administrators during the 1890s, and a new round of violent protests against the status of the Jews in Prague and outlying areas, anti-Semitism had become a basic element in Slovak nationalism as well.

Anti-Semitism from the First Czechoslovakia
Republic to Partition

The birth of Czechoslovakia ushered in better days for the Jews living in the Czech lands. The international Zionist movement had supported Masaryk's lobbying efforts during World War I, and when an independent Czechoslovakia was created after the war he reciprocated by advocating full equality for Jews in the new state. To be sure, anti-Jewish protests did occasionally occur in Prague and adjacent Czech areas prior to the German invasion of Czechoslovakia in 1939; however, it was in Slovakia that anti-Semitism seethed unabated as a component of Slovak nationalism, with that region's Jewish population now being viewed as instruments of Czech rule over Slovakia.

Then came the German occupation of Czechoslovakia. As elsewhere in German-controlled Europe, the ghettos once again became the compulsory locales for Jews, and then their transit point for processing. In Czechoslovakia, a model ghetto was quickly erected in the northwest (the Terezin ghetto), with flowers planted and schools constructed for the benefit of touring International Red Cross inspectors. It too soon became a way station for Jews en route to the death camps. By the war's end, nearly 75 percent of Czechoslovakia's interwar Jewish population (277,000 out of 375,000, and 99.5 percent of those sent to the death camps) had been killed, many with the active assistance of the German-backed First Slovak Republic.

Czechoslovakia's Jewish population declined still further when the Communists seized control of the state and three-fourths of the remaining Jews in the country emigrated. Those who remained—less than 20,000 by 1950—soon became the targets of a Soviet-inspired anti-Semitism, and by 1968 their number had further shrunk to less than 12,000.[8]

Although the coup that brought the Communists to power in Czechoslovakia was conceived by communists of Jewish ancestry, most notably Rudolf Slansky, the Soviet Union justified tightening its control over the country by "discovering" Jewish crimes against the state on the part of Slansky and 11 of his cohorts. All were executed in 1952 in the name of protecting the state from the Jewish fifth column inhabiting it. Sixteen years later the Soviets played the "Jewish card" again in retroactively justifying the dispatch of Warsaw Pact forces to Prague to crush the 1968 revolt against communist one-party rule as a necessary measure to protect Czechoslovakia from international Jewry. Shortly thereafter, as Jewish historical sites, synagogues, and libraries were being destroyed or looted throughout the country, the Jewish ghetto in Bratislava was razed to make space for the poured concrete bridge now spanning the Danube.

Anti-Semitism in the Czech Republic and Slovakia

When the Velvet Revolution ended communist rule, less than 12,000 Jews remained in the country, three-fourths of them in the Czech lands. Yet, anti-Semitism remained strong despite the relative absence of Jews.

In the Czech lands, this lingering prejudice has been part of a broader xenophobia aimed at all "outsiders," itself widely explicable in terms of the region's centuries of defeat, invasion, and occupation by foreign conquerors,[9] its absence of contact with the outside world during most of the era of communist rule, and the postcommunist turmoil of moving quickly from one way of life to another. Political opportunists, however, have also contributed to the growth of this anti-other sentiment. As summarized by Ivan Gabal, who conducted a 1996 poll in the Czech Republic that found 81 percent of his respondents viewing the postcommunist influx of foreigners in negative to very negative terms, "People feel as they are falling out of the transition and look for someone to blame. Their 'xenophobia' is encouraged by the political elites, not inherited from communism."[10] The same arguments also partially explain anti-Semitism in Slovakia, a land very harshly treated by foreign conquerors and whose rural poor had far less contact with foreigners under communist rule than the Czechs.

Whatever the explanation for this rise of xenophobia, policies in postcommunist Czechoslovakia's now independent Republics have evinced a lingering anti-Semitism. Thus, for example, despite the protests of international Jewish organizations that it constituted a desecration of holy ground, in the spring of 2000 the Czech Republic's government chose to erect an insurance company headquarters on the site of a thirteenth-century Jewish cemetery in central Prague.[11]

The picture is not uniformly negative. In September, 2000, the Slovak government agreed to pay approximately US$19 million in compensation to Slovak Jews for the property confiscated from them and for their personal suffering during World War II—an amount perhaps equivalent to 10 percent of the value of the property they lost.[12] On the street, though, it is anti-Semitism which still dominates, occasionally tempered by the drawings on Bratislava's bridge but more often punctuated by anti-Semitic graffiti on the sides of its buildings.

Ethnoclass Conflict and the Romany Issue in
Czechoslovakia

The Romany arrived in Europe later than the Jews, but to much the same greeting. In the case of the Romany, however, from the time of their arrival to the present, there have been far fewer momentary upswings in their history and no instances of actual influence.

Historical Background

Known by various names in the countries to and through which they have traveled—Gypsies, Gitanos, Sinti, Romanichal, and "Egyptians"—the Romany people's point of origin and date of arrival in Europe were long disputed. Macedonian legends tell of their presence as early as the time of Alexander the Great (356–325 B.C.); more conventional sources place their arrival in Europe between the ninth and thirteenth centuries. Most recently, linguistic analysis of the Roma language has produced a general consensus that they probably originated in the northwestern area of the Indian subcontinent and departed it *en masse* sometime during the eleventh century, when the spread of Islam into that region encouraged local tribes to move north and west ahead of the invading Muslim conquerors.

By the early 1300s, they had crossed the Himalayas and edged into southeastern and Central Europe. References place them in present-day Slovakia as early as 1322. A century later, they had established a presence throughout most of Central and Western Europe. Local hostility followed, sometimes immediately after their arrival, sometimes later. In the Czech lands, the turning point came in 1541, when a rash of fires swept through Prague. Blamed for the blazes, the Romany were attacked throughout the immediate region. Eight years later, the first anti-Gypsy law was passed in Bohemia and signs depicting hanged gypsies were posted along the border. Shortly thereafter, country after country banned the Roma from their territories.[13]

Violation of the ban became a capital crime in the Czech lands in 1710, when a degree ordered the hanging without trial of adult Roma men found in Czech territory, and the marking of women and boys. Slightly over a decade later, the Austrian-Hungarian Empire controlling the area ordered the extermination of Roma throughout its domain. The 1721 order formed the basis of the Empire's Romany policy for four decades. Then, in 1761, the policy was reversed when Empress Maria Theresa of Hungary initiated Europe's first effort to settle and assimilate the Roma. The implementation of directives such as those forbidding the wearing of Romany attire or the use of Roma language, and authorizing the taking from their parents of Romany children for placement in foster homes, did little to narrow the trust gap between the Romany and their hosts.

The following century brought additional relief to Central Europe's Romany population, including the abolition of the institution of Romany slavery in 1856. Discrimination against and the persecution of the Romany, however, continued into the twentieth century. Hence, within six years of Czechoslovakia's founding, Romany were being tried for cannibalism in Slovakia. Three years later (1927) the government in Prague outlawed Romany nomadism and authorized anew the taking of Gypsy children from their parents as a means of curtailing the propagation of the Romany way of life.

The Romany Holocaust

By the time Hitler targeted the Romany along with the Jews and other "undesirables" for extinction, the Romany had not so much become an underclass in the countries they inhabited as an *outer*-class of migratory people almost always existing apart from the societies housing them. Unlike the Jewish community, many of whom were proficient enough in the language of the rulers to be a part of the Austrian-Hungarian's civil service and contribute to the culture of Vienna, and who frequently learned the language of the areas to which they were sent, the Romany remained largely illiterate in the Czech and Slovak languages, speaking only in a broken fashion that underscored their outsider status. They were thus easy prey once Germany occupied Czechoslovakia, and although the Anne Frank–like tales of citizens risking their lives throughout Europe to shield the Jews may be exaggerated in number, it is interesting that there are no similar stories of local citizens heroically shielding the Romany.[14]

On the other hand, the wartime fate of the Romany in the Czech lands, where they had a longer history of contact with the majority community, was different from that of the Romany in Slovakia, who at the time of World War II were largely concentrated in the underpopulated parts of eastern Slovakia and had comparatively little contact with the Slovak people. The German occupation of Czechoslovakia began in 1939, six years after Hitler had first ordered the forced sterilization of Gypsies in Germany, two years after the processing camps to which the German Roma were initially dispatched had been gradually replaced by extermination camps, and a year after the June, 1938, roundup of all Roma in Germany and Austria. By 1940, the Lety "reeducation" camp had been established in the Czech lands, officially for those with an aversion to work. The relatively small number (approximately 10,000) of Roma residing in Bohemia and Moravia were its principal targets. As the policy shifted from reeducation in labor camps to extermination, Lety became a concentration camp, then a way station to the extermination centers, and finally, for the at least 300 Roma who were executed there *without explicit orders from Berlin*, a death camp.[15] By the war's end, 95 percent of the Romany in the Czech part of the country had been exterminated, a part of the estimated 500,000 Romany who were executed throughout Europe during the war. "Czech postwar authorities added insult to injury by pardoning the camp commandant and the guards, because they considered the Romany low-class citizens and thieves."[16] More than half a century later, most of Lety's memory had been expunged from Czech history as well. Largely unmarked, its locale has become a working pig farm.

In contrast, though persecuted the Romany not only survived but multiplied in the Slovak portion of wartime Czechoslovakia. There, the combination of their remote locale, infrequent contact with Slovaks, and the autonomy that the Nazis permitted the First Slovak Republic to exercise provided the Romany with a degree of insulation from the fate of their brethren in the Czech lands. Indeed, the relative safety available there drew Romany to Slovakia from neighboring states, and by the war's end the number of Roma in Slovakia had grown to over 100,000.[17]

The Romany under Communist Rule

The ascent of communist rule in postwar Central Europe had a profound if mixed impact on Central Europe's large (now at least 6,000,000) Roma population, and one that has outlasted the reign of communism.[18]

On the positive side, because communist regimes treated the Roma as socially underdeveloped communities, communism offered greater educational opportunity to Romany children and, in guaranteeing employment to all, poked at least minor holes in the "invisible" curtain that had often made it impossible for the Romany to find jobs in Central European countries.[19] Literacy increased, as did the standard of living for those with skills. On the other hand, in several areas the policies inaugurated by communist regimes have had a long-term deleterious effect on the Romany's relationship with their host societies.

First, the implementation of a command economy was accompanied by the curtailment or prohibition of many shady-but-technically-legal market economy occupations from which the Roma had traditionally derived income: for example, fortune telling, playing music in restaurants, and merchandising in used clothes.

Second, and even more disruptive to the Roma's traditional way of life, postwar communist regimes closed their borders to the West and, to a lesser extent, to one another. They thus halted the traditional, nomadic lifestyle of numerous Roma tribes and produced the buildup in the individual states of Central Europe of a permanent Gypsy population whose size has steadily grown more rapidly that than of the indigenous communities.

Finally, inside their borders, Czechoslovakia and other Central European countries committed themselves to a comprehensive effort to assimilate the Romany. In Czechoslovakia, the process involved a two-prong attack on the Romany culture, beginning with a 1958 decree, which prohibited individuals from wandering through the country but which did nothing to ameliorate the reaction of the Czechs and Slovaks to the impact of the law. As one analyst noted:

> Prior to this time the Government had been able to keep the Gypsies out of the sight . . . by tolerating the wandering Gypsies and shunting sedentary Gypsies to slums on the outskirts of cities and towns. The two groups were now expected to coexist, however unrealistic an expectation this was.[20]

With the mobility of the target population frozen, the second part of the assimilation process could be implemented: education and resettlement policies designed to integrate the Romany into the host societies. Frequently harsh in nature and heavyhanded in their execution by biased local authorities, these policies ranged from compulsory education, which was usually meted out in segregated schools, where the Roma children were frequently consigned to remedial learning classes because of their lack of fluency in the national languages, to the banning of Romany associations and the disproportionate targeting of Romany women for sterilization.

The heart of the program was on the resettlement and employment front. In 1959, the Czechoslovakian government drew up an elaborate plan linking these two areas and began a policy designed to move the Roma from their substandard rural housing in Slovakia to state housing throughout the industrialized Czech lands. The policy was meant simultaneously to fulfill an edict mandating that Romany housing be made to conform to the standards governing the rest of the population, to disperse them in order to undercut their capacity to perpetuate their culture, and to help the country's economy by channeling low-cost Romany labor into the jobs vacated by the German people who were expelled after World War II. Eventually, much of the resettlement policy had to be tabled because of the excessive costs involved in relocating tens of thousands across the length of the country, the financial load placed on the local governments charged with providing them with adequate housing, and the not-in-my-backyard resistance that the policy encountered in the resettlement areas.[21] By then, the policy had already heightened tensions between the Czechs and Slovaks on the one hand and the Roma on the other as Roma enclaves grew in the country's urban areas and the local populations complained that the Roma were getting preferential treatment under the government's housing and employment policies.[22]

The Velvet Revolution, the Velvet Divorce, and the Romany

With the fall of communism and the overnight disappearance of the limited protection that communism had given the Romany, resentment against them boiled into the open in much of Central Europe, frequently resulting in violence directed against them in a democratizing region whose citizens continued to view them with a mixture of open hostility and prejudice. At the same time, the Roma's post-partition status in the former Czechoslovakia has not been without a few gains.

As the following tables indicate, both before and after the Velvet Divorce, governments in the Czech Republic and Slovakia have enacted legislation giving the Romany legal status, although both have pointedly stopped short of passing the affirmative action or antidiscrimination measures sought by the local Romany and endorsed by outside actors such as the

EU and UN. Other bright spots have included such gestures as a call for an end to racism in Slovakia by the speaker of the Slovak Parliament (2000), the indictment of an extremist Slovak member of parliament for inciting racial hatred (also 2000), and the Slovak government's commitment to translate Slovakia's Constitution, Criminal Code, Civil Code, and Labor Code into the Roma language (2002). Nevertheless, on balance, as tables 8.1 and 8.2 indicate, the darker side of the ledger has dominated.

The entries on the negative side of the ledger begin with the weakness of the self-help option for Roma in former Czechoslovakia, as throughout Central Europe. Relatively few in number in any region, often living in

Table 8.1   The Romany in the Czech Republic since the Velvet Revolution

Date	Development
1989–92	Roma benefit from legislation officially recognizing the 200,000–300,000 Roma in the Czech lands as a minority entitled to their own political and cultural associations
1992	June: skinhead attack on Gypsy family during eviction proceedings in Brno sparks riots; 200 armed Gypsies protest in town square of Czech Republic's second-largest city
1993	January 1: partition. Czech Republic immediately passes a citizenship law based on parental heritage; Slovaks with two years residency in Czech lands eligible for Czech citizenship; Romany lacking documents or with criminal records ineligible
	January 20: eviction of Romany from illegally held apartments in northern Bohemia begins under new local residency laws aimed at curtailing migration of Slovak Romany into area
1995	May: brutal murder of Romany construction worker by four bat-wielding youth in front of his family prompts Prime Minister Klaus to urge a crack down on racially motivated crimes
1996	National poll finds 69% of respondents harbor ill feelings toward Gypsies. Discrimination by private citizens even in places of public accommodation is common
	August: panhandling law enacted to limit begging in central Prague is widely interpreted as anti-Romany in intent
1996–98	Escalating anti-Romany violence in Ostrava and Olomouc catches other "dark-skinned" foreigners in attacks; public outcry missing
	October 1997: escalating crime leads to tightening of immigration law
	June 1998: depressed industrial town of Usti and Labem erects a wall separating its Czech citizens from Roma tenements. Despite widespread criticism wall is not removed until October 1999
	September 1998: number of Romany seeking asylum abroad continues to increase with 1,000 from Czech and Slovak Republics arriving in Britain
1999	March: in a celebrated case involving the death of a Romany woman, a Czech court reduces the charge to hooliganism and the sentence to 15 months
2000	Czech government forms a Human Rights Council to propose legislation amid still mounting "skinhead" violence against foreigners and Romany
2002	Spring: Roma establish neighborhood patrols to protect themselves from skinhead attacks.
	May: several parties running for office adopt anti-Romany planks pertaining to immigration and forcing the assimilation of Romany; most notorious of these, however, receives only 1% of vote
	October: Czech Republic invited to join enlarged European Union

Table 8.2   The Romany in the Slovak Republic since the Velvet Revolution

Date	Development
1989–92	Velvet Revolution to the Velvet Divorce: Roma benefit from legislation passed in Czechoslovakia, which officially recognizes the 350,000–400,000 Roma in Slovakia as a minority entitled to their own political and cultural associations, and with the same status as other minorities
1993	January 1: partition July: village of Spisske Podhradie imposes curfew on Romanies and "other suspicious persons"; regulation is subsequently nullified by Slovak National Council
1994	January: Romany leaders in Kosice criticize ethnic Hungarian parties for intentionally increasing tension between Roma and Slovak Hungarians
1995	Union of Romani Political Parties formed
1997	August: Slovak Deputy Premier Jozef Kalman blames Romany for not doing enough to improve their position in Slovakia. November: Slovak Romany seeking asylum in France refuse offer to return home
1998	September: number of Romany seeking asylum abroad continues to increase; Office of the Plenipotentiary for Roma Constitutions established and charged with implementing government policy vis-à-vis the Roma
1999	Instances of racial beatings lead to decrease in number of foreign students seeking admission to Slovak educational facilities
2000	September: number of Romany seeking asylum in Czech Republic jumps from 13 in 1999 to 538 during the first 8 months of 2000
2001	January: number of racial beatings again increasing in Slovakia
2002	June: Slovak police officer involved in gang attack on Roma in Kosice July: in a reversal of policy, Comenius University decides not to lower entrance exams to make it easier for Roma to gain admission July 3: government refuses to discuss a draft law to prohibit discrimination based on race, age, religion, and sexual or political orientation, though encouraged to pass it by EU officials. September 25: announcement that Slovakia will be invited to join NATO October: Slovakia invited to join the enlarged EU
2003	January–March: exodus of Romany from eastern Slovakia to Czech Republic exceeds 20,000 April: government considers wide-ranging plan to ease conditions in Romany community May: two high-ranking officers in Slovak army are fined 125 Euros each (approximately US$150 at the time) for arguing that 97% of the country's Romany "are unable to adapt and should be shot"
2004	January–February: Slovakia joins EU, begins drafting required antidiscrimination law; deploys 2,000 police and soldiers to Eastern Slovakia to quell rioting by Romany protesting welfare cuts

small, isolated areas, and internally divided into numerous clans and political associations, they project a weaker voice in political processes than their numbers should allow. For example, in a recent parliamentary election in Slovakia, a country where they constitute between 8 and 10 percent of the population and 4 percent of the eligible vote, the largest Romany party polled only 0.29 percent of the vote, a "catastrophe for the Roma" in the words of the party's chair.[23]

Beyond the instances of abuse detailed in tables 8.1 and 8.2 lies the daily treatment that the Romany receives at the hands of the majority populations. More than a decade after partition, the citizens of Slovakia and the Czech Republic continue to harbor deep prejudices against the Romany, and the latter continue to face persistent discrimination by both private citizens and public officials. Beauty queen contestants seeking the crown of Miss Czech Republic may no longer respond to the question of what they want to do with their life by answering that they want to become town mayor so they can "cleanse" their city of "dark-skinned" residents,"[24] and Slovak demagogues may no longer preach (as Meciar once did) that the best way to handle a gypsy is in a small courtyard with a long whip; however, in both republics, the local police remain almost openly hostile to the Roma and the judicial systems remain disproportionately harsh on any Romany charged with crime.

Outside the justice system, Romany children are still taught in segregated schools and remedial classes, and Romany adults face discrimination in terms of jobs (the Roma have an estimated 70 percent unemployment rate) and housing, and are consequently forced to live in slum conditions with deleterious effects on their health.[25] Meanwhile, in former Czechoslovakia's rapidly privatizing sectors, the Romany are routinely turned away from restaurants and other places of public accommodation. Local politicians and business owners justify their action on the grounds that the Romany commit a grossly disproportionate amount of certain types of property crimes and that the Romany have steadfastly resisted the efforts made to assimilate them. They also continue to cling to a language and lifestyle that places them nearly as far outside of mainstream Czech and Slovak culture as the North Africans' Muslim way of life in France separates them from the culture and lifestyle of the French. Hence, the arguments made to justify the treatment that Romany receive are not entirely without foundation, although depending upon one's point of view the high incidence of crime attributed to the Romany can be seen as either a reason for discrimination against them or the result of their inability to gain honest employment. Whatever the justification most of the policies and practices aimed at the Romany fall far short of the human rights standards expected of advanced democratic societies.

The issue most troubling to outsiders remains the acts of violence against the Roma. In truth, the most outrageous of these acts have not been especially numerous—one or two per year in the Slovak and Czech Republics combined, out of a population of more than 15 million Czechs and Slovaks and 750,000 or more Romany. It would thus be possible to dismiss them as just another facet of antiforeigner sentiment were it not for two aspects of anti-Gypsy violence. First, there is a personal element in the discrimination against the Romany that separates it from more generic xenophobia and acts of violence against the "dark-skinned residents" of the former

Czechoslovakia. Second, despite the official condemnation that the worst of the anti-Romany violence has produced, many of these acts have either involved the police as perpetrators, or a crime that the police have been slow to investigate, and/or the criminal justice system lenient in meting out punishment to the convicted offenders.

The Romany Issue, Ethnopolitics, and the International System

Given the wide diffusion of anti-Romany prejudice throughout the former Czechoslovakia, discrimination against the Roma needs no Le Pen–like public figure to catalyze it. In fact, single-issue, anti-Gypsy parties have done poorly in Czech and Slovak Republic elections. Those involved in policy processes are well aware of anti-Roma sentiment, however, and pander to it. The most enlightened of these leaders, therefore, have tread lightly in proposing pro-Romany legislation that would enhance Romany rights or their visibility in Czech and Slovak societies. Weak in power themselves, the Romany have consequently been forced to look abroad for allies to advance their interests.

Unfortunately for the Romany, the international community has had little success in persuading Prague or Bratislava to be more proactive on behalf of the Roma minorities, although it has been very vocal on the matter. In August of 2000, for example, the United Nations Committee on the Elimination of Racial Hatred urged the Czech Republic to end the pervasive discrimination against Gypsies in housing, education, and employment and prosecute those inciting racial hatred. Similarly, EU administrators once stressed that Slovakia's treatment of its Romany would be an important factor affecting that country's application for admission to the EU. Others joining the chorus have included: the Council of Europe, which issued a report in 2000 attacking intolerance against the Roma in Slovakia; the European Parliament, which as late as October, 2000, found it necessary to pass a specific resolution calling for Slovakia to improve the status of its Roma and other minorities; the United States Congress, whose Committee monitoring compliance with the Helsinki Accords has persistently noted in its annual reports the Czech Republic's ill-treatment of the Roma; Amnesty International, whose 2001 report bemoaned the pattern of racist attacks against Roma in the Czech Republic and the failure of the courts and police to intervene; and even the World Bank, whose April 22, 2002, report noted the continuing high poverty level and welfare needs of the nearly half a million Slovak Roma.

Despite the numerous outsiders interested in the Roma's well-being, the Romany nonetheless lack an outside protector of the type that Slovakia's Hungarian minority has in Hungary; that is, an entity dedicated to vouchsafing their welfare and security. In 1974, Indira Gandhi formally recognized India as the Roma's point of origin, but India has never assumed the role of championing the Romany cause. It has other and more pressing issues. The same can be said for the UN. In a world where India and

Pakistan rattle nuclear sabers over Kashmir, multiple points in the Middle East threaten to erupt into war, and weapons of mass destruction continue to proliferate, the Romany practically fall off the UN's radar screen.

As for the others, they too have their priorities, and however much they may genuinely lament the treatment of the Roma in former Czechoslovakia and elsewhere, the continued plight of the Romany people has not prevented them from pursing *their* objectives. Thus, despite half a decade of Congressional reports critical of the treatment of the Romany in the Czech Republic, an American government committed to enlarging NATO extended an invitation to Prague in the late 1990s, just as post-Meciar Slovakia was placed on the list of eligible countries in 2002. In similar fashion, an EU finally eager to pursue enlargement in 2002 placed both the Czech Republic and Slovakia on its list of countries eligible to join in 2004, in spite of nearly a decade of reviews by international bodies universally critical of their treatment of their Romany minorities.

CHAPTER NINE

Ethnopolitics in Former Czechoslovakia in a Comparative Perspective

It is easier to compare Czechoslovakia's policies toward its ethnoclass Romany and Jewish minorities with the experiences of these communities in other Central European countries than Czechoslovakia's solution to its territorialized Czech–Slovak conflict to the responses of others to eth-noterritorial demands elsewhere in the postcommunist world. Most of these states have continued discriminatory practices toward the Romany despite a decade of international admonishment and urging to do other-wise. In dealing with their ethnoterritorial minorities, however, many have not only taken paths different from the partition route to which Czech and Slovak leaders gravitated but also from the modes of conflict management most frequently used to accommodate restive, territorialized minorities in Western Europe. Thus, while there are instances of postcommunist governments attempting to placate minority groups with enhanced eco-nomic assistance, devolutionary schemes, and consociational arrangements, "management" devices in the postcommunist world have also entailed civil wars, international peacekeeping forces, internationally monitored elec-tions, and outside overseers of minority rights.[1]

Ethnoterritorial Conflict in the Postcommunist World

Ethnonational Conflict in the Former Soviet Union

Although the Soviet Union broke apart peacefully, with its various union republics emerging as sovereign states during 1991–92, its disintegration did not follow the Czechoslovakia model of mutual consent. Moscow would have preferred to have preserved the Soviet Union, but when the governments of its union republics announced their intention to leave, Gorbachev could neither interest them in the confederate-like Commonwealth of Independent States (CSI), which he proposed in a last minute effort to preserve the Soviet Union, nor physically prevent them from seceding *en masse*. Further, the USSR's decomposition did not end ethnopolitical conflict in the former Soviet Union, a state that once contained over 150 different ethnic groups, politically organized in a hierarchical fashion based on their size, territoriality, and degree of national consciousness, with the union republics at the top of the pyramid.[2] Even in those states that emerged from the union republics with relatively high degrees of ethnic homogeneity, territorialized ethnic divisions have frequently produced violent conflicts between the majority and minority populations that have retarded the democratization effort and have sometimes spilt into the international system. These include the following.

The Nagorno-Karabakh Conflict

The Nagorno-Karabakh enclave of Armenians living in the mountains of Azerbaijan generated considerable tension inside the Soviet Union between Armenia (93 percent Armenian) and Azerbaijan (90 percent Azerbaijan) from the beginning of the Soviet system. The area was transferred to Azerbaijan by Moscow in 1923 as a part of Moscow's efforts to consolidate Soviet control of the border regions following a 1918–20 war between independent Armenia and Azerbaijan over Karabakh and other territory. Soon thereafter, the enclave's predominantly Christian, Armenian population fell under the discriminatory control of Muslim Azerbaijani administrators.

The long-simmering conflict reignited during the mid–1980s when Gorbachev liberalized political dialogue. Armenian nationalists used their new freedom of expression to renew long-standing demands that Nagorno-Karabakh be returned to Armenia and that until then the Armenian language be given legal priority in education and public affairs in the region. By 1989, both Armenia and Azerbaijan were openly discriminating against the minorities inside their borders. Three years later, when an Armenian missile shot down an Azerbaijani helicopter during the last moments of the Soviet Union, war was only averted by Russian diplomatic intervention. Subsequently, Armenian separatists have been slow in subscribing to the 1998 ceasefire agreement negotiated for the region. In fact, in 1998, the president of Armenia was forced to resign for making concessions to Azerbaijan in peace talks designed to resolve the conflict.[3]

Separatism in Georgia

Russia has been drawn even more deeply into the process of intercommunal conflict management in the former Union Republic of Georgia. There, too, the ethnoterritorial conflicts long predate the collapse of the Soviet system. Moreover, it was Gorbachev's *glasnost* reforms that opened the door to increasingly open rivalry between contending ethnonationalist movements in a Soviet republic. In the case of Georgia, this high-stakes sparring involved the Georgians, whose nationalist movement against Moscow reemerged in the mid–1980s, along with the nationalist movements against Georgian rule among the minority Abkhazians of northwest Georgia and the Ossetian minority in the south. By 1990, Communist rule was on the way out in Georgia. nationalist spokesmen had assumed leadership positions at the head of all three national communities, ethnic violence was becoming commonplace in Abkhazia and South Ossetia, and South Ossetia had declared its independence. Over the next two years, while the Soviet Union was collapsing and Georgia fought a war to prevent South Ossetia's secession, matters deteriorated further. When the Georgian ultra-nationalist Zviad Gamsakhurdia was ousted from office, a mini-civil war erupted between factions inside the Georgia community that ended only when Eduard Shevardnadze was returned to power in 1992; however, no sooner did the fighting end in South Ossetia in a Russian-brokered ceasefire than Georgia invaded its Abkhazia region to quell the ethnopolitical conflict there between the Abkharians and the Georgian minority in the region. By 1993, that war had ended with essentially a Abkhazian military victory, which left the Abkhazians in control of the province and provoked an exodus of Georgian refugees from the area. The introduction of a Russian-led (nominally Commonwealth of Independent States) peacekeeping force and reintroduction of a UN observer force the following year ended neither this exodus nor the fighting between ethnic Georgians and the Abkhazians.[4] Ten years later, Shevardnadze was again gone but Russian troops were still present, Russia's influence on events had become a source of tension between Moscow and Georgia's new government, and separatist movements still controlled large sections of South Ossetia and Abkharia.[5]

The Civil War in Chechnya

Although 82 percent of Russia's population is composed of ethnic Russians, Russia continues to house numerous, territorialized minorities acquired during Czarist Russia's state-building period. Even before the Soviet Union's collapse, the desire of many of these for ever-greater freedom from Moscow's control occasionally forced Moscow to tinker with the subcategories of autonomous republics and autonomous zones inside the large Russian federation which formed the Soviet Union's core. With the breakup of the Soviet Union, ethnonationalism surged in many of these areas, in some cases leading to the emergence of low-grade civil wars necessitating the intervention of the Russian Army. The most serious of these has raged at the southern tip of the Russian Federation, just north of Azerbaijan and east of Georgia in Russian Chechnya.

Acquired by Russia in the first half of the nineteenth century and only secured by Moscow after nearly a quarter century of aggressive resistance from Islamic warriors in Chechnya and neighboring Dagestan, Russia's Chechen region attained Autonomous Republic status in 1922 and, in 1934, became a part of the Cheneno-Ingush Republic. The area remained restless, however, and concern during World War II over the political loyalty of the Chechens led Stalin to deport them from their homeland. It was not until the 1950s that they were allowed to return, but throughout their years in exile Chechen national identity remained strong.

In 1992, as the Soviet system unraveled and Russian troops were withdrawn from the area, Chechnya declared itself an independent Republic. Two years later, the civil war began when Russian troops shelled the separatist rebels and occupied the region. Chechen freedom fighters, aided by al-Qaeda forces, retaliated by bombing apartment complexes and other civilian targets in Moscow and elsewhere in Russia. That activity continues, including the September, 2004, attack, which resulted in more than 300 children dying when a hostage situation unraveled at a school in Beslan in the North Ossetia area of the Russian Federation.

Civil War and the Collapse of Yugoslavia

The former Soviet Union and portions of its Central European empire are peppered with conflicts of the Chechen, Georgian, and Nagorno-Karabakh ilk. In nearly every instance, the same combustible combination of elements are discernible: religious, linguistic, and other factors reinforcing ethnonational lines of cleavage (the Muslim Chechens and the non–Muslim Russians); simmering national grievances; often fueled by relatively recent moments of bloodletting, and opportunist leaders inciting minority ethnonational communities into pursuits of independence.

These elements, albeit with a twist, are partially evident in the most violent example of separatist politics in postcommunist Europe, Yugoslavia's bloody descent into multiple civil wars, and especially in the former Yugoslav province of Bosnia-Herzegovina, where Muslims, Serbs, and Croats were to a degree territorially intermingled and none of these groups represented a majority.

Meltdown: The Wars in Slovenia, Croatia, and Bosnia

Table 9.1 briefly chronicles both the origins and collapse of the Yugoslav federation. At their core, the conflicts that ripped Yugoslavia apart were rooted in deep grievances separating ethnonational communities often claiming the same soil as their motherland. Differences in economic status also entered into the picture, often reinforcing the cultural differences separating Yugoslavia's national groups and providing the nationalist leaders of the communities with additional justification for secession. Slovenia, for example, was not just Yugoslavia's richest union republic but one of the richest regions in Central Europe, with an average per capita income that is more than three times that of Serbia's. Slovene nationalists could therefore argue not only that an independent Slovenia would be economically viable but that as long as Slovenes remained in Yugoslavia they would be subsidizing their Serbian masters. A similar situation prevailed in Croatia, also a substantially richer republic than Serbia. Meanwhile, Bosnia and, inside Serbia, Kosovo were far poorer than Serbia as a whole—a state of affairs, their nationalists argued, that reflected Serbian indifference to their poverty and hostility to their Muslim culture. Finally, in all of Yugoslavia's national communities, opportunists played a major role in moving their peoples away from accommodative politics and toward open conflict.[6]

Among these opportunists, the central figure was the president of the Federal Republic of Yugoslavia (FRY), Slobodan Milosevic. Unlike Vaclav Klaus, the Czech prime minister who responded to Meciar's threats of secession with almost indifference, Milosevic was a former communist who resurrected his political career as a militant Serbian nationalist fighting to retain Serb control over historical Serbian lands (e.g., Kosovo) and those regions with large Serbian minorities. He was therefore quick to champion the demands of Serbian autonomists in Croatia and the cause of the Serbian minority in Bosnia, and to become increasingly embroiled in the interethnic conflicts in both union republics. Nonetheless, it was outside parties—in particular, Germany—whose advice pushed Yugoslavia into civil wars.

The unraveling began in early 1991, when Western diplomats encouraged Croatia and Slovenia to secede under the mistaken belief that Milosevic's problems with the ongoing insurrection in Kosovo would force him to accept their departure as a *fait accompli*.[7] Instead, when they declared their independence, Belgrade responded militarily. The resultant war against the Slovenes lasted only ten days before Belgrade acquiesced to Slovenia's independence, in part because Slovene units in the Yugoslav army defected to fight on Slovenia's side but also because the negligible number of Serbs in Slovenia and its location in Yugoslavia's extreme northwest made it difficult for Milosevic to mobilize support for the war as a defense of Greater Serbia.[8]

The war between Belgrade and Croatia lasted longer given Croatia's larger Serbian population (11.5 percent), and it did not wind down until Belgrade's large-scale offensive during the winter of 1991–92 left it in control of a third of Croatia. Even then, with a UN-negotiated ceasefire in place and Croatia as well as Slovenia and Bosnia admitted to the UN as sovereign states, the battle between Serbian paramilitaries backed by Belgrade, and the Croatian government in Zagreb continued until the 1995 Dayton Accord ended the first round of civil wars in what was once Yugoslavia.

In the meantime, the center of the conflict shifted to Bosnia, where Serbs constituted nearly a third of the population. Paramilitary units and acts of atrocity quickly proliferated on all sides. By the time the fighting ended, at least 250,000 Bosnian-Muslims had died in the war, millions of Bosnian residents had become refugees, and the ferocity of the various ethnic-cleansing processes had prompted the international community to create a tribunal to prosecute those responsible for the crimes against humanity committed during Yugoslavia's civil wars. The war also produced the worst instance of atrocity since World War II in July, 1995, when Serbs overran the UN-created "safe haven" of Srebrenica and massacred at least 8,000 Muslim men and boys in front of an under-armed, 450-man Dutch peacekeeping force.

It was the brazenness of the attack on Srebrenica and the almost simultaneous Serbian shelling of Tuzla and Sarajevo, two other UN-designated "safe" cities, which finally prompted NATO to intervene with sufficient military force to establish a peace that could be kept by the international forces deployed in Bosnia. By December, the leaders of all communities involved in the conflict had agreed to the Dayton peace plan, which ended the war and provided the legal basis for establishing, under international tutelage, self-governing institutions in Bosnia. It was clear at the time, though, that the peace-building process was going to be a long one, especially on the refugee repatriation front. Two of the signatories of the pact, Croatia's leader Franjo Tudjman and Milosevic, vigorously opposed the repatriation provision in the Dayton Accord in the hope of maintaining those territories under Croatian and Serbian control as ethnically cleansed as the wars had left them.[9] Progress is hard won still, delayed by both corruption within the fledgling new state and the electoral success of the ethnonational parties representing each of Bosnia's ethnic communities in most of the democratic elections that have been held there under international supervision, beginning with the local elections of October, 1997.[10]

Balkan Dominos: The Conflicts in Kosovo and Macedonia

The hand of outside parties is also apparent in the escalation of ethnic conflict in Serbia's Kosovo province and, later, in Macedonia. In both instances, though, their intervention occurred against a backdrop of the same factors that have shaped ethnoterritorial conflict elsewhere in post-communist Europe.

In Kosovo, both the heart of an ancient Serb empire *and* the birthplace of nineteenth-century pan-Albanian nationalism, the combustible materials revolved around the Albanization and Islamization of the province while under Ottoman rule (see table 9.1). By 1990, Kosovo had become 90 percent Albanian Muslim but had lost its right to provincial autonomy and was under the direct control of Belgrade's highly nationalist, Serbian government of Milosevic, with its commitment to keep Kosovo forever Serbian. After agreeing at Dayton to abandon Belgrade's claims on the Serbian populations of Bosnia, Croatia, and Slovenia, it was not a promise that Milosevic could politically afford to break.

On the Albanian side, by the mid-1990s, the principal actor had become the Kosovo Liberation Army (KLA), an outlawed paramilitary organization no more inclined to compromise on the issue of an independent Kosovo than Milosevic. While Milosevic concentrated on harassing the Kosovo Albanians to the point where many would choose to leave the province, the KLA focused on attacking Yugoslav personnel in Kosovo in the hope of provoking Belgrade into so overreacting that the international community would intervene on behalf of the Kosovo autonomists. It took a few years but the strategy worked.

Widely criticized for having delayed too long before responding to the carnage occurring in Bosnia, in 1998, President Clinton's administration began to press Belgrade to restore Kosovo's autonomy and permit the

Table 9.1 Yugoslavia: The Construction and Deconstruction of a State

1389	Ottoman Turks defeat Serbian empire at Battle of Kosovo and rule area until World War I dissolves Ottoman Empire; in interim, heart of old Serbian empire in Kosovo becomes heavily Albanian-speaking and Muslim
19th c.	Nineteenth-century pan-Slavic movements, chiefly in Serbia
1878	Serbia, including Montenegro, achieves independence from Ottoman rule
1901–	Pursuit of a Greater Serbia involving Ottoman and Albanian lands begins
1908	Austria-Hungary annexes Bosnia
1912–13	Balkan Wars; Serbia gains northern and central Macedonia
1914	Serb assassinates Austrian Archduke Ferdinand, igniting World War I
1918	Kingdom of the Serbs, Croats and Slovenes formed following World War I
1929	King Alexander I renames country Yugoslavia, assumes authoritarian powers
1934	King Alexander I assassinated in France by Croatian separatists
1941–45	World War II intensifies Serbian–Croatian animosity as Germany creates a puppet Croatian state and Croats settle old grievances against Serbs
1945–47	Federal Republic of Yugoslavia established; Kosovo is a part of Serbia
1966–71	Secret Police dismantled; nationalist protests grow in Kosovo and Croatia
1974	New Constitution gives autonomy to Kosovo inside Serbia
1980	Tito dies; nationalism increases within all the groups composing the state
1989	Serbian nationalist Milosevic assumes power; Kosovo loses autonomy
1990	Anticommunist revolutions sweep Central Europe; 4 Yugoslav republics elect noncommunist governments; Kosovo Albanians create separatist "government"
1991	Western countries encourage Croatia and Slovenia to secede
1991–92	Four Republics secede; Macedonia exits peacefully but civil wars follow secession of Slovenia, Croatia, and Bosnia
1992	UN creates peacekeeping forces for Croatia (February), Bosnia (September), and Macedonia (December); Yugoslavia expelled from UN for aiding Serb aggressors in Bosnia
1993	Kosovo Liberation Army forms; UN authorizes creation of an international War Crimes Tribunal and six "safe havens" in Bosnia
1994	Croatians and Bosnian Muslims agree to form joint federation in Bosnia
1995	May: United States agrees to permit use of ground forces to protect peacekeepers July: Serbs launch major offensive against safe areas August: Croatia launches offensive against its rebellious Serb region; Serbs attack Sarajevo and NATO responds November 21: Presidents of Bosnia, Croatia, and Serbia reach an agreement to end war in Bosnia (Dayton Accord)
1997	Bosnia holds local elections under international supervision; KLA operations against Yugoslav forces in Kosovo grow
1997	Albania implodes, making weapons available to KLA
1998	Bosnia elects national government, nationalist parties do well; ethnic cleansing begins in Kosovo, producing nearly 300,000 Kosovar refugees
1999	January 28: NATO notifies Milosevic that it is prepared to use military forces to halt the ethnic cleansing in Kosovo March 24: NATO begins 78-day air offensive; the number of refugees soars June: hostilities end; UN authorizes creating Kosovo Stabilization Force (KFOR) and UN Administration Mission in Kosovo
2000	October: municipal elections in Kosovo; voters support Kosovar moderates
2000–1	Safety of Kosovo's Serbs becomes issue. Kosovar Albanians attack Macedonia in defense of its Albanian minority's rights.
2001	Assembly election held in Kosovo; high refugee out-of-country vote

Continued

Table 9.1 Continued

2002	National elections held in Bosnia; nationalists again do well; Kosovo local elections draw light out-of-country refugee vote
2003	February–March: FRY dissolved in favor of looser Montenegro–Serbia relationship; international peacekeeping forces remain deployed in Bosnia, Kosovo, and Macedonia. In Montenegro presidency election 2 separatists win combined 95% of vote
2004	March riots in Kosovo force NATO to increase the size of its peacekeeping forces

deployment there of an international force to guarantee the safety of its Albanian populace. In fact, although rumors of Serbs committing atrocities in Kosovo were rampant, there was little evidence to support these rumors and considerable evidence that the acts of political violence being committed there were not one-sided.[11] Even the increasing deployment of Serbian military personnel in Kosovo during the mid-to-late 1990s was primarily reported as Belgrade's response to KLA attacks on its forces in Kosovo. By then, however, the atrocities committed during the war in Bosnia had also been well reported, and the most famous of these had been executed by the Serbs. Highly exaggerated stories of Serbian massacres of Kosovo Albanians were thus given credence, especially when Belgrade's efforts to crush the KLA produced a steady stream of Albanian refugees during the winter of 1998–99.

Even though each threat of NATO intervention on behalf of Kosovo Albanians emboldened the KLA into hardening its demand for Kosovo's independence and Serbs as well as Albanians were fleeing the province to escape the fighting, the Clinton administration placed full blame on Milosevic. Consequently, when at a March, 1999, summit Milosevic refused to cede sovereignty over Kosovo to an international peacekeeping force, U.S.-led NATO forces initiated a 78-day air campaign against Yugoslav targets to force his compliance. Matters quickly degenerated even further. NATO's bombing of factories, railroads, and communications facilities in Serbia provoked the Serbian forces in Kosovo into escalating their attacks on the province's Muslim Albanians, who NATO had left unprotected when it ruled out deploying ground forces as a part of its campaign. Then, when the war ended and the Albanian refugees returned, the absence of a NATO force in place to prevent revenge attacks on Kosovo's Serb and Romany minorities triggered a massive exodus of non-Albanians fleeing the province.[12]

The absence of a NATO ground force in Kosovo when the conflict ended also precluded NATO from disarming the KLA at that time. Two years later, KLA militants initiated fighting between the Albanian minority and the majority population in Macedonia, the only independent part of former Yugoslavia which had hitherto escaped civil war despite the presence of elements conducive to interethnic conflict. Invariably the Orthodox Macedonians controlled economic and political power and enjoyed a living standard visibly better than that of Macedonia's Albanian Muslims, who possessed a paramilitary liberation force committed to moving them into a "Greater Albania." Nonetheless, the fighting that raged in the mountains along Macedonia's border with Kosovo in the early months of 2001 was clearly instigated by KLA guerrillas, albeit in collusion with allies in the Albanian National Liberation Army (NLA) in Macedonia.[13] Once started, the conflict between the NLA and Macedonian security forces gained momentum and produced yet another stream of refugees from a wartorn area of the former Yugoslavia until, months later, international mediators brokered an uneasy peace in the area. Subsequently, Macedonia's government has extended several output-oriented (economic and educational) packages to its Albanian minority, and has restructured local government to grant them limited local autonomy in Albanian-majority areas. Nevertheless, Macedonia's two communities continue to coexist in a tense relationship, while in Kosovo, Albanian hardliners have begun to improve their showings at the ballot box in a province that itself remains bitterly divided between its Albanian majority and the Serbians, who now live under international (UN) oversight even though officially Kosovo is still legally a part of Serbia.

Ethnoclass Conflict in Postcommunist Central Europe

Private and state-sanctioned discrimination against immigrants and other ethnic "outsiders" is neither uncommon nor new, particularly when their lower economic status is perceived to signal inferiority to their hosts. The unfriendly and sometimes violent environment faced by North Africans, Turks, and immigrants from the "coloured commonwealth" in, respectively, contemporary France, Germany, and Britain echoes the hostility immigrants from Asia and Mexico faced in the United States at the turn of the twentieth century. The "Yellow Peril" campaign against Japanese immigrants in the United States, for example, began in 1899—only one year after the Supreme Court found it necessary to affirm the citizenship of U.S.-born Chinese. Elsewhere, even the late twentieth century witnessed the mass expulsions of peoples from different lands, most conspicuously in Uganda where its Asian population was expelled within a year of the 1971 coup which brought Idi Amin Dada to power.[14] In the short term, some groups have found assistance in the form of an oversight protection exercised by their country of origin. One of oldest American civil rights organizations, the Anti-Defamation League, owes its origin in part to the urging of the government of Italy, which was deeply concerned about lynchings targeting Catholic Italian immigrants in America's heavily protestant, post–Civil War south during the 1880s. Likewise, Algeria's already noted concern about the safety of its citizens abroad led it to halt the exodus of Algerian workers into France in the early 1970s. More recently, Budapest's concern over Slovakia's treatment of its large Hungarian minority prompted the Hungarian government to suspend Bratislava's application for membership in the Council of Europe during the middle 1990s until

Slovakia's government agreed to a series of steps designed to protect the rights of its citizens of Hungarian descent.

In the long term, most migrating minorities have found relief from persecution by assimilating, as much as possible, to the culture of their host country: for example, the core group assimilation practiced by most groups migrating from continental Europe to the United States prior to World War I. They not only embraced the language of the English who colonized the original 13 colonies but adapted to their attire, style of living, and political creed as well. Or, the Russian immigrants to France after the 1917 revolutions in Russia, who likewise chose to melt into the culture of their French hosts.

But what happens to a relatively small number of outsiders who refuse to divest themselves of their distinct culture and assimilate even after centuries, and who lack outside protectors?

The general answer to that question in the case of Central Europe's Jewish and Romany minorities is little different from that provided by our brief examination of their fate in Czechoslovakia: a centuries-long story of banishment, expulsion, discrimination, and even genocide.

The Jews and Romany in Pre-1945 Europe: Personas Non Grata

The parallels between the history of Europe's Jewish and Romany communities are imperfect, as the time lines offered in tables 9.2 and 9.3 indicate. Not only did Jewish migrants arrive a thousand years before the first groups of Romany, but in notable moments European Jews achieved significant prosperity and cultural influence—and hence a higher than average ethnoclass status—never within the reach of the Roma. During the early centuries of Christianity, when it forbade believers from engaging in usury and other economic activities, Charlemagne, William the Conqueror, and other European leaders invited Jews into their domains for the useful functions they could perform. Jews prospered as moneylenders, merchants, and tradesmen until the Crusades created a backlash against non-Christians in Western Europe. Then, stigmatized as heretics, Jews were forced to flee during the Middle Ages into Central Europe, where they had already established a presence in Poland and adjacent areas as early as the tenth century.[15] Later, as in the case of Czechoslovakia's Jewish communities, they were gradually reinvited to return to the countries from which they had once been exiled, and well-educated Jews attained eminence in numerous fields in the Austro-Hungarian Empire, including the administration of Budapest's imperial realm. Even after World War I their influence continued to grow in the newly created states of Central Europe, which often lacked a developed commercial class of their own.[16] Meanwhile, throughout these years, the Romany remained a despised community, existing outside European power structures—enslaved for centuries and used as game as late as Germany's now infamous nineteenth-century Gypsy hunts.

Table 9.2 A brief chronology of the Jewish community in Europe

70	Romans destroy Second Temple in Jerusalem; Jewish Diaspora intensifies as Jews flee first to modern Iraq then Europe. By 300 a million Jews inhabit most of the Roman Empire west of Greece
312	Christianity becomes Roman Empire's official religion, institutionalizing discrimination against Jews
6th c.	Theordoric the Great of Italy (454–526) invites Jews to live in his kingdom
8th c.	Charlemagne invites Jews to live in the kingdom of France and western Germany
1066	William the Conqueror invites Jews to England; outside feudal system, they prosper as moneylenders
1095	Crusades begin, creating a backlash against Jews as part of heresy Christians fighting. Often as result of expulsion, Jews begin eastward migration during the Middle Ages to much of Eastern Europe
1215	4th Lateran Council decrees Jews must don badges or other attire distinguishing them from Christians
1144	Norwich, England: Jews charged with ritual murder of Christian children
1190	Jews in York, England, under siege by Christian fanatics, commit mass suicide
13th c.	Treatment of Jews worsens in medieval England; Edward I (reign 1272–1307) orders mass expulsion of Jews; not readmitted until mid-seventeenth century under Cromwell
1243	Belitz, Germany: series of anti-Semitic massacres follow accusations that Jews are desecrating the Host. Isolation of Jews as an alien socioeconomic class established throughout Europe; more overt discrimination ends in Western Europe with Enlightenment but never fully subsides in Central Europe
14th c.	King Kasimierz the Great welcomes Jewish refugees to Poland as compulsory ghettos begin to appear, first in Spain and Portugal, then Madrid, Barcelona, Venice, Naples, Rome, Florence, Prague, and elsewhere
15c	Jews expelled from Warsaw and Krakow
1521	Protestant Reformation begins in Europe; Jews again welcome in most countries where formerly excluded
1780	Emperor Joseph II abolishes badge, permits Jews to leave ghetto, practice any trade in Hapsburg Empire
1795	Poland partitioned; Jews return to Warsaw, soon all Russian Jews forced to live in Pale of Settlement
1819	First major outbreak of anti-Semitism in Central Europe; Austrians demand return of Jewish ghettos
1867	Emancipation of Jews in Hapsburg Empire; until 1918 "Hungarianized Jews" help administer the Empire
1881	Organized massacres (pogroms) of Eastern European and Russian Jews result in migration of 3 million Yiddish Jews to United States by 1924
1906	Failure of 1905 Revolution in Russia produces intensification of pogroms in Russia.
1918	World War I ends; Poland now independent; Jews reestablish ghetto in Old Town Warsaw
	Paris Peace Conference opens Palestine to Jewish immigration and places in postwar treaties involving Central European states provisions to protect Jewish minorities
1918–39	Jewish professionals gain high status in a postwar Central Europe often lacking a professional class
1924	Anti-Jewish backlash in the United States; immigration limited; Nordics given preference over Slavs and Semitic groups
1933	Hitler takes power in Germany; first concentration camp (Dachau) opened; first inmates are communists
1935–6	German Jews stripped of citizenship and right to vote
1938	November 10–11: *Kristallnacht*, Nazi youth gangs terrorize Jewish communities in Germany and Austria

Continued

Table 9.2 Continued

1939	Germany takes over Czechoslovakia; German Jews required to wear badges, obey curfews
1940	Nazis begin deporting Jews to Poland and executing Polish Jews; Warsaw ghetto established; German Jews ordered into ghettos
1941	Jews throughout occupied Europe forced into ghettos
1942	Final Solution discussed; Warsaw ghetto destroyed, 165,000 Jews sent to death camps in 7-week period
1943	Final Solution in high gear; by February, more than 80% of all Jews who die in Holocaust already slain
1945	World War II ends, leaving Soviet troops in control of much of Central Europe
1946–91	Communist rule in Eastern Europe; anti-Semitism remains high despite decimated Jewish population; Israel is born as a Jewish state in 1948
1979–80	France swept by series of bombings and desecrations of Jewish schools, synagogues, and Israeli facilities
1990–92	End of Communism unleashes pent up ethnonationalism in Central Europe; pursuit of ethnically pure nation-state creates backlash against Jews as well as other minorities; anti-Semitism increases in Western Europe
2002	July: desecration of Jewish graves in Rome cemetery
2003	Spring: French foreign minister uses anti-Semitic rhetoric in seeking Arab support for Paris' foreign policy
	September: right-wing extremists arrested for planning attacks on Jewish targets in Germany
2004	Jewish community center destroyed in Paris; Israeli prime minister urges French Jews to emigrate to Israel

Table 9.3 The Romany: A chronology of an oppressed minority

14th c.	First recorded arrival of Roma in Serbia, Croatia, Bulgaria, Greece, Romania, and Hungary
1330s	King Rudolph IV of Baden establishes first recorded system of Romany enslavement in Europe
1416	Roma expelled from the Meissen region of Germany
1471	Anti-Gypsy laws passed in Lucern; 17,000 Roma deported to Moldavia as slave labor
1482	First anti-Gypsy laws enacted in Brandenburg (1482)
1492	Spain enacts first anti-Gypsy laws
1493	Roma expelled from Milan
1504	Louis XII prohibits Roma from living in France
1512–26	Catalonia expels Roma (1512); first anti-Gypsy laws passed in Holland and Portugal
1532	England enacts its first laws expelling Gypsies
1540	Gypsies allowed to live under own laws in Scotland
1541	First anti-Gypsy laws passed in Scotland
1549	First anti-Gypsy law passed in Bohemia (Czech lands)
1568	Pope expels Roma from domain of Catholic Church
1589	Denmark condemns to death Roma not leaving country
1619	Spain bans all *Gitanos*, as well as Gypsy dress, names, and languages
1637	First anti-Gypsy laws passed in Sweden; expulsion ordered under penalty of death
1666	Louis XIV orders severe punishment for any "Bohemian" found in France
1685	Portugal bans Romany language, deports Roma to Brazil

Continued

Table 9.3 Continued

1710	Prague orders hanging without trial of adult Roma men; women and boys are to be mutilated
1721	Austro-Hungarian Empire orders extermination of Roma throughout its domain
1733	Russia forbids Roma from settling as serfs on land
1761	Maria Theresa, Empress of Hungary, makes first European effort to assimilate Roma, orders removal of Romany children from parents for assignment to foster homes
1776	Prince of Moldavia prohibits marriages to Roma
1782	200 Roma charged with cannibalism in Hungary
1800s	Gypsy hunts become popular sport in Germany
1803	Napoleon prohibits Roma from residing in France
1856	Abolition of Romany Slavery (the *Slobuzenia*)
1880s	Argentina bars Roma from entering country; Roma excluded from entering the United States; Bismarck advocates deporting non–German born Roma
1914	Sweden prohibits further Roma immigration
1921–24	Czechoslovakia recognizes Roma as separate "nationality"; legislation later repealed (1921); Roma tried for cannibalism in Slovakia (1924)
1926–27	Bavaria mandates registration of all Roma; Czechoslovakia prohibits Romany nomadism and permits taking Gypsy children from parents
1933	Hitler orders sterilization of Gypsies and their arrest; by 1937 sterilization orders replaced by extermination orders
1934	Sweden passes sterilization law to keep Swedish pure
1938	June 12–18: roundup of Roma in Germany and Austria
1941	Concentration camps opened in Poland, Croatia, Ukraine, and Serbia
1944	August 2: 4,000 Roma gassed and cremated at Auschwitz in single action
1945–47	World War II ends; Central European communist regimes consolidate and begin policies of assimilating Romany
1953	Roma readmitted to Denmark
1969	Segregated schools established for Roma in Bulgaria
1972	International Romani Union (IRU) affiliates with Council of Europe Czechoslovakia initiates sterilization program for Roma and bans Romany associations
1975	Belgium permits Belgium-born Romany to naturalize
1976	Indira Gandhi supports Roma demand to be recognized as national minority of Indian origin
1986	IRU becomes member of U.N. Children's Fund (UNICEF)
1993	Macedonia introduces use of Romany languages in schools; Austria recognizes Roma as an ethnic group
1994	England abolishes caravan (trailer) sites; 3,000 Roma left without legal homes
1996	5,000 Roma evicted from homes in Istanbul
1998	New Jersey rescinds last anti-Roma law in United States
2002	Dorking, England, council advertises Budapest Gypsies Ensemble show as "the only time you want to see 100 Gypsies on your doorstep"
2003	Despite continuing discrimination against Romany, except for former Yugoslavia states, Central European countries are invited to join the EU and many are invited to join NATO

Beyond these differences in wealth and stature, however, Europe's Jewish and Romany communities had several things in common.

First, both practiced a high degree of intragroup exclusiveness, shunning assimilation to their hosts' cultures, emphasizing intracommunal solidarity, and thus sharing in an "other" identity as much self-imposed as imposed on them by the states in which they lived.[17] For centuries, the insular nature of Jews as the self-proclaimed chosen people of the Lord set them apart from, and incurred the animosity of the peoples among whom they lived, even when their status was more humble than that of their hosts. For their part, the Romany have historically been deemed the *Gadje*, or non-Romany, as unclean and to be avoided.

Second, at least in part because of their unwillingness to assimilate, both communities experienced the same historical pattern of arrival followed by mass expulsion. Only four generations after William the Conqueror opened England to Jews, a local community in Norwich was charged with murdering Christian children in a heretic rite. A few generations later, Edward I became the first leader in Europe to cleanse his country of Jews when he ordered their mass expulsion from Britain, an act that one commentator has labeled the "medieval-style 'final solution.' "[18]

This pattern became a familiar one for Jews living on the continent as well. As anti-Semitism grew in Western Europe, King Kasimierz the Great invited the Jews to Poland in the fourteenth century. By the sixteenth century, Poland had become a center of Jewish culture in Europe, but not in Warsaw, from which Jews were expelled during the fifteenth century and banned again from 1527 to 1768. Then, at approximately the time that Jews were allowed to return to Warsaw (1780), Hapsburg Emperor Joseph II ended the policy of confining Jews to ghettos and excluding them from specified trades in his realm. With the subsequent entry of Jews into important posts in the Austrian Empire's civil service and the field of law and other professions, by 1819 Austria had become the home of the first broad-based anti-Semitic movement in Central Europe.[19] One hundred years later, the same pattern unfolded again when the creation of new states out of the Austro-Hungarian Empire in areas lacking a large professional or middle class of their own allowed Jews to achieve high status in interwar Czechoslovakia, Hungary, Romania, and Poland.[20] Anti-Semitism rose; the Holocaust followed.

Meanwhile, by the early 1400s, the Romany had also spread, albeit uninvited, throughout most of southeastern Europe into the areas now containing Serbia, Greece, Hungary, Germany, Slovakia, Italy, France, Belgium, and Holland. Discrimination, persecution, forced sterilization, impoundment of Romany children, and/or expulsion followed, often immediately, both there and elsewhere in Europe over the centuries that followed.

Third, both the Roma and Europe's Jews were targeted by the Nazis for extermination as inferior races during the Holocaust, and in their extermination policies the Nazis were often abetted by the national populations of Nazi-occupied Europe, with devastating results. Except for Bulgaria, whose small (48,000) Jewish community survived essentially intact, Jewish communities throughout Central Europe absorbed the same devastating blow as those in wartime Czechoslovakia. In Hungary, with an estimated prewar Jewish population of 444,000, only 140,000 remained by 1945. For Romania, the numbers were 757,000 before the war, 428,000 afterward, and in Yugoslavia more than 80 percent of its estimated 68,000 Jews perished. It was in Poland, however, with the largest Jewish concentration in Central Europe, that the most tragic figures were recorded. Nearly 10 percent of Poland's prewar population was Jewish: 3,350,000 people. Of these, only 250,000–300.000 were still alive in 1945, and only 50,000 remained in Poland, the others having survived by fleeing to Russia during the war.[21] Nearly a tenth of the victims came from Warsaw, where in October, 1940, the occupying German forces established the Warsaw ghetto. In July, 1942, they began emptying it, dispatching its 375,000 occupants to the death camps at the rate of 6,000 per day.[22] The remainder of the Polish Jews who died during the Holocaust came from throughout Poland, and the Nazis were not solely responsible for their deaths. A recent report from Warsaw acknowledged that in at least 24 areas of Poland, Poles committed wartime crimes against the Jewish population, including mass murder.[23]

The Holocaust claimed a smaller number of Romany lives, in part because local populations in much of Central Europe collaborated less in the destruction of the Romany than the extermination of their often envied Jewish communities, and in part because Central Europe's Jews were concentrated in highly vulnerable, urban Ghettos whereas the Romany were widely scattered in the more remote areas of Central Europe. On the other hand, because they were a despised underclass, generally perceived as useless, the Romany *were* early targets for forced sterilization by countries concerned with keeping their populations pure, including Sweden in 1934. Accordingly, they became the subject of German purification plans very early (1933) in the Nazi era, and were marked for extermination in Germany in 1938 and, three years later, in German-occupied Poland, Croatia, Serbia, and the Ukraine. Although the data are less reliable than in the case of the Jewish Holocaust, it is generally believed that by the time of the Roma Holocaust at least 500,000 Roma had been executed by the Nazis and their Central European collaborators. Romany estimates place the number in the 1,500,000 range.[24]

Ethnoclass Minorities in a Classless Society: Jews and Romany under Communist Rule

Although the Romany and Jews remain a small minority everywhere, and hence—like Western Europe's foreign workers—more the subjects of public policy than its architects, their history has differed considerably in the post–World War II world, both inside and outside of Central Europe.

In the advanced industrial democracies, knowledge of the Jewish Holocaust, buttressed frequently by shame for not having acted sooner against Hitler, has sharply curtailed anti-Semitic actions and utterances by public officials. In communist-controlled postwar Central Europe, however, anti-Jewish pronouncements remained commonplace. As in Czechoslovakia, when dissatisfaction with the regime grew, the Jewish minority was repeatedly scapegoated for society's ills. The strategy did not always succeed, but it was serviceable. As one analyst noted, shortly after the failure of Czechoslovakia's reform movement in 1968,

> when Soviet propagandists refer to the "zionists," they are speaking to the population in a familiar language. The Zionist is the old, mythical jew, the faceless enemy, the cunning foe . . . [and] Jews can be set apart and defined more easily than, for instance, the intellectuals, the opposition, or the deviationists. Neither a janitor nor a mailman can be 100 per cent certain that an attack on the intellectuals is not also aimed at him in a way . . . but every Aryan knows quite definitely that he is not a Zionist.[25]

Matters were both better and worse for the Romany of communist Central Europe. In deference to an ideology that stressed class over ethnicity and in order to meet the need for low-cost manpower, communist regimes officially sought to contain the Roma within their individual borders and to assimilate them into their respective societies. In most instances the outcome was similar to the results achieved in Czechoslovakia. The Romany were consequently neither officially persecuted nor scapegoated; however, their traditional way of life was disrupted by them being forced to end their nomadic ways. At the same time, despite numerous, self-congratulatory government reports of progress, proportionately few Romany overall were actually resettled from the remote rural areas they favored and in which they established self-segregated enclaves once the borders were closed to them. Furthermore, wherever they lived they continued to practice their traditional professions (e.g., horse-trading and trafficking in used clothing) even when these activities were proscribed.[26] Alternately, when they were relocated among local national communities their presence often intensified anti-Romany prejudices and their children were usually segregated in schools established explicitly for them. Hence, integration plans were unable to dispel the prejudice through which the Roma have traditionally been viewed throughout Central Europe and beyond. And, as in Czechoslovakia, the assimilation policies were often harsh and usually administered by local nationals with little interest in actually improving the Romany's collective status, and the education of Romany children in special education classes was often paralleled by incentive-laden programs aimed at enticing Romany women into availing themselves of sterilization services.

Romany and Jews in Postcommunist Europe

The Romany

The fall of communism abruptly ended the limited protection that communism had afforded the Romany against the more overt displays of discrimination. The result has been a resurfacing of hostility toward the Roma, and not infrequently violence and widespread discrimination against them throughout democratizing Central Europe.[27]

Local grievances against the Romany entail far more than resentment over the favoritism they supposedly received under communism. They include: a general aversion to their lifestyle (extraordinarily high levels of illiteracy, unwillingness to assimilate, willingness to accept living in squalor, and the like); a widespread belief that they profited from illegal activities while local workforces were struggling during the transition to marketplace economies; and hostility toward their communities' growing size and the load that growth is perceived to be placing on the strained welfare systems of postcommunist Europe. The role of the media in sustaining the worst stereotypes of the Romany is also cited, by the Romany and others, to explain the discrimination that they continue to encounter. Governments also contribute to the problem, and not just by exploiting anti-Romany prejudices in campaigning for office. At least as late as September, 2002, for example, the Hungarian Ministry of Education had approved textbooks for public schools containing such passages as, "the life of Romany is marked by crime" and Gypsies "were unable to and did not even want to adapt to a civilized European way of life."[28]

Where they reside, the Romany continue to live in the worst conditions of any community, and their poverty continues to grow.[29] When civil wars occur, they are among the first to be driven out by the victorious parties. They are also usually denied education, health services, and other basic assistance in the states where they find shelter. Meanwhile, as in Czechoslovakia, the widespread dispersion of the Romany communities, the unwillingness of Romany to vote or otherwise participate in politics, and the internal factions within individual Romany tribes have made it difficult for them to gain even those concessions achieved by small, concentrated territorialized minorities such as the Hungarians in Slovakia.

Furthermore, the desired international support for the Romany has not effectively materialized in spite of the Roma's efforts to achieve higher visibility by joining in UN activities and participating in a variety of European conferences (see table 9.3). The memberships offered to the Czech Republic and Slovakia by NATO and the EU have, with the current exception of the states emerging from the former Yugoslavia, also been offered to the remainder of postcommunist Europe despite its continued mistreatment of and discrimination against its Romany minorities.

Europe's Jewish Communities

The fall of communism was also responsible for indirectly contributing to a new round of anti-Semitism in a Central Europe that, by the 1990s, was inhabited by less than a quarter million Jews—approximately 5 percent of its pre–World War II number. In unleashing nationalist movements, which had been generally kept under control during the communist era, the fall of communism created a backlash against not only the national minorities in Central Europe's multinational states, but Jews as well.[30] Across the region *Mein Kampf* and other anti-Semitic books sold out in newly opened capitalist bookstores; in Warsaw, the posting of guards at the memorial erected to honor those who once inhabited the Warsaw ghetto has not prevented its occasional defacing with anti-Semitic markings.

More broadly, the 1990s also ushered in a new round of anti-Semitism in Western Europe, an area in which it never entirely disappeared, as indicated by the occasional anti-Jewish violence in France and elsewhere during the 1970s and 1980s, when Jewish minorities were caught in the right-wing backlash again foreign workers and other "others."[31] In the 1990s, anti-Semitism was reinforced by the increasingly anti-Israeli drift of public opinion in numerous Western European countries, especially those with large Muslim minorities and/or a high dependency on Arab oil and the accompanying fear that its availability could be disrupted because of Israeli intransigence on the Palestinian issue. A poll taken in Italy in the mid-1990s captured the changing mood when it found that one in three Italians did not believe that Jews were true Italians.[32] Twenty-first-century polls taken in Italy, France, and Germany indicate that this trend is developing on a Western Europe–wide basis.[33]

Ethnopolitics in Postcommunist Europe:
Common Threads

Neither territorialized nor territorially intermingled minorities have fared particularly well in postcommunist Europe. Those minorities who have gained states of their own have generally been insensitive to the demands for autonomy and/or civil rights guarantees raised by the minorities in their countries. In addition, the acquisition of national self-determination has frequently triggered an outpouring of nationalism, which in several instances has translated into politics meant to stress the culture of the new rulers, often at the expense of the culture of the new state's minority communities. Score settling has also occurred against minorities akin to those who previously ruled, be they ideological (the hunt for former communist informers in the Czech Republic and Poland) or ethnic/national (the Russians in Estonia, Hungarians in Slovakia). The cases are varied, reflecting historical, demographic, and cultural elements; however, despite the obvious differences separating the multiple instances of ethnic conflict in postcommunist Europe, several common themes bind them together.

The Intoxicating Appeal and Exploitation of National Self-Determination

In numerous instances, territorialized ethnic communities have been mobilized by self-serving leaders casting their appeals in ethnonational terms. Like Vladimir Meciar, Yugoslavia's strong man at the critical moment, Slobodan Milosevic, was a former communist who prolonged his political career by cloaking himself in the robes of majority nationalism. Once awakened, ultra-nationalism of the ilk preached by Milosevic can be a powerful mobilizing force, but also a destructive one—especially when clashing with the ethnonational demands of others, such as Franco Tudjman, the Croatian nationalist who rose to power in Zagreb on his promise to make Croatian a sovereign country. Other examples are not hard to find and they explain much of why the demands of Central Europe's territorialized minorities have focused on independence while the more typical pattern among similarly situated minorities in Western Europe has been to seek regional autonomy within the states they occupy.

The Triumph of the Subjective over Cost–Benefit Analysis

Nationalist jingoism has also been effective in shaping politics in postcommunist Europe because of the difficulty that those caught up in the idea have had in evaluating the full price of pushing a separatist agenda. The same may also be said for majority communities intoxicated by the appeal of a "Greater Serbia" or "Greater Albania" at whatever the cost. Despite the universally literate nature of the peoples in postcommunist Europe, politics since the fall of communism has involved little of the cost–benefit analysis that characterized, for example, the referenda debates in Quebec on the issue of an independent Quebec or those in Scotland involving a devolution of power to a Scottish Assembly.

The Weakness of Crosscutting Ties and Institutions

In addition to repudiating ethnicity as a basis for political organization, communism officially repudiated and/or repressed such other bases of association as religion and social class (beyond the classless society being officially built under the auspices of the communist party). Consequently, even though Slovaks and Czechs and Croats and Serbs sometimes intermarried, a negligible number of formal, communally crosscutting associations emerged outside of the auspices of the communist parties during the communist era in Central Europe. Many of these party affiliates vanished with the fall of communism. Meanwhile, some associations were organized along lines of national identity even under communism. One of the consequences of the federal political framework of communist Czechoslovakia, Yugoslavia, and the Soviet Union, for example, was that even youth groups and such recreational associations as mountain climbing clubs were organized on a state or union republic basis rather than being system-wide. Hence they were dominated by the majority communities in the respective regions.

The Appeal of Grudge-Settling Politics

Ethnopolitics have also been volatile in postcommunist Europe because the meltdown of the Soviet empire removed the cap that formerly contained communal conflict in a region honeycombed with memories of historical injustices and simmering desires to "settle the score." As long as Armenia and Azerbaijan were governed by Moscow, Armenian nationalists could not easily express Armenia's frustration vis-à-vis the Nagorno-Karabakh region. The responsibility for the injustices done to the Armenians there could be divided between Moscow, who transferred the region to Azerbaijan, and the Azerbaijani, who wronged the area's Armenians for generations without Moscow intervening. Moscow's loss of control over its periphery and the subsequent collapse of the Soviet Union simplified the equation. Suddenly only the Azerbaijani were responsible for the persecution of the Armenians. Similarly, freed from the fear of Moscow's intervention, the leaders of Yugoslavia's national communities could engage in previously foreclosed, rancorous personal (Milosevic–Tudjman) and lethal military confrontations.

In a much more muted fashion, the same elements colored the post-communist history of Slovak politics. It was not the Czechs but the Turks and the Hungarians who had committed the great historical injustices against the Slovak people. The dialogue with the Czechs over the terms of continued cohabitation could thus be conducted with a degree of cordiality entirely absent when ethnopolitical discussions in the independent Slovak Republic focused on the political rights of Slovakia's Hungarian minority. Likewise, the collapse of communism opened Central Europe's Romany to violence as these long detested minorities were "repaid" for the preferred status they allegedly enjoyed under communism.

Finally, in the broader context, groups longing for self-determination and political opportunists seeking to exploit ethnopolitical emotions have added a greater rigidity to ethnopolitical bargaining in Central Europe than has been customary in the developed democratic world. Political leaders have had less room in which to compromise even when inclined to do so.

The Problem of Intermingled Nationalities

A story is told in Slovakia, and with local variations throughout much of Central Europe, of a dying family patriarch. In Slovakia, he lives in the east, near the Ukraine border. He is very, very old and surrounded by his aged children, grandchildren, and great-grandchildren, all tearful at his immi-nent demise. In his last words, the old man comforts them, saying: "Do not be sad for me. I have lived a full life. In my youth I wore the uniform of the Russian czar. I was citizen of Hungary before I returned to my roots and served proudly in the army of Czechoslovakia. And now I die a citizen in my native country. Yes, I have had a rich life . . . though, of course, I have never left this village."

All of these tales incorporate considerable poetic license in terms of historical detail, but their point is fundamentally true. Throughout Central Europe the same parcels of land have, over the centuries, passed through multiple foreign hands. Each new ruler usually injected greater multiethnicity into the region as the citizens from the new empire would arrive to govern or farm, and remain behind when history shifted again and the region fell under yet another empire's control. Add migratory groups such as the Romany and—despite the ethnic cleansing that Central Europe has endured—the result is a region honeycombed with national minorities, theoretically transient minorities, and "imperial remnants" from adjacent states that once ruled the land. Hungarians are especially widely distributed in the area, with nearly 20 percent of Central Europe's ethnic and linguistic Hungarians now living outside of Hungary. Russians, who also fall into the imperial remnant category, are equally prolific in Estonia, Latvia, Lithuania, and in other states once a part of Imperial Russia and later Soviet republics. Moreover, as often as not these remnant minorities are spatially intermingled—albeit often in minority enclaves—among the majority communities. It is a distribution that makes the management of ethnopolitical demands more difficult than in the West, where ethnonational minorities tend to be territorialized.

Governments dominated by their national majorities may not be willing to create federal-like systems to meet the demands of their territorialized ethnic groups; however, where these minorities are territorialized that option at least exists. Sensitive issues can be downloaded to regional assemblies (i.e., language issues in Belgium) and demands for self-rule can perhaps be satisfied by regime modifications in a federalist direction before escalating to the separatist level. Where, however, communities are territorially intermingled, the problem of soothing minority fears is much more complicated. Civil rights legislation can be enacted or given constitutional status, but in either case its enforcement requires a good-will commitment by the ruling community minorities may doubt will be forthcoming, especially from people against whom, in earlier days, *they* discriminated.

The Pervasiveness of the International Element in Postcommunist Ethnopolitics

The international dimension of many ethnonational conflicts in postcommunist Europe is obvious. The genocidal elements in Yugoslavia's civil wars visibly raised issues covered by international law, just as the large numbers of refugees who fled these wars into neighboring states gave those conflicts an international element. So, too, did the eventual deployment of international forces in order to contain and end the conflicts, and provide a secure environment for the creation of self-governing institutions. And, as we have seen, conflicts in the postcommunist world have been partially instigated as well as penetrated and affected by outside actors.

Frequently outsiders have had a detrimental impact on political stability in the region. Yugoslavia might have unraveled violently without external prompting, but there is little doubt that Croatia and Slovenia were encouraged to secede by Western countries.[34] Likewise, France was a booster of Slovak independence, with its information office in Bratislava adopting an approving attitude toward the Slovak nationalists and beginning the preliminary work of converting itself into an embassy almost a year before the nationalists took control of the Slovak government in June, 1992.

More constructive have been the oversight activities of NATO and EU countries involved with democratization and economic liberalization efforts in postcommunist Europe, including their policies toward the minority communities. Among the primary reasons cited by both NATO and the EU in explaining their decision to exclude Slovakia from their lists of states eligible for early admission were Meciar's policies toward freedom of expression and Slovakia's Hungarian and Romany minorities. Conversely, Hungary and Romania's shared desire to court the EU played an important role in pushing them toward a formal agreement on the rights of Romania's Hungarian minority.[35]

Diplomatic pressure by the Council of Europe on the Baltic states to treat their Russian minorities fairly and the advice offered by EU officials on the treatment of minorities to countries hopeful of obtaining membership represent perhaps the least intrusive form of external influence on politics in the postcommunist world. Pacts such as the Romania–Hungary agreement, and the similar Slovak–Hungarian State Treaty concluded in 1995 in response to Western pressure on Slovakia, represent a middle-range degree of outside involvement in the politics of a postcommunist European state. Finally, there are the peacemaking and peacemaking missions launched either unilaterally by individual countries or multilaterally by the UN, NATO, and other international organizations to halt civil wars, prevent them from spreading, or otherwise control ethnic violence in postcommunist Europe. Russian activity in Georgia, the UN intervention in Croatia and Bosnia, and NATO's intervention in Bosnia and Kosovo are only a few examples of this most intrusive form of external involvement in ethnic conflict in this region. And, in Central Europe as in the case of the UN's 40-year presence in Cyprus and Britain's continuing mission in Northern Ireland, these peacekeeping and peace-building missions are invariably expensive, long-term ventures offering no guarantees of success in bringing together multinational antagonists in a stable political order.

PART 3

Nigeria: Ethnopolitics in the Multinational Third World

CHAPTER TEN

The Setting of Politics in the Developing World

No single word better characterizes the nature of the developing world than diverse. Even the terminology applied to the states falling into this category varies. During the cold war (1947–92), those emerging from colonialism who sought to disassociate themselves from both the Western bloc led by the United States (the First World) and the Soviet bloc of communist countries (the Second World) were labeled the Third World on the basis of political as well as economic criteria. By 1960, when approximately 20 new states emerged in Africa alone, this group of economically less-developed countries had grown into a major presence in the UN' General Assembly. Because their agenda was less concerned with foreign policy (beyond championing complete decolonization) than economic issues (they demanded preferential access to Western markets for their exports, for example), the Third World designation became progressively less associated with their foreign policy orientation than their level of economic development, and the term is still frequently used in that sense. On the other hand, because so many of these states immediately experienced a high degree of political instability—in particular, the collapse of the Western-styled parliamentary systems they possessed at independence—while continuing to fall further behind the more developed states economically, more frequently these economically and politically struggling countries have come to be known as the underdeveloped or developing world.[1]

Whatever their designation, the countries composing this world span four continents (South America, Asia, Africa, and the lands from Mexico south in North America), house all of the world's races and major religions, and—depending on whether China is included—encompass two-thirds to four-fifths of the world's population. They are also profoundly separated from one another as well as from the countries of the more developed world in terms of history, levels of economic and political development (measured respectively in terms of per capita income and degree of constitutional democracy), and such demographic indicators of quality of life as life expectancy and literacy levels. Above all, they offer a mosaic of ethnic and linguistic diversity. And, in the countries of sub-Sahara Africa and of Asia, the heartland of that diversity as well as the core of our case studies in this section, managing and/or controlling that diversity has frequently been at least as great a challenge as overcoming the obstacles to their economic development.

The Environment of Politics in
the Developing World

Economic Underdevelopment and Ethnic Diversity:
A Spectrum of Diversity

Table 10.1 indicates the broadly different settings of politics in the principal countries discussed in this volume. The gap between the advanced democratic world and the countries of postcommunist Europe are negligible in the area of literacy, moderate in terms of life expectancy and levels of industrialization, and sharp in the area of per capita income. The real gap in these categories, however, is between these two categories and the developing world, with life expectancy in the Czech Republic 20 years longer than in Nigeria, and the average per capita income in the former 20 times greater than in the latter. Yet profound differences also separate the countries of the various regions in the developing world from those in other areas.

The poorest area in the developing world remains sub-Sahara Africa, whose countries were among the last to receive independence and where, even in the more developed area of West Africa, per capita income generally hovers in the US$200–500 range.[2] In contrast, the average in the Arab states of North Africa is two-to-five times greater, with only Egypt falling below the US$1,000 per capita level.[3]

Mass poverty almost on the scale of sub-Sahara Africa's also provides a backdrop to politics in much of Asia, where at the end of the twentieth century only the Philippines, Singapore, South Korea, and Thailand had average per capita incomes greater than US$1,000 and the figure for the majority of the remaining states was under US$500.[4] In fact, excluding the small population/oil-rich states of the Arabian peninsula, only the older, western hemisphere states of Latin America, as a group, have climbed above the US$1,000 per capita income level despite such pockets of significant poverty as Haiti, Nicaragua, Honduras, Bolivia, and Guyana. Several (Mexico, Argentina, Uruguay, and Brazil) fall in the US$3,000+ range, a figure comparable to the per capita income numbers of Hungary and Poland during the 1990s.

An equal range of diversity characterizes the ethnic composition of these states (see table 10.2). The least ethnically heterogeneous area is North Africa, followed closely by the Arabian Peninsula, where much of the non-Arab-Berber population is concentrated in the foreign worker communities

Table 10.1 Comparative developmental indicators—select countries of the developed and developing world

	France	Germany	United Kingdom	Czech Rep.	Slovakia	Yugoslavia	Nigeria	India
Population[a]	58.3	81.9	58.1	10.3	5.3	23.36	115.0	994.6
Density[b]	108	230	238	130	103	91.3	125	267
Per capita income (US$)	22,290	28,880	19,810	4,770	3,400	*	240	380
Literacy(%)	99	99	99	99	99	90.5[c]	50.8	51.2
Male life expectancy	74.6	73.4	74.5	69.8	67.0	67.8	50.8	62.1
Urban population(%)	73	87	89	65	58	35	38	27

[a] Population given in millions of people.
[b] Population density given in people/square kilometer.
[c] Based on 1961 data; by 1990s literacy was 99% outside of the state's Muslim community. Except as indicated, all data is from mid-1980s in Yugoslavia and mid-1990s elsewhere.

Sources: Central Intelligence Service on-line data base; and *The Economist* on-line database from the mid-1990s.

in the region's oil-producing states. Next come the countries of South America, Central America, and the Caribbean basin, whose ethnic homogeneity is paradoxically the product of their heterogeneity. Just as the Arab-Berber peoples of North Africa are the result of the indigenous population of this area absorbing the blood, faith, and language of the warriors from Arabia, who conquered the area in the name of Islam within a century of the death of Mohammed in 632, so the Mestizo and Mulatto populations of the southern Americas are the result of centuries of intermixing between the indigenous native peoples, and the European conquerors/settlers who came voluntarily to the region and the involuntarily imported slave populations and their descendants. To be sure, these countries are not without pockets of indigenous peoples still seeking to avoid immersion in the culture around them—for example, the Chiapas in Mexico. For the greater part, though, their populations are centered on a dominant community, albeit one sometimes intermingled with residual minorities dating from their colonial eras.

At virtually the opposite end of the spectrum are the states of sub-Sahara Africa, most of whose populations are either polarized between majority–minority tribal communities (the Hutus and Tutsis of Rwanda and Burundi) or fragmented into numerous broad groupings, themselves often internally subdivided into smaller communities of tribes. In-between lie the states of Asia—less multiethnic/multinational than the countries of tropical Africa but usually lacking the core ethnic community to be found within the states of North Africa and Latin America.

Beyond the economic and often extreme ethnic diversity of the developing states lie a series of commonly shared factors which have also shaped the societies and histories of these countries and which continue to exert powerful influences on their political processes.

Table 10.2 Ethnic diversity of select states in the principal regions of the developing world

North Africa and the adjacent Middle East	
Algeria	99% Arab–Berber
Egypt	90% Eastern Hamitic; 10% Greek Stock
Iraq	79–80% Arab; 15–20% Kurdish
Jordan	97% Arab
Lebanon	95% Arab; 4% Armenian [59.7% Muslim, 39% Christian]
Libya	97% Berber and other Arab, some with Negroid stock
Morocco	98.9% Berber
Syria	90.3% Arab; 9.7% Kurds, Armenians, and others
Middle East: Arabian Peninsula	
Bahrain	90% Arab; 7% Iranian, Pakistani, Indian
Kuwait	87% Arab; 12% Iranian, Indian, Pakistani
Oman	99+% Arab
Qatar	56% Arab; 23% Iranian; 14% Pakistani
Saudi Arabia	90% Arab; 10% Afro–Asian (estimate)
United Arab Emirates	72% Arab
Sub-Sahara Africa	
Burundi	86% Hutu, 13% Tutsi, 1% Twa
Cameroon	200 tribes, largest tribal grouping represents 31% of population
Central African Republic	80 ethnic groups, largest is Banda (32%)
Chad	240 tribes; 12 broad ethnic groupings
Congo (Dem. Rep. of)	200+ ethnic groups; 4 largest constitute approximately 45% of the population
Congo (Brazzaville)	48% Kongo, 20% Sangha, 12% M'Bochi, 17% Teke
Gabon	4 major groupings of Bantu tribes, plus 4 other major tribal groupings
Gambia	41% Malinki, 14% Fulani, 12% Wolof
Ghana	3 major (Fanti, Ashanti, Ewe) and numerous minor tribes
Ivory Coast	7 major indigenous ethnic grous; no tribe with more than 15% of population
Liberia	95% indigenous tribal Africans; 6 major tribal groups
Nigeria	200+ tribes; 29% Hausa-Fulani, 21% Yoruba, 18% Ibo
Rwanda	84% Hutu, 15% Tutsi, 1% Twa
South Africa	75.2% African (9 official languages), 13.6% white, 2.6% Asian, 8.6% mixed
Tanzania	100+ tribes; 97% native African
Uganda	17% Baganda, 8% Ankole, 8% Basoga, 8% Iteso, 7% Bakiga, 6% Langi, et al.
Asia	
Afghanistan	50% Pushtuns; 25% Taliks; 9% Uzbeks
Bangladesh	98.6% Bengali
Burma	72% Burman, 7% Karen, 6% Shan, 3% Indian, 2% Kachin, 2% Chin
Cambodia	89% Kymen (Cambodian); 5% Chinese, 3% Vietnamese
China	94% Han
India	24 ethnolinguistic communities each comprise 1 m+. people, plus others

Continued

Table 10.2   Continued

Indonesia	45% Javanese, 14% Sundanese, 7.5% Madurese, 7.5% Coastal Malays
Malaysia	44% Malay, 36% Chinese, 8% tribal, 10% Indo-Pakistani
Pakistan	66.4% Punjabi, 12.6% Sindhis, 7.6% Urdu
Sri Lanka	71% Sinhalese, 21% Tamil, 6% Moor
Thailand	75% Thai, 14% Chinese
Latin America	
Argentina	85% European; 15% Mestizo, Indians, and others
Bolivia	30% Quechua, 24% Aymara, 25% Mestizo, 15% white
Brazil	55.8% white, 38%, mixed white and black, 6% Negro
Chile	85–90% Mestizo, 3% Indian, 17% other
Colombia	70% Mestizo, 20% white, 5% Negro
Costa Rica	09% white or Mestizo, 2% Negro
Cuba	51% Mulatto, 37% white
Dominican Republic	73% Mulatto, 16% white
Ecuador	41% Mestizo, 39% Indian
El Salvador	84–88% Mestizo, 6–9% Indian, 6–9% white
Guatemala	44% Indian, 56% Ladino (Westernized Indians and Mestizos)
Haiti	90% Negro, 10% Mulatto
Honduras	90% Mestizo, 7% Indian, 2% Negro
Mexico	55% Mestizo, 29% Indian, 15% white
Nicaragua	75% Mestizo, 15% white, 10% Indian, Negro, or Mulatto
Panama	70% Mestizo, 14% Negro
Paraguay	95% Mestizo
Peru	46% Indian, 38% Mestizo, 15% white
Trinidad & Tobago	39.5% Negro, 40.3% East Indian, 18.4% mixed, 1.6% white
Uruguay	85–90% white, 5% Negro, 5–10% Mestizo
Venezuela	67% Mestizo, 21% white, 10% Negro

Source: CIA *Basic Intelligence Factbook* and CIA *World Factbook*, most recent available on-line at http://www.cia.gov/cia/publications/factbook/geos/cg.html.

The Legacy of Colonialism

"Other-Made" States

With few exceptions, the borders of developing world states are to some degree the product of earlier periods of rule by or contact with outside powers. Their role in state-making can even be seen in the northern boundaries of Mexico and China, which are, respectively, the result of lost wars with the U.S. government and its future state (Texas) and a Czarist Russia expanding into Asia. Elsewhere, the hand of outsiders has been more intrusive. The countries of Central and South America, in terms of early history, lie somewhere between the settler societies to their north in the United States and Canada, and the states that have emerged from European empires in the Middle East, Asia, and Africa, where, except for notable exceptions such as Algeria, the arrival of a large settler community (as opposed to administrators, military personnel, and landholders) was rare. Yet the borders of the New World states continue to reflect the quest for empire and the pattern of settlement that brought the region under the control of Portugal, Spain, the Netherlands, and Britain between 1500 and the early 1800s.

The quest for empire also left much of Africa and Asia with borders drawn with little regard to postindependence viability. The Wilsonian principle of national self-determination was still decades in the future when Britain, France, Italy, Portugal, Belgium, and Germany gathered in Berlin in 1884–85 to carve up Africa into a series of spheres of influence for their respective exploitation. Three-quarters of a century later, when these territories in that most ethnically diverse of continents acquired their independence in the territorial frameworks that evolved out of those deliberations, the result was an outpouring of new, multiethnic, multinational states onto the world stage.

In Asia, too, ease of conquest and great power politics resulted in Britain, France, and (in Indonesia) the Netherlands gaining footholds during the eighteenth and nineteenth centuries. When those areas gained their independence after World War II—peacefully or otherwise—it was usually within their colonial boundaries or in those affixed during the process of decolonization, as in the case of the Indian subcontinent, where colonial rule ended with the fusion of those principalities ruled indirectly through treaty arrangements with local potentates (Princely India) and that portion under more direct British rule (British India), *and* India's partition into predominantly Muslim Pakistan and predominantly Hindu India.[5]

Augmenting Diversity

Within the often already ethnically diverse territories that constituted the core of Europe's empire, European rule sometimes fostered still greater ethnic diversity and widened the ethnocultural and ethnoterritorial cleavages separating the indigenous communities.

On rare occasions, imperial powers encouraged peoples to migrate from one part of their empire to another because they were perceived to be more industrious, commercially gifted, or better suited to specific work conditions than the peoples indigenous to the areas. The Tamil community in Ceylon (now Sri Lanka), for example, was vastly augmented when British administrators on the island imported large numbers from the Tamil region of southern India to work on Ceylon's plantations On other occasions the imperial power simply permitted, often for the same reasons, the migration of outsiders into their colonies Thus, the number of Chinese in Malaya's population grew substantially during that region's era of British rule. Similarly, Ibos from Nigeria—sometimes referred to as the "Jews of Africa" in the same manner that the Chinese are often dubbed the "Jews of Asia"—often moved freely throughout British West Africa during that region's colonial era, and large numbers of migrants from northern India became a substantial part of the population of Trinidad and Tobago, where they are referred to locally as "East Indians."

More frequently, communities within the individual colonies profited from their colonial administrators' first impressions, or actually were culturally more inclined to adapt to Western ways of doing things: for example, the Hindu peoples of Northern India, the Indian and Chinese immigrants in Malaya, and the Ibos in Nigeria, as opposed to the Muslims, whose conservative, all-encompassing religion made them comparatively reluctant to "modernize." Not surprisingly, the former were given opportunities during the colonial era denied to others. The Chinese in Malaya and the Nigeria's Yoruba were seen to be particularly industrious and suited to commercial activity, and given disproportionately large opportunities to advance economically compared to the Malay majority in Malaya and the other tribes in Nigeria. Nigeria's Ibos, too, were seen as particularly industrious; however, like the Bengalis in northern India the educated Ibo were primarily perceived to be endowed with administrative talent, and became the backbone of Nigeria's civil service—a status that reinforced the ethnoterritorial division separating them from the country's other principal regionalized tribal communities and the minority tribes in their own region. Similar examples abound, including in the area now constituting Rwanda, where the colonial agents treated the minority but more prosperous Tutsi "as a superior caste of aristocrats and the [eight time more numerous] Hutu as their vassals."[6]

Above all, location, resources, climate (congenial to the colonizers), and other economic and environmental considerations contributed to the disproportionte development of some parts of the various colonies. Southern Nigeria abutted the sea; Northern Nigeria was landlocked. In India, industrial development was concentrated in the more populous north, reinforcing southern India's feelings of neglect and fear of domination by the north. Meanwhile, in what became Pakistan, most industrial projects after Partition were located in the western wing, leaving poorer, East Pakistan almost entirely dependent on agriculture.

Finally, sometimes differences widened under colonialism simply because of the presence of the colonial system. British colonies were a good place to invest capital in the late nineteenth and early twentieth centuries; in fact, except where seen as areas for settlement, they *were* economic enterprises. If they had seaports it was only logical that those areas would receive disproportionate economic investment and their peoples greater economic opportunities than the country as a whole. Ports also meant access for the missionaries who zealously went forth from Europe to Christianize the subjects of empire; again with cleavage-enforcing results. Landlocked Northern Nigeria therefore still remained overwhelmingly Muslim when Nigeria acquired its independence in 1960; by then, the major tribes of the south had been converted from animistic practices to the Christian faith—a ethnocultural line of cleavage that continues to have profound implications for politics in Nigeria.

Spreading the Gospel of Nationalism and
National Self-Determination

Even where the colonial power opted, as in the case of France, Portugal, and Belgium, for a direct form of rule relying on personnel from the imperial capital, Western ideas of national self-determination eventually seeped into the local communities. Where the colonial power relied heavily on local manpower, and Western educated some of the sons of the empire to prepare them for leadership positions in the bureaucracy, political processes, and military, exposure to Western notions of nationalism and self-determination came much more quickly.[7] Political leaders in India were thus demanding a greater share of decision-making authority before the end of the nineteenth century and—a generation before their counterparts in French North Africa—independence during the 1930s. At the same time, the demands for self-government that they channeled normally rested essentially on the territorial definition of nationality and national self-determination subscribed to by the European powers they confronted, but not necessarily shared by the territorialized, multiethnic communities constituting the states for which they spoke. Early nationalist movements thus tended to be framed in inclusive terms, such as the all-India Congress Party headed by Nehru at the time of India's partition and—despite its Ibo core—the Nigerian National Congress party led by independent Nigeria's first president, Nnamdi Azikiwe.

Viewed from the perspective of the Western world, these [system-wide] nationalist leaders, movements and parties appeared to be the proper heirs to govern the territorial entities constructed during the colonial era. For the most part, however, these images soon proved to be illusory on three counts. First, the size of the nationalist cadre who thought of themselves as Nigerian rather than Ibo, or Indian rather than Punjabi, was thin in the multiethnic colonial world. Second, where an indigenous organization demanding self-government was labeled a nationalist movement (singular), it was quite often a misnomer. More commonly, these associations were coalitions of ethnonational movements (plural) temporarily joined together in common resistance to the colonial authority. Once that external presence vanished with independence, these coalitions tended to break down into their component parts; sometimes earlier when the colonial authority committed itself to a timetable for independence. Finally, almost everywhere the ideal of national self-determination invariably trickled down after independence to the territorialized communities in multiethnic states, to be commandeered by local ethnonational spokesmen who, in turn, began to pressure the newly installed governments in their capitals for autonomy and sometimes for independence.

The Legacy of Political Transition

Politically Volatile States

Politics in the developing world is not entirely played out in conditions that are the mirror opposite of those characterizing politics in the advanced democratic states.[8] Stable, frequently democratic political systems exist in all regions. On balance, though, governments in large portions of the developing world exercise a more tenuous control over their territory and its peoples, encounter more disorderly modes of political participation, including violence where such democratic outlets as parties are denied, and qualify the forms of participation even in democratic systems because of the perceived fragility of their states to a far greater extent than is true in the advanced democratic world.

Economically Dependent States

The economic underdevelopment of the "other world" is not solely the product of colonialism. Other factors include: location, resources and lack thereof, burgeoning populations swallowing economic expansion when it occurs, and political instability discouraging private investment, to list but a few. Moreover, even in the context of empire, contact with the West carried advantages. Although the benefits in part depended on who the colonial power was, in general some modern medical techniques were introduced, economic investment occurred where the rewards were large, system-wide communication grids were installed, and economic management was facilitated through the introduction of administrative structures, common currencies, and transportation networks. To some degree, however, the gap between Third World levels of economic development and that of the colonial power *was* the product of colonial systems, which delayed economic diversification by harvesting raw products for processing in Europe, whether middle east oil to be refined in European ports or Egyptian cotton to be processed in the textile plants of England. In the process, colonialism also tended to distort economies by building up the most profitable sectors disproportionately (most conspicuously in petroleum producing states), and leaving behind societies earmarked by a disproportionate distribution of wealth, weak middle classes, and, often, a continuing economic dependency on the mother country.[9]

Ethnic Diversity, Ethnic Conflict and the Developing World

New State, Old Loyalties

The Political Legacy of Empire

Just as the economic benefits of colonialism depended on who the colonial authority was—Britain investing most in its possessions, Belgium the least in managing the Congo—so too the colonial world's preparation for independence often depended, in both predictable and unpredictable ways, on the identity of the colonial power.

The British system of "indirect rule" was the most likely to result in a widening of differences between indigenous communities by earmarking some for greater education, administrative responsibility, and commercial roles than others, but it was also the one most likely to leave behind military and police forces instilled with a set of professional ethics transcending ethnic lines of identity, a respect for the rule of the law, and a neutral bureaucracy for the benefit of the new states [10] On the other hand, in return for looking after Britain's interest in their respective areas the conscripted local authorities were permitted to retain much of their pre-British power, and local communities retained much of their pre-British autonomy in practice, with traditional life going on under British auspices in substantially the same manner it always had. Consequently, the system frequently served to perpetuate existing linguistic–ethnic distinctions and the prejudices of local political entities.

In addition, the peaceful manner in which the British accepted the independence of its overseas empire made it unnecessary for its subjects to develop a single, goal-oriented independence movement out of the various ethnonational independence *movements* in order to wrest independence from London. Rather, the spokesmen for the ethnopolitical local communities perpetuated by Britain's system of indirect rule could often focus upon building their individual ethnopolitical organizations with an eye to the struggle for power after independence. Indeed, independence was often granted so quickly and easily that national "struggles" scarcely had time to organize, much less draw together the diverse communities in a shoulder-to-shoulder march for a common cause. There were exceptions to this rule, most notably India, where British reluctance to cede independence to the "jewel in the crown of the British empire" not only prolonged the alliance between India's Hindu and Muslim communities until late in the independence struggle—when Britain's acceptance of eventual independence freed the Muslims to push for a partition of the subcontinent—but also left India with nationalist leaders who transcended the ethnonational communities composing India to assume control of the new state. Elsewhere, however, a lack of bitterness toward the British frequently inhibited the development of transcending identities.

In contrast, because the *raison d'etre* of French colonialism was the assimilation of the subjects of empire into the French culture, French colonialism made little effort to prepare the indigenous communities in its possessions for independence. Even administrative and communication structures were so centralized that in parts of French West Africa telephone calls from one point in a colony to another were routed through Paris. Consequently, much of its empire, upon independence, lacked the system-wide infrastructure and local administrative apparatuses of British colonies. The haste with which independence arrived in much of the French empire once France gave up Algeria following Algerian's bloody battle for independence also left France's imperial possessions with too brief a transition period to develop such accouterments of modern states as national education and bureaucratic structures. And what was true for France was truer for Belgium, which terminated its rule in the Congo in less than two years following generations of direct rule by Brussels, as well as for Spain's and Portugal's colonies in Africa. Consequently, the departure of these states from their overseas possessions often left behind politically as well as economically dependent new states whose regimes not infrequently required military intervention by international bodies or the armies of the advanced democratic world to stay in power (French intervention in Chad) and to establish order in the midst of chaos (Haiti, Somalia)

On the other side of the ledger, France forced its subjects to unite in order to throw off foreign rule. Usually that meant developing a well-mobilized independence movement and/or coalition of various communities seeking independence; often (Indo-China, Algeria) it meant fighting the French army.

Whatever their administration style and mode of departure, in state-making the European powers had much in common. By physically integrating in the same state communities with different ways of life and sometimes histories of animosity, the state-making process during the colonial era brought groups into political proximity with one another with results that continue to produce conflict and sometimes civil ethnic warfare (e.g., Rwanda, the Sudan, Mozambique, Nigeria, Burma, Sri Lanka, and elsewhere).

New States, Weak Economies

The combination of political newness and economic dependency and/or deprivation, the frequent absence of democratic options for protesting minority status, discrimination, and other perceived grievances, and the prevalence of governments who are non-conciliatory have given a raw edge to ethnic politics in the developing world. So has the absence of significant crosscutting cleavages as a result of the underdeveloped nature of the economies and the localized nature of life. Still, the economics of ethnopolitics in the developing world is complex. As Latin America illustrates, there can be a relatively high level of economic development and relatively low level of ethnic diversity by Third World standards, but considerable constitutional rollover and even periodic civil wars. The Dominican Republic, for example, has had 32 different constitutions since its independence in 1844, Venezuela 25 since 1811, and Nicaragua 14 since 1821, as well as numerous, violent struggles for power between ideologically divided groups, most recently during the 1980s.[11]

On the other hand, there does appear to be a correlation between economic development, ethnic diversity, and the tendency toward political stability in developing states. The long-term impact of economic development and modernization within the growing globalizing world economy is expected to bolster more cosmopolitan ways of life and indirectly weaken ethnic and other local ties by "exposing people to different ideas, behavior, and material goods," by creating other political interests and bases for political associations, and by generally challenging traditional identity and authority.[12] In the present, however, the forces of political moderation remain weak and the stabilizing presence of a strong middle class is generally lacking. Instead, mass poverty fuels a politics of despair among the dispossessed. Add the absence of cross-cutting identities and the pervasiveness of cultural reinforcement of ethnic identity (religion, language, appearance, and the like) and the result tends to be a greater (uncompromised) purity of the ethnic factor in the politics of the developing world than has normally been true of ethnopolitics in the advanced democratic or postcommunist worlds.

Given the strength of the ethnic identify in its own right and as an element available for political exploitation in developing states, their postindependence history has often been written in terms of riots and regional rebellions met by heavy applications of force. Far less frequent has been the tendency to accommodate ethnic demands found in the advanced democratic world, where—however reluctantly—governments have been willing to bargain with and offer concessions to the moderate spokesmen for ethnopolitical communities. Rather, the danger posed to the stability of multinational states in the developing world by virulent ethnic identities has been one of the causes and excuses for delaying democratization in these countries. Nevertheless, the last quarter of the twentieth century chronicled an upswing in the number of states perceived by internationally recognized criteria to be making the transition to democracy.

The Setting of Ethnopolitics in Nigeria

Given the ethnic, economic, and political diversity to be found in the developing world, no state can claim to be a typical developing country, and certainly not Nigeria. As a sub-Sahara country, it is already prone to greater ethnic diversity than the countries of North Africa, Asia's Pacific rim, Latin America, and the Middle East. As Africa's most populous state it is not surprising that its degree of tribal diversity is far above the average even for sub-Sahara Africa. Given the size of its population, it also confronts greater challenges than those faced by most developing states, despite its oil wealth, in providing health care and education to its citizens. In fact, given a wide arc of other problems, including a long period of political stagnancy and/or turbulence since the mid-1960s, epidemic patronage and nepotism systems under various regimes, and long periods of discrimination against some of its best-educated people because of their tribal affiliation, the country's oil resources have frequently contributed to the corruption long identified with its various regimes.[13] Yet Nigeria does share, both historically and in its search for stable government, many experiences with the multiethnic/multinational states of Africa and Asia, including the generally turbulent political environment in which its governments have functioned.

The Legacy of Colonialism

The impact of colonial rule on the making of Nigeria and the widening of ethnopolitical identities within it has already been noted. In general, Nigeria's cultural contact with the West during the relatively short period of British colonialism (1885–1960) increased the already formidable differences separating northern and southern Nigeria by leaving the Northern Region, for the major part, to its traditional Muslim way of life and Christianizing most of the south, urbanizing the Yoruba West, and concentrating educational development in Nigeria's Eastern Region.[14]

As in the case of India and British colonialism in North America and the Far East, British "administration" in Nigeria began as a commercial enterprise. Even before Britain's right to the area was formally recognized at the Berlin Conference in 1885, a number of treaties had been concluded between British trading companies and traditional rulers in northern and southern Nigeria. The principal actor in north central Nigeria was the Royal Niger Company, and by 1886 it had established an administrative network throughout the region's hinterland.

The interest of the British government in Nigeria increased with the tempo of the trading companies' activity. When, by the end of the nineteenth century, virtually all of the area now constituting Nigeria and the Cameroons had fallen under company control, London revoked the Royal Niger Company's charter. A year later (1900), the British government established its own control over the area, dividing the land into northern and southern protectorates (excluding the colony of Lagos in the south) and opening the area to large numbers of traders and missionaries. British control over the area was consolidated shortly thereafter, beginning with the amalgamation of the Lagos colony and the southern protectorate in 1906.

Critical Moments during the Road to Independence, and the Environment of Politics

Colonial Unification

Much of Nigeria's colonial history, and a large portion of its postindependence history can be traced to two decisions made during its rule by Britain. The first of these, from which all else has flowed, was Britain's decision to consolidate its two protectorates in 1912, the year Lord Lugard became the high commissioner for both, without any corollary plan to integrate the cultures of the two regions into a whole. Hence, although technically Nigeria was governed as a single, unitary state from 1912 to 1950, when the Richards Constitution created a centralized federal system composed of the Northern, Eastern, and Western Regions, the British system of indirect rule in the north versus the more centralized British administration in the south assured the continuance of local languages, customs, and ways of life even as it widened the already existing differences between the non-Muslim peoples of southern Nigeria and the more conservative Hausa-Fulani people in the north.

Given the profound differences separating Nigeria's north and south, whether measured in terms of topography (the north is arid), religion, diversity (most of contemporary Nigeria's more than 200 tribes and 50 broad ethnic groupings live in the south), or ways of life, this moment of state-making set the table for future conflict to the point where the factors that cut across regional lines in the south—the spreading Christian faith, the region's increasing economic development, and access to Western education—served to widen the differences between the northern and southern poles of the country. In doing so, they sparked fear throughout the Northern Region, where a majority of Nigeria's peoples lived, of being dominated by the 80 percent Christian, more educated, and economically prosperous south.

Smoothing the Road to Independence: The Final Years

The decision to unify the administration of the country was designed to make the country more governable and profitable as a colony for the benefit of London. The second decision, to prepare the country for independence, was made two generations later with the best of intentions for the peoples of Nigeria.

Being aware that a Britain in need of postwar recovery would have to cede independence to India shortly after the end of the war, during the last days of World War II the British Foreign Office began to draft plans for the peaceful decolonization, over time, of most of Britain's empire. As the most populous, as well as one of the most ethnically diverse countries in Africa, Nigeria featured prominently in these plans, out of which emerged in 1945 the draft for Nigeria's first transitional constitution. Designed by then governor of Nigeria A.F. Richards to "promote the unity of Nigeria: to provide within that unity for the diverse elements which make up the country; and to secure for greater participation by Africans in the discussion of their own affairs,"[15] the document broadened the role of the local advisory councils, which had been in place since 1922, and created regional councils for each of the colony's three regions. The Constitution was generally unpopular because these councils could only recommend legislation to the governor general, but the structure gave substantial political prominence to local authorities. It also greatly stimulated political competition among the major tribal communities and generated a trans-tribal desire for a greater say in the country's affairs.

As in the case of the 1912 decision to unite the two protectorates, the 1944–45 decision to begin the process of decolonization, even before an independence movement developed, profoundly affected the country's future. Instead of having to pressure Britain for independence, during the fifteen year transitional period political leaders of the principal communities were able to concentrate on mobilizing their respective tribal coalitions along ethnoterritorial/tribal lines.

The process began in the better-organized and more educated Ibo community. In 1943–44 the American-educated future president of Nigeria, Nnamdi Azikiwe, had founded the Ibo State Union, a pan-Ibo organization to advance the interests of Ibos living in the Eastern Region and elsewhere in Nigeria, and had assisted in the birth of the National Council of Nigeria and the Cameroons (NCNC), a loose association of Ibo political, social, and cultural organizations. With the promulgation of the Richard's Constitution, Azikiwe converted the NCNC into Nigeria's first political party and began articulating "nationalist" complaints against political charters imposed from above.[16]

Although the NCNC was officially a pan-tribal coalition, the dominant role played by Ibos in its leadership and membership aroused suspicions in the other politically awakening tribes of the south. As a result, a political–cultural association dedicated to the advancement of Yoruba interests—founded in London in 1948 by its central figure, Yoruba Chief Obafemi Awolowo, and out of which the Action Group party evolved—soon became active in Nigerian politics. In turn, the emergence of a purely Yoruba political association in the Western Region encouraged the Ibos to consolidate their hold on the NCNC and recast it as an Ibo party, and had a major impact on politics in the Northern Region. There, concern with the north's comparative lack of preparation for self-government and the corollary fear that progressive southerners would replace the British in the governance of the Northern Region prompted two British-educated northern leaders, R.A.B. Dikko and Abukabar Balewa, to organize the Northern Peoples Congress (NPC) in 1949 in support of the area's traditional Hausa-Fulani rulers.[17]

The Birth of Federalism: Preserving the Center by Empowering the Regions

Subsequent constitutional developments both accelerated and reflected these ethnopolitical coalitions' growing control over political affairs in their regions. Gradually Nigerian politics were alternately triangularizing along North, East, and West lines and polarizing whenever the East, and West supported proposals deemed prejudicial to the North. Largely left out of the process were the minority tribes in each region, even though many were developing a political consciousness of their own out of their fear of domination by the principal tribal group in their respective regions once the British withdrew. Meanwhile, a consensus developed among the political leaders of the AG, NCNC, and NPC based on their common aversion to the highly centralized nature of the 1945 (Richards) Constitution. All soon came to endorse federalism as the proper form of government for independent Nigeria. Their reasons for doing so and the form of federalism each had in mind, however, varied considerably.

The idea of structuring Nigeria along federal lines with most power in regional hands had been proposed as early as 1943 in Awolowo's pamphlet, the *Path to Freedom*. Inspired by the example of federalism in India, Awolowo urged the adoption of a federal system based on a loose network of autonomous linguistic states as the best means of protecting the diverse cultures of Nigeria's peoples. Azikiwe, on the other hand, saw federalism primarily as a stepping-stone to the eventual creation of a unitary system. Northern leaders were ambivalent on the issue. Possessing a majority of Nigeria's population, the North's interests seemed assured whatever the structure. If the North had had the educational manpower to control such a state, they would have probably supported Azikiwe's position; however, under the circumstances they waffled, supporting a centralized form of federalism, but one in which the British would continue to control the central government until the Northern Region was sufficiently prepared to assume control of both their region and the central apparatus.

By the time the all-Nigerian Conference on the Constitution convened in January, 1950, all three regions were supporting a "federation" based on only the three existing regions. When the resultant 1950 constitution not only accepted this model but augmented the autonomy of the existing regional councils, the die was cast. The 1954 Constitution strengthened the power of the regions in a clearly federalist direction. Elections held between 1956 (the year Ghana became the first independent country in sub-Sahara Africa) and 1957 saw the regional governments fall fully into the hands of the AG, NCNC, and NPC, and by the time Nigeria received independence in 1960, the issue of form of government was no longer being debated. Moreover, with Nigeria's major parties concentrating on consolidating their political control over their respective regions, the central legislature, which materialized during this transitional period, was singularly lacking in any strong, Nigerian nationalist leadership. Rather, the cabinet was essentially a standing committee of the regional governments until the 1959 federal elections when Sir Abubakar Tafawa Balewa, as the leader of the strongest party, accepted the post of prime minister and at last gave the central government a leader of stature. By then, however, British accommodation of Nigerian regionalism had become the rule. Thus, although Chief Awolowo failed to get his proposed "right to secede" incorporated into the independence Constitution, the federation of Nigeria was launched with the individual regions enjoying substantial autonomy and each soundly under the control of its dominant tribal grouping. The state was new, but the political loyalties of those supporting its governing parties were old—tribal identities, with all their incorporated suspicions of the other tribal fellow.

CHAPTER ELEVEN

Ethnopolitics in Nigeria

As a widely cited student of contemporary Nigerian affairs has summarized, Nigerian politics has been the product of a mix of elements, including the country's precolonial history, the impact of British colonialism on its peoples, its constitutional order at independence and, subsequently, the frequency with which its military has assumed power, and its developmental policies, especially with respect to its oil resources. Hence, "conflict in Nigeria . . . has never been simply along ethnic/tribal grounds."[1] Moreover, the ethnic factor in Nigerian politics has been eclipsed sometimes since the collapse of the First Nigerian Republic (1960–66) by the civilian versus military struggle for power at the top, the corruption that has infected the system in general, and the struggle for control of Nigeria's oil wealth in particular. Throughout, however, the tribal identities of its major and minor tribal communities have persisted as reference points for their members and as sources of system-challenging conflict in the Nigerian state.

Ethnoterritorial Politics in Independent Nigeria

Independence Day in Nigeria, October 1, 1960, arrived accompanied by neither woolly, optimistic predictions of tranquility nor pessimistic predictions of imminent disaster. The centrist versus regionalist disagreements between the major, tribal-based parties on the shape of the state during the writing of the independence Constitution had been troubling; however, the former British colony of Ghana (the former Gold Coast) had achieved independence a few years before, and had seemingly developed a stable government under the leadership of the former pan-Africanist Kwame Nkrumah. Certainly independence in Nigeria carried none of the political drama existing in Algeria, where independence came only after a civil war with France, or the aura of pending doom surrounding decolonization in the Belgian Congo, notoriously underprepared for self-government. More importantly, Nigeria seemed to possess the institutional and human resources necessary to overcome tribal rivalries and establish a stable democracy.

Engineering Stability: The Independence Constitution and the First Republic

The hopes for Nigeria's future were pinned on four components of its planned political order. The first and most important was the federal formula adopted in Nigeria, which gave each of its three federal states (regions) considerable independent authority and left each under the control of one of Nigeria's dominant tribal communities. As a result, the Ibos, Yorubas, and Hausa-Fulanis each enjoyed a power base in the system and hence each had a stake in the regime's survival.

Second, the constitutional provisions governing representation and the amendment process were designed to make any reconfiguration of the regime difficult. As before independence, the central parliament continued to have a house whose membership was based on population, thereby giving the Northern Region, with its majority of Nigeria's people, the ability to block action prejudicial to its interests. To allay southern fears of the North using the central government to dominate the Eastern and Western Regions, a second house was added at the 1957 London Conference on the Constitution. Each region was to be represented equally in it, and a two-thirds majority there would be required before the central government could intervene in any region's affairs.

Third, and complimenting this regional balancing act, there was to be an ethnic balancing arrangement in the allocation of the principal offices of the state. The symbolic head of state was to be the father of Nigerian nationalism, Dr. Nnamdi Azikiwe ("Zik" to his countrymen). The head of government was to be drawn from the more populous Hausa-Fulani North, initially the NPC's leader, Sir Abubakar Tafawa Balewa. Finally, the leader of the Action Group, Chief Awolowo, was to serve as both the leader of the Western Region and leader of (along British lines) the "Loyal Opposition" in the federal parliament. All enjoyed countrywide fame, and "Zik" enjoyed a trans-tribal respect when independence arrived..

Finally, confidence in the new state also resided on the professional (i.e., neutral) nature of the Nigerian Civil Service and the army officer corp, despite the disproportionate representation of southerners in both. The former was modeled on India's civil service, which in the more than dozen years that had passed since India achieved independence had not disappointed its British mentors. The Nigerian army had proven itself shortly after independence as the leading African contingent in the UN forces in the civil war–torn, former Belgian Congo.

Constitutional Government and the Presumption of a Democratic Political Culture

Shortly after independence, hopes for democracy in Nigeria began to fade fast, and largely for the reasons perceived by the architects of Nigeria's constitution. The great divide between North and South had worried British parliamentarians both before and after Nigeria received independence. More basically, as befits a country that relies on a trust in the reasonableness of the government and governed alike rather than constitutional details to safeguard democracy,[2] the British Colonial Office had worried about the commitment of Nigeria's politicians to democratic government. In the words of the Commission on Nigeria's independence constitution in rejecting the demands of the small tribes for states of their own to protect themselves from the majority tribes in Nigeria's three regions:

> The whole structure of the proceedings leading to independence is based on the belief that Nigeria means to follow the road to liberal democracy and parliamentary government; to base parts of the structure on the opposite assumption is to invite governments to do their worst.[3]

Yet beyond Zik, Balewa, and a handful of other Nigerians who were to hold key positions at independence, this belief was not only untested but soon to be disappointed.

Ethnoterritorial Politics, Political Opportunism, and the End of the First Republic

As table 11.1 indicates, independent Nigeria's descent into first political instability, then political violence, and finally civil war was the product of a combination of simmering ethnopolitical rivalries, political ambition, political corruption, good intentions, and, finally, the disintegration of the military and destruction of the bureaucracy as all-Nigeria institutions of unity. In the end, no amount of political manipulations or tactical bargains between the spokesmen for the major tribes could peacefully preserve either the regime or the country.

The breakdown began in 1962 with the unraveling of the ability of each of the dominant tribal-based parties to control one of Nigeria's three regions. Insofar as each of these regions contained minority tribes fearful of domination by the majority tribal coalition, the environment was ripe for an electoral raiding of votes by the dominant parties in the other regions. Particularly vulnerable were the tribes in the East, given the Ibo's educational, economic, and numerical advantages over them. Shortly after independence many of these minority tribes, as well as several non-Hausa-Fulani areas in the North, were already being actively wooed by Chief Awolowo's Action Group party.

In response to Awolowo's action, in 1962 the NCNC and NPC, partners in the coalition government at the center, tacitly agreed to neutralize the Western Region's AG, an especially formidable opponent of the NCNC in non-Yoruba, "Midwest" Nigeria—that is, the eastern-most portion of the Western Region. The opportunity came in May, when the leader of a breakaway faction of the AG and his followers caused disorder in the Western Region's Assembly. With the delegates from the Eastern

Table 11.1   Nigeria: from colonialism to the Third Nigerian Republic

1885	Britain's control over area recognized at Berlin Conference; British trading companies already active in area
1900	Heavily Muslim northern Nigerian becomes British Protectorate
1906	Lagos Colony integrated into non-Muslim Southern Protectorate
1914	Northern and southern Nigeria joined under single Royal Governor, Lord Lugard
1914–40	Differences between northern and southern Nigeria widen given economic, educational, and religious changes in the South
1940s	Political awakening in south's Eastern and Western Regions
1945–46	Postwar Britain begins to prepare Nigeria for independence; tribe-based parties form in Nigeria
1951–54	Constitutional structure of pre-independence Nigeria develops along federal lines based on only 3 regions
1956–57	Elections result in control of each region by parties based on each region's dominant tribal group
1960	October 1: Nigeria becomes independent. First Nigerian Republic begins
1962	Political opportunism results in arrest of leader of Western Region, Chief Awolowo
1962–63	Opportunism escalates; Awolowo's rival, Akintola, takes control of party; new region carved out of West
1963–64	Ibo party controlling (NCNC) East gains control of new (Midwest) region
1964	Election based on tainted census favoring North gives its major party (NPC) majority in Federal Parliament
1964–65	Akintola-led AG joins NPC in coalition at center; regional vote in West rigged to favor Akintola. Protests turn violent
1966	January 14–15: First Republic ends when military coup led by Ibo officers strikes at center and in West and North
	January–April: riots in North, whose principal leaders were killed in coup; Ibo General Aguiyi-Ironsi controls the state
	May–June: Ironsi dissolves federal system; rioting intensifies in North, killing numerous Ibo working there
	July 28–29: counter-coup: northern soldiers mutiny, kill Ironsi and hundreds of Ibos in military, seize control of state
	August–September: Lt. Col. Gowon, a non-Ibo Christian, restores federal system; anti-Ibo riots kill 30,000 Ibos in the North
1966–67	October–May: Ibos return to East; Gowon creates federation of 12 states with strong center over objections of East
1967	May 30: East secedes as Biafra
	July: Federal Troops cross into Biafra, beginning Nigerian Civil Wars
1970	January: Civil War ends with surrender of Biafra; rule of Nigeria by military continues
1975	Gowon deposed in military coup led by General Murtala Muhammad
1979–83	Second Republic, a presidential-separation of power system led by President Shehu Shagari, a Hausa-Fulani
1983	Shagari reelected in tainted vote; military led by General Muhnaunadu Buhari, also a Hausa-Fulani, deposes Shagari
1984	Severe religious riots rock 2 of the now19 states in the Nigerian federation
1985	April: General Buhari is removed in coup led by General Ibrahim Babangida from Nigeria's "Middle Belt"
1987	March: significant Muslim – Christian rioting occurs
1989	April: Constitution for a Third Nigerian Republic drawn up by a nonelected Constitutional Assembly
1990	Middle Belt military officers stage coup against continued rule by Hausa-Fulanis; coup fails, officers executed
1991	April: religious rioting in the northern state of Bauchi kills hundreds of Christians

Continued

Table 11.1   Continued

1993	June 12: presidential election, a Yoruba Muslim, Mashood Abiola wins nearly 60% of vote and 19 of now 30 states
	June 23: General Babangida nullifies election, igniting large-scale riots throughout southwestern Nigeria
	August: Babangida pressured into resigning; interim government under Yoruba Chief Ernest Shonekan organized
	November: General Sani Abacha, a northern Muslim, seizes power and appoints himself head of state.
1998	Abacha dies unexpectedly; a northerner, General Abdulsalami Abubakar takes power promising return to civilian rule
1999	February: retired general Olusegun Obasanjo, a Christian/Yoruba from the South who was sentenced to death under Abacha but is now supported by the North, is elected president with a 60% majority
2000	Several northern states formally adopt the *Sharia* as their legal code.
2003	Obasanjo is reelected; for first time two consecutive national elections pass without military intervention

and Northern Regions supporting action by the central government, the Western Region was declared to be in a state of emergency and placed under central control. By the time the "emergency" ended, the AG was in disarray, Chief Awolowo was in prison charged with sedition, and his rival who had led the demonstrations in the Western Region, Chief Akintola, had been installed as regional premier even though he had very little popular support in the region.

Shortly thereafter the NCNC received its *quid pro quo* for opportunistically collaborating with the Northern Peoples' Congress: the Midwest was surgically removed from the Western Region to become Nigeria's fourth state in a move designed to further weaken the AG and enhance the NCNC's strength in Nigeria's south. Having at least momentarily dispatched the AG, the NPC and NCNC then turned on one another. The roots of the clash were buried deeply in the already noted ethnic, religious, and developmental differences separating the Hausa-Fulanis from the Ibos. The immediate cause was Nigeria's efforts to hold a census preparatory to redistributing among the regions the seats in the central parliament before the 1964 general election. Southern Nigerians hoped that the count would conclude that they constituted a majority of Nigeria's population and hence were entitled to the majority of seats in the federal legislature then held by the Northern Region. And they tried hard to make their wishes come true. The first counts turned in by the Eastern and Western Regions, taken before the AG's demise in the West, were so inflated that even politicians from the South quickly agreed to abandon the first census. The figures produced by the second count were even more inflated, and a compromise—parity between North and South in the legislature—had to be brokered to avert a crisis. Nigeria's exact population at that time remains a mystery but three years later, as the First Republic was reaching its violent conclusion, one long-time observer of Nigerian politics anonymously observed, "Nigerians still talk of the census as though it were an election—who won and by how many people." [4]

The Final Days

Nigerian politics deteriorated quickly following Awolowo's arrest and the dispute over the census. Because the NPC could now count on the support of Western Nigeria's delegates at the center, it no longer needed the NCNC's votes. To protect itself, as the 1964 general election approached, the NCNC formed alliances with the remains of the still popular but highly disorganized AG in the West and several minor parties throughout Nigeria, confronting the Northern Region and its ally, Akintola's unpopular but ruling party in the Western Region, with the coalition of the South's major parties and tribal groups which it had always feared. In the campaign that followed, the southern alliance proposed reorganizing Nigeria's federal system through the creation of additional states and an expansion of the autonomy of all states in order to prevent any group or narrow coalition from dominating Nigerian politics. Had it been embraced by the North, the proposal *might* have sufficiently calmed fears among the Ibo, Yoruba, and many smaller tribes to have halted Nigeria's slide toward the brink, but the northern alliance firmly rejected the proposal.

With the election approaching, incidences involving the harassment and intimidation of opposition parties mounted throughout Nigeria, but especially in the Northern and Western regions. When it was announced on the eve of the vote that 61 NPC candidates in the Northern Region would run unopposed because their opponents had "improperly filed," the southern alliance called for an election boycott and politicians in the South began to utter the first threats of secession. Still, the system held together, largely as a result of the personal intervention of President Azikiwe as peacemaker and the forceful presence of Prime Minister Balewa, who convinced his party's leaders of the importance of installing a broad-based, trans-tribal government at the center. In the resultant compromise, election returns were allowed to stand in the North and West on the grounds that the boycotts there were only partially effective. New elections were scheduled for the Eastern and Midwest Regions, where the NCNC eventually swept virtually all seats. In the meantime, a coalition cabinet including all major parties except the AG was constituted.[5]

Attention then diverted to the scheduled 1965 regional election in the Western Region, which was expected to document the unpopularity of Chief Akintola and his followers. Had it restored the AG to office, the election would have eased southern fears of northern domination and prolonged the First Republic's life. Instead, the results were even more flagrantly rigged than in the 1964 general elections and emphasized the extent to which an unpopular state government with central support was able to subvert the country's democratic constitution. AG candidates were denied the right to register, to hold meetings and, frequently, even to meet in public. Ballot boxes disappeared from the AG's stronghold in heavily Yoruba areas, only to reappear in police headquarters nearly overflowing with anti-AG ballots. In the end, the ruling party announced patently false results and declared itself the victor.[6] Insurrections erupted in much of the Western Region.[7]

As the rioting spread, the central government—which had been so quick to respond in 1962 to a few unruly demonstrators disrupting the Western Region's Assembly—forfeited most of its remaining legitimacy by doing nothing. It was thus the army that eventually acted as disorder fed by frustration with the corrupt nature of the government spread throughout the South, reinforced by traditional southern fears of domination by the Hausa-Fulani North. On January 15, 1966, a band of officers struck with Sandhurst-trained precision in the Northern and Western Regions and the federal capital of Lagos. Among the casualties were the central religious leader and the regional premier in the Northern Region, Chief Akintola in the West, and Prime Minister Balewa.

The Road to Civil War

The coup that ended the First Republic was initially greeted with enthusiasm in much of the country, being interpreted as an attack on corruption and provincialism rather than on a particular region or tribe.[8] Its popularity, however, was short-lived. The fact that most of those killed were northerners, combined with the predominantly (27 out of 32) Ibo nature of those staging the coup and the fact that the subsequent regime of General Ironsi, an Ibo, was almost entirely composed of Ibos, kindled northern fears of southern domination both in the Northern Region and among the northerners in the Nigerian army. Their worst suspicions were seemingly confirmed a few months later by General Ironsi's May, 1966, decree eliminating all existing political parties and terminating the country's system of regional autonomy.

Anti-Ibo riots in the North ensued immediately, killing numerous Ibo civilians living there and prompting Ironsi to retreat politically. In June he indicated that the May decree was only temporary and that the final form of Nigeria's new constitution would be determined by a constituent assembly and popular referendum. As a balm to northern anxieties, his promise came too late. Perhaps because of his own all-Nigeria orientation Ironsi had already drifted too far out of touch with the country's political realities. The leaders of all of Nigeria's principal ethnotribal groups viewed regional power as essential to their community's welfare and to *their* personal status.

On July 29, 1966, the country's second coup occurred—this time a military mutiny by northern troops. Although defended by its architects as pro-federalism in nature, it was primarily an anti-Ibo coup, and widely perceived as such despite the fact that the man who took charge of the government, Lt. Col. Yakuba Gowon, was a Christian from Nigeria's

"Middle Belt." As James Wunsch has noted, "some 200 Igbo officers and rank-and-file soldiers were clearly sought out by the coup leaders and swiftly executed."[9] The dead included General Ironsi.

Taken together, the coups of January and July, 1966, not only ended Nigeria's First Republic but irrevocably shattered most of the institutions and arrangements upon which it rested. The always brittle, three-region federal formula for soothing the fears of the Ibos, Yorubas, and Hausa-Fulani of domination by the other tribal fellow became a political football once Gowon justified the military mutiny in the name of restoring Nigerian federalism. The anti-Ibo nature of the second coup also cast a dark shadow over the Ibo-dominated civil service as a durable, Nigeria-oriented instrument for governance, and tribalized the military to the point of ending its utility as an "instrument of [domestic] conflict resolution."[10] And as for the unifying value of the politicians who inherited political power at independence, Balewa was dead, Awolowo had become so associated with Yoruba interests that he had little value as a voice of Nigerian unity even though one of Gowon's first acts was to free him from prison, and "Zik" was soon forced to live in exile out of fear for his safety.

These events did not end the interethnic, interregional politics that led up to the 1966 coups. Northern Muslims continued to attack the Ibos living in their region to the point that, even as Colonel Gowon was reaffirming the country's commitment to the rule of law, Ibos in the North began to trek back to eastern Nigeria. Their migration took on wholesale proportions in September of 1966, when a massive attack claimed at least 30,000 lives.

As inter-tribal violence mounted, the Ibo officer who had been appointed to take charge of the Ibo East, Major Ojukwu, urged Gowon to create a loose, confederate system in which eastern Nigeria would have far greater autonomy than under the former system as the only means of assuring Ibo security.[11] The idea, however, was totally unacceptable to Gowon and the military council ruling the country. As a result, Ojukwu's proposals swiftly escalated into an ultimatum: that the East would take steps of its own to guarantee the safety of its people if the central government failed to adopt the proposed system. In response, Lagos did loosen some of its control over the regions, but retained the ultimate power to assume direct rule should an emergency develop. On May 20, the last compromise effort failed when Ojukwu refused Gowon's offer of withdrawing all northern soldiers from the East in return for Ojukwu pledging to keep the East in a centralized Nigerian federation. Ten days later, the East seceded, declaring itself the independent Republic of Biafra. Thus began the Nigerian civil war (May 1967–January 1970), which claimed over 600,000 lives before Biafra's surrender brought the fighting to a close in January, 1970.'

Although no formula could be found for preventing the East's secession, in the final days of May, Gowon made two decisions which contributed significantly to preserving the country. First, to secure support from the remainder of Nigeria in his stand against Ojukwu, Gowon declared a state of emergency and reorganized Nigeria into a system of twelve states, three of which were carved from the Eastern Region. The result was that minority tribes in the North and West had something to fight for in the approaching civil war and non-Ibos in the East were given an incentive to revolt against that area's majority or—at least—not to fight wholeheartedly in Biafra's defense. Second, civilians from eleven of these areas were integrated into Gowon's government, providing it with direct linkages to the peoples of the new states. In the bargain, Chief Awolowo was co-opted into supporting the center when he was selected to lead one of the Yoruba states in the West and promised the post of prime minister after the war—a move that guaranteed the West would not follow the East in seceding.[12] Consequently, the Ibos of Biafra had to stand alone against most of Nigeria when the war came, unsure of support even within their own region.

Ethnoterritorial Politics in Post–Civil War Nigeria

Cynics argue that Biafra's decision to secede was resisted by Gowon largely because oil had recently been discovered in Nigeria's East; however, the country's leaders were also, perhaps primarily, motivated to act because of the chaos that might have ensued in Nigeria and elsewhere if Biafra had successfully seceded. Given the multinational nature of so many of the states constructed by the departed colonial powers, there was a danger that a successful secession anywhere might trigger a separatist epidemic throughout Africa. Winning the civil war, however, was only Nigeria's first step back toward restoring the system-wide stability it possessed, however tenuously, at independence. In a very real sense, Nigeria is still traveling that path, sometimes aided and sometimes handicapped by the other developments that have shaped its political process since the surrender of Biafra.

By 2005, the search for stability had taken Nigeria through fifteen different regimes since the July, 1966, toppling of Ironsi's government. Of these, seven have been military, one a military–civilian transitional system (1998–99), and only three civilian, with one of those lasting only months. Ethnoterritorial conflict was rarely the primary cause of this change, but it has remained both a prism through which politics continue to be viewed in the country and a persistent presence in Nigerian politics. Meanwhile, the tribal communities occupying centerstage since the First Republic have often been other than those three that dominated politics in newly independent Nigeria and whose members still represent approximately 60 percent of the country's population.

The Frequency of Military Rule

A major change in Nigerian politics since 1966 has been the constant reality or shadow of military rule during most of the past 40 years. As a result, considerable restraints have been placed on political activity, organizations (including the number and names of the parties permitted to operate) and discourse even during republican eras of elected leadership.[13] The Second Nigerian Republic (1978–83) had a shorter life span than the First before being ended by a bloodless coup on the rationale that it had been unable to restore economic and social order, and the first effort at creating a Third Republic ended when the military nullified the presidential vote before the president-elect could assume office. This action ultimately brought an end to General Babangida's regime because of the protests and general strike that followed, but not an end to military rule. It was not until 1999 that the Third Republic—the current era of democratically elected government— finally commenced with the election of former general Olusegun Obasanjo.

Petro-Corruption

Nigerian politics since the First Republic has also accommodated itself to such a high level of political corruption and criminal activity that Nigeria has persistently topped the international list of the most corrupt countries in the world. Some attribute the decline of professional ethics and duty in the military—from the generals seeing themselves as their country's saviors to becoming its exploiters—to the wealth to be siphoned from the oil industry. As Oladimeji Aborisade and Robert Mundt summarized in their text on *Politics in Nigeria:*

> a subculture developed among officer ranks that can be identified as "When do I get my Turn?" Such corruption of values is common in the world, but the availability of oil revenues means that authoritarian leaders need not seek their rents directly from the populace.[14]

The exploitation of political power for personal wealth peaked during the regime of General Sani Abacha, who seized power in 1993 and ruthlessly ruled Nigeria until his unexpected, natural death in mid-1998 brought to office a successor, General Abdulsalam Abubakr, who was genuinely committed to restoring democratic government. Abacha left behind, in addition to a legacy of corruption and brutality, which included the execution of many of his critics, US$654 million in Swiss bank accounts.[15]

The Northern Nigeria–Military Rule Connection

Throughout the 1966–99 period, the ethnopolitical undercurrent of Nigerian politics endured, fueled by the nature of the military regimes governing the country and those institutional reforms designed at least in part to manage the tribal element in Nigerian Politics. Five of the seven military regimes that have governed Nigeria since July 1966 have been led by northerners, compared to only one by a Yoruba, and another by the Middle Belter who staged the July, 1966, takeover, General Gowon. No Ibo or other Easterner has ruled Nigeria in either a civilian or military capacity since Gowon deposed Ironsi. Thus, despite the fact that the Ibo community suffered no systematic punishment following Biafra's failed effort to secede, there has been a persistent southern uneasiness with, and sometimes estrangement from, even the most forthright of those military governments

Similarly, the fact that the president who was elected to lead the Second Republic (1979–83), Alhaji Shehu Shagari, was also a Hausa-Fulani northerner ensured that from the beginning that Republic would be perceived by southerners as a continuation of their country's dominance by the Northern Region.[16] Consequently, by the end of his term, communal unrest was widespread in the South, acerbated by the collapse of energy prices and hence greater chaos in an economy by then dependent on oil for over 80 percent of its foreign earnings. This unrest, coupled with growing Christian–Muslim violence in northern states and the widespread perception that Shagari's reelection in 1983 was fraudulent, provided the only invitation that the military, led by General Buhari, needed to terminate the Second Republic.

General Buhari, in turn, not only continued the northern connection but made his regime "both more Northern and more Islamic," appointing 13 of the 19 members of his ruling council from the North.[17] Things did not improve during the eight-year regime of Buhari's successor, Major General Ibrahim Babangida, whose lasting contribution to Nigerian politics was to move the country's capital from the southern district of Lagos to the Northern locale of Abuja, a city built at the cost of billions of dollars into a gleaming showcase, whose restaurants and hotels Nigeria's citizens cannot afford.[18] Less lasting were Babangida's efforts to try to work around the ethnic division in moving his country toward a democratic Third Republic by permitting only two parties to function and by banning the candidacies of prior elected officials. Once the country's communal groups were again permitted to organize, the long existing, local political bosses quickly infiltrated the two parties with their surrogate candidates, and local power gravitated back into the hands of those bosses and the tribal coalitions they again mobilized.[19] Meanwhile, in the 1993 Presidential election, two Muslims faced one another, one a Muslim Yoruba from the South (Chief Abiola) whose apparent victory with nearly 60 percent of the vote prompted Babangida to nullified the election. Consequently, an election meant to restore democracy in Nigeria culminated in such widespread protests that Babangida was forced to resign in favor of a civilian caretaker government. The latter, however, lasted only a few months (August 27–November 17, 1993) before being overthrown by Sani Abacha, a northerner from the Kanuri region, and his corrupt supporters.

Not until Abacha's 1998 death did the effort to restore democracy resume, and once again the traditional, territorialized tribal coalitions emerged at the center of democratic Nigerian politics. This time the framework was the five-party system permitted by Abacha's eventual successor, General Abubakr. In short order, the three parties tied to political bosses rooted in the Hausa-Fulani, Ibo, and Yoruba communities emerged as the strongest in each of the regions that originally constituted independent Nigeria.[20]

Federal Manipulations and Ethnopolitical Conflicts

The picture in the Third Republic is not entirely an "old wine in new bottles" rendition of politics in the First Republic—one in which the NPC, AG, and NCNC have been reincarnated with new leaders under new titles. Two important additions to the traditional ethnocultural and ethnoterritorial axes of Nigerian politics have evolved since the end of the First Republic, and each has acquired considerable visibility in contemporary Nigerian politics.

The one that has achieved the most international notoriety has been a federalist variation on the Muslim–Christian conflict in the North and the Middle Belt area, where the two faiths often intermingle. Given the relative neutralization of the North's fears of southern domination after 1966, the Muslim states in northern Nigeria have had the political luxury of splitting on the basis of their inclination to join church and state. Those in the northwest have traditionally been more fundamentalist than those to the northeast, and with the restoration of civilian rule in the late 1990s, some of these states have used their federal autonomy to adopt Islamic law as the basis of their criminal codes, complete with such traditional Islamic punishments as flogging, amputation, and death by stoning. When the latter sentence was imposed on a pregnant, illiterate women in 2002 for her adulterous relationship with the father of her unborn child, her pending execution not only intensified the ethnocultural division between Muslim North and Christian South, but resulted in considerable unwanted international publicity before an Islamic court overturned the sentence after the birth of the child.[21]

Meanwhile, the long-term reliance on federalism and state administrative structures in coping with communalism has also had an impact on tribal conflict in Nigeria. By steadily increasing the number of states—from 12 under Gowon to 37 today (plus the capital district in each instance)—Nigerian leaders have perpetuated the differences separating the principal tribal communities and given institutional standing to an expanding number of ethnoterritorial communities. They have also increased inter-governmental competition for public resources and political influence by pitting more states against one another in the competition for the former and exercise of the latter, although the motivation for enhancing the status of the smaller tribes has varied from regime to regime.

The 1979 decision to increase the number of units to 19 was motivated by a desire to integrate Nigeria's minority tribes into its political life by empowering tribes that constituted 29 percent of the population but which had previously been under the control of the majority community in their regions. Their potential influence was also enhanced by changing the form of the state from the parliamentary system of the First Republic to a separation of power, president-based system in which to be elected president a candidate would have to receive both a majority of the overall vote and 25 percent of the vote in at least 12 states.[22] In contrast, the general (Babangida) who overthrew the Second Republic and subsequently increased the number of states to 30, saw federalism as a divide–and–rule device, which would make it difficult for the opponents of his regime to unify.[23]

Whatever the intent, the practical consequences of increasing the number of states in Nigeria's federal system has been to broaden the distribution of political power at the state level to an expanding number of smaller tribes, thereby producing a new and often violent competition between these groups at the state and federal levels. Another new face of ethnoterritorial politics in Nigeria has thus been an increase in conflict involving the smaller tribes, especially in Nigeria's oil-rich Delta region, where the competition for resources between the area's Ijaw and Itsekiris tribes, and between these and the central government, has frequently (1999, 2001, and again in 2003) erupted into violence claiming hundreds of lives.[24]

At the same time, these institutional reforms *have* widened the range of democracy in Nigeria, and diluted the danger of a bipolar struggle between North and South or a three-way competition for power between the Northern, Eastern, and Western Regions. More importantly, the creation of a directly elected president has forced the formation of broad political coalitions by those seeking that office. Hence, despite charges of fraud, incidents of ethnic violence attending the voting, and a general sense among international observers that the reelection of President Obansanjo in 2003 "wasn't a disaster, but it's a long way from an election to be proud of,"[25] his 62 percent of the vote, even if somewhat discounted for fraud, reflected a candidacy that transcended the North–South division of the country and had appeal in much of Nigeria. It was also the first time in the country's history that two consecutive free elections were held, and if Obansanjo finishes his term, the Third Republic will have outlived multinational Nigeria's first efforts at democratic government.

Ethnoclass Conflict in Nigeria

Unlike in many developing areas, no communities of ethnically distinct outsiders were imported into Nigeria during the era of British rule.[26] Except for a scattering of peoples from tribes outside of Nigeria who traveled there for work in its developing South, no immigrant or foreign worker community emerged in Nigeria before or after independence, unless the managerial layer from the outside world involved in the country's oil industry is counted. Consequently, Nigeria has not experienced instances of ethnoclass politics analogous to that involving foreign worker and immigrant communities in Western Europe, the US immigrant communities, or the Romany and pre–World War II Jewish communities in Central Europe. Yet Nigeria has experienced a type of ethnoclass conflict—one involving its Ibo community and other educated southern tribes working outside their home regions in northern Nigeria.

Because of the already noted, uneven manner in which Britain "modernized" Nigeria, the much more educated southerners formed the backbone of its administrative system during the early days of independence. Commercial opportunities also often led the more entrepreneurial southerners to the Northern Region, where they lived ethnically and religiously apart from the Muslim communities, and usually in a more affluent manner. And it was this status of the Ibos and other southerners in northern Nigeria that exposed them to the violent wrath of Muslim northerners in the mid-1960s, including the massacre of tens of thousands of them as they tried to return to the South It was perhaps the inevitable fallout of the different trajectories of politics in independent Nigeria. For the southern tribes, Nigerian politics revolved, at least initially, around an ethnoterritorial axis. The Yorubas always wanted maximum territorial autonomy. After the 1966 coups essentially disenfranchised the Ibos at the center, the lure of territorial autonomy intensified within their community as well, and when that goal was frustrated, secession followed. For the northern tribes, however, politics centered on the threat to their way of life posed by the more educated as well as economically prosperous South, and hence focused on Nigeria's territorialized ethnoclass cleavage. Fear of the "South" had become a code word for the danger of Nigeria being dominated by a more educated, Christian community with whom northern Muslims had little in common.

In a similar fashion, although the contemporary clashes between Christian southerners working in the more fundamentalist areas of the Muslin North on the one hand, and local officials and citizens on the other are most visibly along religious lines (an ethnocultural cleavage), this divide continues to be substantially reinforced by the higher socioeconomic status of the southerners compared to their northern hosts.

CHAPTER TWELVE

Ethnopolitics in Nigeria in a Comparative Perspective

When Nigeria acquired independence in 1960, the literature on the politics of developing areas was replete with optimistic discourses on nation-building possibilities and—in former British colonies—the utility of federalism as a means of purchasing the time necessary to create overarching national identities in the multinational, newly independent world.[1] The 1947 partition of India had produced two federations, India and Pakistan, with the latter being divided into West Pakistan (itself a federation of ethnically distinct states) and East Pakistan, located nearly a thousand miles away on the other side of India. Subsequently, neither the bumpy history of democratic politics in Pakistan nor the collapse of the regimes established after World War II by the French in Syria (overthrown in 1949) and the British in Iraq (overthrown in 1958) had dissipated that optimism. Rather, even as Nigeria was edging toward a political crisis in 1963, federalism's utility as a means of creating "unity" out of (ethnic) diversity was being celebrated as another former British colony, the Federation of Malaya, expanded into the Federation of Malaysia with the addition of the Chinese city-state of Singapore and the isles of Sabah and Sarawak.

By the mid-1970s, both hopes for nation-building and confidence in federalism had faded. Nigeria's first federation had succumbed to civil war. Pakistan had been destroyed by civil war, with East Pakistan successfully exiting to become Bangladesh. Meanwhile, the presence of Singapore had destabilized the Chinese–Malay balance in Malaysia by awakening the political ambitions of the Chinese in the Federation of Malaya, and Singapore had—depending on whose version is credited—either withdrawn or been expelled from Malaysia. Of the former British federations of a decade before, only India continued to function, and at one point or another there, in the name of preserving the public order, Prime Minister Indira Gandhi had placed all but one of its states temporarily under emergency rule.

To be sure, not all states in the developing, multinational world have been so unfortunate in making the transition from colonial rule to stable self-government. Nor have only the multiethnic and/or multinational states in that world suffered violent political shocks. Ideological and religious differences have produced civil wars and prolonged intra-group conflicts in such ethnically homogeneous countries as Algeria, with casualties over time often numbering in the tens or even hundreds of thousands. Still, a large share of the multiethnic states that have achieved independence since World War II *have* been troubled and sometimes traumatized by eth-nopolitical conflict. So many, in fact, that table 12.1 only hints at the num-ber and wide-ranging locales of these conflicts. Even a moderately comprehensive comparison of these conflicts with political conflict in Nigeria is thus well beyond the reach of this chapter. What is offered instead is a broad, generic comparison of the types of conflict that have confronted independent Nigeria's governments with ethnic conflicts else-where in the developing world, with particular attention to the range and utility of those tools of conflict management that have been employed in those states.

Ethnoterritorial Divisions and the Struggle for Stability

Though not comprehensive, table 12.1 is illustrative of the disproportionate number of ethnoterritorial conflicts in developing states, compared to ethnoclass tension and violence. Similarly, although not all conflicts paral-lel the shape of ethnic conflict in Nigeria—there is, for example, the con-flict in Mexico, Peru, and Bolivia between native tribes and the descendants of the European settlers and of their children with African or Indian partners—most conform to the threefold pattern of ethnoterritorial politics that has developed in Nigeria. Some conflicts are between small communities scrambling for local influence similar to the tribal competition for resources involving the smaller tribes in Nigeria's oil-producing Delta region. Some involve struggles between larger groups and minorities in various regions of developing states. And some are based on the competi-tion between larger groups for influence at the center or those seeking to achieve regional autonomy and those groups controlling power. But unlike in Nigeria, several of these conflicts have cross-border dimensions where tribal or ethnolinguistic communities span international frontiers, and/or have resulted in outsiders becoming involved in the internal conflicts of developing world states.

Weak Minorities, Weak States

Table 12.1 chart also offers only a small glimpse of the frequency of ethnic conflict in the developing world, especially in Asia and Africa, where outsider state-making produced the greatest percentage of highly multinational states. It fails entirely to capture the intensity of that conflict and the degree to which interethnic conflict can strip large numbers of their

Table 12.1   A sampler of ethnic conflict in the developing world

Angola	Tribal struggles involving the Bukongo, Kimbundu, and Ovimbundu tribes still shape history
Bolivia	Periodic protests and revolts by indigenous Indians for civil rights and protection of lifestyle
Burma	Long-term low-intensity civil war involving minority communities, especially the Karens
Burundi	Long-term warfare between Hutu and Tutsi
China	Frequent minority demonstrations in Xinjiang Uygar and Inner Mongolia Autonomous Regions
Columbia	Protests and occasional violence involving Native Indians
Congo	Violence persists despite peacekeepers deployed in Congo
India	Periodic use of federalism since 1956 to accommodate the demands of ethnolinguistic minorities
Indonesia	Forceful secession of East Timor after 1999 vote for independence and Jakarta's efforts to block it
Iraq	Long-term, often violent conflict between ruling governments in Baghdad and the Kurdish north
Lebanon	1975 Christian–Shi'ite–Sunni power sharing "National Pact" collapses; civil war results
Liberia	Violent conflict persists between native Africans and ruling Americo-Liberian minority
Libya	Recent violence between Libyans and sub-Sahara immigrants/refugees from south
Malaysia	Despite expulsion of Singapore, Chinese–Malay tensions continue into twenty-first century
Mexico	1994 Rebellion by Chiapas (Indian tribe) in southern Mexico
Nigeria	Long-term tribal tensions often leading to military rule; 1966–69 civil war when Ibos try to secede
Pakistan	Continuing ethnic conflicts in former West Pakistan; secession of East Pakistan (now Bangladesh)
Peru	1980–2000 conflict involving rebel Indian movement claims tens of thousands of lives
Rwanda	Long-term warfare between Hutu and Tutsi; 1994 bloodbath claims 800,000 lives
Sri Lanka	Long-term, low-intensity civil war resulting from Tamil north's struggle for independence
Sudan	1980–present conflict between Muslim tribes in the north and non-Muslim tribes in the south claims 1.5+ million lives
Uganda	In addition to often significant tribal conflict, forced expulsion of 60,000 Asian residents in 1972
Western Sahara	Struggle for self-rule continues by people of Western Sahara resisting rule by Moroccans

humanity. The description of the massacre of Tutsi and moderate Hutus by Hutu extremists in Rwanda in 1994 is as revealing as it is horrifying:

> Because committing murder with a machete is exhausting, the militias were organized to work in shifts. At the day's end, the Achilles tendons of unprocessed victims were sometimes cut before the murderers retired to rest . . . . The genocide continued with astonishing speed. Although the killing was "Low tech," usually performed with a machete or a hoe, and although it was carried out in large part by

amateurs (often the neighbors and workmates of the victims), the "dead of Rwanda accumulated at nearly three times the rate of Jewish dead during the Holocaust."[2]

Dealing with the dangers of unrestrained protracted conflict, much less the violence of ethnic warfare is a daunting task in even the developed world. Moreover, ethnoterritorial movements in the developing world have normally presented challenges much more analogous to the separatist demands raised by the militants in Ulster and Basque Spain in Western Europe than the output- and authority-oriented goals typical of ethnopolitical organizations in developed democratic states. Under the most advantageous of circumstances, these goals have often been extraordinarily difficult to accommodate. Where, as in the developing world, societies lack mitigating, cross-cutting cleavages, where economic, linguistic, and sometimes religious differences reinforce and acerbate ethnic lines of stratification, and where economies are strained, people poor and resources for peacefully accommodating ethnopolitical demands scarce, the task of peacefully managing these demands can seem insurmountable. With limited options, it is therefore not surprising that many governments in the developing world have turned to one or more of the means of conflict management that Nigerian regimes have employed.

The Tools of Management

Repression and Control versus Accommodation

The dominant form of government in the developing world has been some variant of nondemocratic rule. Typically these have included: direct military rule, as in Nigeria, organized either in terms of one-man rule or under the auspices of a governing council; single- or domineering-party rule, as in Mexico; and rule by a civilian dictator backed by the army.

In many instances, military rule has begun with the best of intentions. Usually the most modern force in developing societies, the military often sees its mission as one of rescuing its country from political upheavals, be they the product of communal conflict, ideological warfare, weak parties unable to govern, countryside resistance to land reform, or poverty-induced rioting. Sometimes continuing disorder has made it difficult for the military to withdraw from politics. On other occasions, military regimes have assumed the long-term mission of playing savior to their countries. And sometimes various forms of strong man rule have lingered because of the personal profits to be made from controlling political power.

By the 1960s a pattern of military officers seizing control of the democratically structured governments left behind by departing colonial authorities had become commonplace. Military officers would intervene to restore order, suspend constitutions, promise new elections at an unspecified future date, and commence to rule. Within this framework, or the similar arrangements emerging in civilian dictatorships, the modal response to dissent has been repression, sometimes tempered (as in Nigeria) by the co-optation of spokesmen for potential centers of opposition and/or concessions of limited autonomy to territorialized minorities.

Where ethnopolitical minorities have remained centers of militant opposition to the regime, violent conflict has frequently resulted. In some instances, civil wars have yielded new states: for example, the emergence of Bangladesh from Pakistan and East Timor from rule by Indonesia. In other instances, secessions have decisively failed and the issue of the permanency of the state's borders has been resolved, as in the case of Nigeria. In many cases, however, conflicts between the center and territorialized minorities have evolved into prolonged, low-intensity civil wars. Sometimes with international attention but more often without, conflicts thus continue in the Sudan, the Western Sahara, Burma, and elsewhere in Africa and Asia, and are likely to persist because neither side seems weak enough to lose or strong enough to win.

Democratically Accommodating Ethnoterritorial Demands: Variations on the Theme of Federalism and Democracy in India

Given federalism's general failure to fulfill the lofty expectations many had for it as a means of holding together postcolonial states, its presence in the contemporary developing world is usually in a qualified form. Instead of the nonrevocable constitutional authority to legislate independently of the center in specified areas, territorialized minorities have been given a measure of autonomy as "states" within the unitary framework of military or strongman civilian rule. Still, because federalism remains an attractive idea to territorialized minorities nearly everywhere, the return to democracy in the current (Third) Nigerian Republic has necessarily been federal, just as federalization was a necessary step toward democratization in post-Franco Spain in order to gain Basque and Catalonian support for the new regime.

Federalism has also, for the same reason, been a primary option considered by third parties who have found themselves in the business of writing constitutions for countries rift with contentious ethnoterritorial communities. The case for federalism as a means of accommodating restive territorial minorities does not rest purely on theoretical grounds or its history in the older federations of the Western world. There is a case in the developing world where federalism has played a major role in democratically preserving the state, India, albeit as one part of a congruence of factors whose combination has been to India's great advantage but rarely approximated elsewhere.

India's original provinces were formed in a haphazard manner by British conquest and administrative systems. When territories were conquered, they were frequently grafted onto adjacent areas already under British control, producing provinces composed of numerous peoples with different tongues and cultures. As in the case of imperial state-making in general, no care was taken to form ethnically or linguistically homogeneous provinces, and when they did emerge it was as a byproduct of Britain's pursuit of other goals. The partition of the linguistically homogeneous province of Bengal into Muslim and Hindu parts, for example, was generally motivated by the British desire to insulate its Muslim community from the strong anticolonial nationalism embedded in Bengal's Hindu-dominated west.

Britain's decision to divide Bengal along communal lines was opposed by India's Congress party on the grounds that it violated Bengal's linguistic unity. After independence, when Congress controlled India's government, many leaders were to regret that stance because the risks of redrawing the boundaries of India's states along linguistic lines seemed high. The action was certain to encourage other territorialized communities to press for states of their own, as well as provide recipients with an institution from which to project additional ethnopolitical demands at the expense of India as a whole. Gandhi, in particular, was fearful that such linguistic units would unleash a storm of competing nationalism long before the official-language policy emphasizing. Hindu and English could provide the necessary link languages for the development of durable, all-India consciousness. Nonetheless, in mobilizing the country for the independence struggle, the party of Gandhi not only advocated redrawing India's internal administrative boundaries along linguistic lines but often organized its own grass roots machinery on that basis.[3]

Once in power, Congress quickly began to equivocate, although there were probably comparatively fewer risks in India manipulating federalism to accommodate the demands of territorialized separatist groups in the early years of independence than has been true of most multinational developing world states.[4] India had an underlying cultural unity (Hinduism) shared by the vast majority of its peoples. India also had a handy and serious enemy at its doorstep in Pakistan until the early 1970s, when the successful secession of East Pakistan, aided by India, resulted in Pakistan's dismemberment. When internal threats to India's unity appeared to be getting out of hand, wars with Pakistan (1956, 1962) often diverted attention to the common foe, still vilified for its role in dividing India and the tragedies associated with the migration of Hindus from Pakistan to India at partition.

More importantly, India enjoyed the presence of the Congress Party itself, an all-India political organization under the direction of skillful leaders who blended a commitment to democracy with tight control over governmental machinery all the way down to the district level for nearly two decades. Even later, the party still provided a means by which the central government could exercise substantial influence over states under Congress governments, as well as quasi-consociational machinery for keeping federal–state quarrels within the confines of the party and beyond the ears of the less politically sophisticated public. Only after Congress' mystique as the party of Gandhi, Nehru, and independence faded and a new generation of politicians emerged inside and outside of Congress with roots in their own localities did its integrative value diminish. Until then, a fourth asset enjoyed by India during its first two generations of independence was the continuity of not just the Congress Party but a broadly trusted ruling dynasty in first, Prime Minister Nehru, then his daughter Indira Gandhi, and finally her sons.

India also profited enormously from the all-Indian civil service fashioned by the British and retained after independence. With an elan of their own and distributed throughout all levels of government, this corp of administrators committed to India's survival was woven into governments throughout India.

Nevertheless, the immediate reaction of India's leadership at independence was to stall on implementing the long-promised reorganization of India's states. On the other hand, insofar as Congress had also accepted the principle of universal suffrage while challenging colonialism, it was understood that given the popularity of the linguistic reorganization issue, Congress would have to reorganize India once it honored that commitment. In the meantime, its leaders adopted the option of democratic politicians everywhere who find themselves on the spot. They appointed a handpicked committee to examine the matter, and in December, 1948, the commission dutifully concluded, "The formation of provinces on exclusively or even mainly linguistic considerations is not in the larger interests of the Indian nation and should not be taken in hand."[5]

Although that committee concerned itself with only four of India's states, its conclusions were meant to silence the almost countrywide demand for linguistic provinces. Instead, dissatisfaction with the committee's findings spread throughout India. The decisive moment came in 1953, when yet another commission was considering the reorganization of an Indian state (in this instance, the carving of a new unit out of Madras), with the self-immolation of an advocate of creating the proposed Telegu-speaking state. His death led to widespread disorder and bloodshed in the area, forced New Delhi to create the separate state of Andhra based on the linguistic principle, and eventually led to the comprehensive reorganization of India's federal system along linguistic lines. Three years later, the internal structure of India was halved to fourteen federal states, plus six autonomous territories. Of the fourteen, only two—Bombay and Punjab—were deliberately established on a multilingual basis. Each of the others had a dominant ethnolinguistic community.

In those twelve states where reorganization produced relatively unilingual provinces, the States Reorganization Act of 1956 proved to be a highly successful use of federalism as a means of defusing the centrifugal demands of India's largest linguistic communities. Moreover, in reorganizing India, the Congress Party validated its leadership position and slightly increased its share of the vote at both the state and central levels in the following year's general election. In the large and multilingual/multiethnic states of Bombay and Punjab, though, pressures for reform remained strong, as they did in the minority areas of many of the dominant-community states.

In 1960, Congress decided to end the experiment in multilingual coexistence in Punjab and split the state into the Gujarati-dominant state of

Gujarat and Marathi-speaking state of Maharashtra. That decision began a pattern of accommodation vis-a-vis India's ethnolinguistic minorities, which has continued into the twenty-first century. In spite of the party's reluctance to create a non-Hindu state in northern India, in 1966 Punjab was divided into the state of Punjabi-Suba for the Punjabi-speaking Sikhs and Haryana for the majority of the Hindi-speaking peoples of the area. Concessions to the ethnolinguistic minorities in those states with dominant linguistic majorities followed, beginning with the creation of the separate state of Nagaland to calm separatist demands among some of Assam's non-Assamese. Shortly thereafter, India employed the rather unique device of creating a "federation" out of the remainder of Assam in order to accommodate the desire for autonomy of the non-Assamese-speaking peoples in the state's hill districts.

Forty subsequent years of bargaining over separatist demands and boundaries in India have resulted in numerous concessions to the demands of India's smaller as well as larger ethnolinguistic communities, with the accommodation of one encouraging demands by others. The accommodation process, however, has not been an uninterrupted one, or one that has always worked to the advantage of the central government. Indian governments essentially followed this accommodation approach to separatist demands from 1956 until the late 1970s, and have again during the past decade; however, the intervention of outside governments in Indian affairs during the 1980s revived fears that India might disintegrate and resulted in New Delhi taking a hard stand against the demands for autonomy in the northeast as well as those of Kashmir's Muslims for merger with Pakistan.[6]

Separatism and calls for new states thus remain a part of politics in India.[7] Still, as Myra Chadda has noted, "Ever since India gained its independence in 1947, scholars of India have regularly predicted India's demise."[8] India not only survives but increasingly offers some evidence of a less turbulent future. For more than a half-century, its governments have done more than concede states to ethnolinguistic minorities to prolong India's existence. They have used that time to build an all-India economy and within it a large, well-educated middle class, which transcends ethnolinguistic borders. The process began as early the first Five Year Plan (1951–56), under which national income increased 18 percent and per capita income rose 11 percent even when adjusted to the country's imposing population increases.[9] A half century later, in raw numbers the Indian population contains the largest middle class and holders of advanced degrees in the world—a still growing, system-wide contingent that lives in the Indian and/or global economy, not the regional arenas where separatist agendas find their greatest appeal.[10]

Accommodation at the Center: Consociational Government, Co-optation, Proportionality, and Ethnic Balancing in the Developing World

Noncoercive means of responding to ethnopolitical demands in the developing world have also included, as elsewhere, a series of other individual and mix-and-match devices. The least prevalent and least successful of these have been consociational arrangements in which leaders with system-wide orientations have sought to prevent ethnoterritorial issues from gaining ground on the public agenda. Consociational government is always tenuous in multinational states. As occurred in Belgium during the 1970s, once an ethnoterritorial issue becomes salient—and they were usually salient *before* independence in the developing world—containing them becomes very nearly a lost cause. Ethnoterritorial organizations invariably spring up as ambitious political leaders seek to increase their influence by mobilizing the ethnic factor, and their co-optation into consociational systems is highly unlikely because *their* influence rests on keeping the ethnoterritorial lines of segmentation in their countries salient. Furthermore, if co-opted, the likelihood is high that they, in turn, will be rhetorically outbid by more regionally attuned political organizers in the next round of elections.

Personal ambitions have also eroded, either quickly or over time, efforts to control ethnopolitical divisions through ethnic balancing and representation schemes. The division of significant national offices in Nigeria among the leaders of its principal tribal communities during its First Republic, and the rotation of government offices among spokesmen for a wider network of tribal communities during the Second Republic ("Zoning") have had parallels elsewhere, most notably in Lebanon.[11] There, a "National Pact" allocating the principal offices according to ethnic identity provided the foundation for interethnic/intersectarian rule from the time Lebanon became independent in 1943 until its breakdown more than 30 years later. Under its terms, the president was to be a Maronite Christian, the prime minister a Sunni Muslim, the speaker of the Chamber of Deputies a Shia Muslim, and the chief of staff to the (Maronite) commander of the military was to be a Druze. As in the case of Nigeria's original leaders, there was a quasi-consociational presumption that Lebanon's leaders would have a system-wide [all-Lebanon] identity and try to minimize ethnic and sectarian divisions, even though they held their own offices by virtue of their affiliation with those identities. In the end, again as in the case of Nigeria, political leaders who saw more advantage in emphasizing their communal roots than defending the cause of Lebanon toppled the arrangement.

The unraveling began in the aftermath of the 1970 civil war in Jordan between Jordanians and the Palestinian refugees there. Under the terms of the settlement brokered by Egypt's President Nasser, the Palestinians moved into Lebanon, where they simultaneously injected the Arab–Israeli conflict into Lebanon policies and changed the balance of numbers in the country between Lebanon's Christian and Muslim communities. Previously, no group had represented a significant majority. Suddenly the Muslims did, and when they demanded that political power be redistributed to reflect this changing balance and the Maronites refused, the Pact broke down, unable to adapt to the changing world around it (the growing

Israeli–Palestinian conflict) or the changing environment of politics inside Lebanon, including politicians who saw greater personal opportunities in cultivating the ethnic division in their country than by trying to manage it.[12]

Proportionality formulas for distributing government power, resources, and jobs overcome many of the weaknesses of consociational and ethnically balanced governments in managing ethnic conflict; however, given the disproportionate access to education of some groups in the developed world, proportionality and parity systems received relatively little consideration when the multinational states of Asia and Africa received independence. Instead, governments have tended to speak more in terms of "equitable" or "fair" distribution of resources, not the more inflexible principle of proportionality as a basis for allocating political rewards.

Peacekeeping Missions and Communal Conflict

The one device that has not been a part of the conflict-management process in Nigeria but which elsewhere has gathered currency involves the deployment of peacekeeping forces by outside parties as a means of controlling communal violence. Indeed, peacekeeping was one of the major growth areas in international politics during the 1990s. The UN alone undertook more peacekeeping missions between 1990 and 1995 (nearly 30) than during the previous 45 years. To be sure, not all of these operations involved ethnic conflict—for example, the mission in a Haiti where law and order had broken down;[13] however, most of those undertaken by the UN, NATO, the Economic Community of West African States Monitoring Group (ECOMOG), and other international bodies have, and a growing number have involved the developing world.[14] Of the latter, the most instructive as well as complex and well known remains India's failed peacekeeping operation in neighboring Sri Lanka during the late 1980s.

The crucial events involving both the development of communal conflict in Sri Lanka and the deployment there of a peacekeeping force of approximately 80,000 Indian troops can be summarized easily. Sri Lanka is an essentially bicommunal state composed of a 72 percent Sinhalese majority, concentrated in the island's south, and an indigenous, 12 percent Tamil minority concentrated in the north and east, where they are the local majority and plurality respectively.[15] During the struggle for independence in the 1920s, Sinhalese leaders talked of the country's future in federal terms, with regional autonomy for the Tamils. Only eight years after independence in a still unitary Sri Lanka, however, its government passed the 1956 "Sinhala Only Act," ending the official status of English in the country and placing Tamils at a disadvantage in obtaining employment in the civil service, where they had previously held a disproportionate share of the jobs. Tensions abated momentarily when the prime minister agreed to devolve some form of regional autonomy to the territorialized Tamil minority, but when communal violence in 1958 prompted the prime minister to disavow the federal option, Sinhalese–Tamil relations begin their long-term downward slide.

In 1976, with laws favoring the Sinhalese majority growing in number, Tamil spokesmen redefined their objectives. Instead of federal astronomy they now demanded a country of their own. Running on a separatist platform, the Tamil United Liberation Front (TULF) won all seats in the north and eastern areas, only to forfeit them when those elected refused to take the required oath against secession. Elsewhere, the Sinhalese United National Party won 85 percent and, using its control of parliament, in 1978 it assured Sinhalese control of government by abandoning the Westminster model of cabinet government in favor of a president-centered system. Although violence continued to grow, the only sop offered to Tamil spokesmen over the next several years was the promise to hold legislative elections on a proportional representation basis, but in 1982 President Jayawardene used a referendum (overwhelmingly rejected in the Tamil areas) to postpone the implementation of that pledge. Interethnic relations nosedived thereafter, and in that context, between 1983 and 1989, India's role in the Sinhalese–Tamil conflict evolved from that of an outside mediator operating in its sphere of influence, to interventionist under the terms of the July 1987 Indo-Sri Lankan Accord (which promised the Tamils regional astronomy) to participant-policemen in the growing conflict between *Tamil* groups during the period between its intervention and its July 1989 decision to withdraw its peacekeeping contingent.

By the time India's peacekeeping force (IPKF) was deployed in July 1987, both the Sri Lankan police force and army had lost their capacity to function as neutral law and order agencies, given the government's previous efforts to "Sinhalize" them and their post-1983 reputation for conducting excessive reprisals against the Tamil community. Even the British-trained Special Air Services had become so identified with wanton retaliatory massacres of Tamil civilians that it was useless as a device for conflict resolution.[16] Moreover, extremist elements in the Sinhalese and Tamil communities had joined or eclipsed the more moderate spokesmen for these groups by the time the IPKF touched ground. The ruling Sinhalese party was under pressure from a nationalist-religious party in its own community, and the extremist, Tamil Tiger guerrilla organization (Liberation Tigers of Tamil Eelam, or LTTE) was in open warfare against the moderate Tamil leaders who had negotiated the autonomy-for-peace Accord with the Sinhalese that the IPKF was sent to enforce. Consequently, India's peacekeeping operations required both the deployment of troops and the harmonization of dual levels of mediation: diplomatic mediation between spokesman for the minority and majority communities in Sri Lanka (Tamil moderates and the Colombo government), and mediation between the moderates and the extremists in each community. It was a multitask challenge probably beyond the ability of any peacekeeper to achieve.

A successful peacekeeping operation (as opposed to side-taking) requires that the third party maintain an image of neutrality, but from the beginning

India had image problems within the Sinhalese community because of its prior, semi-open support of Sri Lankan Tamils.[17] Further, the terms of the Accord did not win India much favor among the Sinhalese insofar as it seemingly gave India a veto over several portions of Sri Lankan foreign policy. However, as the IPKF began to operate against the more radical Tamil organizations and to pressure their leaders to accept local autonomy instead of fighting endlessly for a separate state, New Delhi was able to develop an image of fairmindedness, at least within the government in Colombo.

Unfortunately for the operation, the actions that gave India credibility in Colombo deprived it of the aura of neutralism necessary to broker the conflict between moderate and extremist Tamil factions. Given its opposition in principle to separatism because of the separatist groups in India itself, New Delhi inevitably sided with the Tamil moderates in Sri Lanka. Hence, from the outset within Sri Lanka's Tamil community, the Indian troops received a cool reception. Once the IPKF focused on pacifying the internecine conflict between Tamil extremists and moderates, and engaged the Tamil Tigers' liberation army, India's ability to mediate the conflict disintegrated. The Tigers closed their bases in India and returned to their camps in northern and eastern Sri Lanka. Once entrenched there, the insurgents not only refused to disarm, as required by the Accord, but began to fight both moderate Tamil factions *and* the IPKF for control of the land that they had previously gained in battles against the Sri Lankan military. Gradually, Tamil opinion became as polarized on whether to trust India as on the issue of trusting Colombo, and the longer that normal life had to be suspended, the less popular the IPKF became. Meanwhile, India became increasingly frustrated with the Tigers' unwillingness to disarm, the IPKF's inability to defeat them decisively, the declining support for its policy among southern (Tamil) Indians and the perceived unwillingness of Sri Lanka's government to offer enough concessions to satisfy most Tamil groups and thus permit a political settlement of the conflict.

In the end, Colombo's frustration with India's inability to install a stable, moderate Tamil administration in the island's north and east prompted Colombo to request the IPKF's withdrawal. India troops were evacuated from the country the following year, leaving behind a country to this day ravaged by ethnic conflict that continues unabated despite the frequent international condemnation of the Tigers' use of children as soldiers.[18]

Ethnoclass Politics in the Developing World

Ethnoclass conflict in the developing world has predominantly involved prejudice and policies directed against minorities who either arrived during, or profited from, a colonial era that left them with a higher socioeconomic status at independence than their respective country's population as a whole. Thus, ethnoclass politics in the developing world more closely parallels the discriminatory policies aimed at Europe's Jewish community than the ethnoclass politics involving such economic under-classes as Europe's Romany.

One dimension of developing world ethnoclass politics centers on the problems faced by communities such as Nigeria's more educated southern tribes when working in Northern Nigeria. A similar ethnoclass element characterized Tamil–Sinhalese conflict in Sri Lanka before it escalated. Hence the discriminatory nature of the language and education laws enacted by the Sinhalese that, over time, resulted in the movement of large numbers of Tamils to Sri Lanka's already heavily Tamil areas. Similar patterns of ethnoclass conflict involving indigenous minorities can be found throughout much of the developing world. The major exception is Latin America, where ethnoclass politics more often favors those with the blood-lines of the European settlers than the indigenous people who fell under their rule.

Second, and more often the recipient of headlines, there is that category of ethnoclass politics that focuses on those minorities who originated elsewhere and prospered in their new homelands during the colonial era. In many instances they achieved greater economic status than the host populations, and their visibility often made them a despised upper tier of their countries' socioeconomic ladders at independence.[19] Although numerous immigrant communities fall into this category (including the Ibos and Lebanese in much of West Africa), by far the largest two group-ings are the Asians from the Indian subcontinent, who spread across East and South Africa, the Pacific islands, and even into the West Indies, and the Chinese of Asia.[20] Though only between 1 and 3 percent of the population in Cambodia, Indonesia, Vietnam, the Philippines, and Burma (now Myanmar), 14 percent of the population in Thailand, and a third of Malaysia's people, the Chinese in particular have come to be an "affluent ele-ment of the population who constitute both a significant influence beyond their numbers and a convenient target for possible ethnic conflict."[21]

Frequently, these "foreign" communities, who are often citizens of the states in which they now live, are far from cohesive. The Chinese of Malaysia, for example, are divisible on the basis of the geographical and linguistic areas of China from which they came. In addition, the various Chinese immigrants tended to drift into different occupations upon arrival. Cantonese and Hakkas, at Malaysia's independence, tended to be miners, Hokkiens were usually storekeepers or traders, and Hailmans were to be found in the more menial areas of farming, domestic employment, and laboring on the rubber estates. Similarly, within Malaysia's Indian commu-nity, caste differences reinforced by occupational differences have tended to break down any all-Indian cohesiveness in normal times, despite their high degree (90 percent Tamil speaking) of linguistic unity; however, these internal differences fade quickly when these "outsiders" feel threatened by the majority community. And as in the case of the more educated Tamils in Sri Lanka, discrimination and political violence are often parts of their lives. The most egregious act of discrimination against them remains

Uganda's decision to expel its Asian community in the early 1970s, shortly after Idi Amin gained control of the government.[22] In times of economic adversity, however, the transplanted Asian and Chinese communities of Africa and Asia are still often singled out as scapegoats for the economic woes and targets for local frustration—a fact of ethnoclass political life underscored by the riots directed against the Chinese in Indonesia and elsewhere during Southeast Asia's economic crisis of the late 1990s.[23]

Finally, although developing states since the 1950s have been more donor countries than recipient countries in global immigration patterns, regional wars, catastrophic acts of nature, and the lure of better economic opportunities have propelled refugees and unwanted illegal immigrants from one developing state to another, where the short supply of jobs in the domestic market has usually kindled ethnoclass conflict between them and their hosts. Thus, tensions are reportedly high between Libyans and the refugees who have migrated there from wartorn areas in Africa (especially Chad), and until it bowed to international pressure, deportation was Malaysia's response to the political tensions created by the arrival there of thousands of refugees from Indonesia who had lost their homes when a tsunami ravaged the Indian Ocean region in December, 2004. In short, in the developing world, as in the advanced democratic and democratizing postcommunist worlds, ethnoclass minorities are most often the target of popular dissatisfaction and political processes, not the initiators of proposals or participants whose objectives receive accommodation-oriented hearings.

Conclusion

Reflections on the Management of Ethnopolitical Conflict in the Contemporary World

We conclude our study much as we began it, with recognition of the continued vitality of ethnicity in both domestic politics and international relations in our world. Tribal conflict continues to beset numerous African states. Separatists still take lives in areas as diverse as Spain's economically developed Basque region, Serbia's relatively poor Kosovo district, and India's northeast periphery. Terrorist attacks by homegrown members of Britain and Holland's Muslim communities have recently heightened the tense relations between native Europeans and nonassimilating Muslim communities throughout Western Europe. Concerned conservatives in the United States speak with alarm of the growing "Mexicanization" of the American southwest. Refugees are still squeezed from country to country; even Bangladesh, itself the product of a war for liberation, is no long willing to shelter the millions from Indonesia encamped on its borders. And in Afghanistan, Iraq, and the former Yugoslavia, international workers speak optimistically of nation-building as though such projects had not repeatedly failed in the past in both the Third World and multinational communist states.

As this short inventory suggests, ethnic issues continue to be manifested in many forms, though with a durability rooted in the interrelationship among ethnicity, culture, and identity, and in the elemental fact that for most people, socialization in ethnic identity predates the more structured socialization processes encountered in schools and later in life. Given this diversity, our examination of that world can lay no claim to being exhaustive or to answering all of the questions related to the causes and consequences of contemporary ethnic conflict. Similarly, because our focus has been on the impact and management of ethnic conflict as it most often emerges *within* contemporary political processes, we have only lightly touched upon irredentism, diaspora, and other international dimensions of ethnic politics. Our study does suggest, however, several observations about the nature of ethnic conflict in general, the emergence and susceptibility to accommodation of ethnoclass and ethnoterritorial conflicts in particular, and contemporary efforts to manage them.

Ethnoclass and Ethnoterritorial Conflict:
Common Threads, Distinct Dynamics

Ethnicity: A Fluid Political Force

To summarize earlier observations, the content and political manifestations of ethnicity in our world are the evolving products of the forces that have shaped that world. The multiethnic and multinational states of today are the consequence of the historical state-making processes, be they of the European model of expanding centers conquering ethnically distinct communities on the periphery, the settler society model in which Europeans intermingled with or displaced indigenous peoples as rulers and opened the door to immigrants from different points of origin, or the developing world format, where Europe's imperial outposts have retained their multinational character as independent states. More recently, ethnopolitics has been further reshaped by the postwar recovery of Europe and an accelerating globalization process, both of which resulted in the movement of large numbers from their (usually) developing world homelands to immigrant lifestyles in the more developed regions of the world.

Under the weight of these forces, the basis of ethnicity has been affected. In some areas—for example the more rural subcultures of Nigeria and newer, immigrant neighborhoods in the cities of the developed world—ethnicity can still be defined genetically. In advanced democratic and economically advanced postcommunist countries, ethnoterritorial minorities long integrated into their respective states' borders and the third-generation descendants of immigrants are more likely to measure their "otherness" by their pre-union history, areas of origin, and/or cultural barometers of ethnic distinctiveness.

As to *how* ethnopolitical communities become mobilized, given the number of variables involved it is not surprising that our case studies are inconclusive as to even the relative weight of such macro-elements as changes in the economic environment versus such micro-variables as the role of political elites in the emergence of ethnopolitical self-awareness, demands, and conflicts. Ethnic clashes have occurred without the immediate presence of instigators in advanced democracies; for example, the Los Angeles riots related to the Rodney King case and the 2005 clashes between Romany and Muslim underclasses in the south of France. Conversely, even in Africa's deepest backwaters, the greatest carnage has usually been associated with the presence of radical voices inciting violence, as in the 1994 massacres in Rwanda, where radio broadcasters were urging Hutus to massacre their Tutsi neighbors.

The safest conclusion at this juncture is that the relative weight of various elements in inducing and shaping ethnic agendas and conflict varies in terms of area (i.e., *jus soli* immigrant societies such as the United States versus countries defining citizenship in terms of parental ethnicity), circumstance (the different political environments of 1960s Britain, Franco's Spain, de Gaulle's France, and Gowon's Nigeria vis-à-vis ethnoterritorial movements), and time (Europe's Muslims before and after the twenty-first-century terrorist attacks in Spain, Holland, and Britain). On the other hand, whatever the time, place, or circumstance, it *is* clear that a different set of elements shapes the emergence of politically salient ethnoclass issues than ethnoterritorial ones, and that once mobilization has occurred ethnopolitics evinces quite different characteristics and trajectories when the ethnic cleavage is linked to the economic cleavages in societies than when it is reinforced by territorial lines of segmentation.

The Emergence of Politically Salient Issues

Although the diversity of variables of potential importance in explaining why ethnic issues become politically salient remains astounding, the bedrock factor is the sense of ethnic identity itself. To be sure, as Paul Collier reminds us, "Conflicts in ethnically diverse countries may be ethnically patterned without being ethnically caused";[1] however, once the ethnic element is infused into the conflict, its character fundamentally changes. Additional members of the ethnic community may join in the conflict because of the instrumental utility of ethnic identity in mobilizing support for a cause—particularly when that cause can be portrayed in terms of the group's ability to gain control of its destiny. Likewise, once invoked the ethnic factor can significantly affect the tractability of the conflict, regardless of its fundamental cause.

Further, as we have seen, ethnic identity does not have to be persistently active to be politically significant. It may be relatively latent in comparison to other forms of social identification. This is especially a feature of ethnoterritorial conflict in Western Europe, and one of the reasons why the 1950s and 1960s witnessed considerable scholarly disagreement over whether the regional movements there reflected a resurgence of older identities, new ones in the process of formation, or some combination of the two. For our purposes, whether the movement represents a resurgence of older identities or a development of a new, regionalized one is less important than the fact that there was, even if latent, an ethnic self-identity present upon which these movements were launched and which subsequently affected their ability to achieve a significant political impact. Recognition of this relevance focuses attention away from historical considerations and on those factors that have subsequently affected the activation of ethnic identity and its salience in policy processes—for example, the importance of the region to the parties controlling the state, the openness of the political leadership to accommodation, the political skill of the ethnopolitical spokesmen in exploiting their advantages, the intensity of the grievances, and the nature of the demands being articulated.

There is a similar need for a sense of ethnic identity (and community) to exist amongst nonspatial minorities, immigrants, refugees, or foreign workers before their concerns become politically important *as a result of their own actions*. Otherwise, members of these categories are dependent upon non-members to articulate their interests, and although this has frequently occurred, these exterior champions of minority causes have not been particularly successful. Yet, left to themselves, the structural and political developments surveyed in our cases do not support much confidence in the ability of ethnoclass minorities to mobilize in defense of their interests. To the contrary, their individual ethnic identities have worked against cross-communal mobilization on the basis of their common interest as "outsiders." Even where given political standing, their presence is often characterized by their vertical segmentation from one another: for example, the members of France's recently convened Muslim advisory council are as much representatives of their associations' respective ethnic communities (Algeria, Moroccan, Arabian, and so on) as of the diverse threads of the Islamic faith in France.

What is evident from our studies is that political and structural developments occurring in countries hosting ethnoclass minorities have activated in the majority populations an *ethnic* (not just class) reaction. A list of these developments in the advanced democratic world—prior to and following 9/11—includes the rapid expansion of postwar economies, which necessitated the addition of outside workers to the domestic work force in developed countries, the gradual trend of the guest workers becoming permanent parts of their host countries' economies, the resulting social conflict between host country nationals and the foreign workers and their families, the economic downswing in most European states that negated the need for large numbers of foreign workers, and the emergence of globally organized, anti-Western Muslim organizations launching terrorist acts in countries containing Muslim minorities. Meanwhile, in Central Europe it is the often internally divided Romany community who have felt the greatest discrimination since the fall of communism, suddenly becoming the unprotected targets of frustrations that built up in majority communities during the communist era, when socialist-styled affirmative action policies seemingly gave the Romany preferential treatment. And in the developing world, ethnoclass consciousness has fueled postindependence conflicts whose roots are traceable to such developments during the colonial era as European decisions to import workers from outside the states being created and economic and educational policies that favored some communities over others.

Political Dynamics: Ethnopolitical Demands and

the Policy Process

Our study suggests three bases for meaningfully differentiating the demands of ethnopolitical communities: the content of those demands; the range of actors involved in the demand process; and the means by which the demands are conveyed. All affect the reception that these demands may receive in the political process, and noteworthy differences separate ethnoclass and ethnoterritorial politics in each area.

Ethnoterritorial demands cover a wide range, although all require central government concessions to the ethnoterritorial community and some can lead to dissolution of the state and/or international involvement in a country's ethnopolitical conflicts. As previously noted, they include output-oriented demands (i.e., financial assistance for a downward spiralling regional economy), essentially nationalistic (authority- and regime-oriented) demands for a share of decision-making authority and/or some form of political autonomy, and—at the extreme—groups seeking to purge their land of other communities or separate from the states containing them. In none of the cases examined is there complete consensus over the content of the demands to be placed before political authorities. Each case exhibits a diverse range of factions with varying opinions about the goals to be pursued and how stridently they are to be pushed. In this sense, ethnoterritorial politics tend to be more groups politics than a category of group politics in which a government is addressed by a single, goal-oriented organization.

In contrast, ethnoclass conflicts involve two distinct types of issues: those involving the conditions of the indigenous, territorially dispersed, and immigrant ethnic minorities, and those concerned with the *presence* of these groups. To recap, issues related to the status of foreigners and indigenous underclasses include their need for more and better housing, health care, and educational facilities, civil rights protection, and affirmative action policies. Where ethnoclass minorities *are* the issue, however, debate revolves around such issues as the presence of large numbers of foreigners as a threat to a country's unique character and indigenous job market, and—more recently—the danger of foreign communities becoming breeding grounds for terrorists.

Most complex are the issues to be found in ethnoclass-territorial conflicts of the type found in Northern Ireland. These often combine demands found in both ethnoclass and ethnoterritorial politics. Ultimately, however, these conflicts tend to raise on all sides the issue of the political entity's legitimacy; in the case of Ulster, the issue is the legitimacy of Ulster's political institutions in the eyes of its Catholics and of the Catholics presence in Ulster to its Protestant militants.

Regarding the range of political actors involved in the conveyance of policy demands, again some differences between our categories have quite clearly emerged. Collectively, the ethnoterritorial communities we have examined have both produced a wide range of different types of organizational spokesmen and have utilized most conceivable means of influencing their respective political processes, from cultural associations and regionalist parties to direct action organizations practicing civil disobedience (e.g., the Welsh Language Society) to clandestine groups employing overt violence aimed at symbolic (the French national banks targeted by Corsican and

Breton extremists) and human targets (i.e., ETA militants' activities in Spain) to declarations of secession and the fighting of civil wars to achieve independence. In the developed democratic world, these actors have also included factions or wings of broader, system-wide, political organizations, such as the Labour Party in Scotland.

The modes of expressing demands related to ethnoclass issues depend on the nature of a conflict. Demands raised on behalf of foreigners can come from the minority community itself, interest groups within the host country, the countries of the immigrants' origins, the host country's government, and transnational organizations. When the foreign communities themselves are the issue, policy demands tend to originate in three sources: domestic nationals (public opinion), domestic interest groups and parties such as Le Pen's, and the government of the host country, usually when it is seeking to placate its majority's sentiments. Contrary to the pattern prevalent in ethnoterritorial politics, the principal system-wide parties in the developed world have tended not to play a particularly active role in the generation of these demands but have functioned more as their recipients with the expectation that they will act upon them.

Among those participating in ethnoclass politics there is a considerable variance in the amount and intensity of activity. Understandably but also paradoxically, the groups most directly affected today by policy responses to ethnoclass demands (the foreign workers, immigrants, Romany, and others) tend to be the least active, in part because these communities are often of such a diverse mixture of nationalities and so mutually competitive in the economy that they have remained politically disorganized. But it also reflects the even more fundamental weakness of their bargaining condition as politically powerless minorities generally lacking in economic influence and the power of numbers in elections, while their opponents in the Western world have been quite willing to use the leverage of the ballot box to promote their exodus. Consequently, except in those instances where their frustration explodes in spontaneous public demonstrations, their grievances remain most often articulated by concerned (indigenous) citizens in the host countries, who speak for what is distinctly a minority viewpoint in their states. And, where leaders have emerged from within to articulate issues on their behalf, their demands have been essentially defensive—that they not be deported, dispossessed, or flagrantly discriminated against.

Most fundamentally, ethnoclass minorities frequently suffer from a perceived "otherness" that, at least in older states, ethnoterritorial minorities do not. A citizen of Glasgow can appear as both a Scot and British to the man in the street in Leeds; a Muslim in France is a Muslim in France. Hence, the amelioration of ethnoclass conflict requires double-sided adaptation. Not only must there be a willingness on the part of the besieged minority to adapt to their minority condition (and in some instances that will is lacking) but the host population must often adapt to their own cultural shock in dealing with "foreigners" and reorganize their attitudes toward that minority, often a generation-consuming task. The durability of racist attitudes toward African Americans and Native Americans in large portions of the United States offers a case in point. So too do the continuing negative attitudes toward Europe's Romany, especially in Central Europe, where Andrej Skolkay recently found 65 percent of the Slovaks opposed to having a Romany neighbor, and a hard core, self-declared intolerant element of between 15–25 percent of the population in both contemporary Slovenia and Slovakia likely to engage in hate speech and public action against "dark" foreigners.[2]

As for those rare instances where ethnic identity, class, and territoriality converge, virtually every conceivable category of participants and means of conveying demands can frequently be found. Of particular note, though, are two categories of active participants that are found far more frequently in this arena of ethnopolitics than others: terrorist groups and the system-wide governments. In Northern Ireland, for example, both the Protestants and Catholics have had terrorist organizations committed to their respective cause. In some instances, their die-hard members continue to operate. As in the case of the Ku Klux Klan in the United States, the presence of such extremist, extra-constitutional, paramilitary organizations tends to interject an erratic and uncontrollable element into the policy process. It was, in part, in reaction to the terrorists that the British government had to become an active, direct participant in Ulster politics in its effort to manage the communal conflict there, much as the United States government eventually had to challenge the "states' rights" position of the southern states in its federal system in order to end racial segregation in America a century after its civil war ended.

The Nature of Policy Responses to Ethnoclass and Ethnoterritorial Demands

There are two particular areas involving policy responses to ethnopolitical demands where our study suggests the need for further research: Who receives the demands? And, potential patterns of response to them? We will thus limit our observations here to a few brief reflections on the comparative role of governmental actors in this area, and—more broadly—to some of the problems related to studying policy responses.

In the case of ethnoterritorial conflict, the central government and the system-wide political parties are almost invariably the recipients of demands. This is especially true, as would be expected, in unitary political systems, but also holds for federalized countries such as the United States and Canada, though in these instances the state/provincial/cantonal level is often as involved in the policy process as the central government. A similar pattern emerges when one considers ethnoclass conflicts over immigrants and foreign nationals; however, a broader range of demand-recipients appear to be also involved in these issues. Conflicts over the rights of immigrants, for example, frequently involve the legal system, unions, or employers more than high-level governmental institutions or system-wide political parties, except where the latter choose to co-opt the "foreigner" issue.

How the recipients of the demands respond is a more difficult matter to summarize. With regard to ethnoterritorial conflicts, a diverse set of policy responses have been utilized in Western societies. These, however, can be grouped into two broad (and largely self-evident) categories. Recipients of demands have either tried to accommodate the demands of ethnoterritorial spokesmen by granting at least some concessions or they have responded with hostility to such demands. On balance, the states in the advanced democratic world and postcommunist Central Europe have generally gravitated towards the pragmatic position that accommodation is preferable to conflict. Indeed, the only form of institutional accommodation that was long rejected by system-wide leaders in most Western states involved proposals to federalize fully their polity, federalism being initially equated with separatism by system-wide elites. Even here exceptions abound, beginning in the mid-1970s when post-Franco Spain accepted federalism for its Basque and Catalonian provinces as a necessary step toward democratization and continuing in the volatile climate of democratic politics in postcommunist Europe when the Czechs and Slovaks moved beyond federalization and split their country.

In part, the nature of the response has reflected the degree of mobilization exemplified by the ethnopolitical group and the economic or political importance of their region as much as the specific demands being conveyed. Those regions with the greatest mobilization and of greater importance have, predictably, received the most accommodative responses in advanced democratic systems.

Partisan considerations also weigh heavily in explaining ethnoterritorial policy in the democratic world. The importance of the Welsh and Scottish seats in Parliament to the Labour Party's ability to remain competitive with the Tories in British elections, and of Quebec's vote to the ability of Canada's Liberal Party to govern in Ottawa have thus led these parties to endorse, respectively, assemblies for Scotland and Wales and greater federal autonomy for Quebec.

Lastly, on our short list, the economically measurable value of a region to the center *and/or* its psychological importance can become a powerful consideration in weighing options when faced with separatist demands and the prospects of civil war. The large Serbian minorities in Croatia and Bosnia versus their very small number in Slovenia and Macedonia goes far in explaining the different levels of military commitment that Belgrade made between 1991 and 1995 to retain these diverse parts of the former Yugoslavia, just as Kosovo's status as the cradle of the Serbian nation continues to explain Belgrade's unwillingness to part with that now almost entirely Albanian-speaking and Muslim province. Quite apart from any general commitment to the concept of unity, the discovery of oil in eastern Nigeria made Biafra's secession unthinkable in the late 1960s. Conversely, Slovakia's need for investment capital made it easier for Czechoslovakia's

Czech leadership to contemplate the partition of their country in 1991–92. The choices that have been made have varied, but circumstances have generally made those choices decisive ones even when they have proven to be wrong, as in the case of Belgrade's 1991–95 efforts to hold onto Bosnia and Croatia and 1999 resistance to international intervention in Kosovo.

The issues generated by the presence of large numbers of foreign workers and immigrants in the advanced democratic world have, comparatively, been approached with greater ambivalence by political leaders. As we have seen, the flow of foreign workers into Europe, and to a lesser degree of citizens from the "coloured commonwealth," in Britain, was initially greeted with a policy of "studied neglect," justified in the case of the foreign workers by the rationale that they were only temporary additions to the domestic work force. As the permanency and number of foreigners became issues in their own right, governments found it increasingly difficult to retain a policy of passive neutrality.

As in most cases of politics, context was a major factor affecting policy response even in the pre–9/11 world. It was easier to use restrictive measures where the foreign presence was concentrated in foreign workers on work visas than immigrants who entered Britain as Commonwealth citizens or—for that matter—against the illegal immigrants from Mexico in the United States, given the generally delicate nature of U. S.–Mexican relations. With the rise of electorally successful anti-immigrant parties, the balance shifted in the 1990s with anti-immigrant rhetoric streaming from the mouths of the leaders of established parties as well as from the Le Pens. It is too early to speculate on the effects that the current instances of terrorism in Europe will have on policy toward Europe's "foreign" communities; however, a further tightening of oversight is already discernible.

Context has also significantly affected ethnoclass politics in the postcommunist and developing worlds, again with the "foreign" element being the target of the political process rather than the instigator of political demands despite the limited, outsider protection that the Romany enjoyed as long as the governments of postcommunist Europe were courting NATO and the EU for membership. Under less scrutiny, and sometimes belligerently self-assertive of their independence, developing world states have addressed the "foreigner" issue with even less ambivalence.

Finally, as to the pivotal role of governmental institutions reacting to ethnopolitical demands, even within democratic systems it differs depending upon the nature of the conflict. In the area of ethnoterritorial politics, governments most often find themselves in the position of *responder* to the demands. In the area of ethnoclass politics, however, as the focus of various types of demands from a variety of sources, governments will more often see their role as that of a *mediator* or *broker* of competing interests. Hence the occasional schizophrenic appearance of policies involving immigrants, foreign workers, and refugees where the government concurrently pursues policies designed to assure foreign nationals, immigrants, and sometimes international overseers of their civil rights while simultaneously seeking to placate domestic opinion by halting the inflow of additional foreigners and even encouraging those present to return to their home countries. Yet, even where the government adopts a clear and decisive policy in response to ethnopolitical issues, there is inevitably a problem of measuring its "responsiveness" to the matter at hand. What may seem speedy progress to a majority community making concessions to what it perceives to be a noisy minority may seem indecently long to those who have been historically discriminated against or reside at the bottom of a society's socioeconomic ladder. Alternately, if the decision is to do nothing, considerable time may pass before the conveyers of the demands realize it.

The Impact of Policy Decisions

The two most basic aspects of ethnopolitics likely to be affected by policy developments are (1) the nature of ethnopolitical movements and their mode of operation, and (2) the nature of subsequent ethnopolitical demands. The emphasis on these areas underscores our operating presumption throughout this study: that ethnic-laden issues normally defy permanent settlement. This does not mean that ethnic issues are by definition nonbargainable; in fact, most of our studies underscore the high degree of bargainability characterizing ethnopolitical issues. Moreover, political elites seem to have considerable latitude in terms of policy implementation, especially as long as the majority of the public remains unmobilized. But political settlements are almost never permanent. Even the partition of Czechoslovakia did not end tension between the derivative governments, although it did downgrade the issues from concern with the form of the state to such matters as the disposal of public properties and the access of Czechs and Slovaks to universities in the resultant states. Generally, ethnopolitical decisions are always subject to changing social, economic, and international conditions; consequently, they are subject to renegotiation. It is only when the contrary presumption is adopted, that the current political status quo is the *proper* base for comparison, that these issues become no longer susceptible to political bargaining.

In the area of ethnoterritorial conflict, the impact of policy responses has taken several directions. Generally, though, the key variable in determining the mode to be used for articulating demands has been the degree to which the existing regime is willing to entertain and, at least in part, respond to them. Thus, in Britain, where political leaders were willing to negotiate most of the last quarter century, the principal means selected to express ethnoterritorial demands have been system-participatory, primarily ethnoterritorial parties. Conversely, where the relevant political leadership seemed to be insensitive to ethnoterritorial demands or repudiated their legitimacy, ethnopolitical organizations tended to develop as clandestine, system-challenging actors. The specific level of political violence employed, in turn, has tended to correlate in the advanced democratic world with (a) the degree of insensitivity exhibited by the established leadership,

(b) the number of overlapping cleavages encapsulated in the political conflict between ethnic groups within the same region, and between the ethnoterritorial actors and the central authorities, and conversely (c) the degree to which the members of these ethnoterritorial communities share cross-cutting ties and interests with the other members of the broader political community.

The impact of policy responses to ethnoterritorial demands also affects—even generates—subsequent demands for additional action. Responses involving institutional accommodation are likely to create a basis for new demands for further administrative or decision-making autonomy. Even primarily symbolic gestures may increase expectations and desires, and a seemingly favorable reception to ethnoterritorial demands followed by little substantive action may increase the ante the next time around. Alternately, it might deflect ethnoterritorial pressure for a substantial period of time. The introduction of violence into the conflict, however, essentially complicates the situation, because the violence itself becomes a focal point for demands and responses. That, in turn, tends to steer governmental responses away from the avowedly more basic issues of the conflict, and invariably diminishes a government's inclination toward accommodation.

What seems to be most important vis-à-vis the nature of subsequent ethnoterritorial demands is the ability and willingness of elites from each perspective to reach mutually agreeable rules of the game or patterns of interaction. This need not result in a full-blown consociational resolution; in fact, as our case studies suggest, that option is usually time-limited because collaborative ethnonationalists are highly vulnerable to being outbid by more militant spokesmen for their communities. Still, it can be something akin to consociational politics—a bargaining process based on mutually accepted principles of cooperation.

As for ethnoclass conflict, the impact of public policies there appears to depend on whether the conditions affecting the lives of the "outsiders" (including those holding citizenship) or their *presence* in the host country is the central question. Policy responses regarding the former do not appear to have had a major impact on those raising such issues, perhaps because these issues have been too diffuse in character to be satisfied by specific governmental policies. However, policy responses involving the latter have had an impact on subsequent demands, and equally importantly, the morale of the targeted communities. Most commonly, as minority demands have increased in scope, public support for the parties opposed to their presence has grown. Yet the civil rights protection they have received has never fully satisfied the concerns of these communities, largely because believing in that protection has required them to trust in the long-term goodwill of a host population that in large measure continues to support anti-immigrant and anti-Romany laws. In a worse-case scenario, the ambivalent policies aimed at protecting "outsiders" may have gradually hardened the frustration of many of these communities by awakening expectations that have been grievously disappointed.

Further, the policy responses when the foreigners themselves are the issue do not appear to have had much of an impact on the nature of the antiforeigner, anti–Romany, movements actively promoting this perspective in advanced democratic and postcommunist states. At most, such policies as those suspending further immigration have modestly deflected the potential growth of these organizations. The most important variables involving polices in this area, however, remain not the presence of the antiforeigner parties but the dynamic nature of the economic and political conditions in which the policy processes function. To date these have consistently kept the "foreigner" issue salient, if not ever more significant in the political systems of the developed world.

Managing Contemporary Ethnic Conflict

The Changing Face of Ethnic Conflict

The origin and dynamics of ethnoclass and ethnoterritorial issues in these early days of the new century are little different than those described in our case studies. Ethnoclass minorities are still more the target of political action than the originators of proposals designed to improve their status; territorialized minorities in the advanced democratic world, the democratizing post-communist world, and developing world are still the primary spokesman for their own cause. The tools of management still stress accommodation in the economically developed states of North America, Western Europe, and postcommunist Central Europe, although in the realm of ethnoclass politics the groups whose demands are to be accommodated are more often the domestic majorities rather than the minority communities. Meanwhile, repression remains the major tool of control in the developing world, particularly with respect to dissatisfied minorities with a territorial base seeking greater control over their own affairs.

That stated, the *face* of ethnic conflict in today's world has altered considerably from what it presented half a century ago or even a generation ago. During the 1950s, the most visible manifestation of ethnoclass politics in the developed world was the quest by black Americans for equality in American society, and their struggle to end segregation was gradually being achieved, albeit still primarily in courtrooms rather than the halls of Congress. As for the ideal of "national self-determination," prior to decolonization—when the idea of nation-building was first gaining currency—discourses involving self-determination were generally restricted to either the right of the "captive peoples" of Eastern Europe to throw off the communist regimes imposed on them by Soviet occupation or the right of European colonies to gain independence, not the right of the territorialized minorities in the colonial possessions to Balkanize Asia and Africa into hundreds of economically nonviable but more or less ethnically homogenous states.

By the 1970s, the issue of self-determination had been commandeered by Western Europe's regionalized minorities, as well as dissatisfied territorialized minorities in developing countries; however, for the most part, the demands of those groups seemed tractable. Sri Lanka's Tamil minority was still seeking regional autonomy. Following Nigeria's civil war, its tribes were accommodating themselves to military rule and whatever representation the expanding number of tribally organized states in that country gave them. And regionalist and nationalist movements throughout Europe and Canada were generally focused on regional or federal autonomy, representation in the cabinet, the right to preserve their tongues, or simply acquiring a larger share of the budget controlled by the central governments. Moreover, although the growing size of the immigrant and foreign worker communities was beginning to become an issue in Europe, the political debate was still focused on such issues as the need to protect foreign workers from job and housing discrimination and the need to limit immigration to protect the domestic work force. To be sure, unresolvable or apparently unresolvable conflicts were present. Bangladesh had just successfully seceded from Pakistan; the protracted conflict continued in Northern Ireland and was heating up again between an Israel occupying largely Palestinian areas in the West Bank and Gaza strip and in Arab world. For the most part, however, the ethnic conflicts of a quarter century ago continued to hover around demands of an output-, authority-, or regime-centered nature subject to, if not necessarily receiving, accommodative responses in the policy-making processes of the time.

By contrast, whether because the global communications revolution has brought ethnic warfare into Western homes (Rwanda), communal conflicts are emerging in core areas (Yugoslavia), or of the core issues they embrace (homeland security), recent ethnic conflicts seem to be more violent and substantially less susceptible to peaceful management. Our study points tentatively toward an explanation for these perceptions. Contemporary ethnic conflicts increasingly challenge the nature of the political community. Consequently, they revolve around issues far less subject to compromise than those earlier demands of ethnopolitical leaders. The trend is most visible in instances of ethnoterritorial politics. There, the hardline extremists represented in Europe by diehard Basque and Irish separatists are joined across the globe by the mainstream spokesmen for territorialized communities who define their self-determination objectives in terms of ethnically cleansing the land they hold and/or separating from the states they see holding them captive. Furthermore, such community-centered demands are not limited to ethnoterritorial conflicts. They are also at the heart of the "foreigner" debate in France, where French nationalists want to protect the French community as they perceive it, secular and Catholic, from growing numbers of Muslims who appear unwilling to assimilate to either, and in the debate over immigration in a growing number of small population, northern European states, where the issue is no longer jobs or even security but the survival of the Finnish, Swedish, and other such nations.

The Drift toward Extra-Systemic Conflict Management

The emergence of such community-centered issues, coupled with the continued presence of protracted political violence in areas such as Basque

Spain, Ulster, and Sri Lanka and of unsettled if nonviolent conflicts such as that between Greek and Turkish Cypriots over the future of their island has gradually altered the conflict-management processes involving ethnic conflict. Whereas formerly states saw ethnic conflict in internal terms and sought to respond to it inside their borders, their constitutional system, and alone—France and Spain, for example, each dealt individually with their Basque communities—conflict-management options now include a growing number of extra-systemic approaches toward ethnopolitical issues.

As table 13.1, and several of our case studies indicate, a considerable number of "options" can be grouped under the "extra-systemic" rubric. Some involve decisions voluntarily reached by the parties to the dispute to resolve or manage it in a controlled if sometimes unconventional manner. The decision to split Czechoslovakia into two states is perhaps the most conspicuous example of this approach, but so too are the Indian–Sri Lankan Accord and the Good Friday Agreement in Northern Ireland, both of which involved bringing outsiders into the conflict-management process. Also falling into this loose category would be the willingness, at least prior to 9/11, of several European states to "upload" decisions involving the rights of non-EU citizens in EU member states to the decision-making bodies of the EU. These devices can be of an imposed nature, however: for example, when outside force is used to restore order where governments have been unable either to accommodate or repress successfully the demands of militant ethnopolitical communities and disputes are escalating toward civil warfare.

Table 13.1 Systemic and extra-system responses to communal conflict

Mode of response

A. Systemic responses
  1. Ignore or challenge the legitimacy of the ethnopolitical groups
  2. Accommodative responses
    a. Output concessions
    b. Authority concessions
    c. Regime modification
  3. Repression

B. Extra-systemic responses/outcomes
  1. Separation of ethnopolitical community
    a. Negotiated division
    b. Coerced separation
  2. Unrestrained separatist violence
  3. Unrestrained border conflicts
  4. Third-party peacekeeping/coping mechanisms
  5. Non-codified international pressure
  6. Treaty arrangements with outsiders
  7. International tutelage and community-building activities

The most *extra*-systemic devices as well as the fastest growing area of extra-systemic conflict management are those involving the injection of outside actors into ethnic conflicts via peacemaking and peace-enforcing military activity, peacekeeping action, postconflict institution-building, and sometimes the prosecution of war criminals. Indeed, it was the severity of ethnic conflict in Rwanda and the former Yugoslavia that prompted the reevaluation of the provision in Article II (7) of the UN Charter, which formally prohibited the UN from intervening in matters falling "essentially within the domestic jurisdiction of any state." Civil wars were once routinely viewed as falling under this provision, and peacekeeping forces had to be approved by a member state before they could be deployed on its soil. Now, international law permits action where refugee flows into neighboring states render civil wars international, as well as where internationally defined war crimes are taking place.[3] As for the deployment of peacekeeping forces in areas of communal unrest, although the practice is not recent—the UN entered the fray in the Congo in 1960 and Cyprus four years later, and British troops have been performing a peacekeeping mission in Northern Ireland since the early 1970s—the pace at which the UN and others have launched these operations sharply increased during the 1990s. In the first five years of that decade, the UN alone undertook as many peacekeeping operations as it had in its previous history. Moreover, unlike its previous peacekeeping operations, most of which involved patrolling cease-fire zones between states, the majority of these involved the particularly costly (in finances, lives, and duration) area of communal peacekeeping.[4]

Finally, among the extra-systemic conflict-management devices involving outside parties, by far the most ambitious undertakings are the postconflict institution- and community-building operations in areas of continuing communal conflict (e.g., the UN's position in post–civil war Bosnia and Rwanda). This expansion of responsibilities beyond the peacekeeping activity of interposing troops between opposing sides is understandable. In most of these areas, communal warfare has destroyed the legitimacy of such preexisting institutions for conflict control as the courts, police forces, and the military, if not the institutions themselves. Moreover, while the reconstruction processes are underway, these duties too customarily fall on the intervening parties, especially where such delicate tasks must be performed as part of a peace settlement agreement as the repatriation of refugees to their former homes in zones that have been "ethnically cleansed." In two instances, Bosnia and Kosovo, the UN has even undertaken tasks of political tutelage and exercises tight control over the process of democratization, complete with the right to dismiss duly elected officials.

State-Building in the Postconflict World and the Search for Models

To date, this shifting nature of communal conflict management, especially in the area of ethnoterritorial conflict, has encountered difficulties at two levels. First, as in the case of India's peacekeeping venture in Sri Lanka, it has often been difficult to keep the peacemakers out of the conflict. Second, the models available for use in these extra-systemic approaches to conflict management have been essentially the same (usually authority-centered or regime-centered) devices, which have often accommodated ethnic demands in advanced Western democracies but whose track record is weak beyond that world.

The Delicate, Costly, and
Thankless Business of Peacekeeping

Under any circumstances, peacekeeping operations in areas on the verge of, in the midst of, or just emerging from communal warfare is politically sensitive and extraordinarily difficult. Even if the intervening party enters the fray in a neutral capacity—and much intervention has been done under the guise of peacekeeping by actors with personal agendas in the outcome of the dispute—the challenge is onerous and gratitude hard to find and usually fleeting when found.[5]

The problem begins with the multiple tasks confronting the individual peacekeeper. Neither police nor soldiers, peacekeepers perform roles that simultaneously require them to have automatic weapons on their shoulder to transmit a sense of security to the world around them, the personal tact necessary to negotiate street quarrels between members of formerly warring communities, and a tool belt at the waist should a child's bicycle require repairs. Unfortunately, as the need for peacekeepers and the danger of peacekeeping operations have grown, the number trained for this specialized task has dwindled.

The most serious problem confronting peacekeeping units nonetheless remains retaining the aura of neutrality necessary to function in the heated environment of communal conflict. Their missions are invariably structured in terms of implementing and/or preserving some form of status quo. It may be an imposed or negotiated cease-fire line, as in Croatia, or an agreement like the one the Indian Peacekeeping Force operated under in Sri Lanka, or a curfew law like the one British troops enforced in Ulster. The problem is the same. In communal conflicts, *the* issue is the legitimacy of the status quo itself, however it may be defined. Enforcing cease-fire lines established while one paramilitary was in retreat, or international agreements that require the resettlement of the displaced to their homes in ethnically cleansed areas have the effect if not the intent of identifying the peacekeepers with "the other side" in the minds of at least some of the people.[6] Where peace has been imposed by outside forces, the peacekeepers may lose their image of neutrality before they are even on the disputed territory. Hence, the leverage of international mediators brokering intercommunal conflict is usually at its peak before the peacekeepers are deployed and when their violence-ending presence is most likely to be interpreted as beneficial by all parties.

Lastly, both as a tool of preventive diplomacy designed to prevent conflicts from spreading or rekindling, and as a part of postconflict rebuilding processes, peacekeeping forces have become essential components of recent extra-systemic approaches to managing communal conflict. Only in the atmosphere of security that they provide can individual rights be secured and institutions of governance and justice capable of acquiring legitimacy be constructed. The rebuilding process, however, can also become too heavily dependent upon them. Those returning to ethnic minority enclaves in areas of Bosnia and Kosovo, in particular, have tended to become psychologically dependent on their presence—a recent trend in refugee returns that is likely to extend the stay of peacekeeping missions which in general tend to be openended in areas of communal violence.[7]

Institution-Building: Old Wine in New Bottles?
Western Institutions in Non-Western Settings
In these institution-building arenas, the removal of peacekeepers is usually linked to the emergence of institutions of not just democratic government, but "constitutional government" in which the rights of minorities are protected. In fact, there is no instance in our case studies or beyond in which peacekeeping forces have been withdrawn from areas of communal conflict where the conflict has not flared up again or, as in the case of the removal of the IPKF from Sri Lanka, intensified. Yet, there are no tested models available to today's community-builders, even when backed by a coercive military presence. Consequently they have turned to the models of constitutional government and procedural arrangements of the developed world for their principal designs. To date, however, the ideal of national self-determination has traveled into these areas well ahead of the environmental conditions in which constitutional government gradually developed in the advanced democratic world. To the contrary, cross-cutting ties have been historically weak and unemployment very high (in the 50 percent range and above) in Bosnia, Kosovo, and other postconflict settings, feeding both local insecurities and ethnonational parties, just as the high rate of unemployment and underemployment in France during the 1980s fueled the growth of Le Pen's anti-immigrant party. Furthermore, many of these areas do not have any history of government based on the rule of law or tolerance of the views of others.

Even if models did exist, state-building processes would still be plagued by many of the problems that have beset them in the former Yugoslavia, occupied Iraq, Lebanon, and elsewhere. Some of these revolve around the third party state-builders. As Stanley Hoffman has observed, "preventive intervention by the United Nations or a regional organization is a highly intrusive affair."[8] It has certainly been so in Bosnia, where international overseers of its democratization process have closed radio stations for inflammatory nationalist broadcasts and nullified the elections of ultra-nationalist candidates deemed unlikely to participate constructively in the country's evolving political institutions. In the short term, such intrusiveness generates its own resentment and opposition to international tutelage, even when the international community is providing the promised resource assistance, and often, as has been conspicuously true in Kosovo, it does not. In fact, given the costliness of postconflict peacekeeping and institution-building operations, the see-through commitment of the international community, and the potentially conflicting personal agendas of its major actors are also at issue. Loss of military personnel prompted the United States to drop out of peacekeeping missions in both Lebanon and Somalia between 1982 and 1992 and, as we have seen, both NATO and the EU ultimately placed their desire to expand into postcommunist Europe ahead of their commitment to improve the status of the Romany in postcommunist Europe.

Perhaps the most serious obstacles to postconflict reconstruction are the communities and conflicts themselves. Moving beyond the traumatic memories of violent ethnic conflict requires generations, developing the trust across communal lines that is necessary for durable constitutional government will require at least as long. Some conflicts are so entrenched and zero–sum in nature that they are beyond outsider—or inside—management: for example, the conflict in Chechnya, where grievances have reached the point on both sides where permanent warfare and/or secession may seem to be the only alternatives. In still other instances, circumstances may defy existing models for conflict resolution. Territorial autonomy in exchange for refugee return, for example, will be unacceptable where a separatist minority has achieved majority status in its region only by driving out large numbers of the former majority community, as has occurred in parts of Georgia.

Finally, there are the limitations inherent in the institutional arrangements available to those constructing constitutional governments in postcommunal conflict arenas. Military forces have—in their own right—proven to be useful but limited components of peace-building processes beyond providing a shield around endangered minorities. Military occupation can be valuable in assisting the short-term transition to civilian rule as an instrument for quickly implementing reforms and overcoming entrenched opposition.[9] In building institutions for the long haul, however, reformers have generally relied on the three macro-level approaches to organizing government authority that have been most frequently utilized to manage ethnic conflict in the advanced democratic world: (a) ethnically inclusive modes of allocating political offices; (b) consociational-like arrangements, typically involving power-sharing constitutional designs and parties organized on a cross-communal basis; and (c) federal-like distribution of power systems where ethnic divisions are territorialized.

All of these arrangements have utility, but as we have seen each also has its limitations or costs. Power-sharing, ethnic-based allocation of offices, and variations on consociational forms of managing societal cleavages require an enduring goodwill on the part of those making the bargain. Ultimately, all can be undone by outsiders mobilizing ethnic cleavages and/or outbidding the ruling cartels in appealing to their ethnopolitical communities. Consociational schemes, in particularly, are inherently weak means of managing ethnic conflict in the midst of democratization processes where system-wide parties are not already established and a mobilization of voters along ethnic lines is, as in Slovakia, almost inevitable. Once that occurs. because ethnonational and ethnoclass parties alike derive their strength by exploiting the ethnic divisions in their countries, consociational systems have very diminished chances of survival. Indeed, the collapse of that system in Belgium, once its ethnoterritorial division became politicized in the late 1950s, suggests the vulnerability of these arrangements even where system-wide parties have long existed.

At the same time, arrangements territorializing decision-making authority like those that Belgium implemented during the 1970s offer only a limited, long-term potential for managing ethnoterritorial cleavages. The utility of devolution, regionalization, and federal formulae in accommodating ethnoterritorial demands has been noted throughout our studies. They have proven useful in a variety of settings where the demands are focused on reshaping the regime in a federal direction. There are, however, both short- and potentially long-term costs in adopting this approach even where the territorialized communities are not ethnically diverse. Federalism provides an institutional base for territorialized centrifugal forces; it does not neutralize them. The system was "invented" in the United States not by ethnically distinct colonies who had recently fought against one another, but by a set of colonies largely in the hands of ethnically similar, English-speaking elites who had collaborated with one another a few years previously against a common enemy. Yet, within its framework different economic systems and philosophies about the ownership of human beings were perpetuated until they were finally resolved by a civil war. Where the units are ethnically and perhaps linguistically diverse, as in Canada, even if their respective communities lack a recent history of animosity, ethnoterritorial objectives can reach a separatist level.

Especially in the fragile and volatile climate of politics in the aftermath of communal conflict and in the developing world, federalism is best viewed as not so much a mode of conflict resolution or even conflict management as a means of buying time. Peacekeeping forces, consociational arrangements where possible, and ethnic balancing acts also function as essentially time-purchasing, manipulative devices vis-à-vis ethnoterritorial movements in such environments, just as advisory Muslim councils do with respect to the ethnoclass demands of those communities in Britain and France. For territorialized communities desiring control over their own affairs, however, federalesque modes of accommodation are the ones most likely to be successfully negotiated in a postconflict, institution-building process. But, in the long term, unless other forces are actively set in motion to build cross-cutting cleavages and to facilitate the development of non- or cross-communal parties and a sense of shared identity among the members of a political system, the prognosis is not good. Thus, in most instances the process of conflict management only begins when federalism is adopted or forced upon the conflicting parties. Further manipulations designed to purchase additional time are almost inevitable, reflected in Nigeria and India's case in the steady growth in the number of, respectively, tribal and linguistically organized states in those federations. For long-term stability, that time must be used profitably, as India appears to have done in fashioning a middle class that transcends the borders of its linguistically drawn states.

In brief, contemporary institution- and community-building, like the management of ethnic conflict in general, is a work in progress, and necessarily so. Just as ethnicity itself is a fluid concept with a proven ability to survive as an important basis of identity and political activity in a changing world, so the search for means of managing the conflict is an evolving undertaking. As ethnoterritorial and ethnoclass conflicts increasingly partake of a greater—indeed, international—dimension unknown in Aesop's time, it is a sign of our age that the struggle to manage these conflicts in modern political systems is becoming as extra-systemic as the conflicts themselves.

NOTES

Chapter One   Ethnicity and Politics in
the Contemporary World

1. Thomas Spiro, *Nationalism and Ethnicity Terminologies: An Encyclopedic Dictionary and Research Guide*, Volume I (Gulf Breeze, Fla.: Academic International Press, 1999), 207, with reference to Rodolfo Stavenhagen's definition in *Conflicts, Development, and Human Rights* (Tokyo: United Nations University, 1990).
2. Rupert Emerson, *From Empire to Nation: The Rise of Self-Assertion of Asian and African Peoples* (Cambridge, Mass.: Harvard University Press, 1960), 95–96.
3. See, especially, Connor's landmark essay, "The Politics of Ethnonationalism," *Journal of International Affairs*, 22 (1973): 1–21. The nation-state model usually carries the collateral benefits of the people also identifying with their territory as *their* country, entitled to their love and support (patriotism), and sharing a core political culture and hence a political consensus useful in resolving conflict over the ends and means of the state. Connor estimated in 1973 that less than a third of the states in the world fit this model; the percentage is no higher today.
4. New York: Columbia University Press, 1981.
5. See, especially, Newman's book, *Ethnoregional Conflict in Democracies: Mostly Ballots, Rarely Bullets* (Westport, Conn.: Greenwood Press, 1996), and his article on "Nationalism in Post-Industrial Societies: Why States Still Matter," *Comparative Politics*, 33 (2000): 21–41. Earlier, developed world–focused studies include: Milton J. Esman (ed.), *Ethnic Conflict in the Western World* (Ithaca, N.Y.: Cornell University Press, 1977); and Edward A. Tiryakian and Ronald Rogowski (eds.), *New Nationalism of the Developed West* (New York: Allyn and Unwin, 1985).
6. New York: Oxford University Press, 1993.
7. Typical of this literature would be such widely used works on the United States as Paula D. McClain and Joseph Stewart, Jr., *"Can We All Get Along?" Racial and Ethnic Minorities in American Politics* (Boulder, Colo.: Westview Press, 2000).
8. See, for example, Paula S. Rothenberg, *Race, Class and Gender in the United States: An Integrated Study* (New York: St. Martin's Press, 1995); and Joseph F. Healey's standard sociology text, *Race, Ethnicity, Gender, and Class: The Sociology of Group Conflict and Change* (Thousand Oaks, Calif.: Pine Forge Press, 1995), with its suggestively cross-national title but map of the United States on its cover.
9. See Anthony D. Smith's analyses of this approach, especially his *Theories of Nationalism* (New York: Holmes and Meier, 1983); and *The Ethnic Origins of Nations* (Oxford: Basil Blackwell, 1986). For a succinct summary of the basic approaches to the study of ethnicity, see Raymond C. Taras and Rajat Ganguly, "Chapter 1—Ethnic Conflict on the World Stage," *Understanding Ethnic Conflict: The International Dimension* (New York: Longman, 2002).
10. Spira, *Nationalism and Ethnicity Terminologies*, 112, relying extensively on the discussion of constructionist and instrumentalist theory in M. Crawford Young, "The Dialectics of Cultural Pluralism: Concept and Reality," in M. Crawford Young (ed.), *The Rising Tide of Cultural Pluralism: The Nation-State at Bay?* (Madison: University of Wisconsin Press, 1993).
11. Instrumental theory was widely used to explain the reawakening of ethnoterritorial movements in the developed democratic world in the 1960s and 1970s, and has recently seen much use in explaining recent ethnic conflict affecting the international system. See, for example, David A, Lake and Donald Rothchild, "Spreading Fear: The Genesis of Transnational Ethnic Conflict," in Lake and Rothchild (eds.), *The International Spread of Ethnic Conflict: Fear, Diffusion, and Escalation* (Princeton, N.J.: Princeton University Press, 1998), 5–32.

12. Martin O. Heisler, "Ethnicity and Ethnic Relations in the Modern West," in Joseph V. Montville (ed.), *Conflict and Peacekeeping in Multiethnic Societies* (Lexington, Mass.: D.C. Heath and Company, 1991), 26.

13. The role of leadership in the breakup of both Czechoslovakia and Yugoslavia is examined in chapters six and nine respectively, in this book.

14. See, for example: Ronald Ingelhart, *Modernization and Post-Modernization: Cultural, Economic and Political Change in 43 Societies* (Princeton, N.J.: Princeton University Press, 1997), esp. 248f.; and Michael Keating, *Nations against the State: The New Politics of Nationalism in Quebec, Catalonia, and Scotland* (London: Macmillan, 1996).

15. I. William Zartman "Sources and Settlements of Ethnic Conflicts," in Andreas Wimmer et al. (eds.), *Facing Ethnic Conflicts: Toward a New Realism* (New York: Rowman and Littlefield, 2004), 141–159, esp.146–148.

16. Milton J. Esman, "Perspectives on Ethnic Conflict in Industrial Societies," in Milton J. Esman (ed.), *Ethnic Conflict in the Western World* (Ithaca, N.Y.: Cornell University Press, 1977), 377.

17. See Saul Newman's "Ideological Trends among Ethnoregional Parties in Post-Industrial Democracies," *Nationalism and Ethnic Politics*, 2 (1997): 28–60.

18. See, especially, Saul Newman, "Ethnoregional Parties: A Comparative Perspective," *Regional Politics and Policy*, 4 (1994): 28–66.

19. On the relationship between the macro-level conditions (economic change, postindustrial attitudes, and the like) that give rise to ethnic issues, the micro-level behavior that follows (support for ethnopolitical organizations), and the impact of the policy process' response to ethnopolitical demands on both these conditions and political behavior, see Robert J. Thompson, "The Ebb and Flow of Ethnoterritorial Politics in the Western World," in Joseph R. Rudolph, Jr. and Robert J. Thompson, *Ethnoterritorial Politics, Policy, and the Western World* (Boulder, Colo.: Lynne Rienner, 1989), 4–9.

20. Aristides R. Zolberg, "Culture, Territory, Class: Ethnicity Demystified," a paper presented at the International Political Science Association Congress, Edinburgh, Scotland, August 16–21, 1976.

21. See, as an earlier application of this approach to the study of ethnopolitics, Robert J. Thompson and Joseph R. Rudolph, Jr., "Ethnic Politics and Public Policy in Western Societies: A Framework for Comparative Analysis," in Dennis Thompson and Dov Ronen (eds.), *Ethnicity, Politics, and Development* (Boulder, Colo.: Lynne Rienner Publishers, 1986), 25–64.

22. For more extensive discussions of these developments, see chapters three and five, in this book.

23. Cynthia H. Enloe, *Ethnic Conflict and Political Development* (Boston: Little, Brown and Company, 1973), 17–18.

24. It should also be observed that the various minorities are even more divided vis-à-vis one another. Thus, despite the efforts of U.S. politicians such as Jesse Jackson, who ran for the American presidency in 1988 by appealing to a "Rainbow Coalition," an effective political coalition of the county's ethnic minorities has yet to emerge.

25. Leaders of Jewish civil rights organizations were among the founding fathers of the National Association for the Advancement of Colored Peoples (NAACP) and continued to work with and support NAACP leaders such as Dr. Martin Luther King, Jr., until the late 1960s. At the same time, large numbers of Jewish Americans personally combated discrimination by pursuing careers in the professions. Consequently, by the 1960s, they held a disproportionately large share of the positions in such professions as law, higher education, and medicine. Affirmative action programs aimed at benefiting groups traditionally shut out of such areas promised to work against future Jewish American job seekers in these fields.

26. I remain indebted to Professor Wildgen for suggesting this typology long ago in reviewing a draft of my article on "Ethnic Sub-States and the Emergent Politics of Tri-Level Interaction in Western Europe," *Western Political Quarterly*, 30 (1977): 537–557.

27. See Brewton Berry and Henry Tischler, *Race and Ethnic Relations* (Boston: Houghton Mifflin, 1979), 375–402.

Chapter Two   The Setting of Politics in the Advanced Democratic World

1. See Patrick O'Neil, *Essentials of Comparative Politics* (New York: W.W. Norton and Company, 2003), 176–181.

2. Social scientists discuss these accomplishments in terms of the success of developed democracies in overcoming, respectively, the crises of identity, participation, legitimacy, penetration, and

distribution—crises that must be faced by all politically developing polities. For a succinct discussion summary of the concept of political development, see Gregory S. Mahler, *Comparative Politics: An Institutional and Cross-National Approach* (Upper Saddle River, N.J.: Prentice Hall, 2003 edition), 41–51.

3. O'Neil, *Essentials of Comparative Politics*, 149.

4. See Carl J. Friedrich's classic study, *Constitutional Government and Democracy: Theory and Practice in Europe and America* (Boston: Ginn, 1946). Friedrich sees the development of constitutional government, or constitutionalism, as a multifaceted process rooted in developing a political culture which demands that government operate within established rules of the game based on the rule of law.

5. See Michael J. Sodaro, *Comparative Politics: A Global Approach* (New York: McGraw-Hill, 2001), 165–171. In most democracies, a minimal list of these rights by century's end came to include: (1) basic individual rights, such as freedom of speech, press, association, and religion; (2) basic political rights such as the right to vote, assemble, and hold office; (3) and such social and economic rights as education, unfettered access to jobs, and the right to own and sell property (178).

6. For a discussion of declining party identification in the West, see Russell J. Dalton, "Political Support in Advanced Industrial Democracies," in Pippa Norris (ed.), *Critical Citizens: Global Support for Democratic Governance* (Oxford, U.K.: Oxford University Press, 1999), 57–77, esp. 65–72.

7. The reverse situation can also feed ethnoterritorial sentiments if minority regions richer than the state as a whole—for example, Flemish Belgium and Basque Spain—feel that their wealth is being exploited for the benefit of the politically dominant ethnic communities.

8. Guy Heraud, *L'Europe des Ethnies* (Paris: Presses d'Europe, 1963), 284–293. On the same topic, see also Alexandre Marc and Guy Heraud, *Contre les Etats, les Region d'Europe* (Nice: Presses d'Europe, 1973).

9. Heraud's listing of the principal, territorialized groups has not changed greatly or appreciably over time. If, however, the list is extended to include those very small enclaves of ethnic minorities living along the borders of European states or slightly intermingled with the larger populations, the number of entries grows at least fourfold. The current website for the flags of the minorities of all of Europe, for example, contains 272 entries. See http://www.eurominority.org/version/fr/drapeaux.asp, accessed last on August 4, 2004.

10. The website for the minorities of Europe currently lists over 100 parties currently operating in the countries of Western Europe on behalf of territorialized minorities. Of these 27 were a part of the Free Alliance in fall 2004. See http://www.eurominority.org/version/cartes/carte-parties.asp.

11. See Christopher Hewitt and Tom Chechtam (eds.), *Encyclopedia of Modern Separatist Movements* (Santa Barbara, Calif.: ABE-CLIO Press, 2000), Regional Map on Western Europe.

12. Hewitt and Chechtam, *Encyclopedia of Modern Separatist Movements*, Regional Map on Western Europe.

13. Daniel R. Headrick, *Tools of Empire Technology and European Imperialism in the Nineteenth Century* (New York: Oxford University Press, 1981), 3.

14. In contrast to the European settlers who migrated to the islands in the Caribbean Sea and Latin America, and who frequently intermingled with the native peoples and one another, nineteenth-century American immigrants frequently settled in ethnic enclaves in older American cities. Interethnic marriages among even European immigrants were often rare outside of the frontier until the twentieth century. A marriage with a Native American was even rarer, and marriage across racial lines was the rarest of all until the second half of the twentieth century.

15. For a brief discussion of nationalism in Quebec and Canadian efforts to manage it, see Saul Newman, "Canada: The Nationalist Movement in Quebec," in Joseph R. Rudolph, Jr. (ed.), *Encyclopedia of Modern Ethnic Conflicts* (London and Westport, Conn.: Greenwood Press, 2003), 27–35.

16. The 1990 U.S. census recorded a population of more than 3.5 million in Puerto Rico, but only 133,000 in Guam, the largest of the other remaining acquisitions of the Spanish–American War. In terms of area, Puerto Rico is nearly 3,500 square miles; none of the others is larger than 210 square miles and the smallest, American Samoa, is only 77 square miles. In all areas, the citizens enjoy the status of being U.S. citizens with full access to the United States. Data reported in *Whitaker's Almanack* (London: J. Whitaker & Sons, 1995), 1049.

17. For a brief summary of U.S. politics involving Puerto Rico, see Lynne-Darrell Bender, "The United States–Puerto Rico Relationship," in the *Encyclopedia of Modern Ethnic Conflicts*, 319–327.

18. "Mayor Giuliani Makes Case for Immigration in Lawsuit," *The Washington Post*, October 12, 1996.

19. William Appleman Williams, *Empire as a Way of Life* (New York: Oxford University Press, 1980), 31.

20. For a more detailed treatment of the struggle of Native Americans for their constitutional rights, see John R. Wunder, *"Retained by the People:" A History of American Indians and the Bill of Rights* (New York: Oxford University Press, 1994).

21. Cited in Rennard J. Strickland, "Native Americans," in Kermit L. Hall et al. (eds.), *The Oxford Companion to the Supreme Court of the United States* (New York: Oxford University Press, 1992), 578.

22. Most of these reservations still exist; the largest (the Navaho Reservation spanning the corner of Arizona, New Mexico, and Utah) contains over 120,000 residents, the largest single concentration of Native Americans in the United States.

23. For additional details of the fate of Australia's native peoples, see H.W. Reece, *Aborigines and Colonists* (Portland: Sydney University Press, 1974), and on-line, the Department of Aboriginal and Torres Strait Islander Policy, "Aboriginal History—Protocols for Consultation and Negotiation with Aboriginal People," at http://www.indigenous.qld.gov.au/pdf/asection1.pdf.

24. "Canada Pressed on Indian Rights: Commission Urges Self-Rule for Tribes," *The Washington Post*, November 22, 1996.

25. The Rhine River provides much of the sixth side of the hexagon, but being less a barrier to communications and invasion it was less a natural brake on France's extension than the predominantly Germanic nature of the people living to the east of the Rhine.

26. James E. Jacob and David C. Gordon, "Language Policy in France," in William R. Beer and James E. Jacob (eds.), *Language Policy and National Unity* (Totowa, N.J.: Rowman & Allanheld, 1985), 106–113.

27. Sanche de Gramont describes his countrymen as "The Great Codifiers," and lists, along with the great chef Careme's 12-volume treatise, which codified the rules of gastronomy, the work of the nineteenth-century diplomat Govineau in codifying racism, of Louis XIV in codifying slavery, and of the marquis de Sade in cataloging the variants of sex. *The French: Portrait of a People* (New York: G.P. Putnam's Sons, 1969), 301ff.

28. These parties included regionalist associations. The implications of popular sovereignty and political participation in post-Revolutionary France are succinctly discussed in Kay Lawson, *The Comparative Study of Political Parties* (New York: St. Martin's Press, 1976), 28–29.

29. See Lowell G. Noonan, *France: The Politics of Continuity in Change* (New York: Holt Rinehart and Winston, 1970), 178–234.

30. Frank L. Wilson, *European Politics Today: The Democratic Experience* (Englewood Cliffs, N.J.: Prentice Hall, 1994), 105f.

31. See Wilson, *European Politics Today*; Noonan, *France*; Henry W. Ehrmann, *Politics: France* (Boston: Little, Brown, and Company, 1976); and Kenneth Christie, *Problems in European Politics* (Chicago: Nelson-Hall Publishers, 1995). The citation is from Noonan, *France*, 179.

32. I am indebted to Professor Lawson for her comments here, as elsewhere, in reviewing an earlier copy of this manuscript.

33. See chapter three, in this book, for a discussion of the state's efforts to assimilate its regionalized linguistic minorities during the Third French Republic.

34. See Charles Trueheart, "French Proudly Hold Fast to Benevolent Central Rule: Nation Defies Trend in Preserving Traditions," *The Washington Post*, July 14, 1997.

Chapter Three   Ethnoterritorial Politics in France

1. For detailed discussions of France as a multiethnic, multilingual state, see especially James E. Jacob and David C. Gordon, "Language Policy in France," in William R. Beer and James E. Jacob (eds.), *Language Policy and National Unity* (Totowa, N.J.: Roway & Allanheld, 1985), 106–133; and William R. Beer, *The Unexpected Rebellion: Ethnic Activism in Contemporary France* (New York: New York University Press, 1980).

2. William Safran, "Language, Identity and State-Making: A Comparison of Politics in France, Israel, and the Soviet Union," *International Political Science Review*, 13 (1992): 397–414.

3. Sue Ellen Charlton, "France: Ethnic Conflict and the Problem of Corsica," in Joseph R. Rudolph, Jr. (ed.), *Encyclopedia of Modern Ethnic Conflicts* (London and Westport, Conn.: Greenwood Press, 2003), 69–78, 70–71.

4. Jacob and Gordon, "Language Policy in France," 110; and "Languages of France," available on-line at http://www.ethnologue.com/show_country.aspname = France, accessed December 13, 2004. Most of the figures given in the latter source conform with data from the early to mid-1990s, Jacob and Gordon's estimates from the previous decade. The most conspicuous exception to this rule is Corsica, which Jacob and Gordon estimated to be in the 100,000–200,000 range but where the current number speaking the Corsican language is estimated at 281,000 of the 341,000 people living on the island.

5. Jacob and Gordon, "Language Policy in France," 109f. Nice and Savoie, in southeastern France, were added in 1860, completing the physical boundaries of the Hexagon. For a concise discussion of state-making in France, see Thomas M. Poulsen, *Nations and States: A Geographic Background to World Affairs* (Englewood Cliffs, N.J.: Prentice Hall, 1995), 30–48.

6. Jacob and Gordon, "Language Policy in France,"111–112.

7. Jacob and Gordon, "Language Policy in France," 113.

8. Jacob and Gordon, "Language Policy in France," 114–115, citing statistics drawn from E. Weber, *Peasants and Frenchmen: The Modernization of Rural France, 1870–1914* (Stanford, Calif.: Stanford University Press, 1976), 67–70; and Carlton J. Hayes, *France: A Nation of Patriots* (New York: Octagon, 1930), 297.

9. Walker Connor, "Nation-Building or Nation-Destroying?" *World Politics*, 22 (1972): 319–355.

10. Mary Jane Adams, *Ethnic Subnationalism, Regional Devolution, and European Integration* (Unpublished M.A. Thesis, Carleton University, 1979), 118–120. France's post–World War II economic boom further aggravated this situation, with 80% of the postwar foreign investment between 1947 and 1960 going into France's northeast quadrille.

11. Jacob and Gordon, "Language Policy in France," 117.

12. In a concerted movement to detribalize the Indians and dissolve their Native American culture, Indian youth were assigned to strict schools on and off the reservation for (re)education. The schools invariably applied extremely rigid codes of military discipline to every aspect of the students' lives; further, their ceremonial braids and other symbols of their native culture were shorn off and they were forbidden to speak in their tribal tongues. See Edward Lazarus, *Black Hills, White Justice* (New York: Harper Collins, 1991), 103f.

13. Michael Keating, "Regionalism, Peripheral Nationalism, and the State in Western Europe: A Political Model," *Canadian Review of Studies in Nationalism*, 18 (1991): 117–130.

14. Keating, "Regionalism, Peripheral Nationalism, and the State," 120; and Jacob and Gordon, "Language Policy in France," 118.

15. William Safran, "Language, Ideology, and the State in French Nation-Building: The Recent Debate," *History of European Ideas*, 15 (1992): 794.

16. Jacob and Gordon, "Language Policy in France," 118.

17. Valery Giscard d'Estaing, *French Democracy*, Vincent Cronin (trans.) (Garden City, N.J.: Doubleday, 1977), xi.

18. By contrast, time has not altered France's policy to defend the French language against franglais. In the early 1990s, France's Commissariat General de la Langue francaise industriously prosecuted American fast-food franchises for serving "hamburgers" instead of *boeuf hache*. The mid-1990s saw the focus shift to prohibiting English-only pages on the Internet.

19. See Emmanuel Gottmann, "Concealed or Conjured Irredentism: The Case of Alsace," in Naomi Chazan (ed.), *Irredentism and International Politics* (London: Adamantine Press, 1991*).

20. See Maryon McDonald, *"We Are Not French! Language, Culture and Identity in Brittany* (New York: Routledge, 1989).

21. Jacob and Gordon, "Language Policy in France,"125.

22. William Safran, "The French State and Ethnic Minority Cultures," in Joseph R. Rudolph, Jr. and Robert J. Thompson (eds.), *Ethnoterritorial Politics, Policy, and the Western World* (Boulder, Colo.: Lynne Rienner, 1989), 115–157, 217.

23. Safran, "The French State and Ethnic Minority Cultures,"125–126.

24. William Safran, "The French State and Minority Cultures," a paper presented at the meeting of the Midwest Political Science Association, Chicago, Illinois, April 11–12, 1989.

25. Safran, "The French State and Ethnic Minority Cultures," 115–57. Safran, in Rudolph and Thompson, 127.

26. Cited in "Regional Languages Debate Threatens French Stability," *The Sun* (Baltimore), June 30, 1999.

27. Charlton, "France: Ethnic Conflict and the Problem of Corsica," 72–73.

28. Charlton, "France: Ethnic Conflict and the Problem of Corsica," 72.

29. Charlton, "France: Ethnic Conflict and the Problem of Corsica," 74–75.

30. Charlton, "France: Ethnic Conflict and the Problem of Corsica," 74–75; and Elaine Sciolino, "In Blow to Paris, Corsica Rejects French Restructuring Plan," *The New York Times*, July 7, 2003.

31. Sciolino, "In Blow to Paris."

32. For a more detailed account of the election, see Martin Buckley, "Turbulent Corsica spurns autonomy," BBC News World Edition, July 12, 2003, available on-line at the BBC's website.

33. Cited in Sciolino, "In Blow to Paris."

Chapter Four   Ethnoclass Politics in France:
Multiculturalism in an Assimilationist Republic

1. Gerard Noiriel, "Difficulties in French Historical Research on Immigration," in Donald L. Horowitz and Noiriel (eds.), *Immigrants in Two Democracies: French and American Experience* (New York: New York University Press, 1992), 66–67.

2. Myron Weiner, *The Global Migration Crisis: Challenge to States and to Human Rights* (New York: Harper Collins, 1995), 21–25.

3. See Kimberly Hamilton, Patrick Simon, and Clare Veniard, "The Challenge of French Diversity," Migration Information, at http://www.migrationinformation.com/Profiles/display.cfm?ID=21. and the French government's homepage, http//www.France.diplomatic.fr/France/geo/popu.gb.html.

4. Hamilton et al "The Challenge of French Diversity." Most commentators placed the number of foreigners at much higher levels. Milton Esman, for example, estimated that the number in 1990, legal and illegal, was closer to 5 million than the government's estimate of 3.5 million. See Milton Esman, *Ethnic Politics* (Ithaca, N.Y.: Cornell University Press, 1994), 199.

5. All second-generation births in France are subsumed within the count of French citizens and do not show up as "foreigners" in the politically sensitive tabulation of France's official population.

6. Because the "foreigner" issue is popularly defined less in terms of those who are legally foreigners for census purposes (i.e., citizens of other countries residing in France) than those who are perceived to be "foreign" because they do not share a European point of origin, quotation marks are used here and elsewhere to refer to the "foreigner" factor in contemporary French politics.

7. Hamilton et al., "The Challenge of French Diversity."

8. Available at http//www.France.diplomatic.fr/France/geo/popu.gb.html.

9. Weiner, *The Global Migration Crisis*, 100, table 16.

10. Esman, *Ethnic Politics*, 199

11. For an extensive discussion of postwar population change in France, see Philip E. Ogden, "Immigration to France since 1945: Myth and Reality," *Ethnic and Racial Studies*, 14 (July 1991): 294–317.

12. Rene Tempest, "France Is the Immigration Litmus Test," *Los Angeles Times*, September 22, 1996.

13. See Weiner, *The Global Migration Crisis*, 100–101.

14. See Ronald Tiersky, *France in the New Europe: Changing Yet Steadfast* (Belmont, Calif.: Wadsworth, 1994), 191.

15. See Milton Voirst, "The Muslims of France," *Foreign Affairs*, 75 (September/October 1996), 85f.

16. See Esman, *Ethnic Politics*, 200–205.

17. See Tiersky, *France in the New Europe*, 33–38.

18. See Tiersky, *France in the New Europe*, 33; and "Jospin's Win Follows Years of Peaks and Valleys," *The Washington Post*, June 3, 1997. The unemployment rate did not drop appreciably until the late 1990s and has been running in the 9% range (approximately 2.3 million people) in the early years of the twenty-first century.

19. Cited in Rachel K. Gibson's outstanding treatment of *The Growth of Anti-Immigrant Parties in Western Europe* (Lewiston, N.Y.: Edwin Mellen Press, 2002), 7 in the on-line version of the Introduction, at http://www.espch.salford.ac.uk/politics/rg/chapter1.html.

20. Tiersky, *France in the New Europe*, 190–191. The unemployment figures cover the 1991–93 period.

21. Tiersky, *France in the New Europe*, 110.

22. Cited in Tiersky, *France in the New Europe*, 110.

23. Early 1990s polls showed 71% of the population believing that there were too many Arabs in France. "Race for Votes, Votes for Race," *The Economist*, September 28, 1991, 58. A decade later, when Le Pen had ridden his anti-immigrant platform into the run-off election for the French presidency, the numbers remained largely unchanged, with 59% expressing the view that France had too many immigrants and that its government was not sufficiently protecting French values. See Bruce Crumley, "The Le Pen Effect," *Time Europe*, June 10, 2002.

24. See Tiersky, *France in the New Europe*, 111f.

25. Tiersky, *France in the New Europe*, 112,

26. See "The Far-Right Factor," *The Economist*, March 4, 1994, 53–54.

27. Tiersky, *France in the New Europe*, 114; and Jim Wolfreys, "The Programme of the French Front National," *Parliamentary Affairs*, 46, 3 (July 1993): 415–429.

28. "The Radical Right Gains Legitimacy in France," *Peace Watch*, 1, 5 (August 1995), 4–5.

29. Cited in Tiersky, *France in the New Europe*, 36. Giscard d'Estaing's comments appeared in *Le Figaro*.

30. Peter Fysh and Jim Wolfreys, "Le Pen, the National Front, and the Extreme Right in France," *Parliamentary Affairs*, 45 (1992): 313.
31. "French Center–Right Parties in Disarray," *The Washington Post*, March 21, 1998. Furthering the unraveling process, two major national figures, in turn, resigned in protest when their party expelled its local members for collaborating with the FN. "French Rightists Hit by Resignations," *The Washington Post*, April 15, 1998.
32. "French Rightist Is Barred from Office for a Year," *The Washington Post*, November 18, 1998.
33. See Adrian Adams, "Prisoners in Exile: Senegalese Workers in France," *Race and Class*, 16 (1974): 157–181; and Mahfoud Bennoune, "The Maghribin Migrant Workers in France," *Race and Class*, 17 (1975): 39–55. Recent legal immigrants tend to be less overwhelmingly male, less overwhelmingly from North Africa, and more skilled. Only the illegal immigrants fit the earlier profile. See the "Population" entry in the "About France" Fact Sheet, available from the Embassy of France in Australia, http://www.ambafrance-au.org/aboutfrance/paes/population.en.htm.
34. Bennoune, "The Maghribin Migrant Workers in France," 44–45. Bennoune notes that 90% of the North African laborers who had arrived in France by the early 1970s came from peasant backgrounds; 97.6% became wage laborers, with 43.7% working in the Paris metropolitan area.
35. A broad discussion of the immigrants' conditions written during this period can be found in Andre Vieuget, *Francas et immigres* (Paris: Editions sociales, 1975).
36. Esman, *Ethnic Politics*, 199.
37. See Danielle Lochak, "Discrimination against Foreigners under French Law, in Horowitz and Noiriel, *Immigrants in Two Democracies*, 391–410, esp. 401–404.
38. William Safran, "Sociopolitical Context and Ethnic Consciousness in France and the United States: Maghrebis and Latinos," in Anthony M. Messina et al. (ed.), *Ethnic and Racial Minorities in Advanced Industrial Democracies* (New York: Greenwood Press, 1992), 67–90, 71. Safran attributes much of the difference between U.S. Latinos and the Maghrebis in France to two factors. First, the former have been in America longer (three to four generations) and hence are exposed longer to the socialization process than even the earliest postwar Algerian immigrants to France. Second, the U.S. federal system has given Latino Americans access to genuine political power at the state and local levels unavailable to North Africans born or naturalized in unitary France.
39. Cited in Elaine Sciolino, "A Maze of Identities for the Muslims of France," *The New York Times*, April 9, 2003.
40. Safran, "Sociological Context", 82.
41. *Ibid*.
42. Julie Read, "Rift over French Immigration Laws," *The European*, April 18–24, 1996.
43. "France and Algeria—Partners Again," *The Economist*, March 8, 2003, 50.
44. See Michel Wieviorka, "Tendencies to Racism in Europe: Does France Represent a Unique Case or Is It Representative of a Trend," in John Wrench and John Solomos (eds.), *Racism and Migration in Western Europe* (Oxford: Berg, 1993), 55–65, esp. 56–57.
45. Wieviorka, "Tendencies to Racism in Europe," 187–188.
46. William Safran, *The French Polity* (White Plains, N.Y.: Longman, 1995), 37.
47. See chapter three and chapter five, in this volume.
48. "Terror in the Paris Metro," *U.S. News and World Report*, accessed on-line August 27, 2004 at http://www.keepmedia.com:/Register.do?oliID = 225.
49. Reported in Jon Henley, "France Sets Up Muslim Council," *The Guardian*, April 7, 2003, on-line at http://www.freerepublic.com/focus/f-news/886762/posts.
50. See Elaine Sciolino, "France Creates Muslim council to Handle Diverse Minority," *New York Times*, January 15, 2003; and "France Creates Muslim Council," BBC News on-line, December 20, 2002, at http://www.freerepublic.com/focus/news/809785/posts
51. See "French Official Takes On Muslim Radicals," *The Sun* (Baltimore), September 20, 2003.
52. The expulsion was reported in the News in Brief section, captioned "Lyon, France," *The Washington Post*, October 6, 2004.
53. "France to Silence Hezbollah TV Station," *The Sun* (Baltimore), September 20, 2003.
54. See Didier Fassin, "The Biopolitics of Otherness: Undocumented Foreigners and Racial Discrimination in French Public Debate," *Anthropology Today*, 17 (February 2001).
55. See "France's Lower House Affirms Head Scarf Ban," *Washington Post*, February 11, 2004.
56. Cited in Keith B. Richburg, "French President Urges Ban on Head Scarves in Schools," *Washington Post*, December 18, 2004.
57. See "French Legislators Pass Secularization Law," *The Sun* (Baltimore), February 11, 2004.

Chapter Five   Ethnopolitics in France in a
Comparative Perspective

1. See chapter one, in this volume.
2. See Joseph R. Rudolph, Jr. and Robert J. Thompson, "Ethnonational Movements in the Policy Process: Accommodating Nationalist Demands in the Developed World," *Comparative Politics*, 17 (1985): 291–311, at 308–309.
3. See especially in this context Saul Newman's study of ethnopolitics in Western Europe, *Ethnoregional Conflict in Democracies: Mostly Ballots, Rarely Bullets* (Westport, Conn.: Greenwood Press, 1996), esp. 4–5 and chapter 7, "Ethnic Conflict and Political Order."
4. Only in Corsica have administrative and electoral boundaries in France routinely coincided with ethnoterritorial borders.
5. The weakness of the ethnoterritorial parties was shown clearly in the 1974 presidential election, when Guy Heraud ran on a platform focusing on France's "national minorities" and pledged to work toward the creation of a Europe of Regions. At a time when France's ethnoregional minorities accounted for approximately 35% of the country's population, Heraud received only 1.7% of the vote. Mary Jane Adams, *Ethnic Subnationalism, Regional Devolution, and European Integration* (Unpublished M.A. Thesis, Carleton University, 1979), 139 and 177.
6. See, for example, this author's early work on "Ethnonational Parties and Political Change: The Belgian and British Experience," *Polity*, 9 (1977): 401–426.
7. See chapter three, in this volume.
8. See Saul Newman, "Losing the Electoral Battles and Winning the Policy Wars: Ethnoregional Conflict in Belgium," *Nationalism and Ethnic Politics*, 1, 4 (1995): 44–72. The other principal ethnoregional parties in Belgium, the *Front democratique des Francophones bruxellois (FDF)* and the *Volksunie (VU)* in Flanders have also experienced sharp decreases in support, leading to intense factionalism in the latter and eventually the breakaway of one of its cliques to form its own pro-Flemish, antiforeigner party.
9. Arend Lijphart, "Consociational Democracy," *World Politics*, 21 (January 1959): 207–225, citation at 216.
10. See Raphael Zariski, "Ethnic Extremism among Ethnoterritorial Communities in Western Europe: Dimensions, Causes, and Institutional Responses," *Comparative Politics*, 21 (1989): 253–272.
11. See Keith B. Richburg, "Long Basque Rebellion Losing Strength: International Effort Squeezes Underground Separatist Group," *The Washington Post*, December 11, 2003. Richburg cites figures showing a sharp drop in ETA activity, from the high water years between 1977 and 1980, when it still had legitimacy.
12. Concerning the use of referendums as tools for managing ethnonational conflicts, with particular reference to the referendums held in democratizing Spain, Britain, Jura, Switzerland, and Quebec during the 1970s and 1980s, see Robert J. Thompson, "Referendums and Ethnoterritorial Movements: The Policy Consequences and Political Ramifications," in Joseph R. Rudolph, Jr. and Robert J. Thompson, *Ethnoterritorial Politics, Policy, and the Western World* (Boulder, Colo.: Lynne Rienner, 1989), 181–220.
13. "Right-Wingers Break Through in Eastern Germany State Vote," *The Sun* (Baltimore), April 27, 1998.
14. "New Anti-Asian Party Shows Strength in Australian State," *The Sun* (Baltimore), June 14, 1998.
15. "Kohl Govern Rejects Citizenship Law Reform," *The Washington Post*, March 28, 1998.
16. "California Rejection a Big Blow to Bilingualism," *The Washington Post*, June 4, 1998.
17. Milton Esman, *Ethnic Politics* (Ithaca, N.Y.: Cornell University Press, 1994), 176.
18. By way of contrast, the 850,000 "ethnic Germans" who entered Germany from Poland and other points to the east between 1990 and 1992, many of whom did not speak German, were instantly eligible for German citizenship.
19. On racism in Europe's past, see Benjamin P. Bowser (ed.), *Racism and Anti-Racism in World Perspective* (Thousand Oaks, Calif.: Sage Publications, 1995).
20. See Anthony Mark Messina, "United Kingdom: The Making of British Race Relations," in Joseph R. Rudolph, Jr. (ed.), *Encyclopedia of Modern Ethnic Conflicts* (London and Westport, Conn.: Greenwood Press, 2003), 243–250.
21. Gerhard Schmidt, "Immigration in Europe: How Much 'Other' Is Too Much?" *Social Education*, 57, 4 (April–May, 1993): 181–183. Because of the numbers involved, Germany has usually

received the harshest criticism of any country for its failure to come to terms with the foreigner issue and its government's tendency to deny the existence of problems related to the foreigner issue, which Bendix argues continued into the 1990s. See John S. Bendix, "Germany: the Foreign Worker Issue," in *Encyclopedia of modern Ethnic Conflicts*, 85–92, 89–90.

22. William Drozdiak, "Passions Feeding Europe's Far Right Parties Leave German Politics Unfazed," *The Washington Post*, June 23, 1997.

23. Rachel K. Gibson, *The Growth of Anti-Immigrant Parties in Western Europe* (Lewiston, N.Y.: Edwin Mellen Press, 2001), 2–9. Professor Gibson identifies 38 parties who carried an anti-immigrant banner in the European elections between 1970 and 1999 in her 14-country study.

24. "Poll in Germany Finds Many Hostile toward Foreigners, Jews," *The Washington Post*, March 8, 1994. The same poll found 22% preferring not to live near Jews and 68% opposed to having Gypsies as neighbors.

25. Donald Kommers, "The Government of Germany," in Michael Curtis (ed.), *Introduction to Comparative Government* (New York: Longman, 1997), 174.

26. By 1997, when Germany began to evict its Bosnian refugees, its states contained 300,000 Bosnians, four times the number residing in Austria and more than the total number of Bosnian refugees living in the rest of Europe combined. "Germany Escalates Drive to Repatriate Bosnians," *The Washington Post*, April 3, 1997.

27. Myron Weiner, *The Global Migration Crisis: Challenge to States and to Human Rights* (New York: Harper Collins, 1995), 46.

28. See David M. Keithly, "Berlin's Difficulties: Shadows of Germany's Authoritarian Past," *Orbis*, 38, 2 (Spring 1994): 207–224; and "Blaming the Victim," *The Economist*, June 5, 1993, 47–48.

29. See Marc Fisher, "Neo-Nazi Attack Kills Three Turks in Germany," *The Washington Post*, November 24, 1992. The most notorious incident in Germany occurred four years later, when ten died in an arson incident targeting a refugee hostel in the port of Luebec in January 1996.

30. Eugene Robinson, "Immigrants Gunned Down, Raising specter of Racism in Spain," *The Washington Post*, November 18, 1992.

31. Shortly after the 1979 elections, for example, the Thatcher government ordered doctors manning the health stations at entry points in Britain to turn back any refugees or asylum seeker of "abnormal sexuality."

32. These developments were not limited to Europe. As early as 1986 Canada began to require visas of tourists from Turkey and Portugal that were not required of travelers from other states in Western Europe.

33. See, for example, Eugene Robinson, "European Nations Coordinate Limits on Refugee Influx," *The Washington Post*, December 1, 1992.

34. Germany, for example, tied its "right to reside" guarantees in its Foreigners Act of 1991 to positive action by its foreign community to adapt to German conditions, which, among other things, meant availing themselves of the specially provided German-language classes and otherwise "Germanize." See Bendix "Germany" and Sarah Collinson, *Europe and International Migration* (New York: Pinter Publishers, 1994), 96

35. See "Sweden's Unmelting Pot Teaching Nation Not to Lecture," *International Herald Tribune*, October 7, 1998.

36. "The New Face of France," *The Washington Post*, January 16, 1999.

37. See Marc Fisher, "Gypsy Influx Comes as Germany Faces Dilemma Over Immigrants," *The Washington Post*, October 22, 1990; and chapter four, in this book.

38. See Keith B. Richburg, "Illegal Workers in W. Europe Do Continent's Heavy Lifting: Increasingly Scorned Immigrants Help Secure Standard of Living," *The Washington Post*, August 3, 2002.

39. Concerning the emergence of a "Euro-Islam," see Nicholas le Quesne, "Islam in Europe: a Changing Faith," *Time Europe*, 158, 26 (December 24, 2002); and Daniel Williams, "Immigrants Keep Islam— Italian Style: 'Modern Muslims' Forge Hybrid Culture," *The Washington Post*, July 24, 2004.

40. See Craig Whitlock, "Poor Moroccans Drawn to Militant Networks," *The Washington Post*, October 14, 2004.

41. See, for example, Eugeen Roosens, "Migration and Caste Formation in Europe: The Belgian Case," *Ethnic and Racial Studies*, 11, 2 (1988): 207–217.

42. Carlyle Murphy, "Distrust of Muslims Common in U.S., Poll Finds," *The Washington Post*, October 5, 2004.

43. William Kates, "Nearly Half in U.S. Say Restrict Muslims," article available on-line at wysiwyg.//38/http://cnn.netscape.cnn.com...0002%2F20041218%2F09436069.htm&sc=1110, accessed on December 18, 2004.

44. See, for example, Peter Finn, "A Turn from Tolerance: Anti-Immigrant Movement in Europe Reflects Post-Sept. 11 Views on Muslims," *The Washington Post*, March 29, 2002; and Keith B. Richburg, "Europe's Muslims Treated as Outsiders," *The Washington Post*, November 27, 2003.

45. See, for example, Peter Ford, "Across Europe, the Far Right Rises," *Christian Science Monitor*, May 15, 2002; John Burgess, "Far Right Party in Austria Gains Regional Victory," *The Washington Post*, March 8, 2004.

46. In admitting the new states from the postcommunist world, in order to protect domestic workforces from an influx of cheap labor, the EU agreed to a compromise measure in which the citizens of the new member states would receive freedom of movement into Western Europe but still have to apply for work permits in EU member states in order to work in them.

Chapter Six The Setting of Politics in Postcommunist Europe

1. Most analyses of the preconditions for successful democratic government owe a huge debt to Robert Dahl's landmark work in this area, *Polyarchy: Participation and Opposition* (New Haven: Yale University Press, 1971). For more recent discussions of the nature of democracy and democratization, see Laurence Whitehead, *Democratization: Theory and Experience* (New York: Oxford University Press, 2002), esp. 1–35.

2. Hans-Georg Heinrich, "Russian and Central European Political Culture," in Fritz Plasser and Andreas Pribersky (eds.), *Political Culture in East Central Europe* (Brookfield, Vt.: Ashgate Publishing Company, 1996), 223–236, at 233.

3. Chief Justice John Marshall, who had been President John Adams' Secretary of State before receiving his appointment as Chief Justice of the Supreme Court, ruled that Marbury was entitled to the appointment even though it had not been formally delivered to him, but that the act of Congress which gave Marbury the right to sue to obtain that commission was unconstitutional and hence the Supreme Court could not provide the relief that Marbury sought. See *Marbury v. Madison*, 5 U.S. (1 Cranch) 137.

4. For the details involved in the Cherokee cases—*Worchester v. Georgia*, 6 Pet. (31 U.S.) 515 (1832)—see Joseph R. Rudolph, Jr., "American Indians," in David Bradley and Shelly Fisher Fishkin (eds.), *The Encyclopedia of Civil Rights in America* (Armonk, N.Y.: M.E. Sharpe, Inc./Sharpe Reference, 1998), 57–61.

5. See Anthony D. Smith, "The Reconstruction of Community in Late Twentieth Century Central Europe," in Peter J.S. Duncan and Martyn Rady (eds.), *Towards a New Community: Culture and Politics in Post-Totalitarian Europe*, (London: University of London, 1993): 65–74.

6. See, for example, Jerzy Jedlicki, "Historical Memory as a Source of Conflicts in Eastern Europe," *Communist and Post-Communist Studies*, 32 (1999): 225–232.

7. See Michael G. Roskin, *The Rebirth of East Europe* (Upper Saddle River, N.J.: Prentice Hall, 1997), 159–163.

8. Michael J. Sodaro, *Comparative Politics: A Global Introduction* (Boston: McGraw Hill, 2002), 215–225.

Chapter Seven Ethnoterritorial Politics in Czechoslovakia and the Creation and Dissolution of a State

1. The 1910 figures are taken from Carol Skalnic Leff's renowned study of *National Conflict in Czechoslovakia: The Making and Remaking of a State, 1918–1987* (Princeton, N.J.: Princeton University Press, 1988), 15.

2. The works are, respectively, *Slovensko* (Matica slovenska v. Turc. Sv. Martine, 1949), and *Praha* (Ceska Graficka Unie A.S. V Praze, 1947).

3. Miroslav Kusy, "Slovak Exceptionalism," in Jiri Musil (ed.), *The End of Czechoslovakia* (New York: Central European University Press, 1995), 138–155, 140. Kusy is translating A. Jurovsky, "Slovenska narodna povaha" ("Slovak National Character") in *Slovenska vlastiveda* ("Slovak Homeland Study"), Volume 2 (Bratislava: 1943), 365–366.

4. Until the end of the Czech–Slovak union, Czech nationalism remained positive, while Slovak nationalism retained a distinctly defensive quality. Even the national anthems of the Czech and Slovak Republics reflected the stark difference. The Czechs sing of the 'paradise" that is their "splendid" country, their "great country." The Slovak anthem is far less tranquil, singing of the Tatra Mountains being "filled with fir-y lightning," and promising, "Slovaks ne'er will sun-der."

5. Given the linguistic similarities and common Slavic stock of the Czechs and Slovaks, it has been argued that the Czech–Slovak conflict was not so much ethnic as *sub*-ethnic. See, for example, Stanley Hoffmann, *World Disorders: Troubled Peace in the Post–Cold War Era* (Cumnor Hill, U.K.: Rowman & Littlefield Publishers, Inc., 2000), 224. Whatever the degree of ethnic difference, it *was* sufficient to produce competing senses of *national* consciousness, render Czechoslovakia a multinational state, and ultimately lead to its breakup.

6. At its inception, Czechoslovakia also contained significant numbers of Ruthenes, Hungarians, Jews, and Poles. Czechs were the largest community but at best constituted only a slight majority of the population. The ethnic Germans were the second-largest group, outnumbering the Slovaks 3:2 in the country's first census in 1921. Together, however, the Slovaks and Czechs composed a solid Slavic majority of approximately 65% of the population. See Stanislav J. Kirschbaum, "Czechoslovakia: The Creation, Federalization and Dissolution of a Nation-State," in John Croakley (ed.), *The Territorial Management of Ethnic Conflict* (London: Frank Cass, 1993), 69–99, at 91, fn.3.

7. Oldrich Dedek et al., *The Break-up of Czechoslovakia: An In-depth Economic Analysis* (Aldershot, U.K.: Avebury, 1996), 27.

8. Leff, *National Conflict in Czechoslovakia*, 31. Leff notes that the 1910 census showed only 164 of the 8,185 civil servants in Slovakia were Slovaks, and that this number declined during World War I.

9. See Kirschbaum, "Czechoslovakia," 71.

10. Walker Connor, "The Politics of Ethnonationalism," *Journal of International Affairs*, 27 (1973): 1–21, at 21.

11. See especially on this topic Vera Olivova, *The Doomed Democracy: Czechoslovakia in a Disrupted Europe, 1914–1938* (Montreal: McGill-Queens University Press, 1972).

12. Kirschbaum, "Czechoslovakia," 74.

13. Jiri Musil, "Czech and Slovak Society," in Musil, *The End of Czechoslovakia*, 77–94, at 92.

14. Kirschbaum, "Czechoslovakia," 78

15. On Czech–Slovak relations following the Velvet Revolution, see Carol Skalnic Leff, *The Czech and Slovak Republics: Nation versus State* (Boulder, Colo.: Westview Press, 1997).

16. Translated and cited in Dan De Luce, "When Meciar Promises, People Listen," *The Prague Post*, June 2, 1992.

17. The initials stand for *Hnutie za Demokraticke Slovenkso*, the Movement for Democratic Slovakia. Other nationalist parties included the *Slovenska Narodna Strana*, the Slovak National Party, which like the HZDS continued to enjoy success in Slovakia's 1994 national elections and actually improved its fortunes in Slovakia's 1998 elections in which the HZDS—blamed for the country's economic decline—was voted out of office.

18. Voting turnout for the election was 85% of the eligible vote, until that time the largest voting turnout in any election held in postcommunist Central Europe.

19. All figures were provided by the Slovak Statistical Office, as of December 1992. Figures documenting standards of living indicate similar differentials at the time of the country's breakup; e.g., 60% of all Czech households had color televisions and 46% owned cars. The numbers for Slovak households were, respectively, 43 and 34%. For a brief summation, see Peter Passell, "An Economic Wedge Divides Czechoslovakia," *The New York Times*, April 19, 1992.

20. Ivan Gabal, the campaign leader of the Civic Movement, which prior to the elections had been the dominant force in the Czech lands, cited by Ross Larsen, "Experience a Scarcity after Incumbents Are Ousted," *Prague Post*, June 16, 1992.

21. In early November, 1992, only 40% of Slovak respondents felt splitting the country was necessary, and only 50% of those questioned in the Czech lands gave that answer. See Boris Gomez, "Splitting the Country still Lacks Majority Support," *The Prague Post*, December 2, 1992. There is another side to the issue, however. Those who criticized the fact that Czechoslovakia was dissolved without a referendum place too much emphasis on the absence of a public opinion majority favoring partition. The polls usually involved a small sample—645 Czechs and 665 Slovaks in the case of the November survey—and hence had a rather wide margin for error. The phrasing of questions was often suspect: e.g., in this poll, respondents were often asked if they felt the split was necessary, not whether they favored an independent Slovakia. Finally, Meciar retroactively chose to interpret the June election victory by nationalists as a referendum and conducted no campaign after it to win an ersatz referendum in public opinion polls. In contrast, those opposed to splitting the country aggressively tried to mobilize public opinion in support of their views.

22. For a discussion of the decision to split Czechoslovakia set in a comparative framework, see Robert A. Young, "How Do Peaceful Secessions Happen?" *Canadian Journal of Political Science*, 27 (1994): 773–792.

23. During the twentieth century, partition was most frequently utilized by outsiders confronting communal unrest; e.g., Britain's decision to partition India upon independence as a means of coping with Muslim–Hindu conflict and the UN decision to partition Palestine in 1948 as a means of resolving the conflicting Jewish and Arab claims on that tract of land. The closest parallel to the Czechoslovakia case was the 1905 separation of Norway from Sweden, to which it had been attached in 1814 following Denmark's military defeat during the Napoleonic Wars. More recent examples are suspect. Singapore did not voluntarily depart from the Federation of Malaysia; it was expelled. Likewise, the Soviet Union's demise was more the product of an uncontrollable implosion than peaceful negotiations.

24. The choice did not merely involve travel documents. Following partition, Prague linked study in Czech universities and other former perks of Czechoslovakian citizenship to Czech citizenship.

25. Ross Crockford, "Different Republics but Same Blood," *Prague Post*, December 29, 1993. The end of all-Czechoslovakia programming and declining access of Czechs to Slovak radio and television stations has resulted in a sharp decline in the number of Czechs able to speak or easily comprehend Slovak, despite its similarities with the Czech language. See Lukas Fils, "Two Countries that Share a Past and a Future," *The Slovak Spectator*, January 13–19, 2003, available on-line.

26. Todd Bensman, "Hungarians in Slovakia Wonder: 'Who Will Protect Our Rights?' " *Prague Post*, June 23, 1992.

27. A parallel can also be drawn with the need of African Americans in the United States to seek protection from the federal government against the persecution facing them from southern whites between the end of the American civil war in 1865 and the successful civil rights movement of the 1960s.

Chapter Eight   Ethnoclass Politics in Former Czechoslovakia

1. This definition of ghetto is the primary one offered by *Webster's New Twentieth Century Dictionary of the English Language Unabridged*, 2nd edition (Collins World, 1977), 769. The secondary definition reflects the term's more common meaning in the contemporary world: "any section of a city in which many members of some national or racial group live, or to which they are restricted."

2. See Robert S. Wistrich, *Antisemitism: The Longest Hatred* (New York: Pantheon Books, 1991), esp. 54–55.

3. "A Teacher's Guide to the Holocaust: Summary of Geographical Movement of European Jews in the Past 2,000 Years," at http://fcit.coedu.usf.edu/Holocaust/PEOPLE/displace.htm.

4. Harry Zohn, "A Cultural Tale of Two Cities: The Jews of Vienna and Prague," in Hazel Kahn Keimowitz and Wolfgang Mieder (eds.), *The Jewish Experience of European Anti-Semitism: Harry H. Kahn Memorial Lectures (1990–1994)* (Burlington, Vermont: Center for Holocaust Studies at the University of Vermont, 1995), 1–18, at 13.

5. Wistrich, *Antisemitism*, 149.

6. Wistrich, *Antisemitism*, 149–153.

7. Cited in Wistrich, *Antisemitism*, 153.

8. The latter figure is taken from Paul Lendval, *Anti-Semitism without Jews: Communist Eastern Europe* (Garden City, N.J.: Doubleday & Company, Inc., 1971), 25.

9. See, for example, Joel Blocker's article, "Attitudes to foreigners Have Been Centuries in the Making," *The Prague Post*, May 14, 1997.

10. Cited by Ross Larsen in "Foreigners, Unloved and Unwanted," *The Prague Post*, December 11, 1996. Gabal's poll also found that those finding value in the presence of foreigners had declined abruptly, from the 40% in 1994 to 14% by 1996.

11. "Prague Police Break Up Jewish Cemetery Protest," copyright Reuters, Ltd., Central Europe Online, June 16, 2000, at http://centraleurope.com/news.php3?id=169598.

12. Tom Nicholson, "Cabinet Approves Jewish Compensation," *The Slovak Spectator*, September 23–29, 2002.

13. For a detailed study of the topic, see David M. Crowe, *A History of the Gypsies of Eastern Europe and Russia* (New York: Saint Martin's Pres, 1995).

14. For a discussion of the Romany in Nazi-occupied Europe, see Donald Kenrick's translation of Karola Fings, Herbert Heuss, and Frank Sparing, *The Gypsies during the Second World War* (Hatfield, Hertfordshire, U.K.: Gypsy Research Center, University of Hertfordshire Press, 1997).

15. See David Short, "Group Strives to Keep Lety Memory Alive," *The Prague Post*, May 7, 1997, available on-line; and David J. Kostelancik, "The Gypsies of Czechoslovakia: Political and Ideological Consideration in the Development of Policy," *Studies in Comparative Communism*, 22, 4 (Winter 1989): 307–321, esp. 308–309. Most executions at Lety were conducted between August 1942 and January 1943.
16. Short, "Group Strives to Keep Lety Memory Alive."
17. Kostelancik, "The Gypsies of Czechoslovakia," 309.
18. The number of Roma in Central Europe, as elsewhere, can only be estimated. Governments have historically undercounted the Romany, especially when efforts were being made to assimilate an officially "small" Romany element. Meanwhile, the Roma have tended to exaggerate their numbers in public utterances, though they often try to pass as non-Roma in private. See Klara Orgovanova, "The Roma in Slovakia," available on-line at http://www.newschool.edu/centers/ecep/fift.htm.
19. Public opinion polls persistently indicate that the overwhelming majority of Czechs, Poles, and other Central Europeans do not believe that the Roma want to do honest labor and would not hire them if free to do otherwise.
20. Kostelancik, "The Gypsies of Czechoslovakia," 311.
21. For a discussion of the Roma under communism in Czechoslovakia, see Will Guy, "Ways of Looking at Roma: The Case of Czechoslovakia (1975)," in Diane Tong (ed.), *Gypsies: An Interdisciplinary Reader* (New York: Garland Publishing, Inc., 1998), 13–68. The dispersal and transfer policies are examined on 32f.
22. Kostelancik, "The Gypsies of Czechoslovakia," 311–315.
23. "Roma Leaders Abandons [*sic*] politics," *The Slovak Spectator*, September 23–29, 2002.
24. The contestant was from Usti And Labem in the Czech Republic's 1993 Miss Czech contest.
25. The demographic statistics for the Romany reveal the consequences of these patterns of discrimination. In addition to having an average unemployment rate at least four times that of Slovakia as a whole in 2003, Romany men had a life expectancy (54.5 years) that was five years shorter than that of Slovak men and Romany women lived eight years lesser than their Slovak counterparts. Recent, comparative figures on education in Slovakia are unavailable; however, even at the end of the communist era of trying to upgrade the status of Czechoslovakia's Roma, the 1991 census indicated that less than 1% (0.84%) of the Roma had completed a secondary education. Martina Pisarova, "Cabinet Unveils Roma Strategy," *The Slovak Spectator*, April 14–20, 2003.

Chapter Nine   Ethnopolitics in Former Czechoslovakia in a Comparative Perspective

1. See Robert Bruce Ware, "Ethnic Parity and Democratic Pluralism in Dagestan: A Consociational Approach," *Europe-Asia Studies* (January 2001), available on-line at http://www.findarticles.com/cf_0/m3955/1_53/69495284/print.jhtml.
2. See John A. Armstrong, "Nationalism in the Former Soviet Empire," *Problems of Communism* (January–April 1992): 121–133.
3. See Stuart J. Kaufman, *Modern Hatred: The Symbolic Politics of Ethnic War* (Ithaca, N.Y.: Cornell University Press, 2001), esp. chapter 3.
4. See Kaufmann, *The Symbolic Politics of Ethnic War*. In addition to Russia and the UN, outside parties in the conflict management process in Georgia have also included the Organization for Security and Cooperation in Europe, which has helped maintain the ceasefire in South Ossetia.
5. See Susan B. Glasser and Peter Baker, "Leader Pledges to Unite Georgia: Two More Rebel Provinces Targeted," *The Washington Post*, May 7, 2004; and "Separatist Violence Flares in Republic of Georgia," *The Sun* (Baltimore), August 5, 2004.
6. On the inadequacy of Tito's successors in preserving the state after his death and the role of nationalists in choosing "the worst of all possible ways for dissolving the federation," see Silvo Devetak, "The Dissolution of Multi-Ethnic States: The Case of Yugoslavia," in Kumar Rupesinghe and Valery A. Tishkov (eds.), *Ethnicity and Power in the Contemporary World* (New York: United Nations University Press, 1996), 159–177, citation at 161.
7. See Heinz-Jurgen Axt, "The Impact of German Policy on Refugee Flows from Former Yugoslavia," in Rainer Munz and Miron Weiner (eds.), *Migrants, Refugees, and Foreign Policy: U.S. and German Policies toward Countries of Origin, Volume II* (Providence, R.I.: Berghahn Books, 1997), 1–34, esp. 7–15 and 25–26.

8. At approximately the same time, Yugoslavia's southernmost province, Macedonia, declared its independence. Like Slovenia, Macedonia contained a very small percentage of Serbs (2%). Moreover, at the time it withdrew the Serbs were heavily bogged down in fighting in Croatia and Bosnia. Consequently, its exit was entirely peaceful.

9. International Crisis Group (ICG), *Bosnia Refugee Logjam Breaks: Is the International Community Ready?* (Washington: ICG Balkan Report No. 95, 2000), 1.

10. Settlement of the conflict has also been complicated by the frequent electoral success of Serbian hardliners in Serbia, which has reduced Yugoslavia's ability to pressure the Serb nationalists in Bosnia to collaborate in the peace-building efforts there. For an analysis of post-Dayton Bosnia, see especially Elizabeth M. Cousens and Charles K. Cater, *Toward Peace in Bosnia: Implementing the Dayton Accords* (Boulder, Colo.: Lynne Rienner, 2001).

11. Beginning in the early 1980s, for example, there were reports of arson at Serbian Orthodox churches and nunneries and maiming attacks against Serbian farmers. See Henry Kamm, "In One Yugoslav Province, Serbs Fear the Ethnic Albanians," *The New York Times*, April 28, 1986.

12. See United Nations Office for the Coordination of Humanitarian Affairs (OCHA), *Humanitarian Risk Analysis No. 18—Humanitarian Situation, Protection and Assistance: Internally Displaced Persons in Serbia and Montenegro* (Belgrade: OCHA, 2002), 5–6.

13. See Peter Beaumont, "Albanians Wage War of Race Hate," *The Observer* (London), February 25, 2001.

14. See Thomas Patrick Melady and Margaret Badum Melady, *Uganda: The Asian Exiles* (Maryknoll, N.Y.: Orbis Books, 1976).

15. Robert S. Wistrich, *Antisemitism: The Longest Hatred* (New York: Pantheon Books, 1991), 101f.

16. Wistrich, *Antisemitism*, 145.

17. As late as 1970, even in the United States only approximately one Jew out of eight married outside the Jewish community. See Alan Cooperman, "Jewish Intermarriage Still Rising: But Rate Leveling Off, Survey Finds," *The Washington Post*, September 11, 2003.

18. Wistrich, *Antisemitism*, 101.

19. Wistrich, *Antisemitism*, 55.

20. Wistrich, *Antisemitism*, 145.

21. Paul Lendvai, *Anti-Semitism without Jews: Communist Eastern Europe* (Garden City, N.J.: Doubleday & Company, 1971), 25.

22. The details pertaining to the establishment and destruction of "The Warsaw Ghetto" are available on-line at http://www.scrapbookpages.com/Poland/WarsawGhetto/WarsawGhetto01.htm.

23. See "Poles Guilty of Crimes against Jews, Report Finds," *The Sun* (Baltimore), November 3, 2002.

24. For a detailed study of the Roma Holocaust, see Karola Fings, *The Gypsies during the Second World War* (Hatfield, U.K.: Gypsy Research Center, University of Hertfordshire, 1997).

25. Lendvai, *Anti-Semitism without Jews*, 20.

26. Many of the names by which the Romany are known in Europe, such as *Tshingani,* are derived from the Byzantine word *atsinganoi,* which means "untouchable" in the sense of being beyond the influence of those around them. Tracy Brand, *Eastern Europe's Gypsy Minority* (Unpublished M.A. Thesis, Johns Hopkins University, 1996), 18.

27. See Zoltan Barany, "Democratic Changes Bring Mixed Blessings for Gypsies," *RFE/RI Research Report*, 1, 20 (May 15, 1992): 41.

28. "Roma Department Counter Prejudices," *Budapest Sun*, September 7, 2002. Retrieved on-line September 8, 2002, at http://www.centraleurope.co...arytoday//localpress/bpsun. php3?id.=196414. When challenged about such racist passages, an official in the Hungarian Education Ministry only agreed to consider scraping "such books from the official list if they prove to be prejudiced."

29. See Peter S. Green, "U.N. Report Shows Growing Poverty among European Gypsies," *The New York Times*, January 17, 2003.

30. See Robert S. Wistrich, "Anti-Semitism Worldwide, 1997/98: Nationalist Challenges in the New Europe," Stephen Roth Institute on Anti-Semitism and Racism, at http://www.tau.ac.il/Anti-Semitism/asw97–8/wistrich.htm.

31. See Josef Joffe, "The Enemy Within," *Time Europe Magazine*, June 17, 2002, posted on-line at http://www/time.com/time/eu...agazine/2002/061//antisemitism/view.htm.

32. "Anti-Jewish Feeling Found Common in Italy," *The Sun* (Baltimore), November 2, 1995.

33. A five-country poll covering Britain, France, Germany, Belgium, and Denmark—the current home of more than 1 million Jews—found that 45% of those polled felt that their Jewish population was

more loyal to Israel than their own state. See Abraham H. Foxman, "Europe's Anti-Israel Excuse," *The Washington Post*, June 27, 2002; and Robert Mendick, "One in Three Europeans 'Is Anti Semitic,' " *The Independent* (London), June 30, 2002.

34. Not only did Belgrade respond to the June 25, 1991, declarations of independence by Slovenia and Croatia by attacking these areas to prevent them from seceding, but international recognition came much more slowly than Slovene and Croatian leaders had expected. It was not until January 15 of the following year that the EU diplomatically recognized the two breakaway states.

35. For the details of the agreement, see Stanley Hoffman, *World Disorders: Troubled Peace in the Post–Cold War Era* (Lanham, Maryland: Rowman & Littlefield Publishers, Inc., 1998), 227.

Chapter Ten   The Setting of Politics in the Developing World

1. With the collapse of communism in the Soviet Union and Central Europe (i.e., the Second World) and the movement toward democratic government and marketplace economies in much of that area, some commentators in the mid-1990s began referring to the economically and politically developing world as simply "the other world." See Joseph N. Weatherby et al., *The Other World: Issues and Politics of the Developing World* (New York: Longman, 1994).

2. See *World Development Indicators, 2004* (Washington, D.C.: World Bank, 2004). The economic gap separating Africa as a whole, with its more than 700 million people, from the remainder of the world continues to grow. The most recent report of the World Economic Forum, for example, found that the average per capita income in all of sub-Sahara Africa is below US$200, less than three decades ago. This downward slide was attributed to a combination of factors, including high population growth, military conflicts, corruption, poor infrastructure, and very low levels of foreign investment. "Nearly Half the World's Poor Are African," *The Sun* (Baltimore), June 3, 2004.

3. Weatherby et al., *The Other World*, 152–153,

4. Weatherby et al., *The Other World*, 193.

5. The partition process resulted in a truncated Pakistani state composed of a multiethnic West Pakistan on India's northwestern border and an ethnically homogeneous East Pakistan a thousand miles away on India's northeastern border, where the ethnically and linguistically homogeneous Bengali province itself split on the basis of religion.

6. Stephen D. Wrage, "Rwanda: Hutu-Tutsi Conflict and Genocide in Central Africa" in Joseph R. Rudolph, Jr. (ed.), *Encyclopedia of Modern Ethnic Conflicts* (Westport, Conn.: Greenwood Press, 2003), 183–190, at 185.

7. See Weatherby, *The Other World*, 39f.

8. See chapter one, in this volume.

9. Weatherby, *The Other World*, 10–14.

10. On the positive legacy of British colonialism, especially in Britain's smaller colonies in the Caribbean, see Richard L. Payne and Kamal R. Nassar, *Politics and Culture in the Developing World: The Impact of Globalization* (New York: Longman, 2003), 235.

11. See Payne and Nassar, *Politics and Culture in the Developing World*, 233f.

12. See especially Payne and Nassar, 297–304, citation at 297.

13. See chapter eleven, in this volume.

14. Except for that small portion of the North's aristocracy that was educated, often abroad, even the Western Region was better educated than Nigeria's North.

15. A.F. Richards, cited in *Proposals for the Revision of the Constitution of Nigeria, 1945* (London: H.M.S.O., 1945).

16. The history of Nigeria's early political parties was captured in detail at the time of Nigeria's independence in Wale Ademcyega's *The Federation of Nigeria: From Earliest Times to Independence* (London: Harrap & Company, 1962). As for the Ibo tribe, scholars have more recently substituted the phonetically more correct "Igbo" spelling; however, because historical documents were often used in researching this chapter, the older "Ibo" spelling is used throughout our study.

17. In 1947, 251 student were enrolled in secondary schools in the north, versus nearly 10,000 (9,657) in the south. Ten years later, the ratio was still approximately 8:1 (3,643 to 28,208). Hans Carol, "The Making of Nigeria's Political Regions," *Journal of Asian and African Studies*, 3 (1968): 277.

Chapter Eleven   Ethnopolitics in Nigeria

1. James S. Wunsch, "Nigeria: Ethnic Conflict in Multinational West Africa," in Joseph R. Rudolph, Jr. (ed.), *Encyclopedia of Modern Ethnic Conflict* (Westport, Conn.: Greenwood Press, 2003), 169–182, 171.

2. As A.V. Dicey phrased the matter nearly a century ago in his *Introduction to the Study of the Law of the Constitution* (London: Macmillan and Company, 1908); "If Parliament decided that all blue eyed babies should be murdered the preservation of blue eyed babies would be illegal . . . [But] legislatures must get made before they could pass such a law, subjects be idiots before they would submit to it." It was only when Britain joined the European Community that the absolute sovereignty of Parliament became qualified by Parliament's contracted obligations to act within the framework of European Community (now EU) law.

3. *Nigeria—Report of the Commission Appointed to Enquire into the Fears of Minorities and the Means of Allaying Them* (London: H.M.S.O., 1958), section 10.

4. "Reflections on the Nigerian Revolution," *South Atlantic Quarterly*, 65 (Autumn 1966): 421–430, 423–424.

5. "Waiting for the West," *The Economist*, 214 (January 16, 1965): 211.

6. K.W.J. Post, "The Crisis in Nigeria," *The World Today*, 22 (February 1966): 45–47.

7. Wunsch, "Nigeria," 174.

8. W. Schwartz, "Tribalism and Politics in Nigeria," *The World Today*, 22 (November 1966): 460–467, 460. See also Wunsch, "Nigeria," 174–175.

9. Wunsch, "Nigeria," 175

10. See, for example, Martin Dent, "Nigeria: The Task of Conflict Resolution," *World Today*, 24 (1968): 273–274.

11. Ross K. Baker, "The Emergence of Biafra: Balkanization or Nationbuilding," *Orbis*, 12 (Summer 1968): 518–533, 528. One proposal would have left the center with control over only railways, airlines, and telecommunications.

12. The deal between Awolowo and Gowon was reported by John Hatch, "The Dissolution of Nigeria," *New Statesman*, 73 (1967): 750.

13. On the party systems of post–civil war Nigeria, see Monte Palmer, *Comparative Politics: Political Economy, Political Culture, and Political Interdependence* (Itasca, Ill.: F.E. Peacock Publishers, 2000), 448–455.

14. New York: Longman, 2001; citation at 247.

15. Palmer, *Comparative Politics*, 454.

16. Timothy D. Sisk, "Nigeria and South Africa," in Michael J. Sodaro et al. (eds.), *Comparative Politics, A Global Introduction* (Boston: McGraw-Hill, 2001), 809–846, 834.

17. Palmer, *Comparative Politics*, 450.

18. Sisk, "Nigeria and South Africa," 825.

19. See Palmer, *Comparative Politics*, 151–152.

20. Palmer, *Comparative Politics*, 454. By the 2003 legislative and presidential elections, the 5-party limit had been lifted and more than 20 parties contested the presidential election.

21. See "Planned Stonings Reflect Political Split in Nigeria: Islamic North's Sentences Defy Christian South," *The Sun* (Baltimore), September 15, 2002. Despite the outcome of this case, the death penalty is still being imposed on those convicted of adultery in some northwestern Nigerian states.

22. Palmer, *Comparative Politics*, 448–449. The Second Republic also required the equitable representation of diverse ethnic groups in state institutions and the military, and in the distribution of oil income to the states, and added to the legislature a Senate whose members would represent the states. See Sodaro et al., *Comparative Politics*, 824f.

23. Sodaro et al., *Comparative Politics*, 450. The general also tactically co-opted the leaders of many tribal groups into his ruling council.

24. "Tribal Militants in Nigeria Call for Cease Fire," *The Washington Post*, March 27, 2003.

25. Ross Herbert, South African Institute of International Affairs, cited in "Opposition Demands that Nigerian Leader Step Down," *The Sun* (Baltimore), April 24, 2003.

26. See chapter twelve, in this volume.

Chapter Twelve   Ethnopolitics in Nigeria
in a Comparative Perspective

1. See, for example, William Livingston, *Federalism and Constitutional Change* (Oxford: Clarendon Press, 1956); D.S. Rothchild, *Toward Unity In Africa: A Study of Federalism in British West Africa*

(Washington, D.C.: Public Affairs Press, 1960); and William Riker, *Federalism: Origin, Operation, Significance* (Boston: Little, Brown Company, 1964). Riker identified ten states with federal systems in the developing world in the mid-1960s: Argentina, Brazil, Mexico, Venezuela in the Americas, the Congo, Ethiopia and Nigeria in Africa, and India, Pakistan, and Malaysia in Asia (1–11).

2. Philip Gourevitch, *We Wish to Inform You that Tomorrow We Will Be Killed with Our Families: Stories from Rwanda* (New York: Farrar Straus, 1998), at 26, cited in Stephen Wrage, "Rwanda: Hutu-Tutsi Conflict and Genocide in Central Africa," in Joseph R. Rudolph, Jr. (ed.), *Encyclopedia of Modern Ethnic Conflicts* (Westport, Conn.: Greenwood Press, 2003), 183–190, at 187–188.

3. See S.K. Arora, "The Reorganization of the Indian States," *Far Eastern Survey*, 25 (1956): 27–30. The key moment was the 1928 publication of the Nehru Report, which explicitly accepted the linguistic reorganization of India as a political objective.

4. As Gandhi summarized the thinking of many Congress leaders in November of 1947, following the partition of India, "the reluctance to enforce linguistic redistribution is perhaps justifiable in the present depressing atmosphere. The exclusive spirit is ever uppermost. . . . No one thinks of the whole of India." Cited in Vasudeva Kamath, *Linguistic Vivisection of India: Why Not Stop It Still?* (Bombay: Bharatiya Vidya Bhavan, 1866), at 9.

5. *Report of the Linguistic Provinces Commission* (Delhi: Government of India Press, 1948), paragraph 152(2).

6. Maya Chadda, "India: Ethnic Conflict and Nation-Building in a Multiethnic State," in *Encyclopedia of Modern Ethnic Conflicts*, 93–100, 96.

7. See, for example, "40 Killed in Bomb, Gun Attacks in Indian States," *The Sun* (Baltimore), October 3, 2004, reporting on violence then in Nagaland and adjacent areas of northeast India.

8. Chadda, "India," at 93.

9. See G. Mehta, "Can India Finance Her Five-Year Plan?" *Atlantic Monthly*, 202 (1958): 77. Industrial production rose 39% for the same period, with the five-year targets being reached or surpassed in most existing industries.

10. On India's growing middle class and its potential impact on India's future, see Gurcharan Das, *India Unbound: The Social and Economic Revolution from Independence to the Global Information Age* (New York: A.A. Knopf, 2001).

11. The process of giving minorities a highly visible and sometimes proportional presence in decision making is not limited to postcolonial countries. Quebec is well represented on the Canadian Supreme court and in the federal cabinet, as are French- and Flemish-speaking Belgians in that country's cabinet. Similarly, however unwritten it is equally well understood that the U.S. Supreme Court will continue to have an African American member whenever Justice Clarence Thomas (who replaced the first African American appointee, Justice Thurgood Marshall) hangs up his robes.

12. On the disintegration and post–civil war reconstruction of Lebanon, see Charles Winslow, *Lebanon: War and Politics in a Fragmented Society* (New York: Routledge, 1998).

13. See Chetan Kumar, "Sustaining Peace in War-Torn Societies: Lessons from the Haitian Experience," in William J. Lahneman (ed.), *Military Intervention: Cases in Context for the Twenty-First Century* (New York: Rowman and Littlefield, 2994), 105–132.

14. Peacekeeping activity in the postcommunist and advanced democratic world includes the intervention of Russian troops in the civil wars in postcommunist Georgia, the UN's 40+-year mission in Cyprus, and the continuing presence of the British troops deployed in Northern Ireland more than 35 years ago.

15. There was also a third group in Sri Lanka during the 1980s: the Indian Tamil descendants of the approximately 800,000 Tamil imported from India during the colonial period to work in Ceylon's plantations. Indian citizens comprised 9% of the population. As a further means of winning India's support, the Sinhalese government, in February, 1986, extended full Sri Lankan citizenship to them. See Robert N. Kearney, "Territorial Elements of Tamil Separatism in Sri Lanka," *Pacific Affairs*, 60 (Winter 1987/88): 561–577; and Kumar Rupesinghe, "Ethnic Conflicts in South Asia: The Case of Sri Lanka and the Indian Peace-keeping Force (IPKF)," *Journal of Peace Research*, 25 (1988): 337–350.

16. See especially Angela S. Burger, "Policing a Communal Society: The Case of Sri Lanka," *Asian Survey*, 27 (July 1987): 822–833, esp. 822f.

17. India, for example, frequently looked the other way while Tamil rebels trained in southern India.

18. It is estimated that worldwide approximately 300,000 children have been conscripted into war, and that 1 out of 6 of these children (51,000), some as young as 8, are involved in the war in Sri Lanka. "Forgotten Casualties of War," available through the Konrad Adenauer Foundation–supported Asian News Network website.

19. A notable exception to this rule was the flow of workers from Yemen, Pakistan, and other poor areas in the region into the oil fields of the Saudi Peninsula. They took jobs that either the local

communities would not take, or their governments preferred they not take lest their absorption into a more modern work force destabilize the conservative, patrimonial regimes in the area. Although paid well, they have remained second-class citizens in the states employing them and a distinct social underclass.

20. Both communities have also migrated in large numbers to states in the developed world, where the Chinese have normally maintained a low profile and been less politically active than the immigrants from India and Pakistan. See Amy L. Freedman, *Political Participation and Ethnic Minorities: Chinese Overseas in Malaysia, Indonesia, and The United States* (New York: Routledge, 2000); and Hugh Tinker's older study, *The Banyan Tree: Overseas Immigrants from India, Pakistan and Bangladesh* (New York: Oxford University Press, 1977).

21. Earl D. Huff, "Asia." in Joseph N. Weatherby et al., *The Other World: Issues and Politics of the Developing World* (New York: Longman, 1997), 190–226, at 195.

22. See Thomas Patrick Melady and Margaret Badium Melady, *Uganda: The Asian Exiles* (Maryknoll, N.Y.: Orbis Books, 1976).

23. See, for example, Keith B. Richburg, "Ethnic Chinese: Indonesia's Scapegoats—Ethnic Chinese Feel Brunt of Indonesia's Economic Ills," *The Washington Post*, December 23, 1998.

Chapter Thirteen   Reflections on the Management of Ethnopolitical Conflict in the Contemporary World

1. Paul Collier, "The Market for Civil War," in Robert J. Art and Robert Jervis (eds.), *International Politics, Enduring Concepts, and Contemporary Issues* (London: Pearson, Longman, 2004), 489–495, at 490.

2. See Andrej Skolkay's 2003 study, "Xenophobia: A Catalyst of Hate Speech in Slovakia and Slovenia," 30–40. on-line at http://www.ceu.hu/cps/eve/eve_xenophobia_skolkay.pdf.

3. The permanent War Crimes Tribunal in the Hague is an outgrowth of the first court of this nature, which emerged as a result of the carnage in Rwanda and provided the precedent for creating a similar international court following the atrocities in Yugoslavia.

4. Peacekeeping operations by the UN, other international agencies, and neighboring states during the past 20 years include the deployment of UN forces in Bosnia, Croatia, Kosovo in Serbia, and Macedonia in the former Yugoslavia as well as Central Africa and East Timor, IPKF operations in Sri Lanka, international peacekeeping forces in Lebanon, Russian peacekeepers in Georgia, the continuing presence of British troops in Northern Ireland, and West African peacekeepers in Liberia.

5. See Joseph R. Rudolph, Jr., "Intervention in Communal Conflicts," *Orbis*, 34 (Spring 1995): 259–293

6. The resettlement process is a particularly delicate issue; in ethnically cleansed areas it can substantially alter the ethnic mathematics of the democratization process, and hence the local balance of political power. See, for example, International Crisis Group (ICG), *The Continuing Challenge of Refugee Return in Bosnia and Herzegovina* (Sarajevo: ICG Balkans Report No. 137, 2002).

7. The psychological as well as physical dependency on their presence of returnees to Bosnia and Kosovo is discussed in ICG, *Return to Uncertainty: Kosovo's Internally Displaced and the Return Process* (Pristina, Kosovo: ICG Balkan Report No. 139, 2000), 27f.

8. Stanley Hoffman, *World Disorders: Troubled Peace in the Post—Cold War Era* (Oxford: Rowman and Littlefield, 2000), 229. For critiques of "coercive diplomacy" in general, as well as in tutelage contexts, see Robert J. Art and Kenneth N. Waltz (eds.), *The Use of Force: Military Power and International Politics* (Oxford: Rowman and Littlefield, 2004).

9. For commentary on the military's role in state-building, see John A. Tures, "Operation Exporting Freedom: The Quest for Democratization via United States Military Operations," *The Whitehead Journal of Diplomacy and International Relations*, 6, 1 (Winter/Spring 2005): 97–112.

INDEX